Thanks for choosing this book! All the fan letters and
handmade crafts I get from fans are a real source of
power for me. They really make me happy!
All that power!!!

KOHEI HORIKOSHI

MY HERO ACADEMIA

14

SHONEN JUMP Manga Edition

STORY & ART KOHEI HORIKOSHI

TRANSLATION & ENGLISH ADAPTATION **Caleb Cook**
TOUCH-UP ART & LETTERING **John Hunt**
DESIGNER **Julian [JR] Robinson**
SHONEN JUMP SERIES EDITOR **John Bae**
GRAPHIC NOVEL EDITOR **Mike Montesa**

BOKU NO HERO ACADEMIA © 2014 by Kohei Horikoshi
All rights reserved.
First published in Japan in 2014 by SHUEISHA Inc., Tokyo.
English translation rights arranged by SHUEISHA Inc.

Printed in the U.S.A.

Published by VIZ Media, LLC
P.O. Box 77010
San Francisco, CA 94107

10 9 8 7 6 5 4 3 2
First printing, August 2018
Second printing, September 2018

PARENTAL ADVISORY
MY HERO ACADEMIA is rated T for Teen
and is recommended for ages 13 and up.
This volume contains fantasy violence.

shonenjump.com

MY HERO ACADEMIA

Overhaul

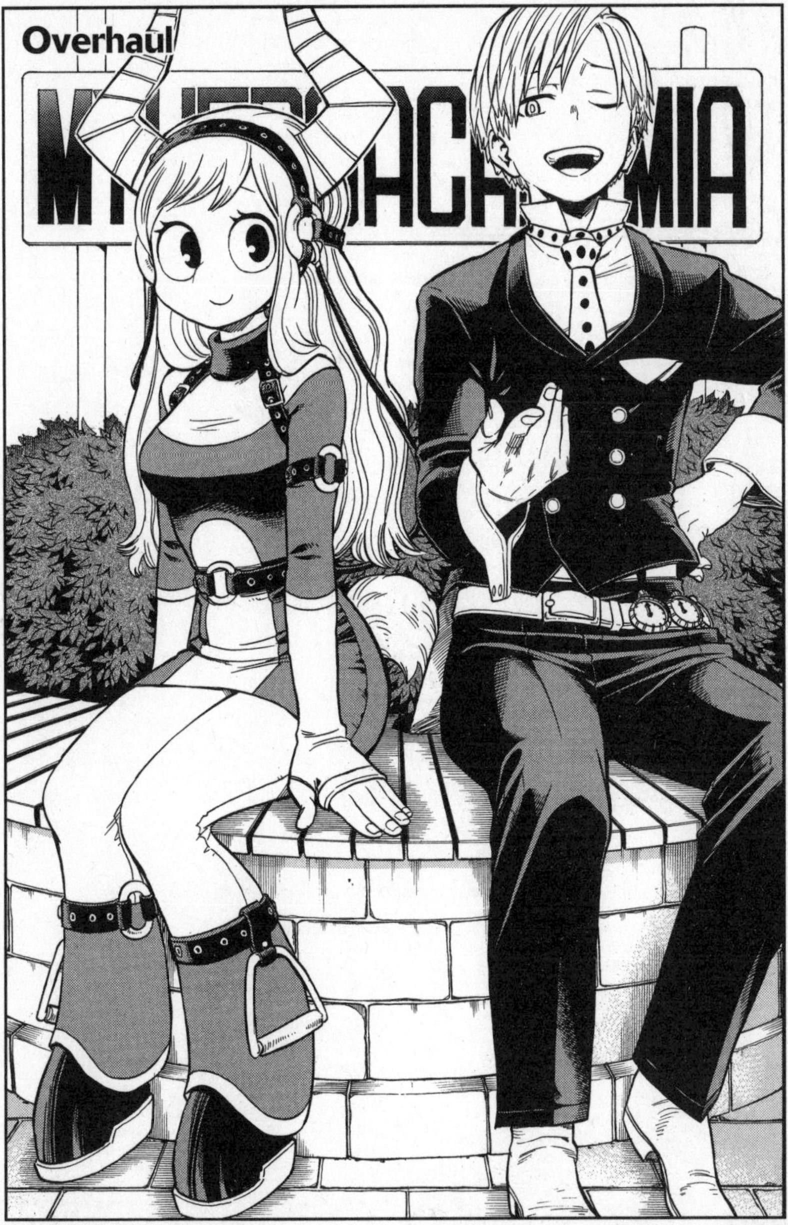

KOHEI HORIKOSHI

SHONEN JUMP MANGA

STORY

One day, people began manifesting special abilities that came to be known as "Quirks," and before long, the world was full of superpowered humans. But with the advent of these exceptional individuals came an increase in crime, and governments alone were unable to deal with the situation. At the same time, others emerged to oppose the spread of evil! As if straight from the comic books, these heroes keep the peace and are even officially authorized to fight crime. Our story begins when a certain Quirkless boy and lifelong hero fan meets the world's number one hero, starting him on his path to becoming the greatest hero ever!

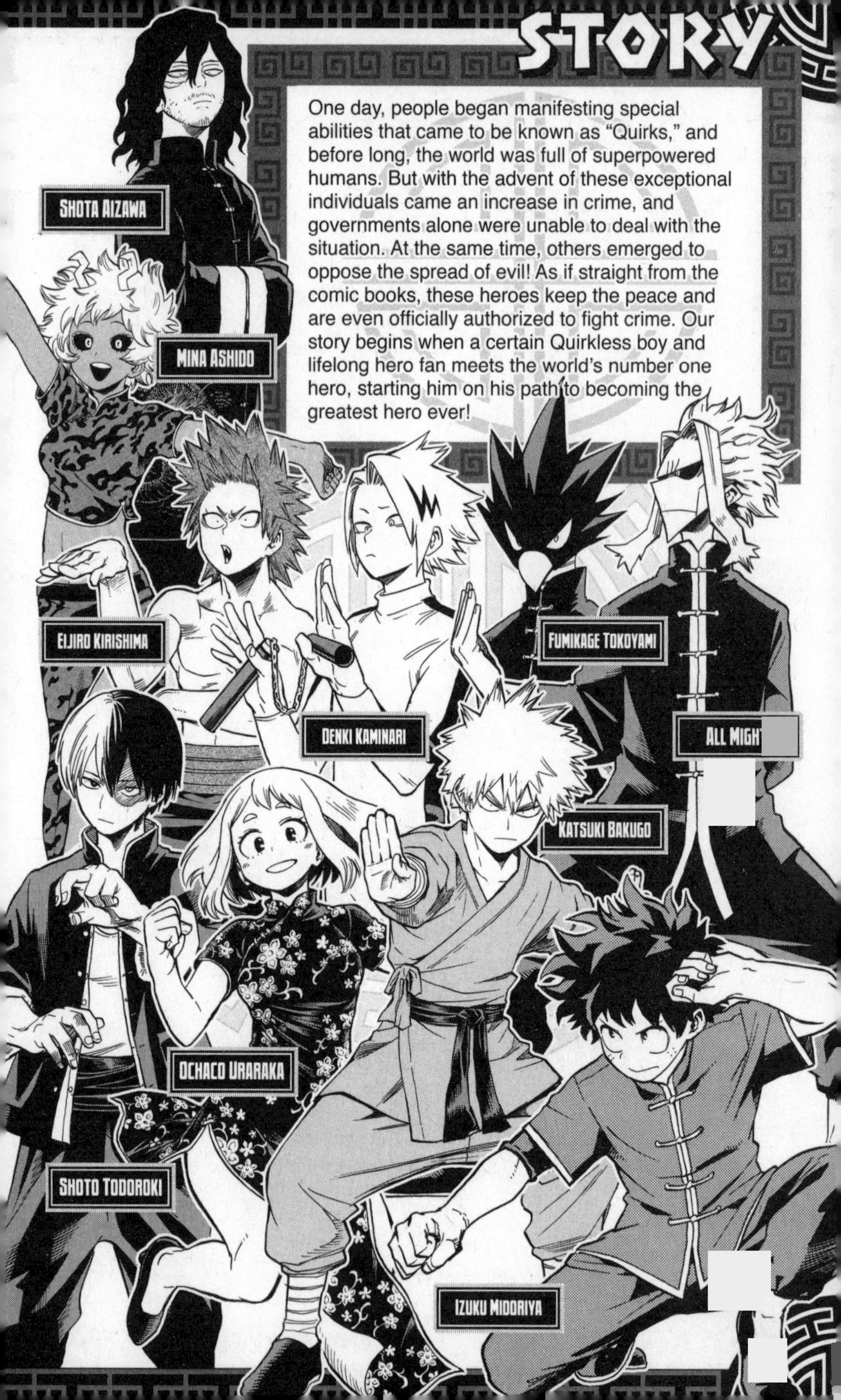
SHOTA AIZAWA
MINA ASHIDO
EIJIRO KIRISHIMA
FUMIKAGE TOKOYAMI
DENKI KAMINARI
ALL MIGH
KATSUKI BAKUGO
OCHACO URARAKA
SHOTO TODOROKI
IZUKU MIDORIYA

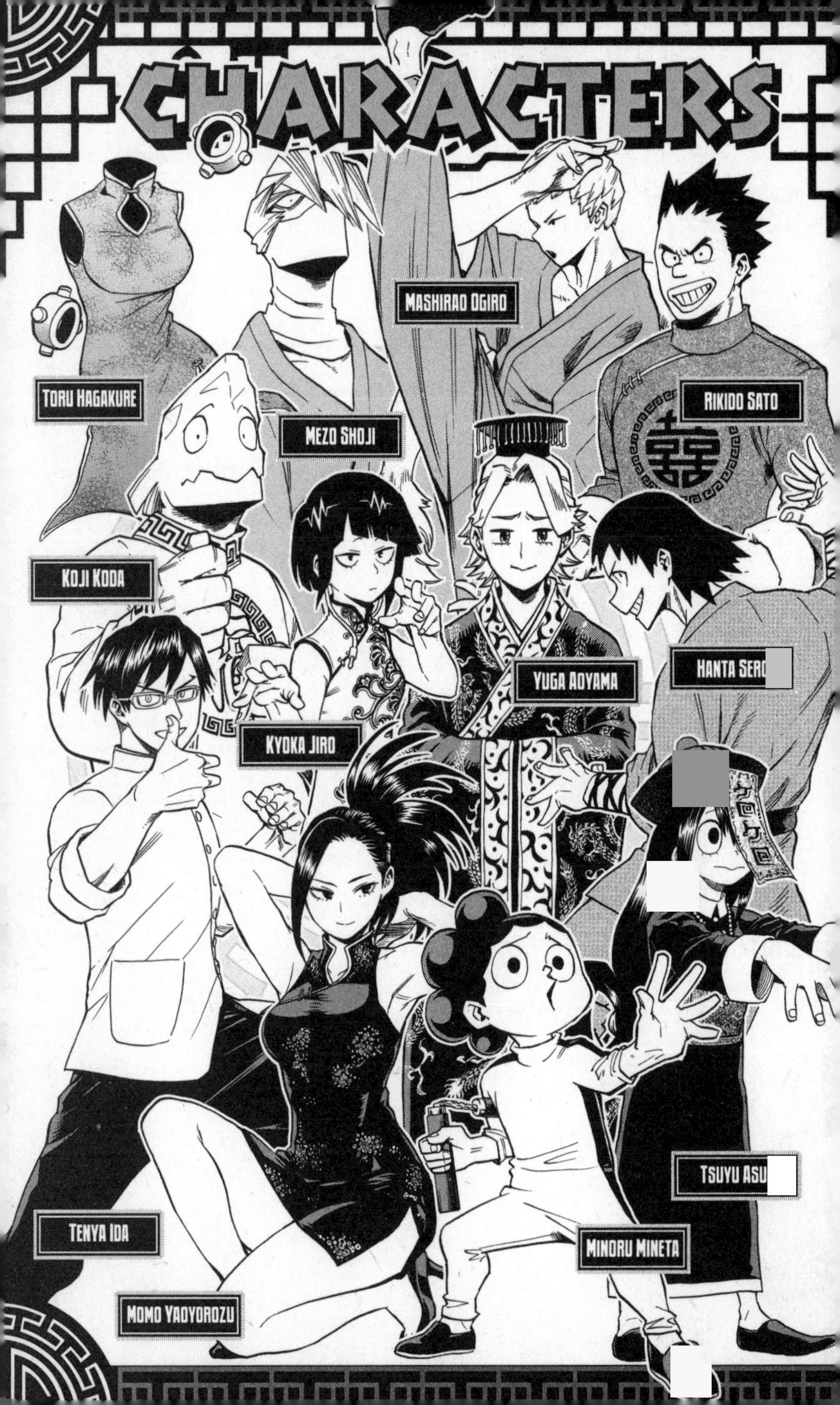
CHARACTERS
MASHIRAO OGIRO
RIKIDO SATO
TORU HAGAKURE
MEZO SHOJI
KOJI KODA
HANTA SER
YUGA AOYAMA
KYOKA JIRO
TSUYU ASU
TENYA IDA
MINORU MINETA
MOMO YAOYOROZU

Vol. 14

MY HERO ACADEMIA

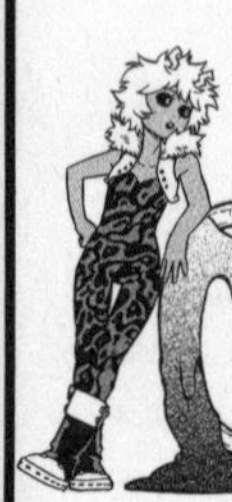

CONTENTS

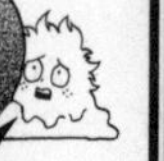

Overhaul

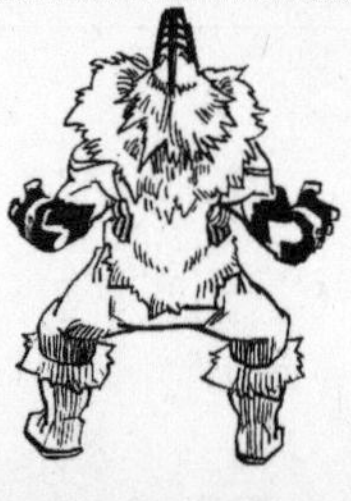

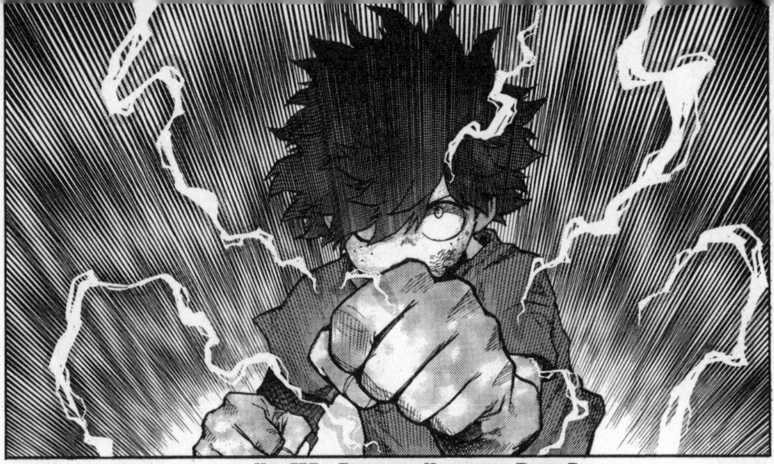

No. 119 - Deku vs. Kacchan, Part 2

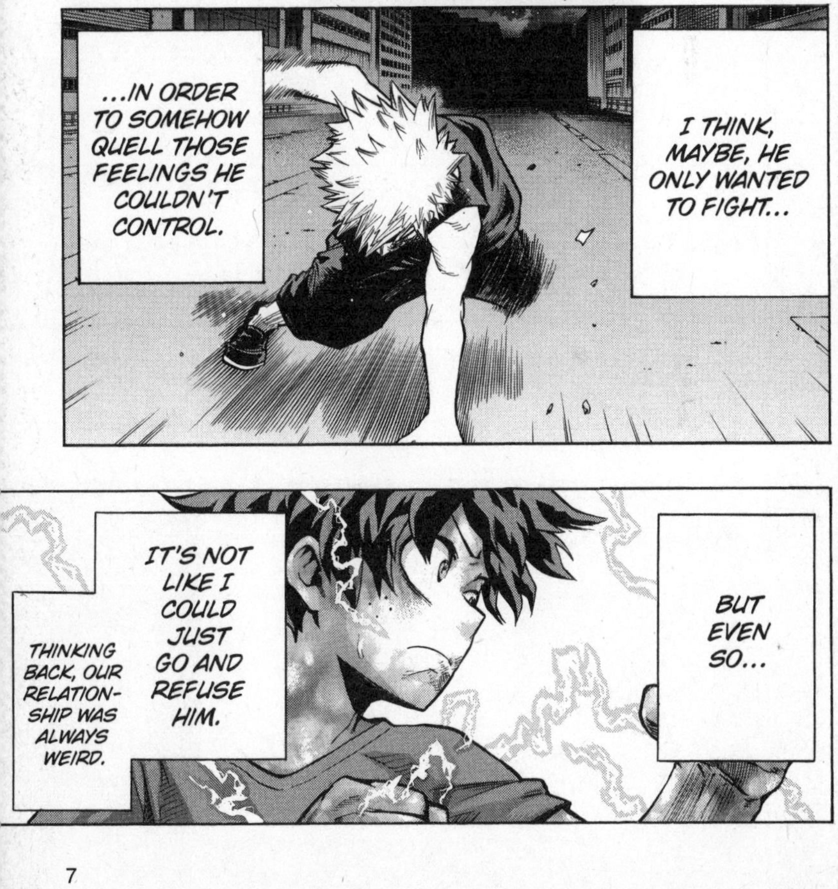
I THINK, MAYBE, HE ONLY WANTED TO FIGHT...
...IN ORDER TO SOMEHOW QUELL THOSE FEELINGS HE COULDN'T CONTROL.
BUT EVEN SO...
IT'S NOT LIKE I COULD JUST GO AND REFUSE HIM.
THINKING BACK, OUR RELATION-SHIP WAS ALWAYS WEIRD.

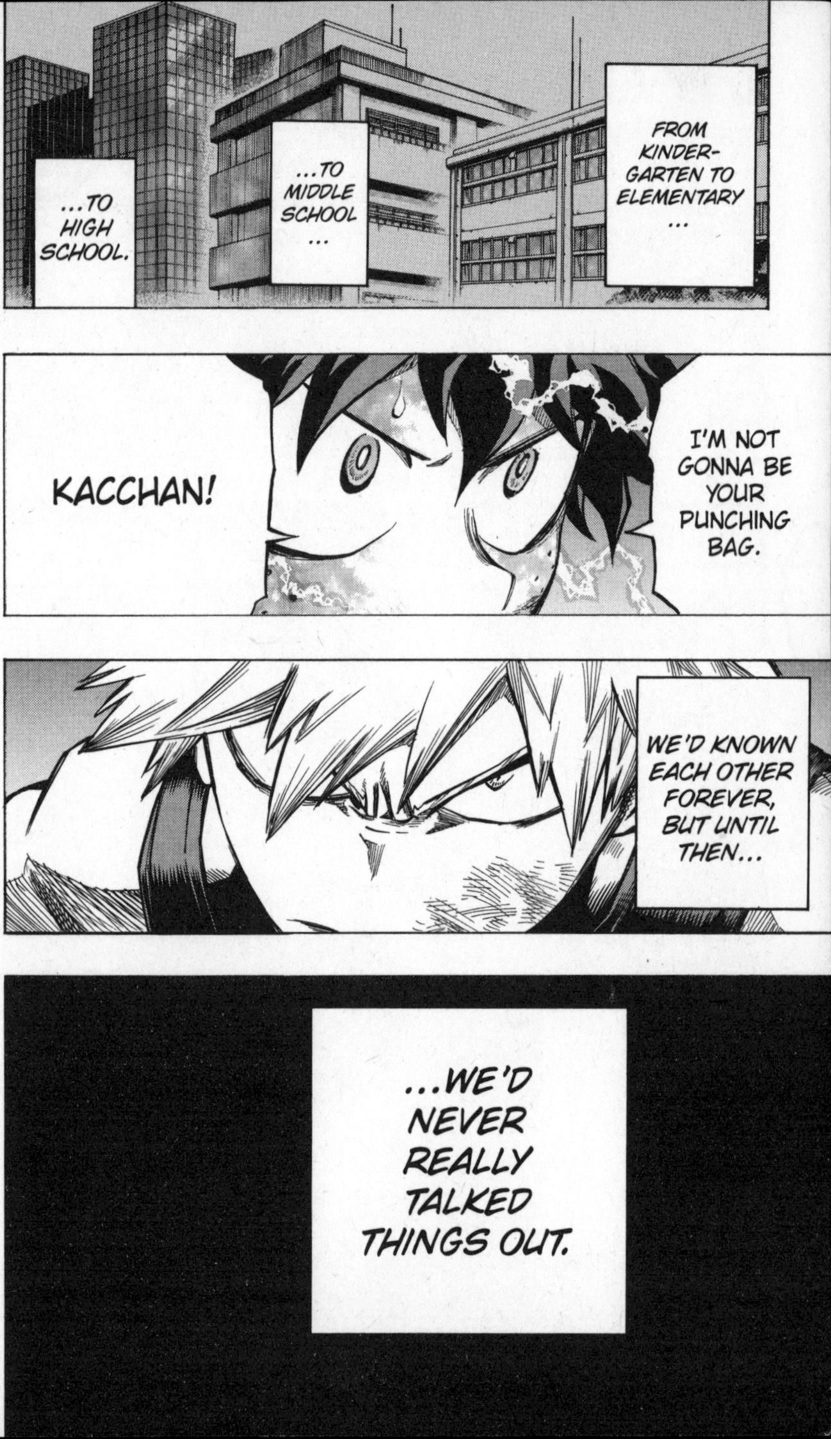
FROM KINDER-GARTEN TO ELEMENTARY...
...TO MIDDLE SCHOOL...
...TO HIGH SCHOOL.
I'M NOT GONNA BE YOUR PUNCHING BAG.
KACCHAN!
WE'D KNOWN EACH OTHER FOREVER, BUT UNTIL THEN...
...WE'D NEVER REALLY TALKED THINGS OUT.

No. 119 - Deku vs. Kacchan, Part 2

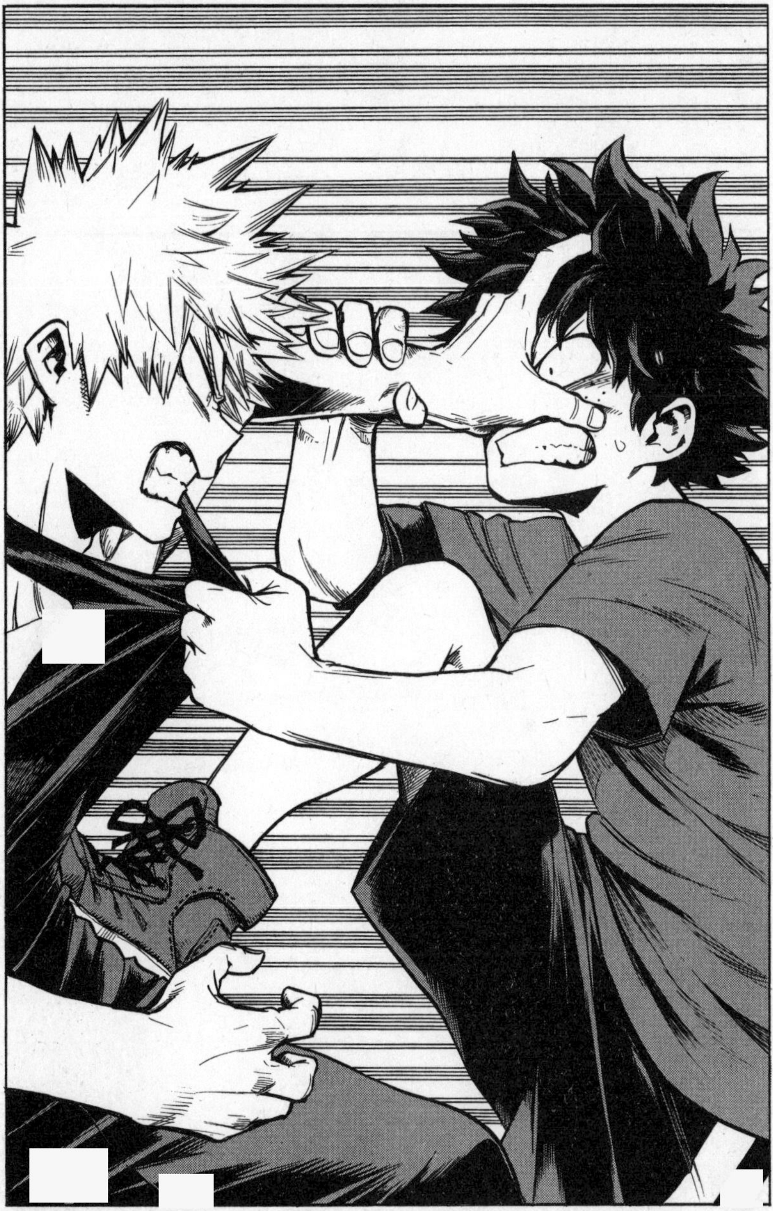

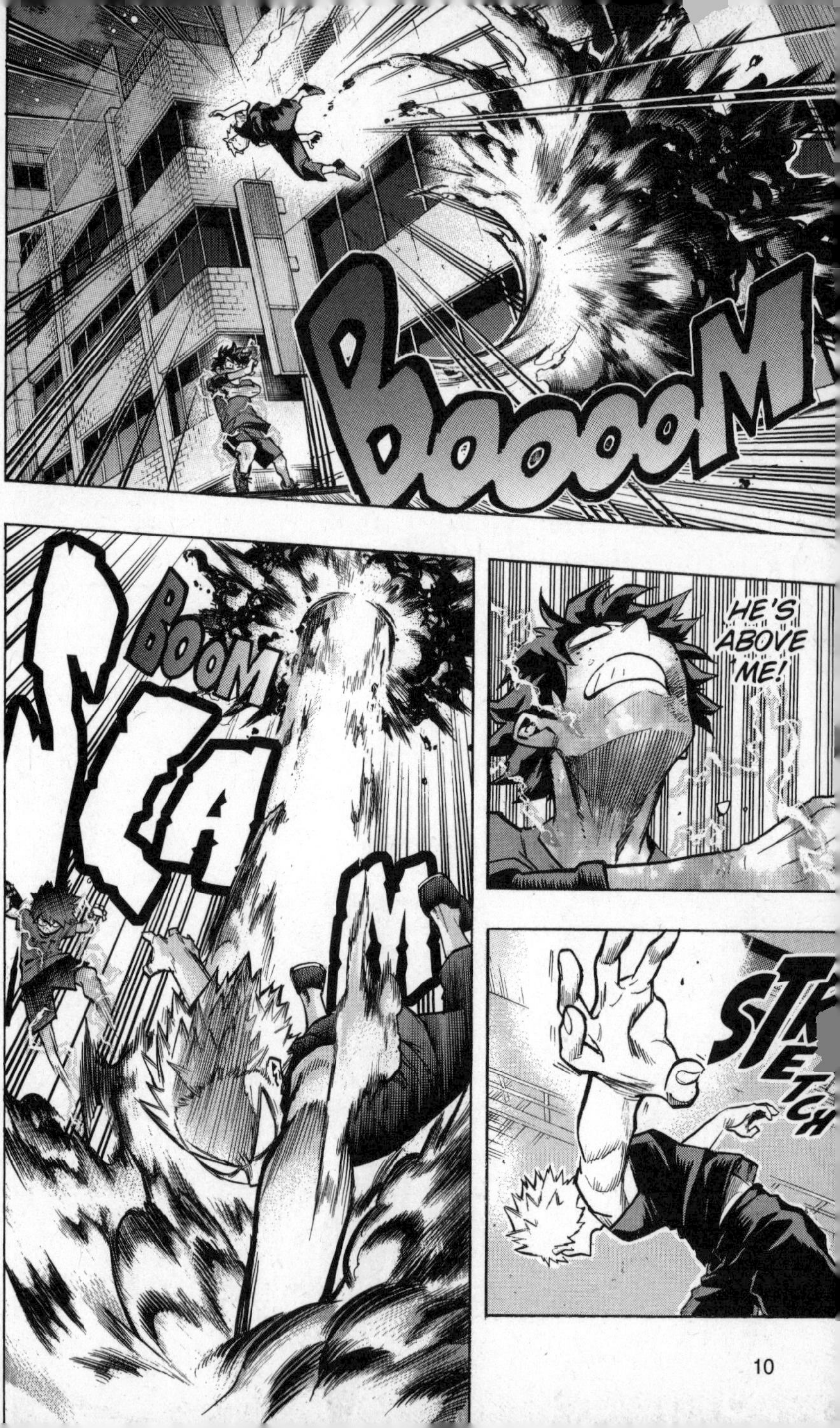
BAOOOM
HE'S ABOVE ME!
STRETCH
BOOM

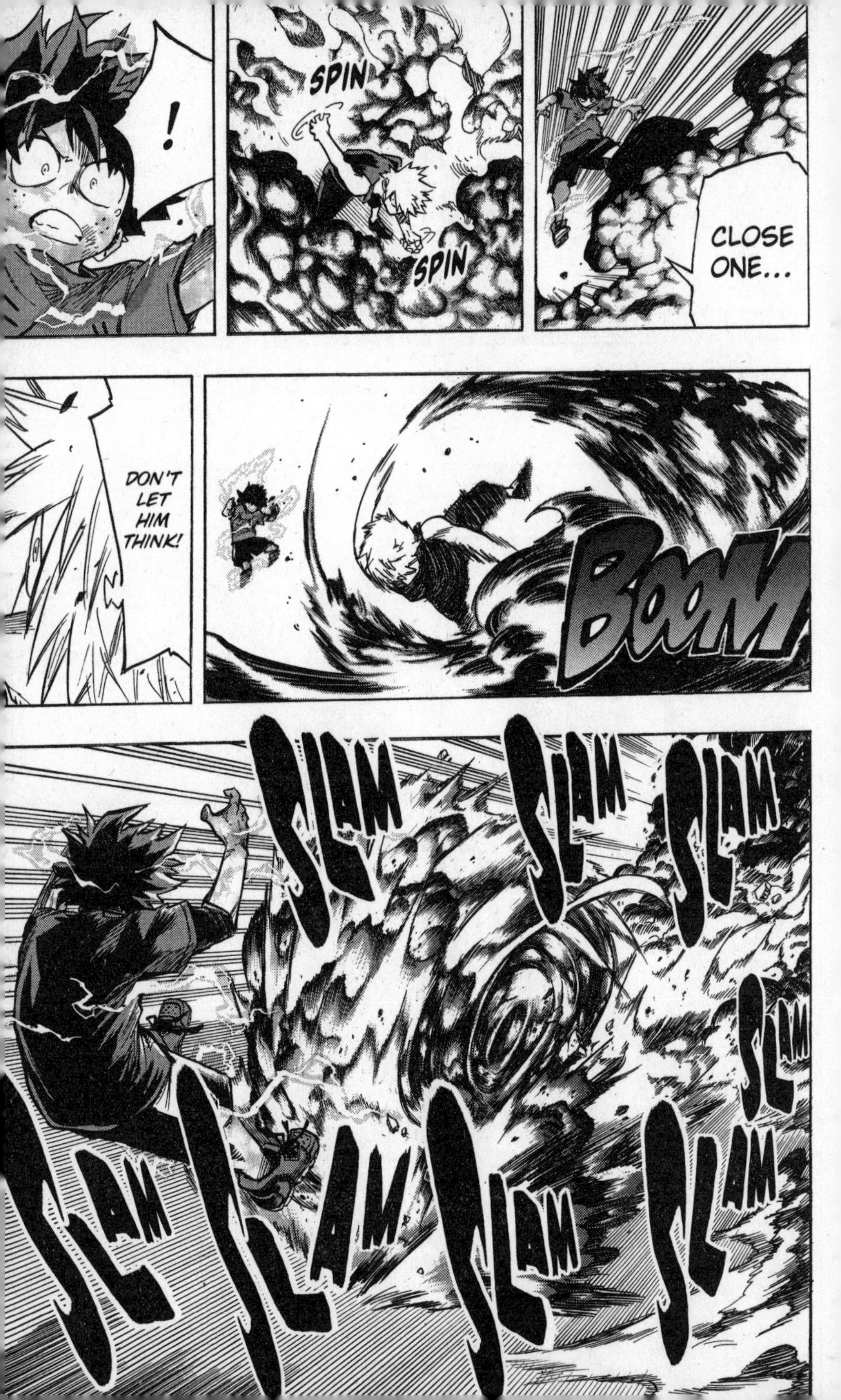
CLOSE ONE...
SPIN
SPIN
!
BOOM
DON'T LET HIM THINK!
SLAM
SLAM
SLAM
SLAM
SLAM
SLAM
SLAM
SLAM
SLAM

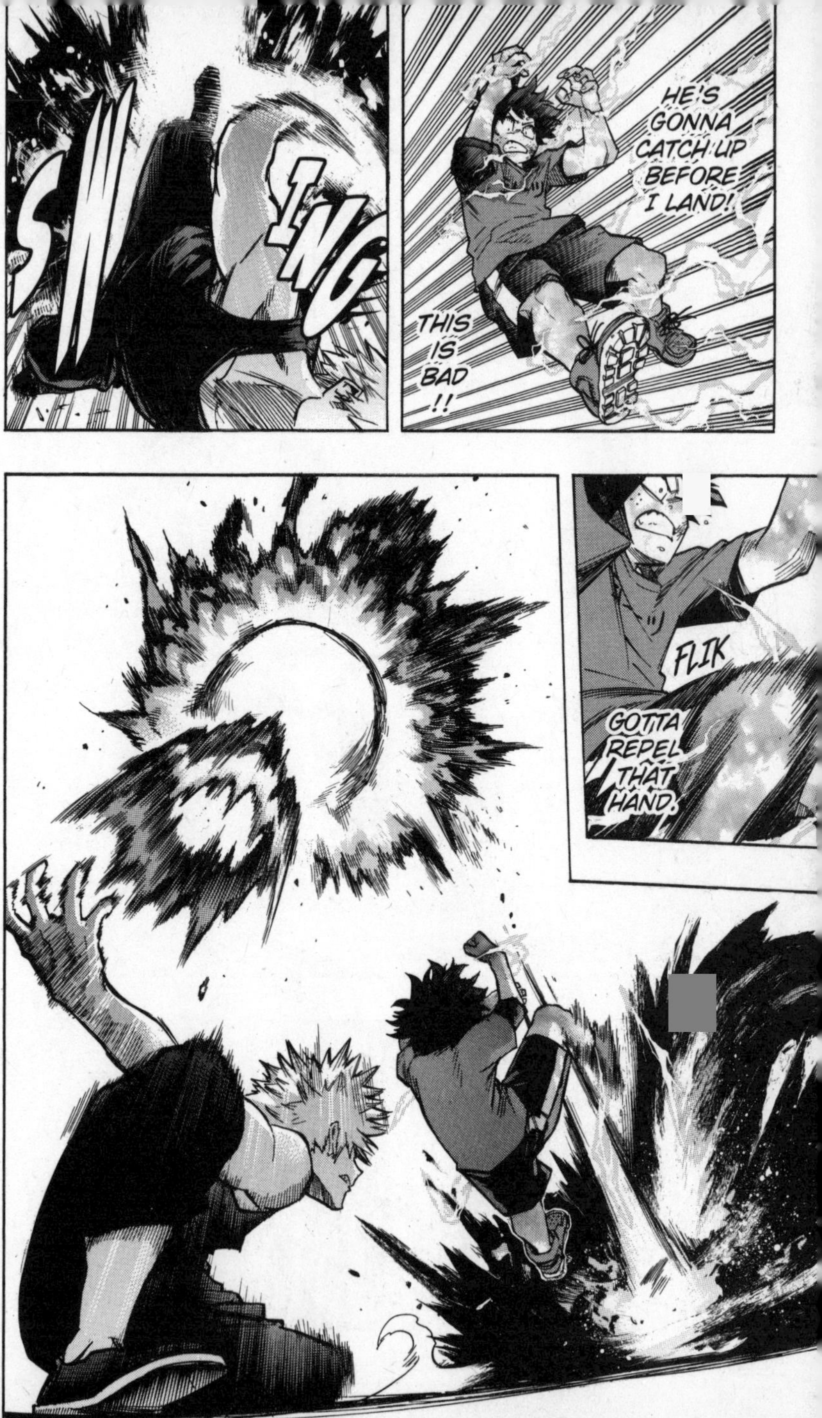
HE'S GONNA CATCH UP BEFORE I LAND!
THIS IS BAD!!
SHING
FLIK
GOTTA REPEL THAT HAND.

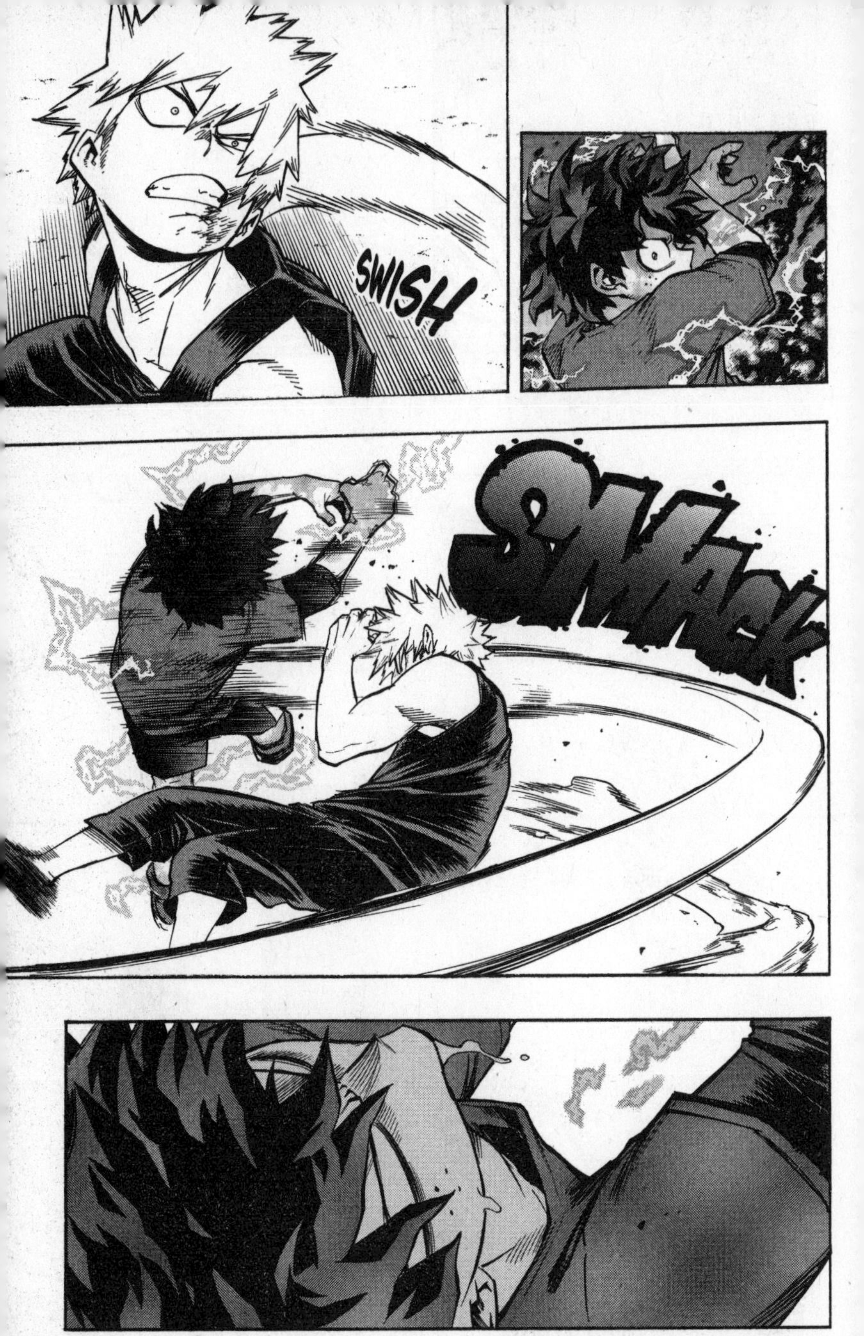
SWISH
SMACK

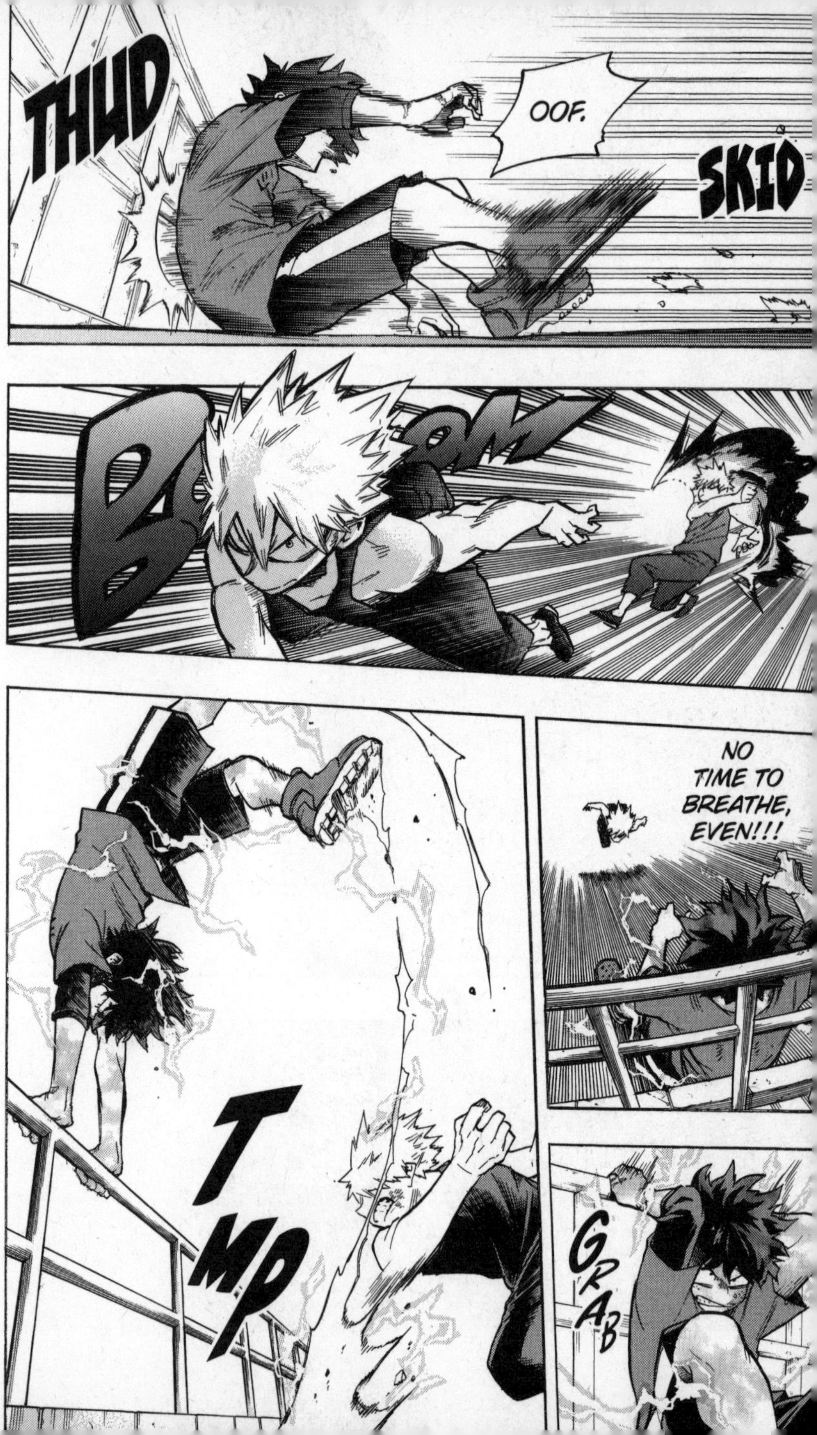
SKID
OOF.
THUD
BOOM
NO TIME TO BREATHE, EVEN!!!
GRAB
TMP

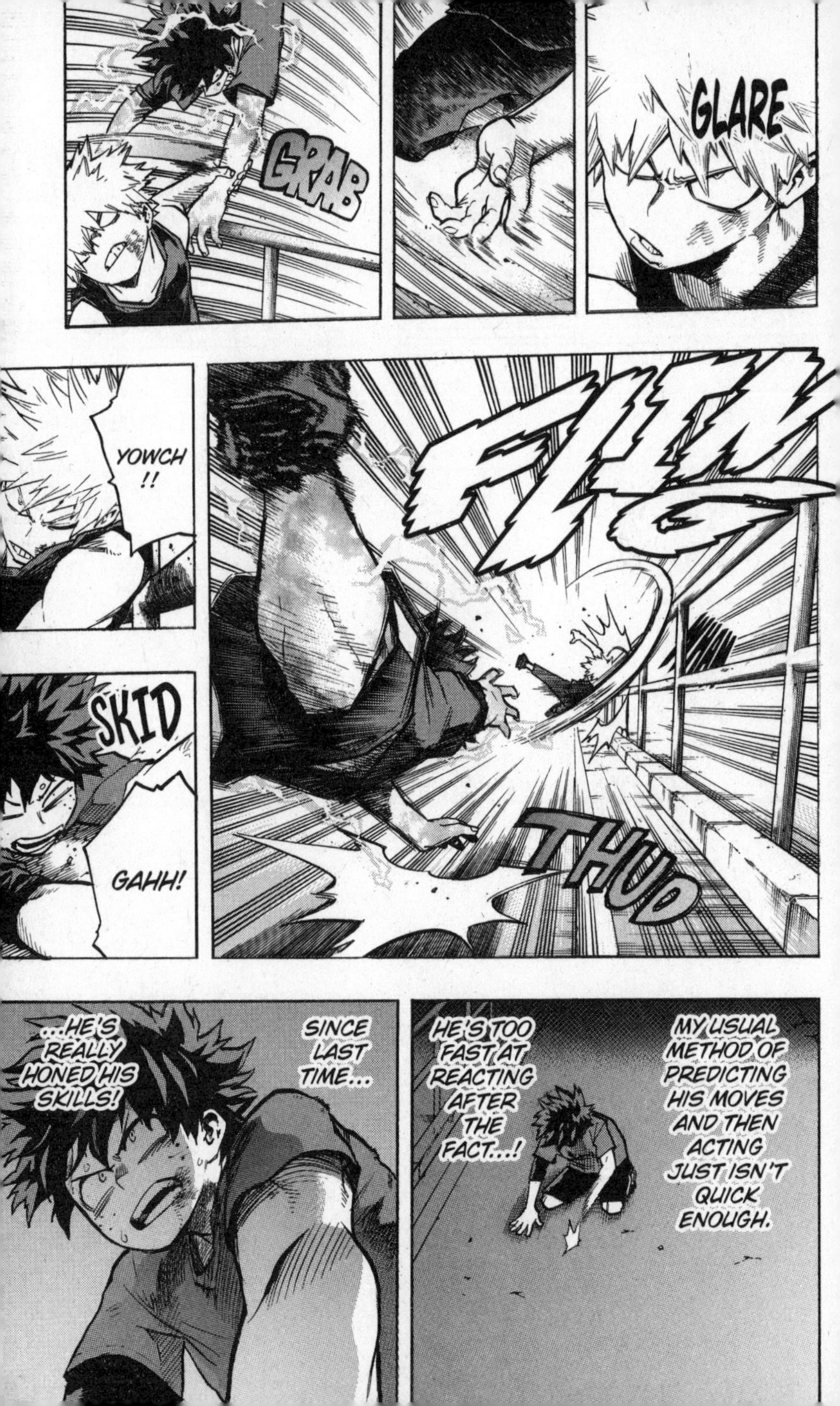
GLARE
GRAB
THUD
YOWCH!!
SKID
GAHH!
MY USUAL METHOD OF PREDICTING HIS MOVES AND THEN ACTING JUST ISN'T QUICK ENOUGH.
HE'S TOO FAST AT REACTING AFTER THE FACT...!
SINCE LAST TIME...
...HE'S REALLY HONED HIS SKILLS!

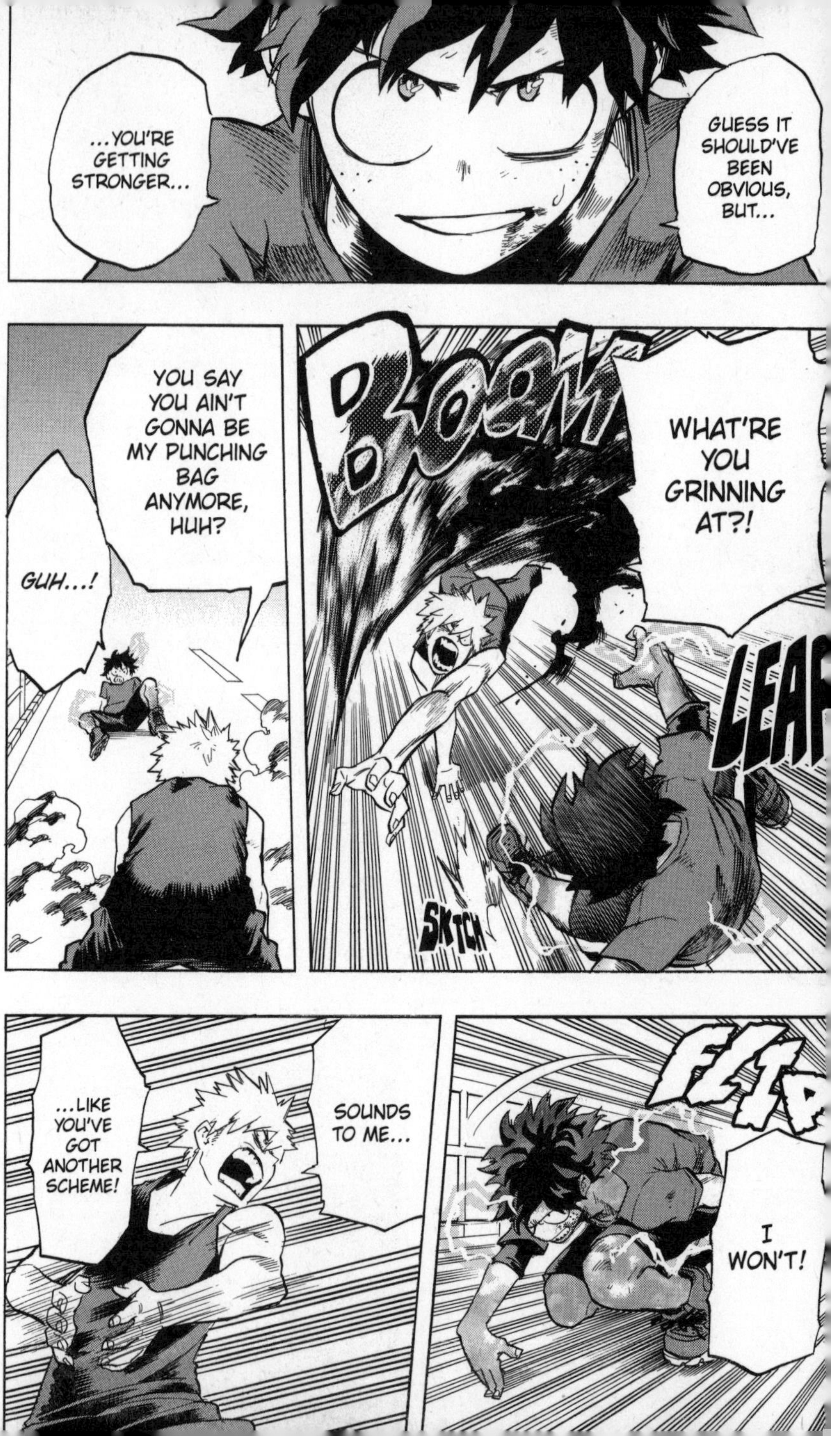
GUESS IT SHOULD'VE BEEN OBVIOUS, BUT...
...YOU'RE GETTING STRONGER...
BOOM
WHAT'RE YOU GRINNING AT?!
SKTCH
YOU SAY YOU AIN'T GONNA BE MY PUNCHING BAG ANYMORE, HUH?
GUH...!
I WON'T!
SOUNDS TO ME...
...LIKE YOU'VE GOT ANOTHER SCHEME!

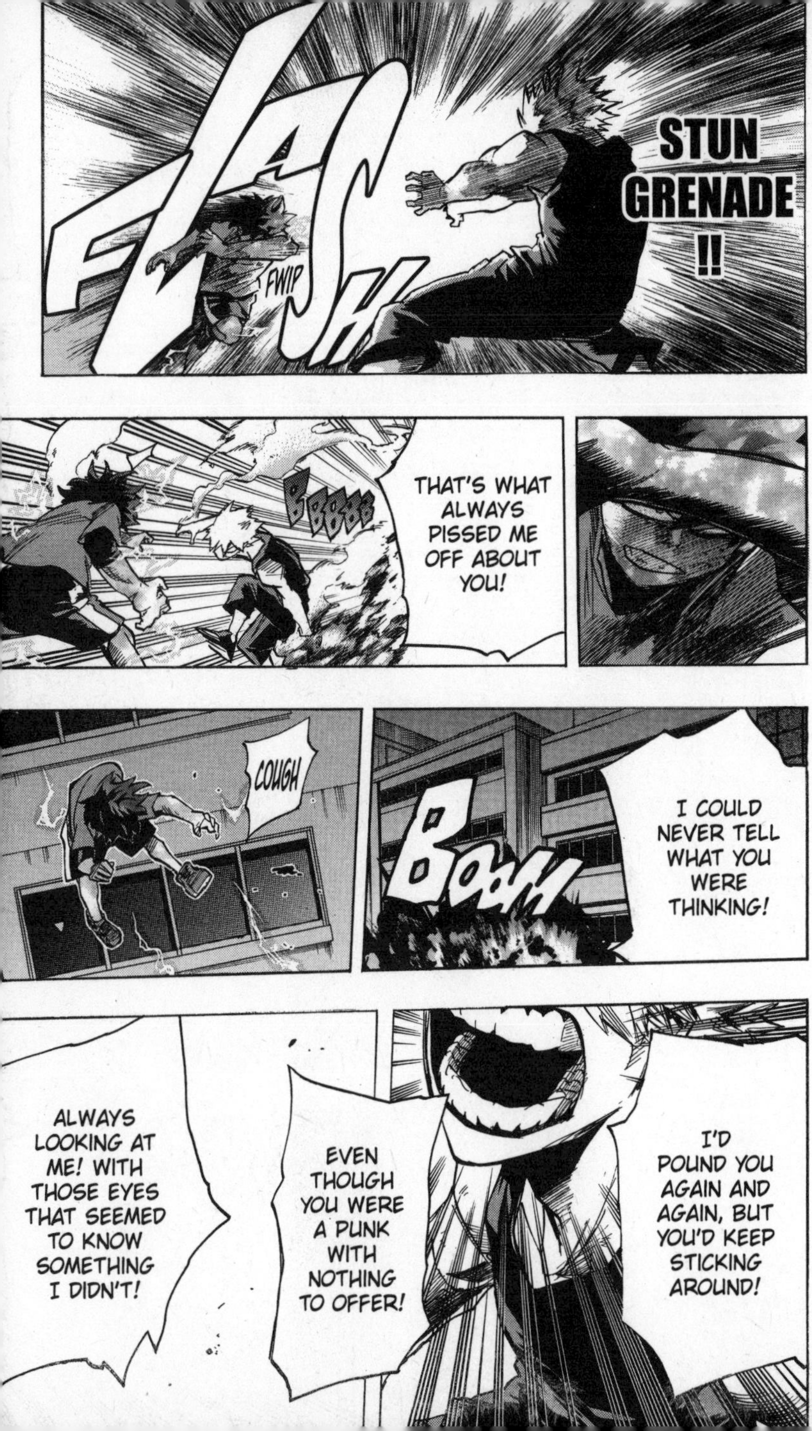
FWIP
STUN GRENADE !!
THAT'S WHAT ALWAYS PISSED ME OFF ABOUT YOU!
I COULD NEVER TELL WHAT YOU WERE THINKING!
COUGH
I'D POUND YOU AGAIN AND AGAIN, BUT YOU'D KEEP STICKING AROUND!
...
EVEN THOUGH YOU WERE A PUNK WITH NOTHING TO OFFER!
ALWAYS LOOKING AT ME! WITH THOSE EYES THAT SEEMED TO KNOW SOMETHING I DIDN'T!

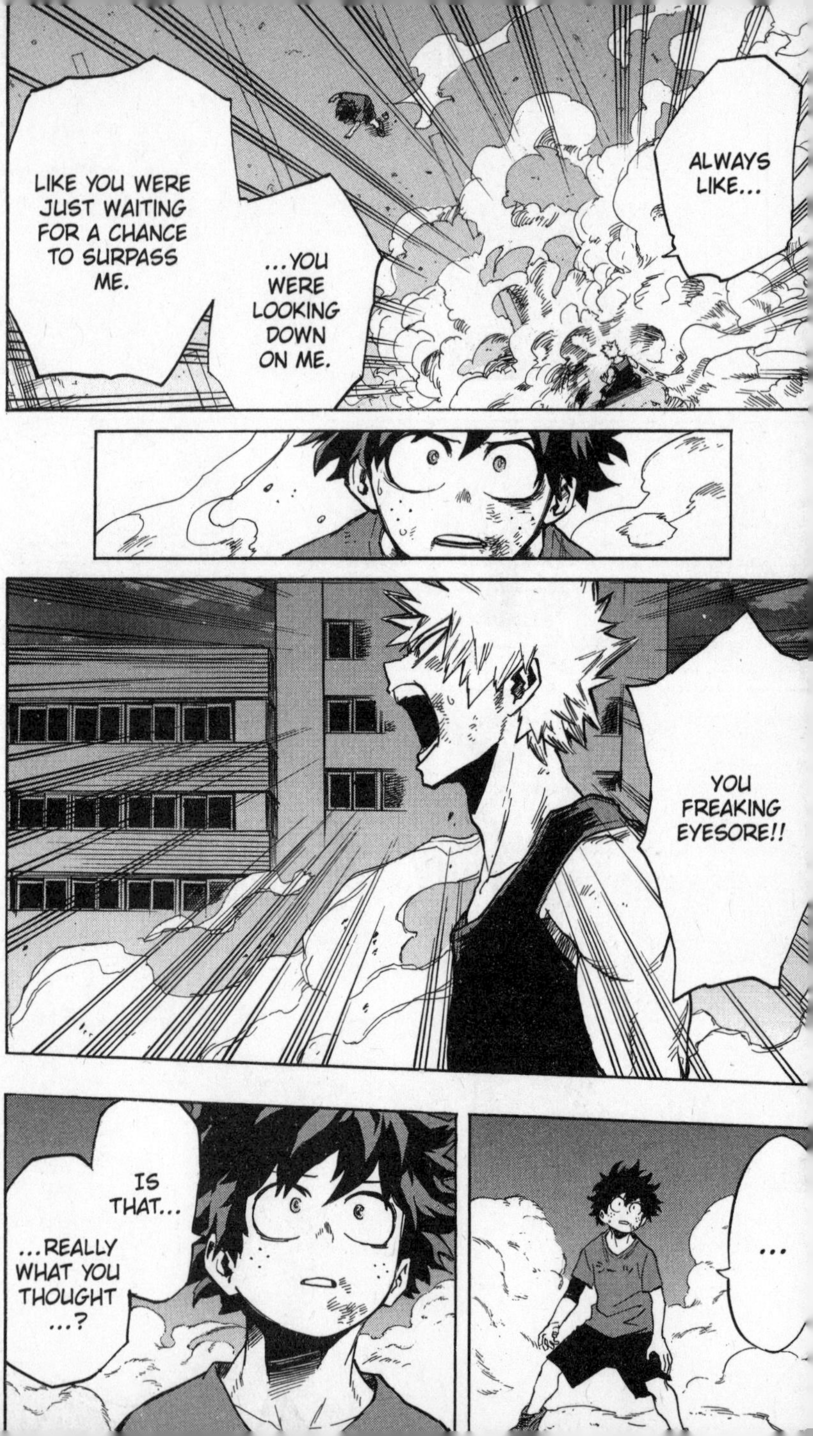
ALWAYS LIKE...
...YOU WERE LOOKING DOWN ON ME.
LIKE YOU WERE JUST WAITING FOR A CHANCE TO SURPASS ME.
YOU FREAKING EYESORE!!
...
IS THAT...
...REALLY WHAT YOU THOUGHT ...?

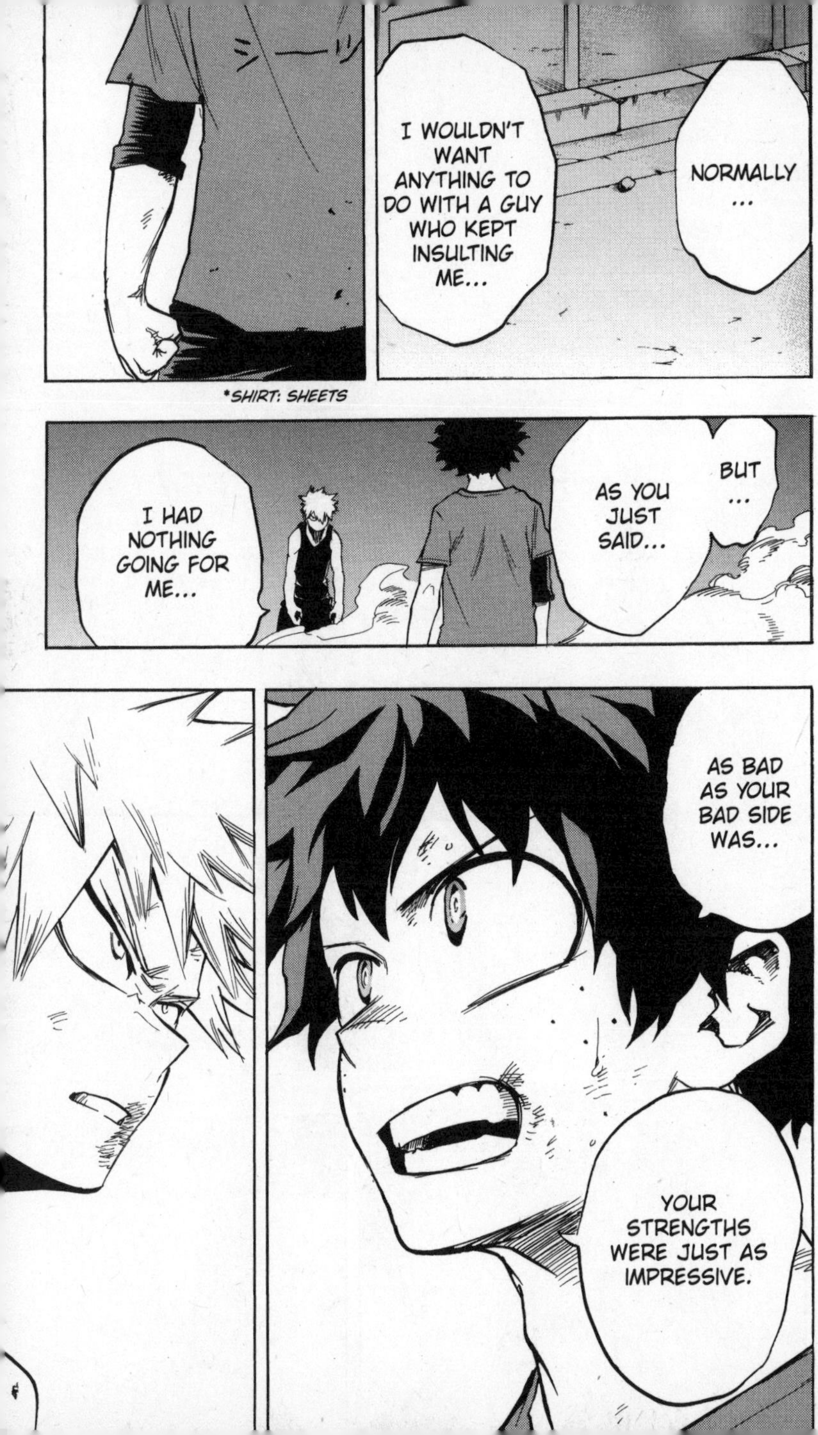
NORMALLY...
I WOULDN'T WANT ANYTHING TO DO WITH A GUY WHO KEPT INSULTING ME...
*SHIRT: SHEETS
BUT...
AS YOU JUST SAID...
I HAD NOTHING GOING FOR ME...
AS BAD AS YOUR BAD SIDE WAS...
YOUR STRENGTHS WERE JUST AS IMPRESSIVE.

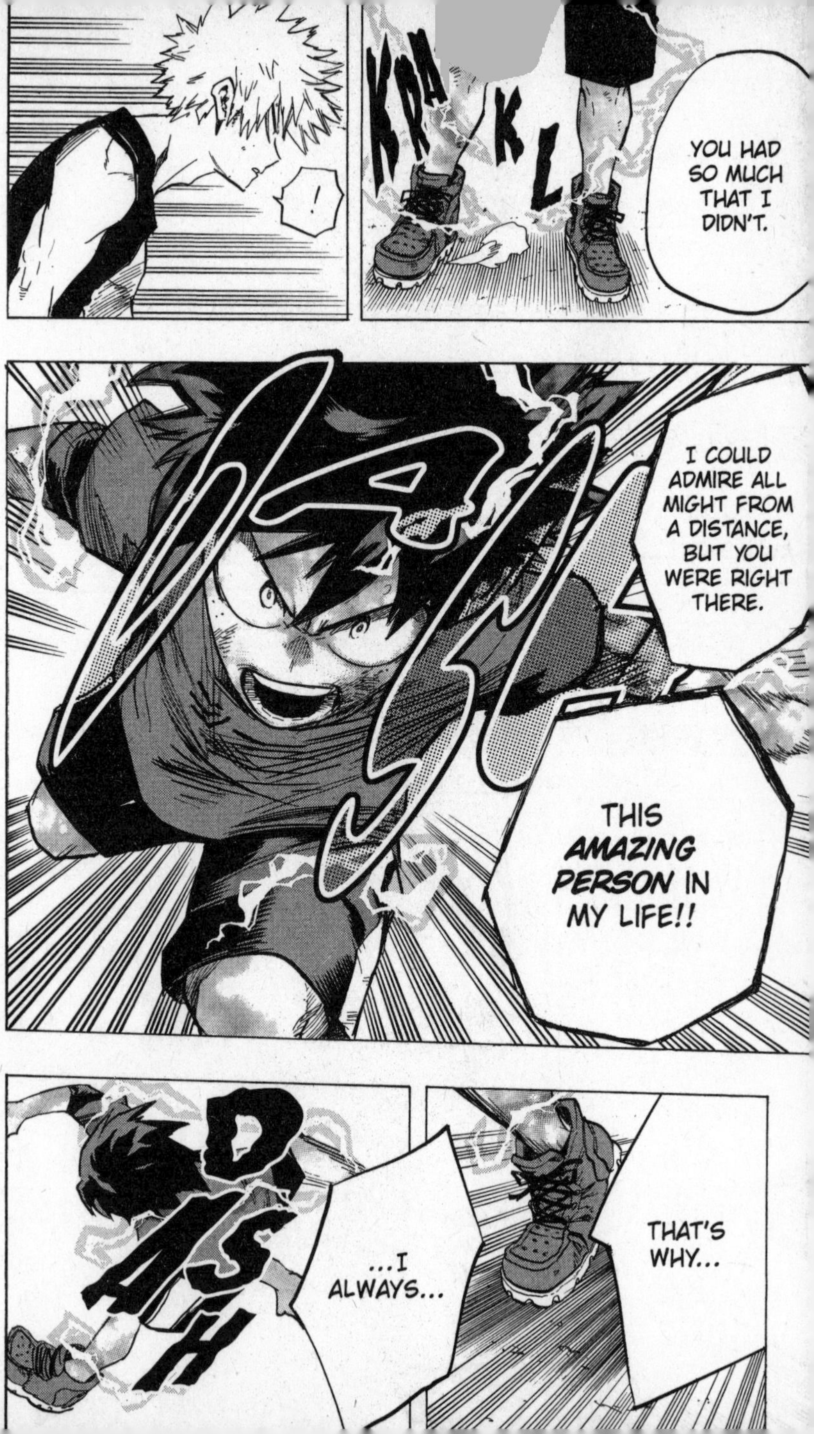
YOU HAD SO MUCH THAT I DIDN'T.
KRAKL
!
I COULD ADMIRE ALL MIGHT FROM A DISTANCE, BUT YOU WERE RIGHT THERE.
THIS *AMAZING PERSON* IN MY LIFE!!
THAT'S WHY...
...I ALWAYS...

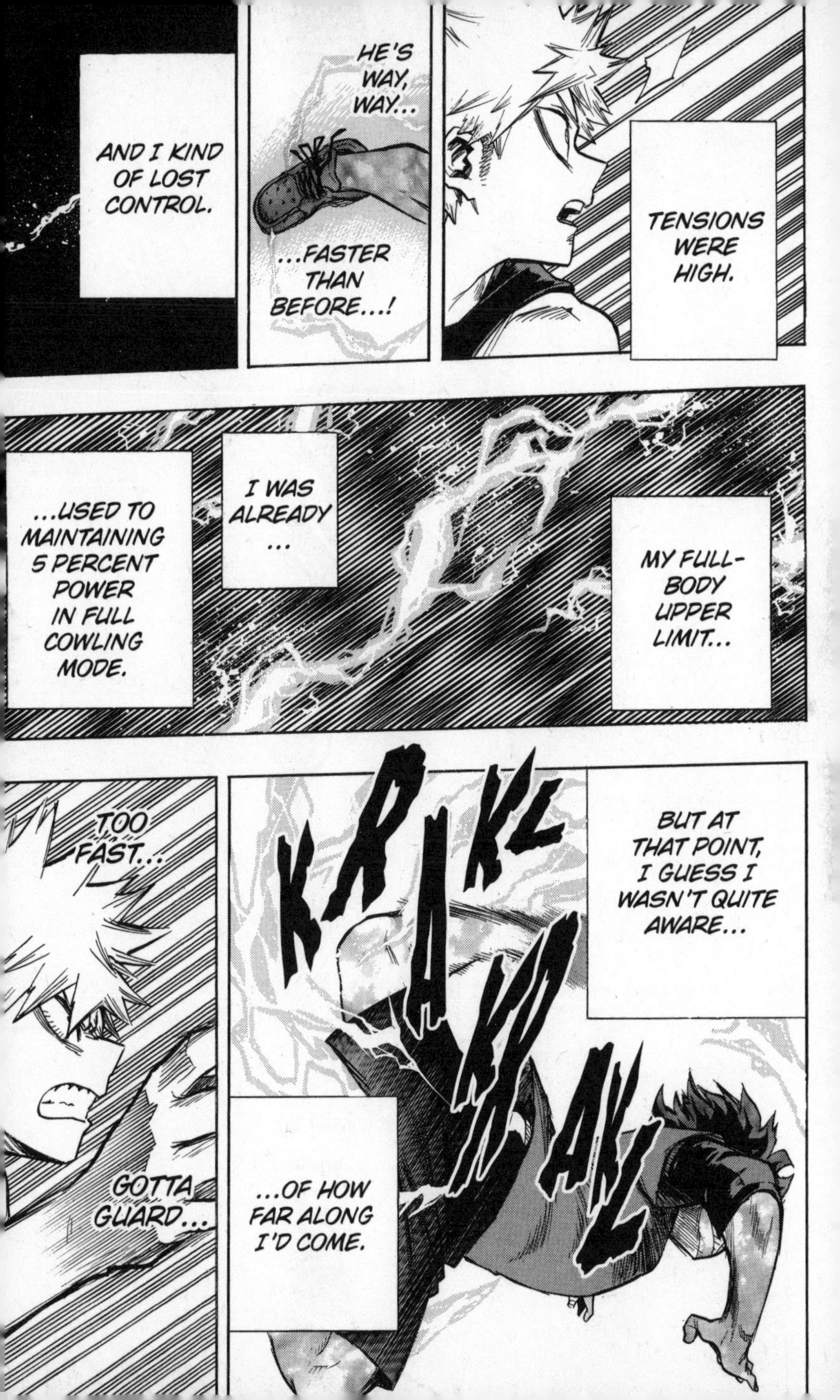
TENSIONS WERE HIGH.
HE'S WAY, WAY...
...FASTER THAN BEFORE...!
AND I KIND OF LOST CONTROL.
MY FULL-BODY UPPER LIMIT...
I WAS ALREADY ...
...USED TO MAINTAINING 5 PERCENT POWER IN FULL COWLING MODE.
BUT AT THAT POINT, I GUESS I WASN'T QUITE AWARE...
...OF HOW FAR ALONG I'D COME.
TOO FAST...
GOTTA GUARD...

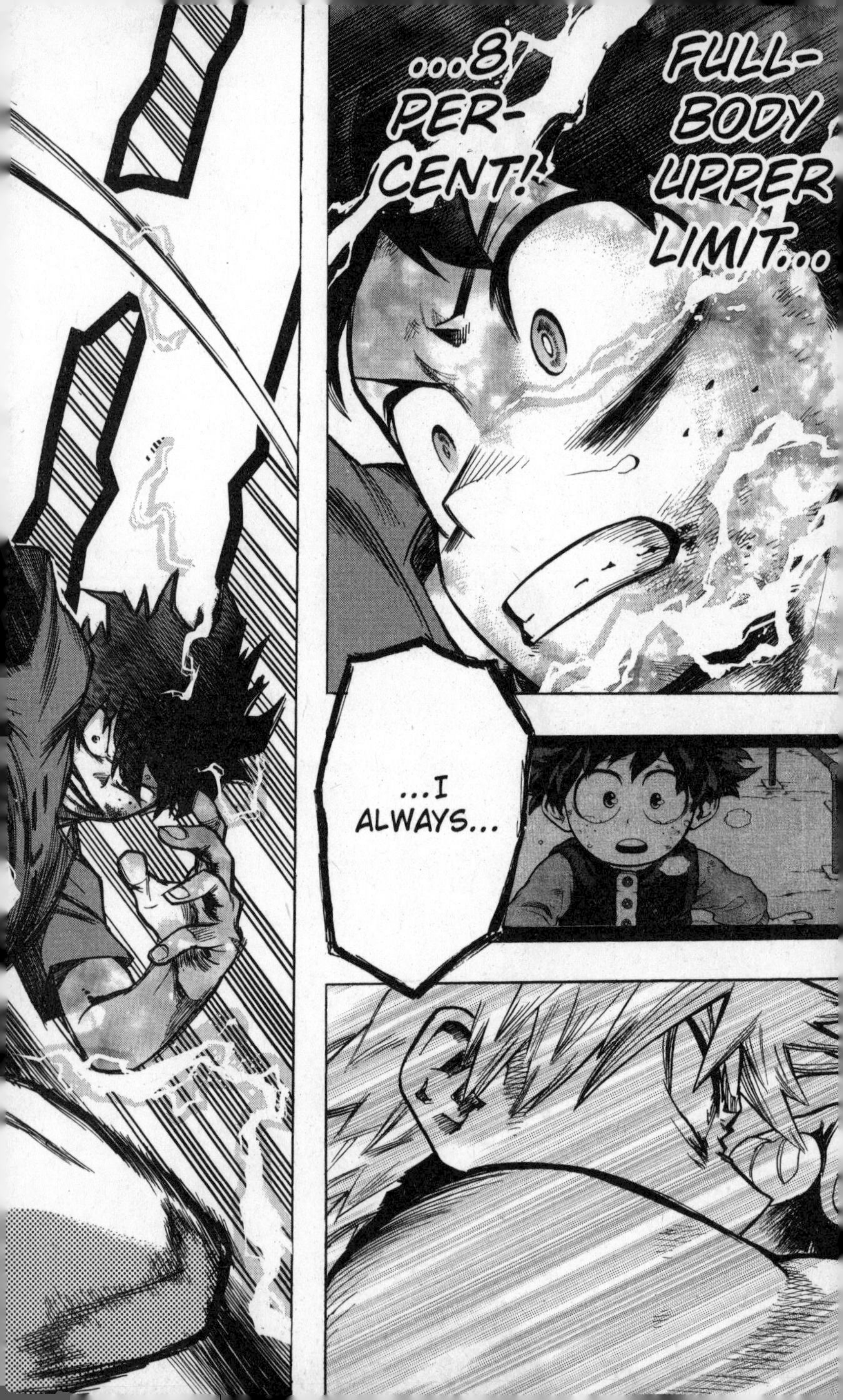
FULL-BODY UPPER LIMIT...
...8 PER-CENT!
...I ALWAYS...

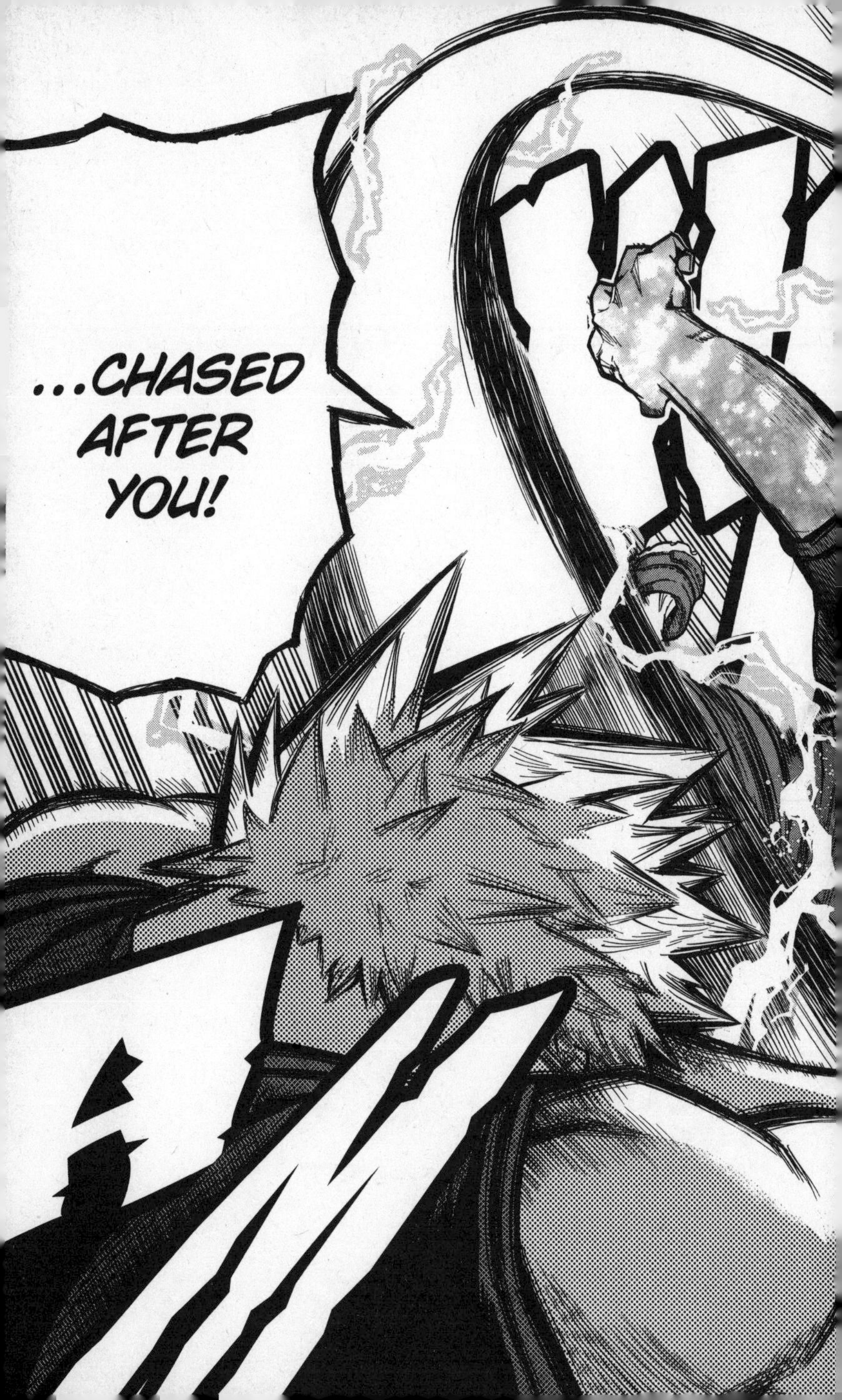
...CHASED AFTER YOU!

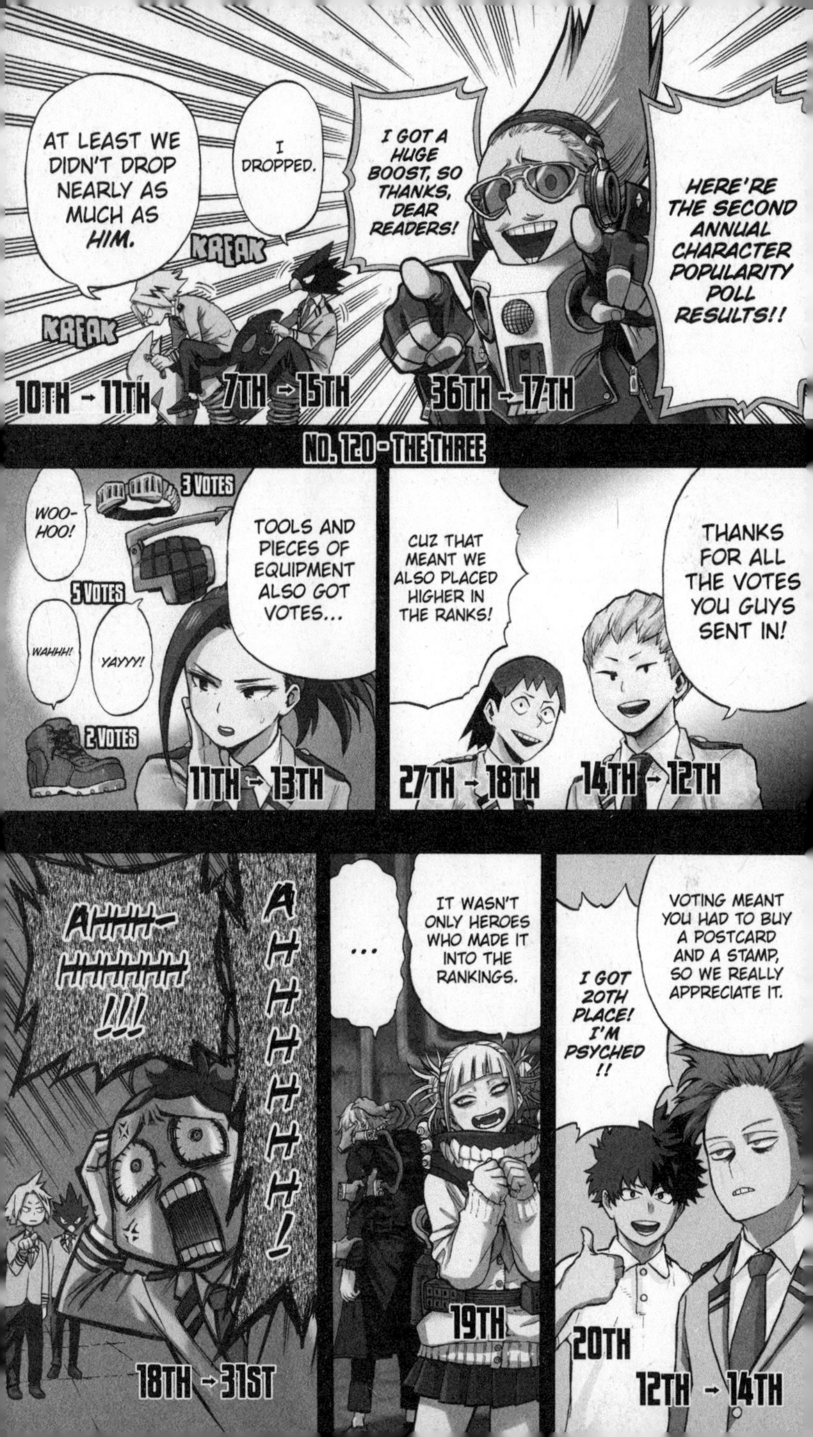
HERE'RE THE SECOND ANNUAL CHARACTER POPULARITY POLL RESULTS!!
I GOT A HUGE BOOST, SO THANKS, DEAR READERS!
36TH → 17TH
I DROPPED.
AT LEAST WE DIDN'T DROP NEARLY AS MUCH AS HIM.
KREAK
KREAK
7TH → 15TH
10TH → 11TH
No. 120 - The Three
THANKS FOR ALL THE VOTES YOU GUYS SENT IN!
CUZ THAT MEANT WE ALSO PLACED HIGHER IN THE RANKS!
14TH → 12TH
27TH → 18TH
TOOLS AND PIECES OF EQUIPMENT ALSO GOT VOTES...
3 VOTES
WOO-HOO!
5 VOTES
YAYYY!
WAHHH!
2 VOTES
11TH → 13TH
VOTING MEANT YOU HAD TO BUY A POSTCARD AND A STAMP, SO WE REALLY APPRECIATE IT.
I GOT 20TH PLACE! I'M PSYCHED!!
20TH
12TH → 14TH
IT WASN'T ONLY HEROES WHO MADE IT INTO THE RANKINGS.
...
19TH
AHHHHHHHHH!
AHHH-HHHHHHH!!!
18TH → 31ST

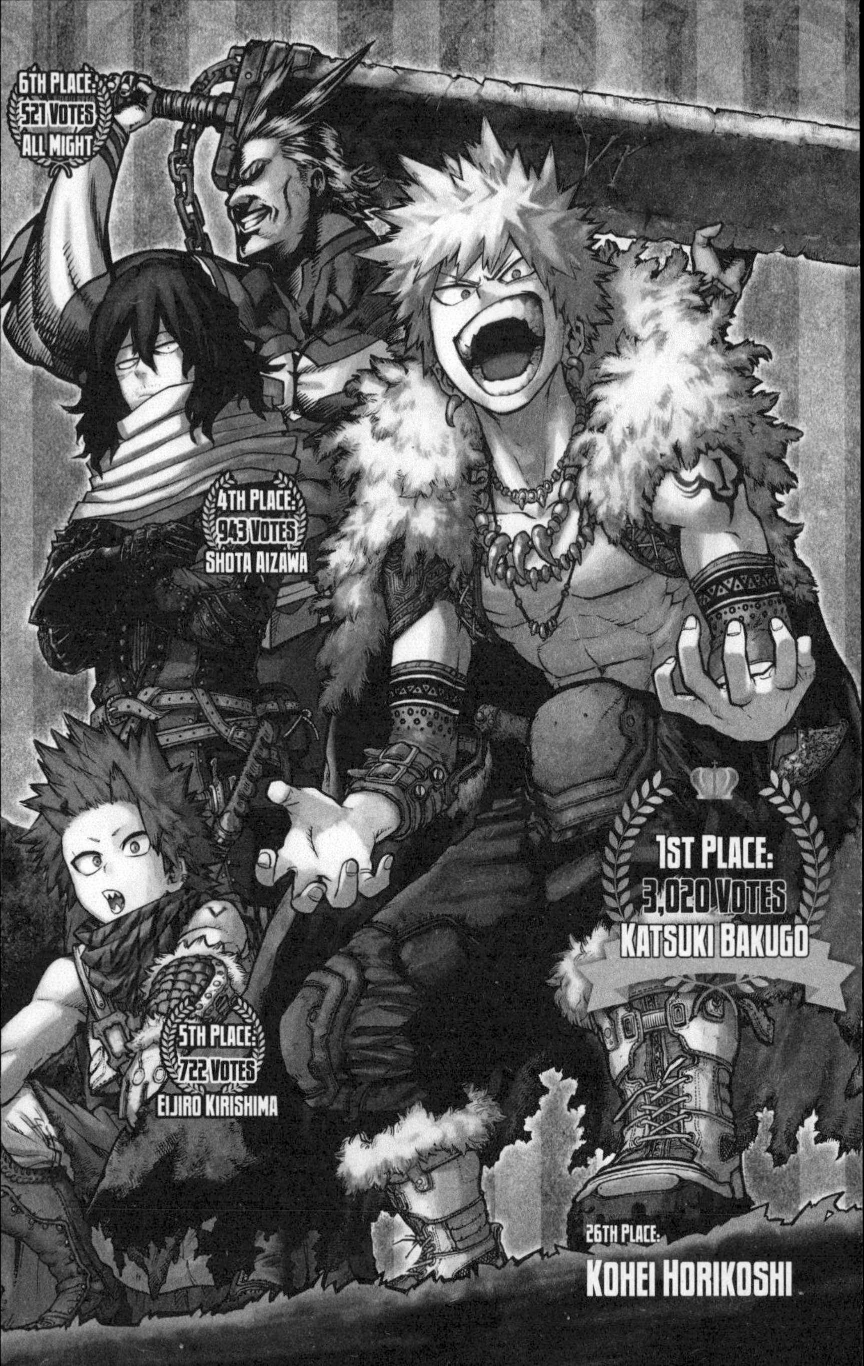
6th Place:
521 Votes
All Might
4th Place:
943 Votes
Shota Aizawa
1st Place:
3,020 Votes
Katsuki Bakugo
5th Place:
722 Votes
Eijiro Kirishima
26th Place:
Kohei Horikoshi

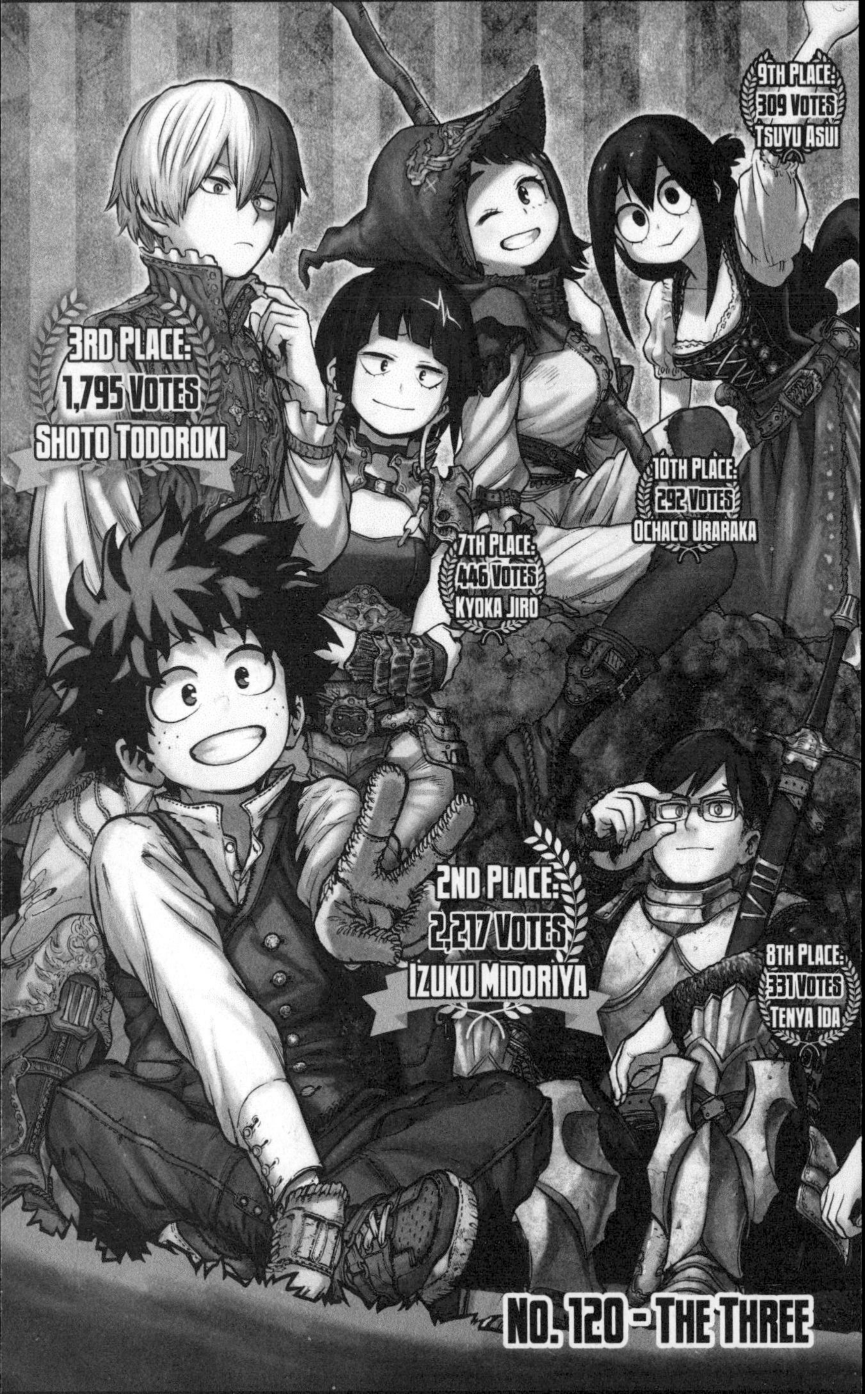
9th Place:
309 Votes
Tsuyu Asui
3rd Place:
1,795 Votes
Shoto Todoroki
10th Place:
292 Votes
Ochaco Uraraka
7th Place:
446 Votes
Kyoka Jiro
2nd Place:
2,217 Votes
Izuku Midoriya
8th Place:
331 Votes
Tenya Ida
No. 120 - The Three

MY HERO ACADEMIA

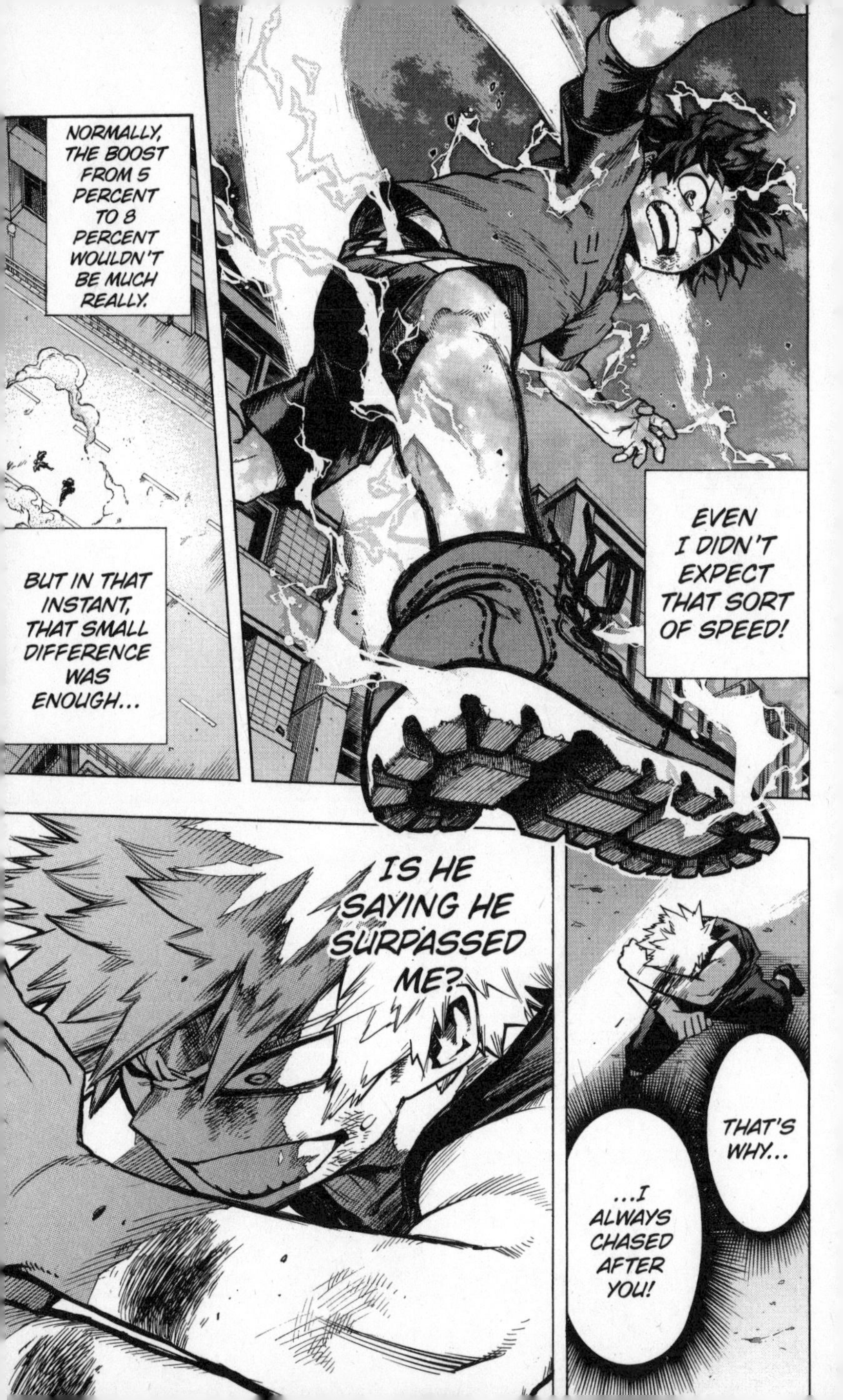
EVEN I DIDN'T EXPECT THAT SORT OF SPEED!
NORMALLY, THE BOOST FROM 5 PERCENT TO 8 PERCENT WOULDN'T BE MUCH REALLY.
BUT IN THAT INSTANT, THAT SMALL DIFFERENCE WAS ENOUGH...
THAT'S WHY...
...I ALWAYS CHASED AFTER YOU!
IS HE SAYING HE SURPASSED ME?

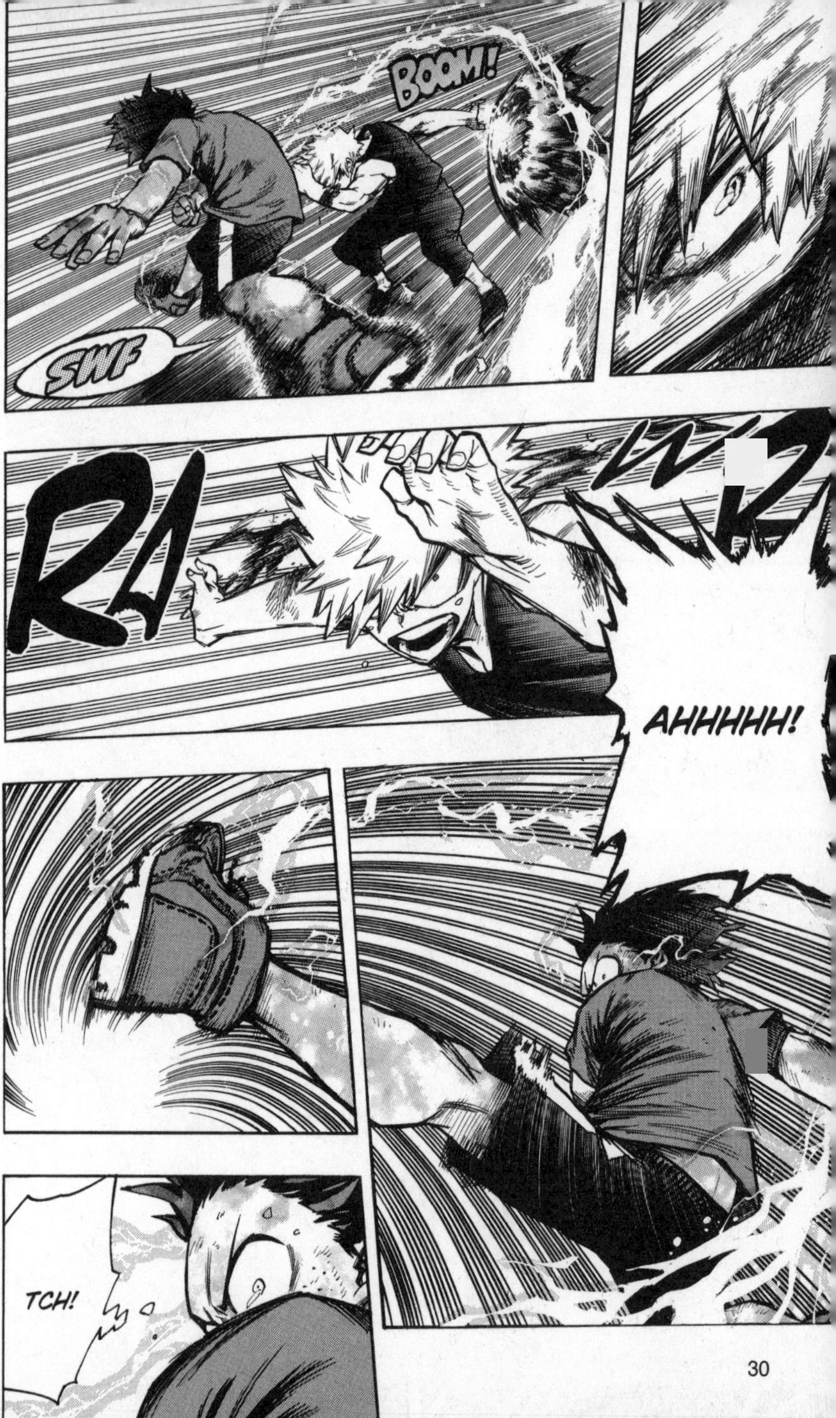
BOOM!
SWF
RA
AHHHHH!
TCH!

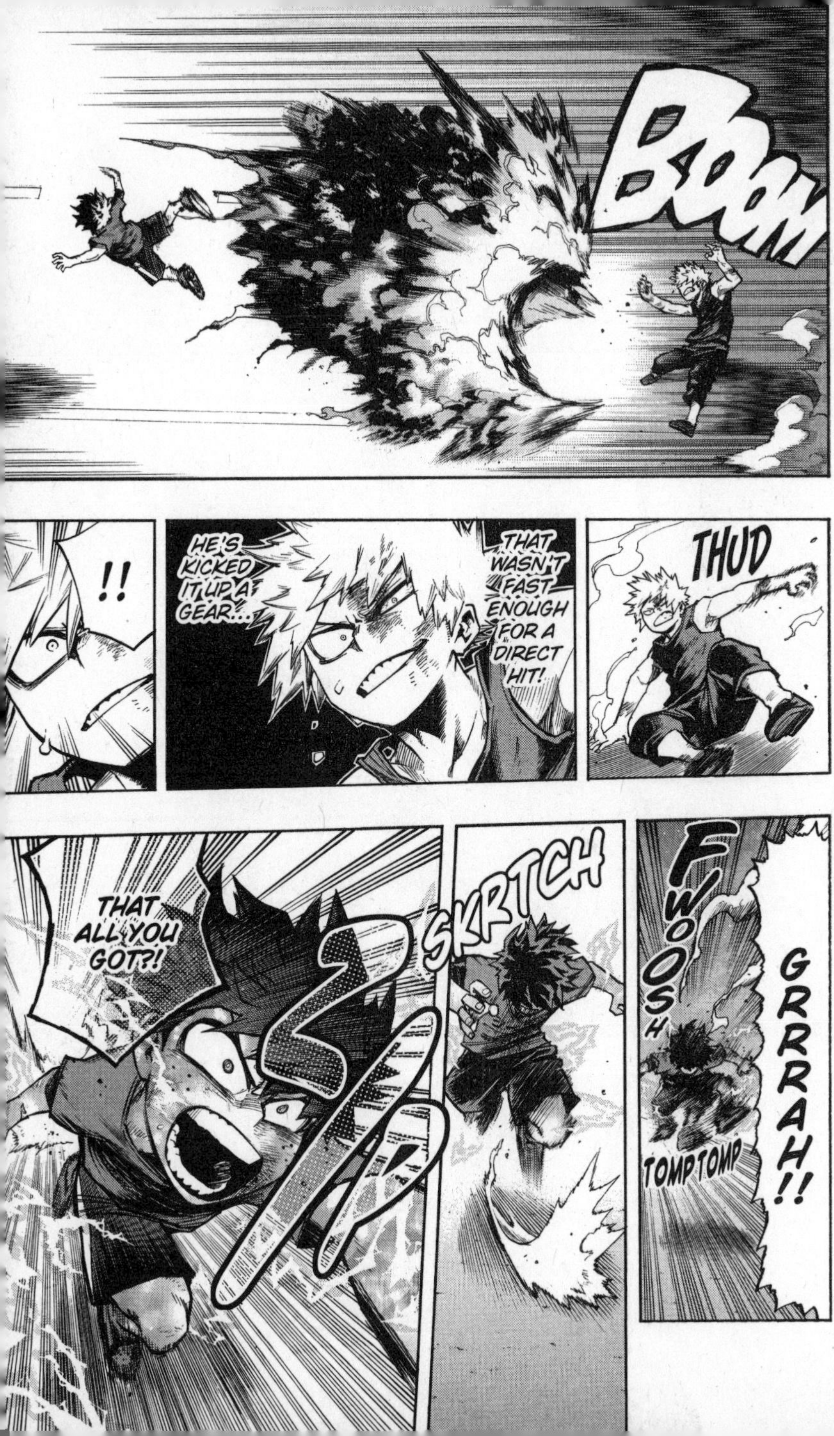
BOOM
THUD
THAT WASN'T FAST ENOUGH FOR A DIRECT HIT!
HE'S KICKED IT UP A GEAR...
!!
FWOOOSH
GRRRAH!!
TOMP TOMP
SKRTCH
THAT ALL YOU GOT?!

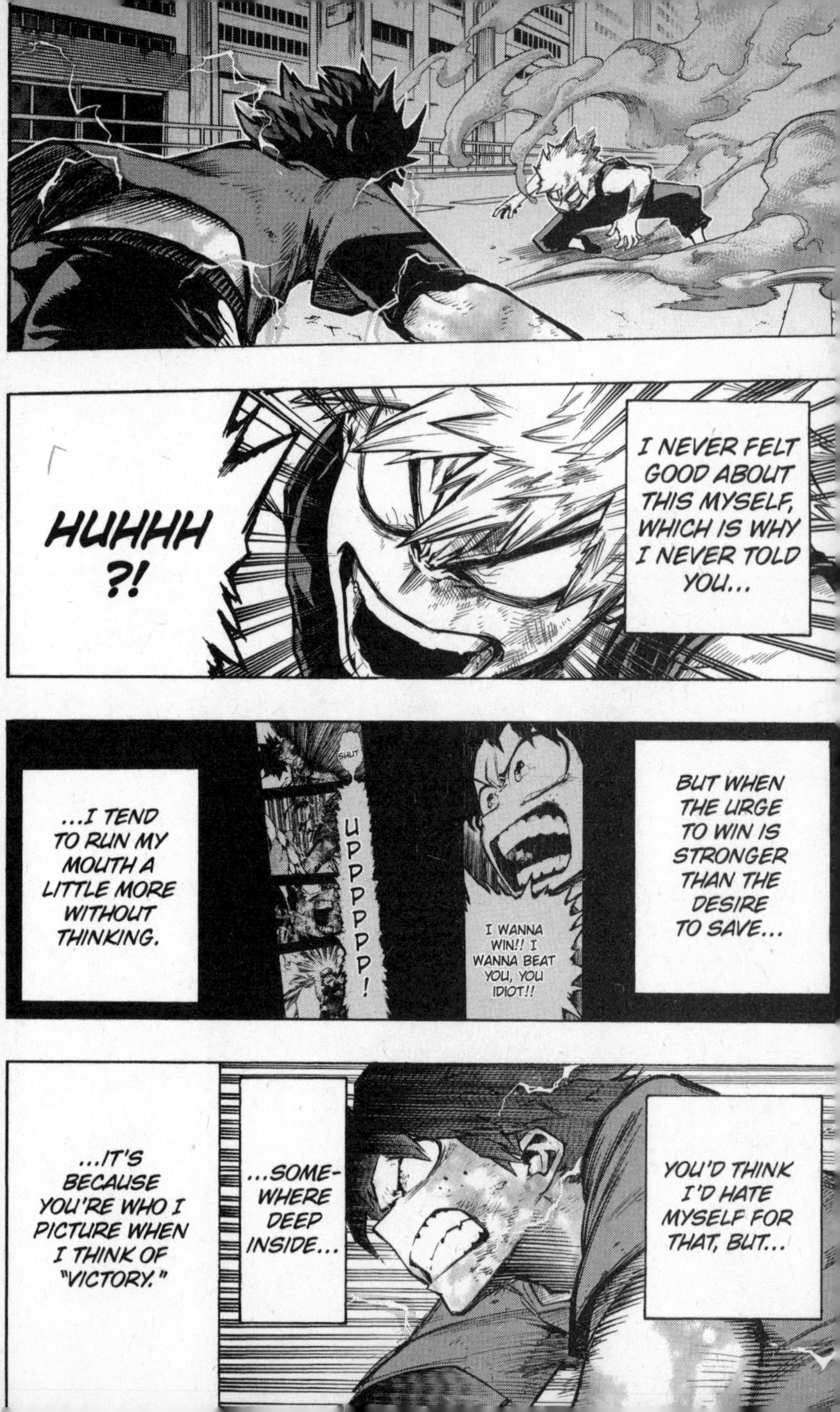
I NEVER FELT GOOD ABOUT THIS MYSELF, WHICH IS WHY I NEVER TOLD YOU...
HUHHH ?!
BUT WHEN THE URGE TO WIN IS STRONGER THAN THE DESIRE TO SAVE...
I WANNA WIN!! I WANNA BEAT YOU, YOU IDIOT!!
SHUT UPPPPPP!
...I TEND TO RUN MY MOUTH A LITTLE MORE WITHOUT THINKING.
YOU'D THINK I'D HATE MYSELF FOR THAT, BUT...
...SOME-WHERE DEEP INSIDE...
...IT'S BECAUSE YOU'RE WHO I PICTURE WHEN I THINK OF "VICTORY."

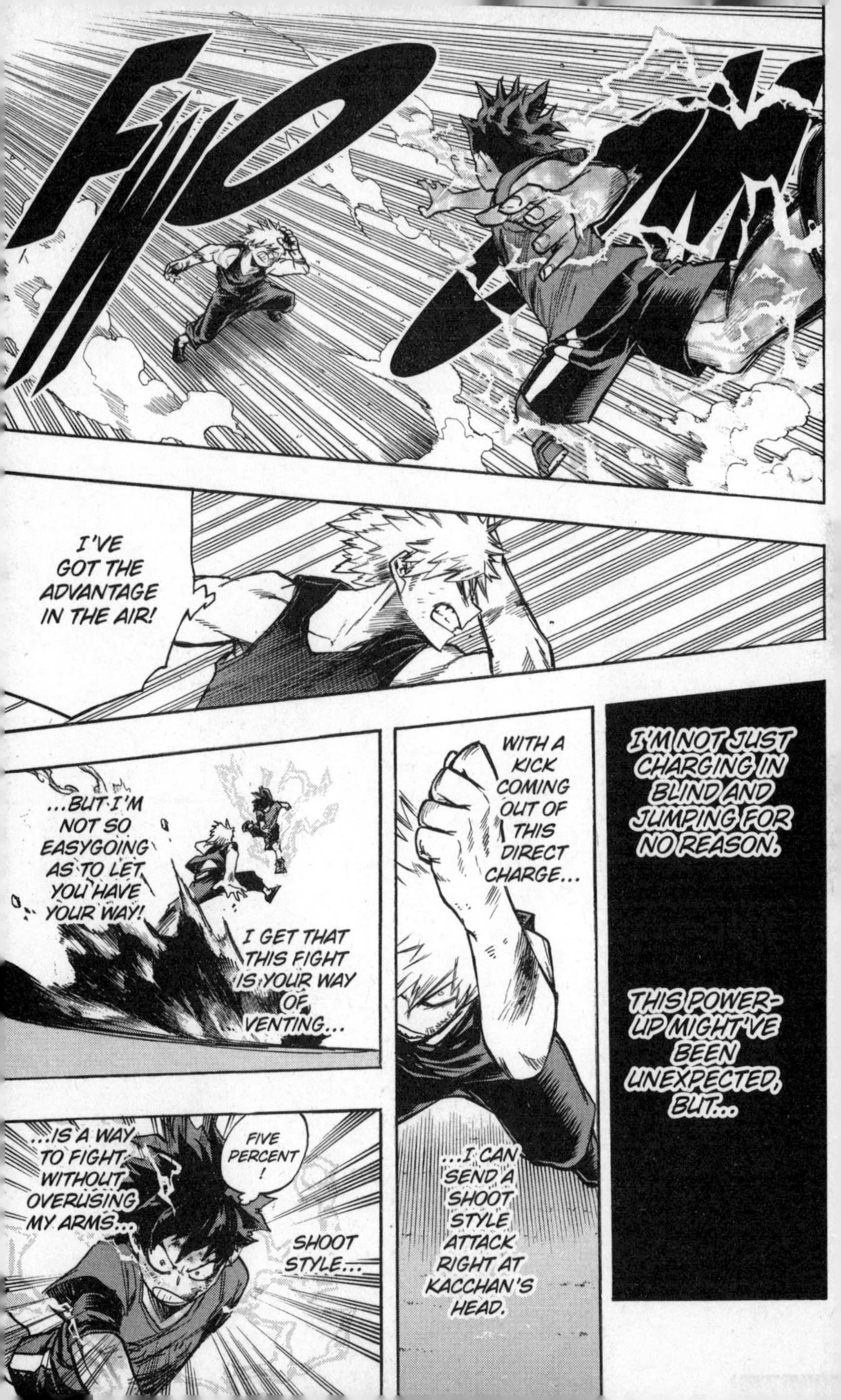

I'VE GOT THE ADVANTAGE IN THE AIR!
I'M NOT JUST CHARGING IN BLIND AND JUMPING FOR NO REASON.
THIS POWER-UP MIGHT'VE BEEN UNEXPECTED, BUT...
WITH A KICK COMING OUT OF THIS DIRECT CHARGE...
...I CAN SEND A SHOOT STYLE ATTACK RIGHT AT KACCHAN'S HEAD.
I GET THAT THIS FIGHT IS YOUR WAY OF VENTING...
...BUT I'M NOT SO EASYGOING AS TO LET YOU HAVE YOUR WAY!
FIVE PERCENT!
SHOOT STYLE...
...IS A WAY TO FIGHT WITHOUT OVERUSING MY ARMS...

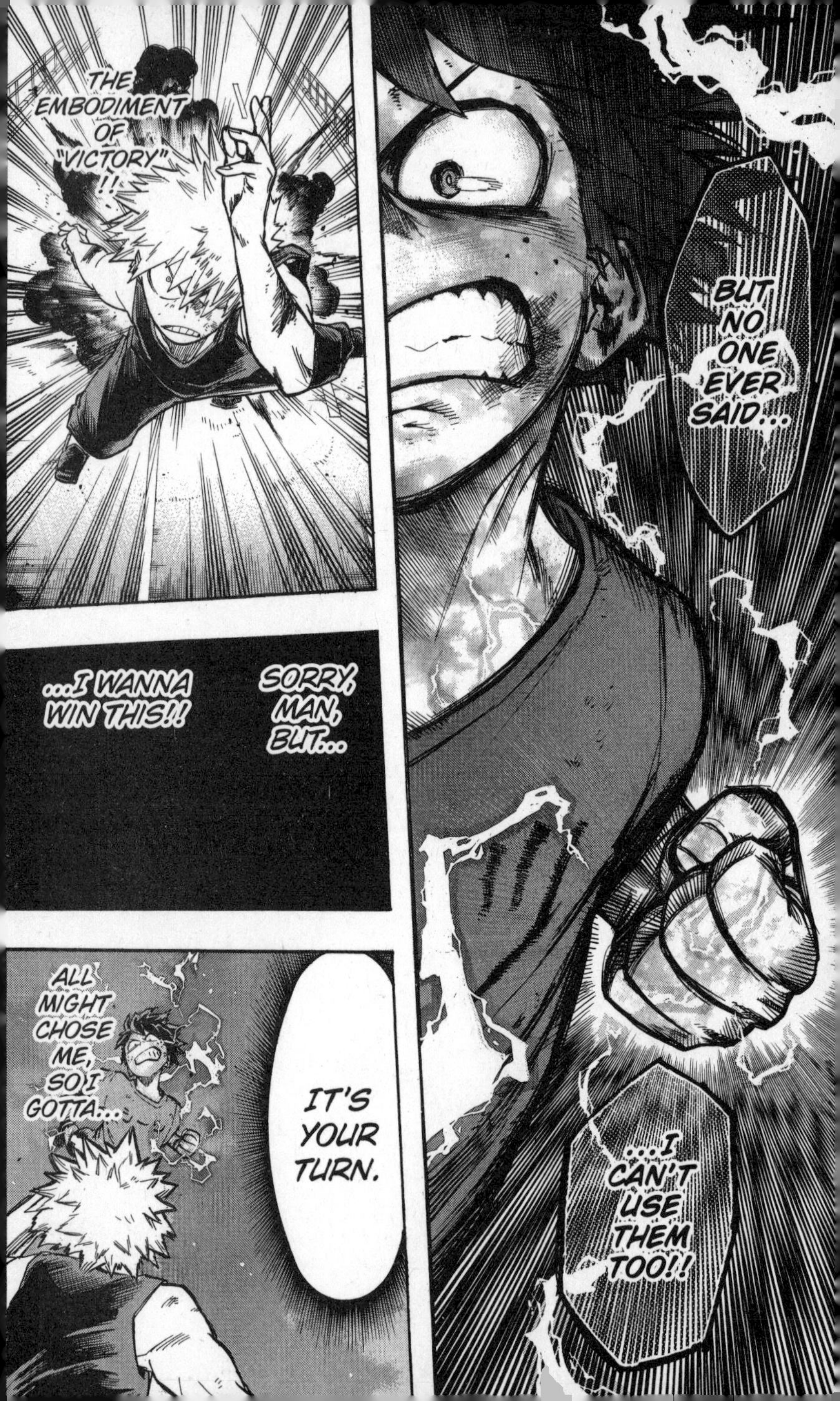
BUT NO ONE EVER SAID...
...I CAN'T USE THEM TOO!!
THE EMBODIMENT OF "VICTORY"!!
SORRY, MAN, BUT...
...I WANNA WIN THIS!!
IT'S YOUR TURN.
ALL MIGHT CHOSE ME, SO I GOTTA...

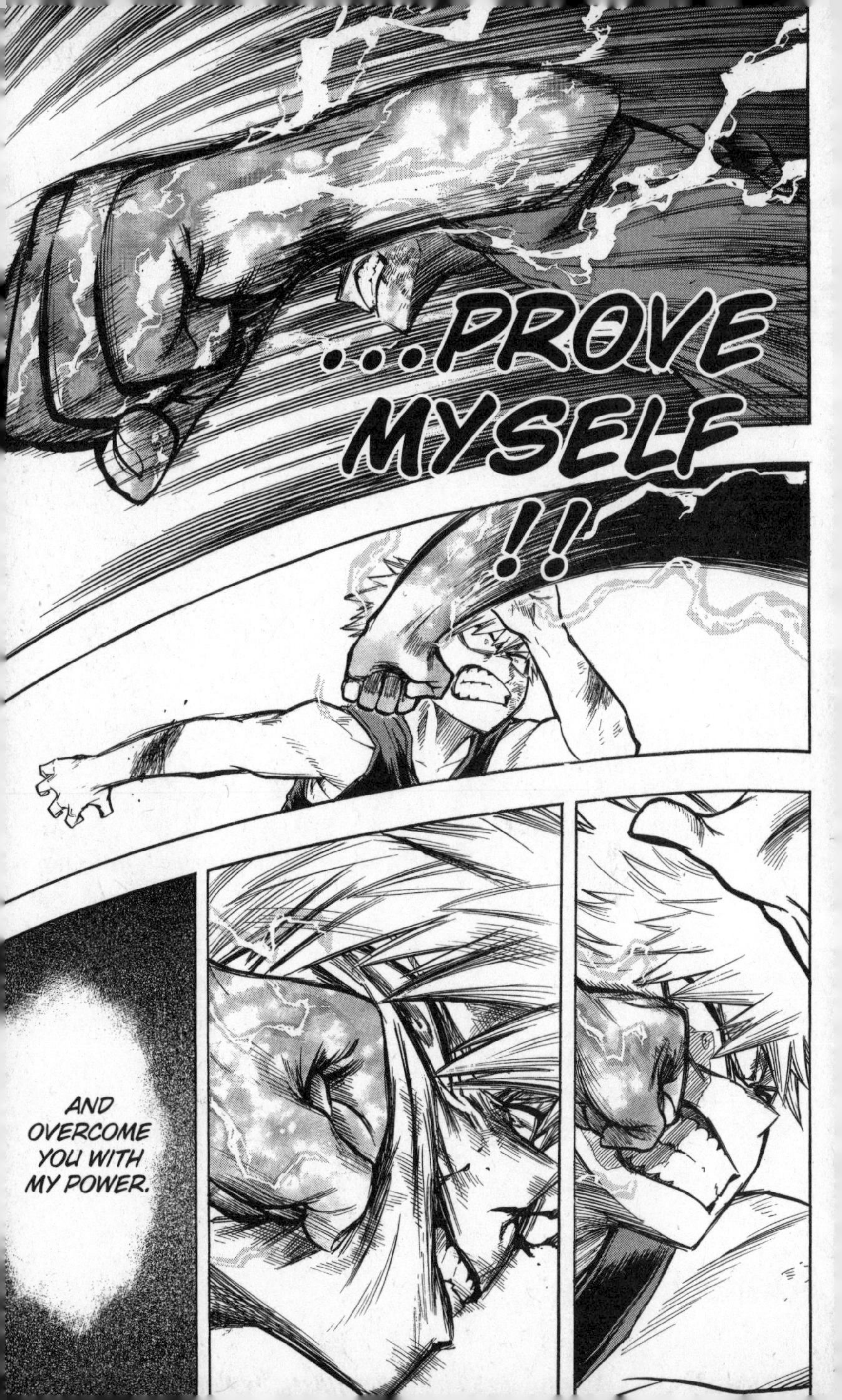
...PROVE MYSELF !!
AND OVERCOME YOU WITH MY POWER.

GRAB

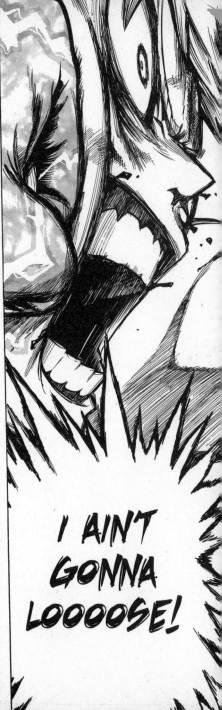

I AIN'T GONNA LOOOOSE!

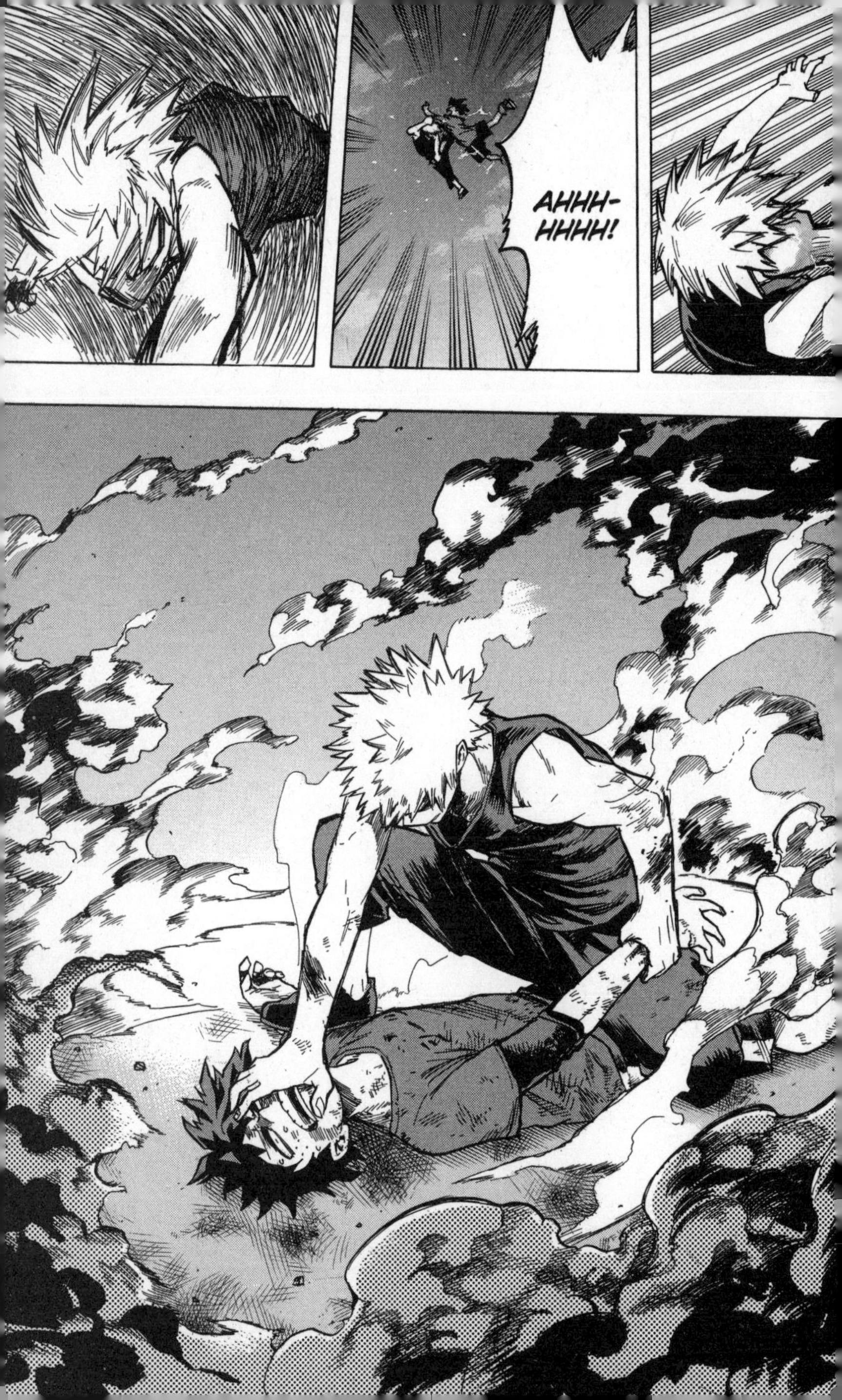
AHHH-
HHHH!

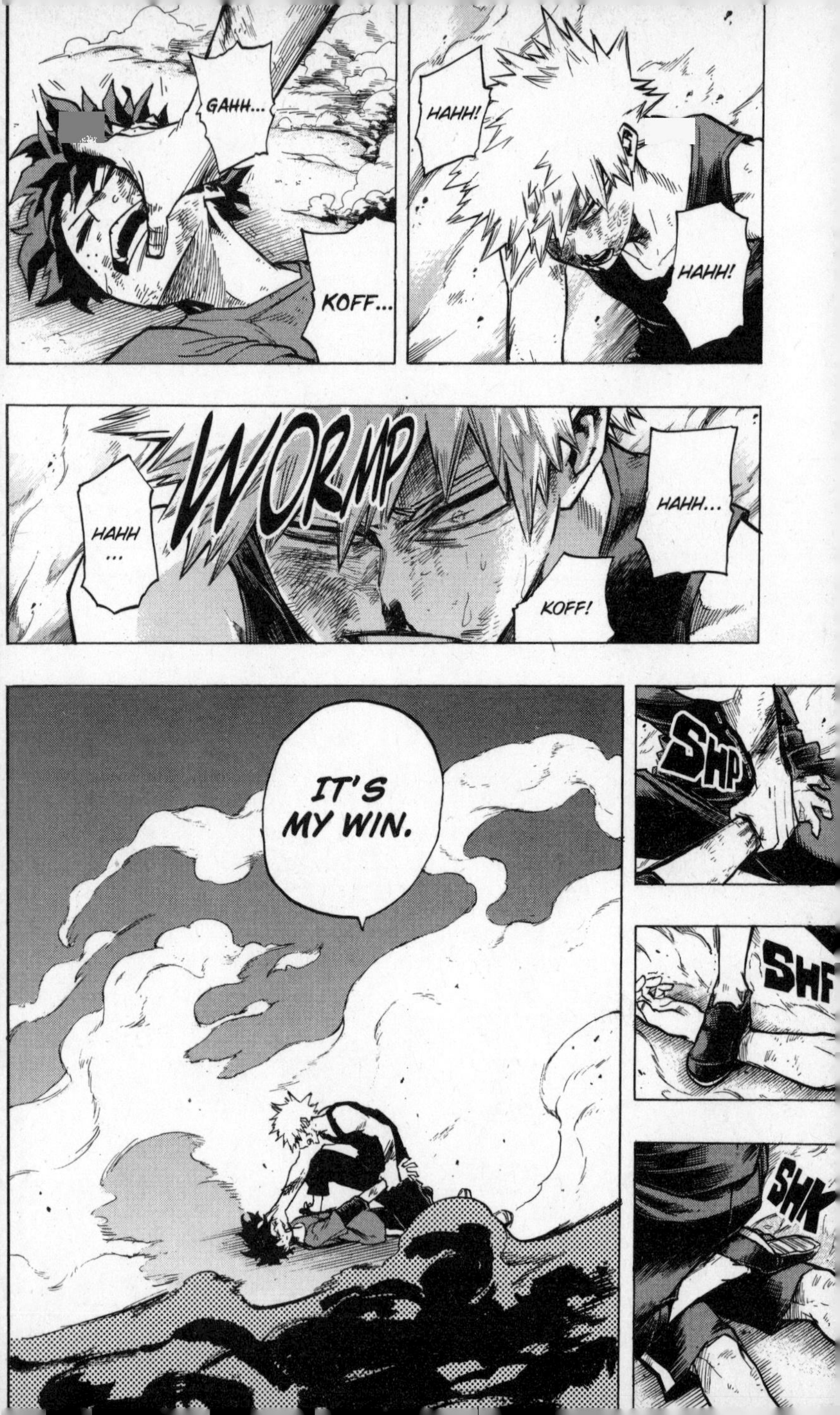
HAHH!
HAHH!
GAHH...
KOFF...
HAHH...
KOFF!
WORMP
HAHH ...
SHP
SHF
SHK
IT'S MY WIN.

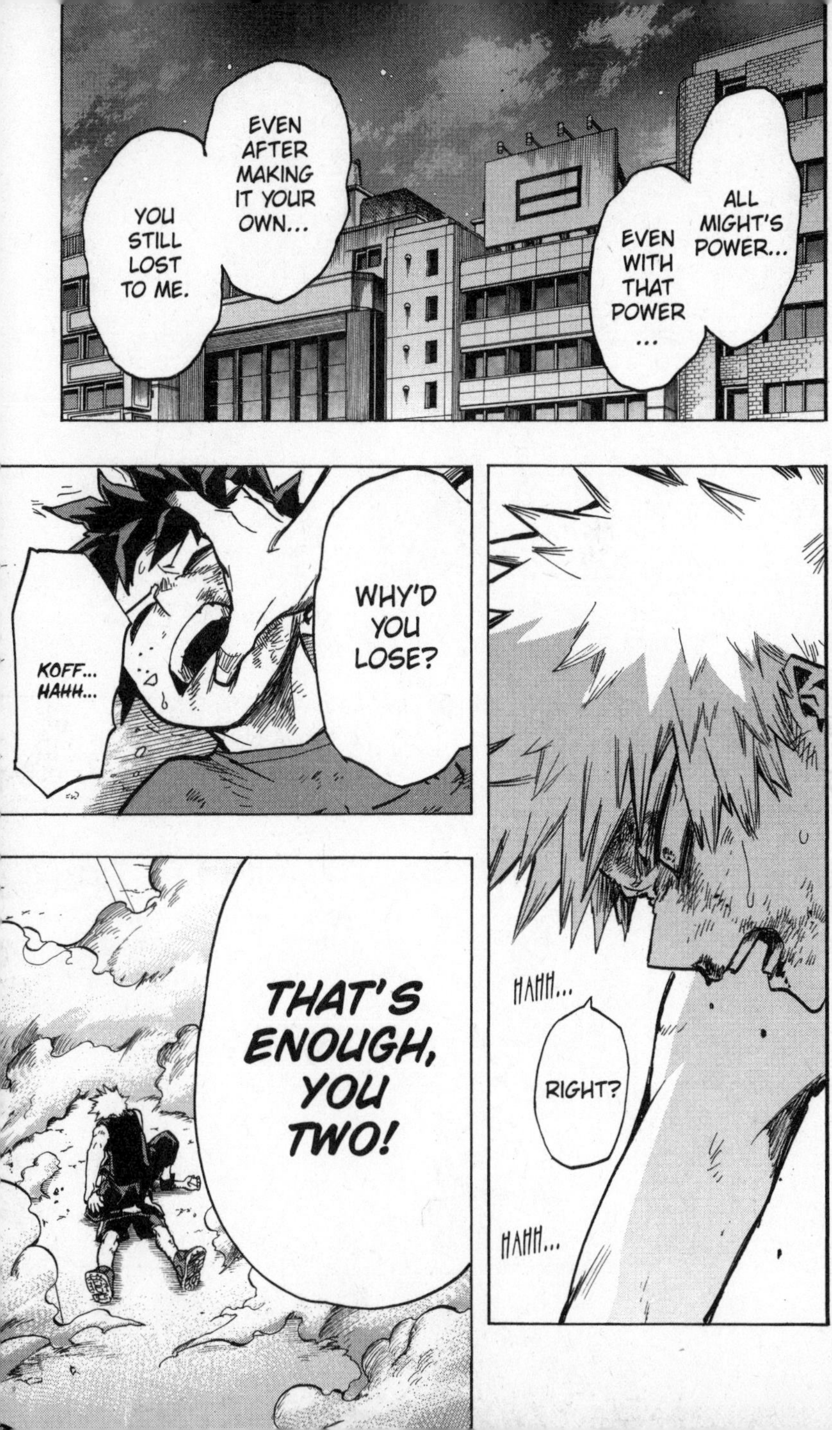
ALL MIGHT'S POWER...
EVEN WITH THAT POWER ...
EVEN AFTER MAKING IT YOUR OWN...
YOU STILL LOST TO ME.
HAHH...
RIGHT?
HAHH...
WHY'D YOU LOSE?
KOFF... HAHH...
THAT'S ENOUGH, YOU TWO!

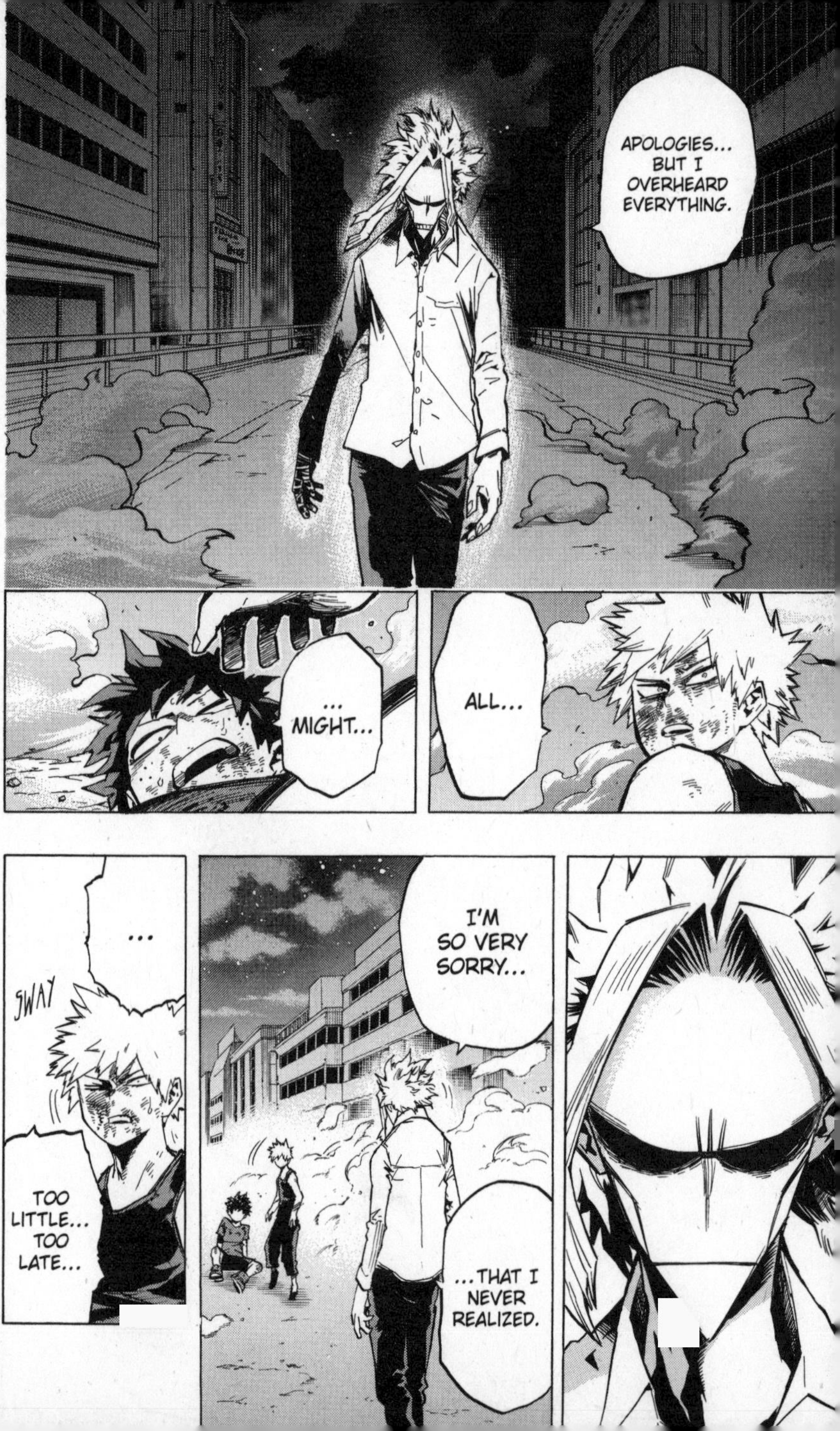
APOLOGIES... BUT I OVERHEARD EVERYTHING.
ALL...
... MIGHT...
I'M SO VERY SORRY...
...THAT I NEVER REALIZED.
...
SWAY
TOO LITTLE... TOO LATE...

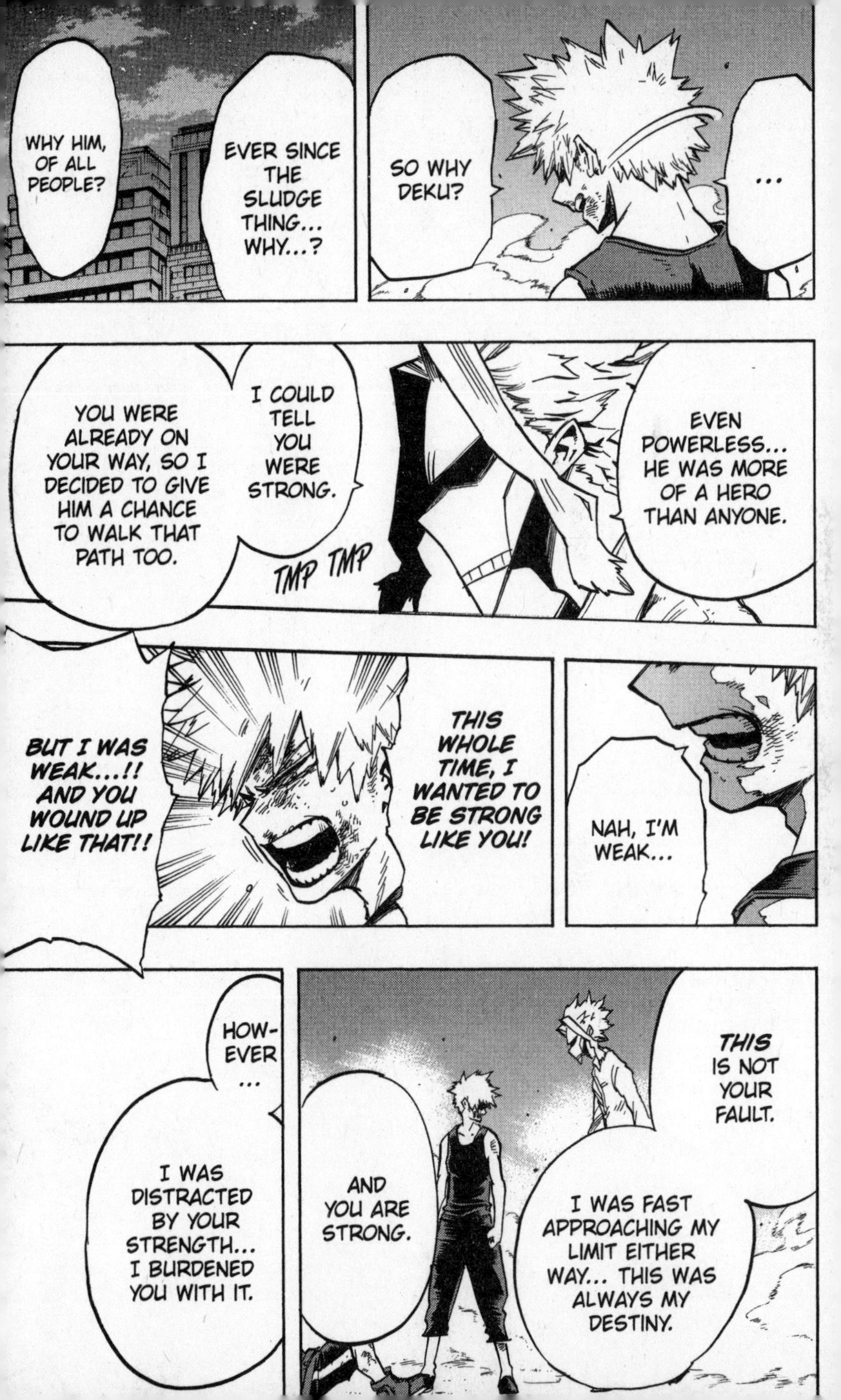
...
SO WHY DEKU?
EVER SINCE THE SLUDGE THING... WHY...?
WHY HIM, OF ALL PEOPLE?
EVEN POWERLESS... HE WAS MORE OF A HERO THAN ANYONE.
TMP TMP
I COULD TELL YOU WERE STRONG.
YOU WERE ALREADY ON YOUR WAY, SO I DECIDED TO GIVE HIM A CHANCE TO WALK THAT PATH TOO.
NAH, I'M WEAK...
THIS WHOLE TIME, I WANTED TO BE STRONG LIKE YOU!
BUT I WAS WEAK...!! AND YOU WOUND UP LIKE THAT!!
THIS IS NOT YOUR FAULT.
I WAS FAST APPROACHING MY LIMIT EITHER WAY... THIS WAS ALWAYS MY DESTINY.
AND YOU ARE STRONG.
HOW-EVER...
I WAS DISTRACTED BY YOUR STRENGTH... I BURDENED YOU WITH IT.

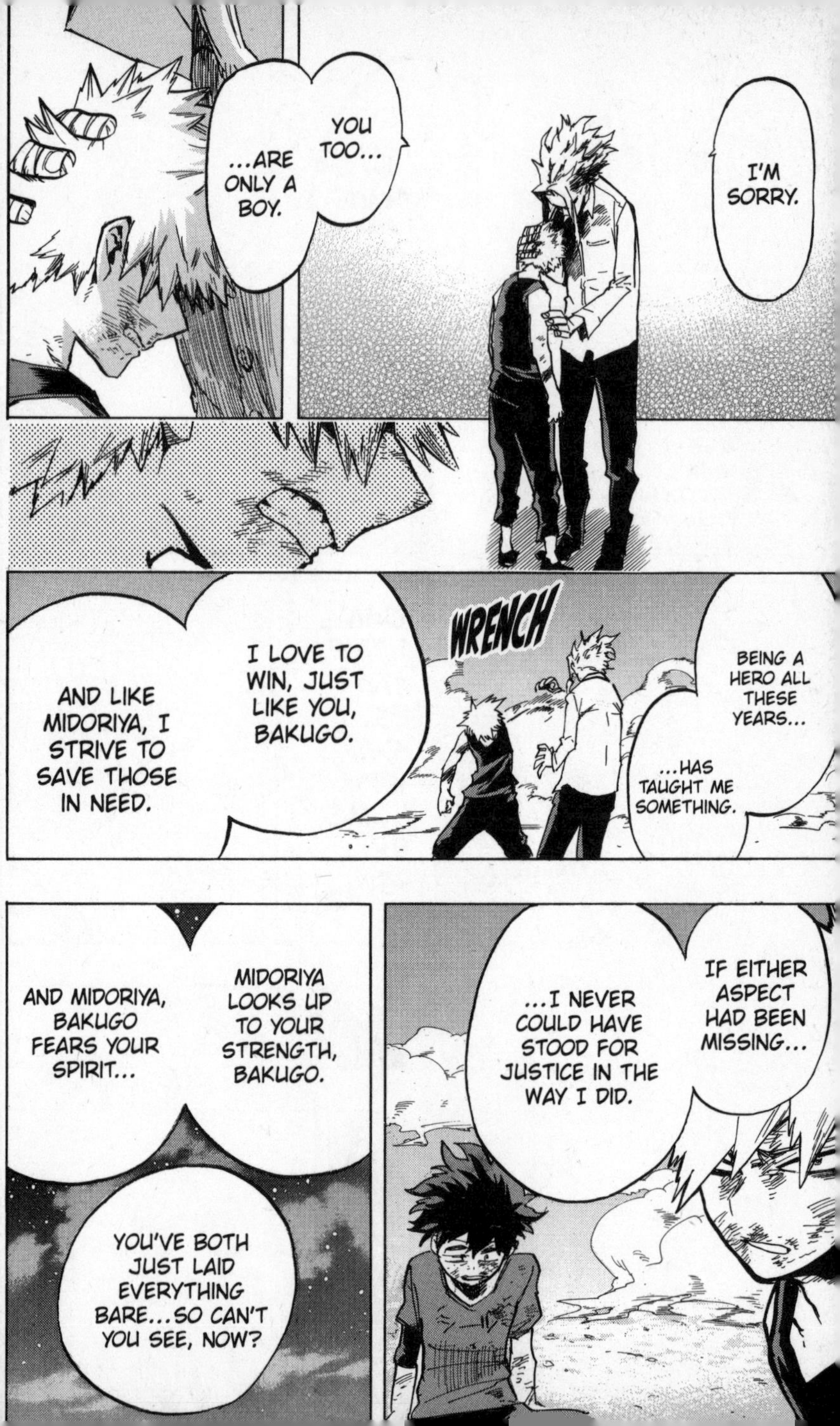
I'M SORRY.
YOU TOO...
...ARE ONLY A BOY.
BEING A HERO ALL THESE YEARS...
...HAS TAUGHT ME SOMETHING.
WRENCH
I LOVE TO WIN, JUST LIKE YOU, BAKUGO.
AND LIKE MIDORIYA, I STRIVE TO SAVE THOSE IN NEED.
IF EITHER ASPECT HAD BEEN MISSING...
...I NEVER COULD HAVE STOOD FOR JUSTICE IN THE WAY I DID.
MIDORIYA LOOKS UP TO YOUR STRENGTH, BAKUGO.
AND MIDORIYA, BAKUGO FEARS YOUR SPIRIT...
YOU'VE BOTH JUST LAID EVERYTHING BARE...SO CAN'T YOU SEE, NOW?

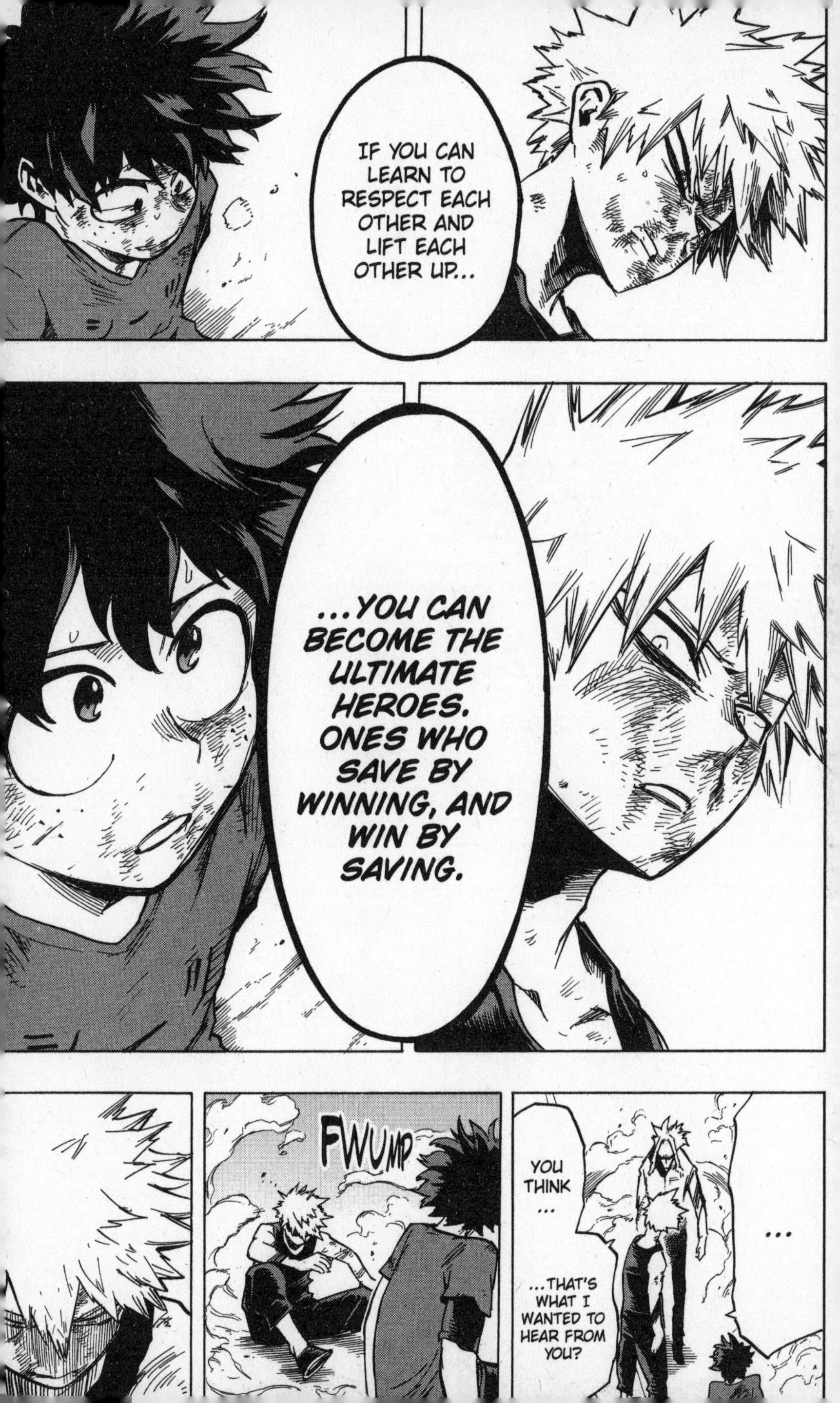
IF YOU CAN LEARN TO RESPECT EACH OTHER AND LIFT EACH OTHER UP...
...YOU CAN BECOME THE ULTIMATE HEROES. ONES WHO SAVE BY WINNING, AND WIN BY SAVING.
YOU THINK ...
...THAT'S WHAT I WANTED TO HEAR FROM YOU?
...
FWUMP

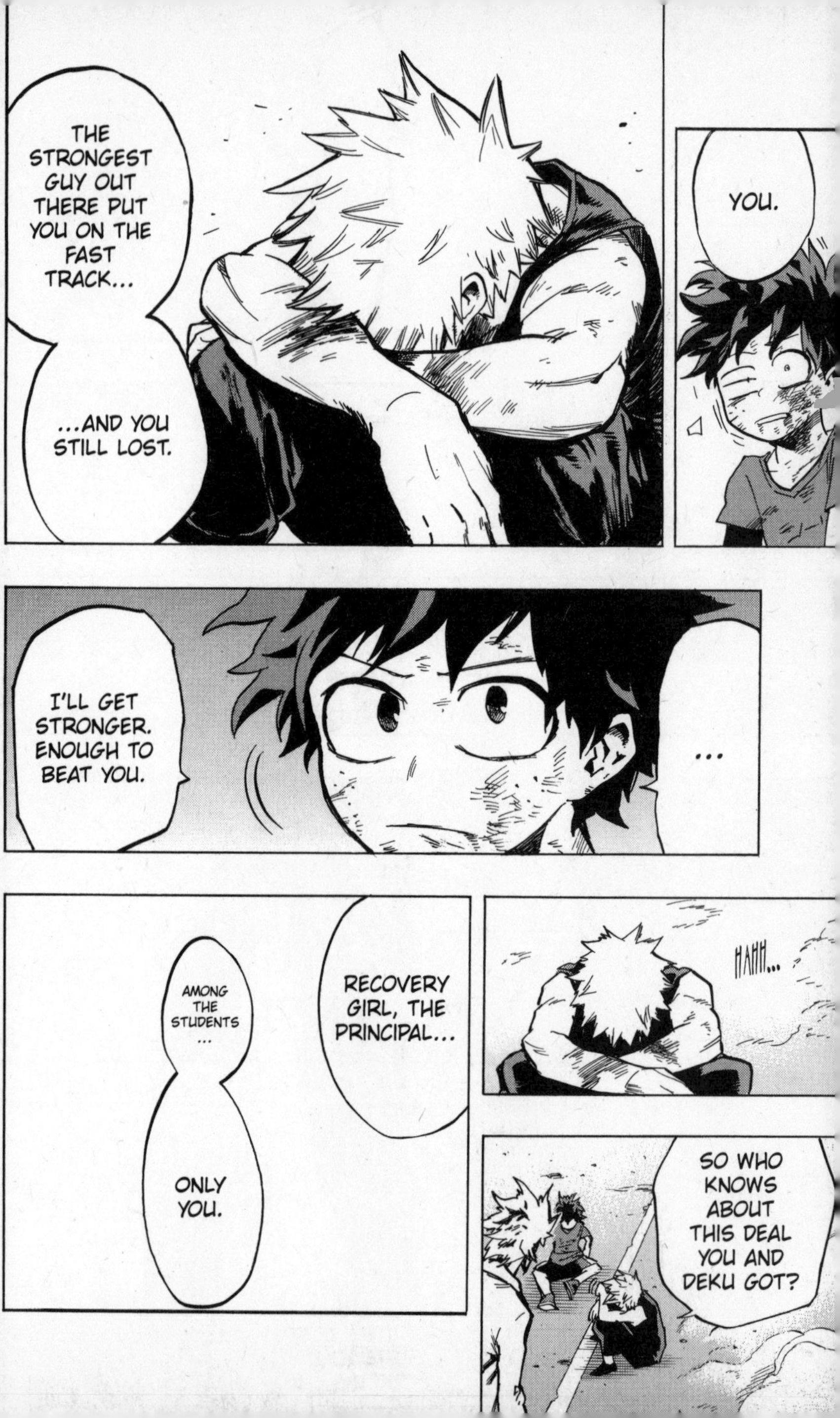
YOU.
THE STRONGEST GUY OUT THERE PUT YOU ON THE FAST TRACK...
...AND YOU STILL LOST.
...
I'LL GET STRONGER. ENOUGH TO BEAT YOU.
HAHH...
SO WHO KNOWS ABOUT THIS DEAL YOU AND DEKU GOT?
RECOVERY GIRL, THE PRINCIPAL...
AMONG THE STUDENTS...
ONLY YOU.

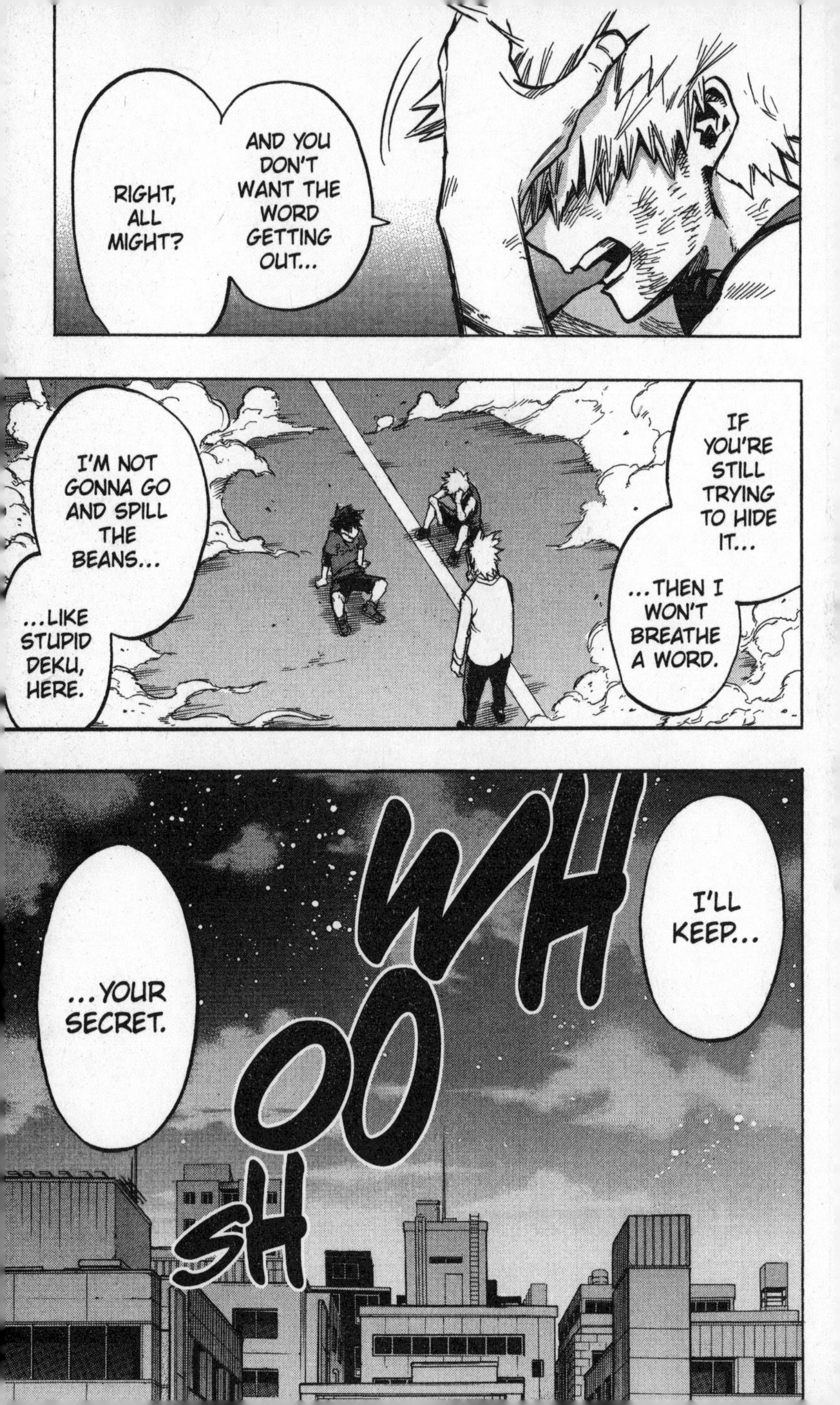
AND YOU DON'T WANT THE WORD GETTING OUT...
RIGHT, ALL MIGHT?
IF YOU'RE STILL TRYING TO HIDE IT...
...THEN I WON'T BREATHE A WORD.
I'M NOT GONNA GO AND SPILL THE BEANS...
...LIKE STUPID DEKU, HERE.
I'LL KEEP...
WHOOSH
...YOUR SECRET.

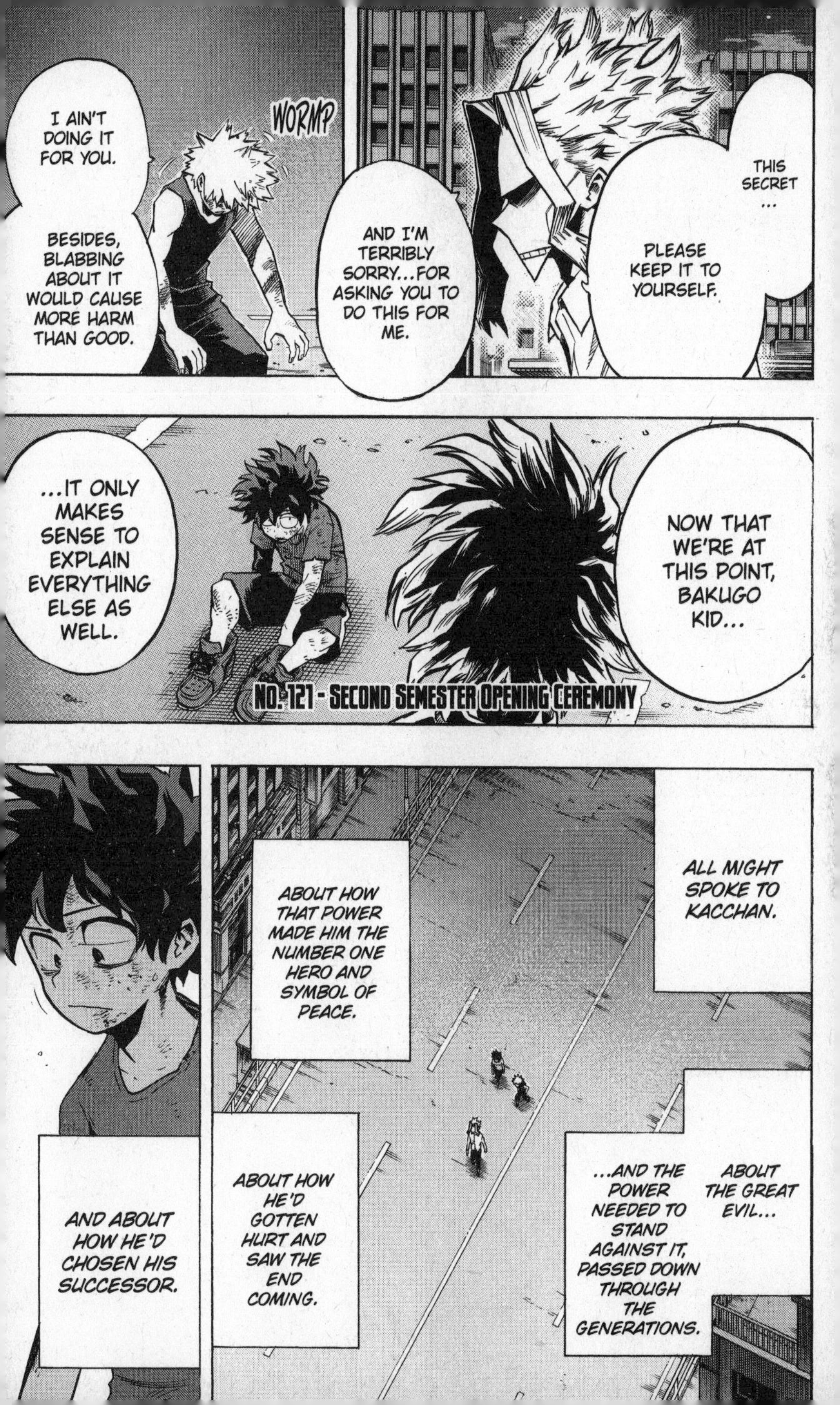
THIS SECRET ...
PLEASE KEEP IT TO YOURSELF.
AND I'M TERRIBLY SORRY...FOR ASKING YOU TO DO THIS FOR ME.
WORM?
I AIN'T DOING IT FOR YOU.
BESIDES, BLABBING ABOUT IT WOULD CAUSE MORE HARM THAN GOOD.
NOW THAT WE'RE AT THIS POINT, BAKUGO KID...
...IT ONLY MAKES SENSE TO EXPLAIN EVERYTHING ELSE AS WELL.
No. 121 - Second Semester Opening Ceremony
ALL MIGHT SPOKE TO KACCHAN.
ABOUT HOW THAT POWER MADE HIM THE NUMBER ONE HERO AND SYMBOL OF PEACE.
ABOUT THE GREAT EVIL...
...AND THE POWER NEEDED TO STAND AGAINST IT, PASSED DOWN THROUGH THE GENERATIONS.
ABOUT HOW HE'D GOTTEN HURT AND SAW THE END COMING.
AND ABOUT HOW HE'D CHOSEN HIS SUCCESSOR.

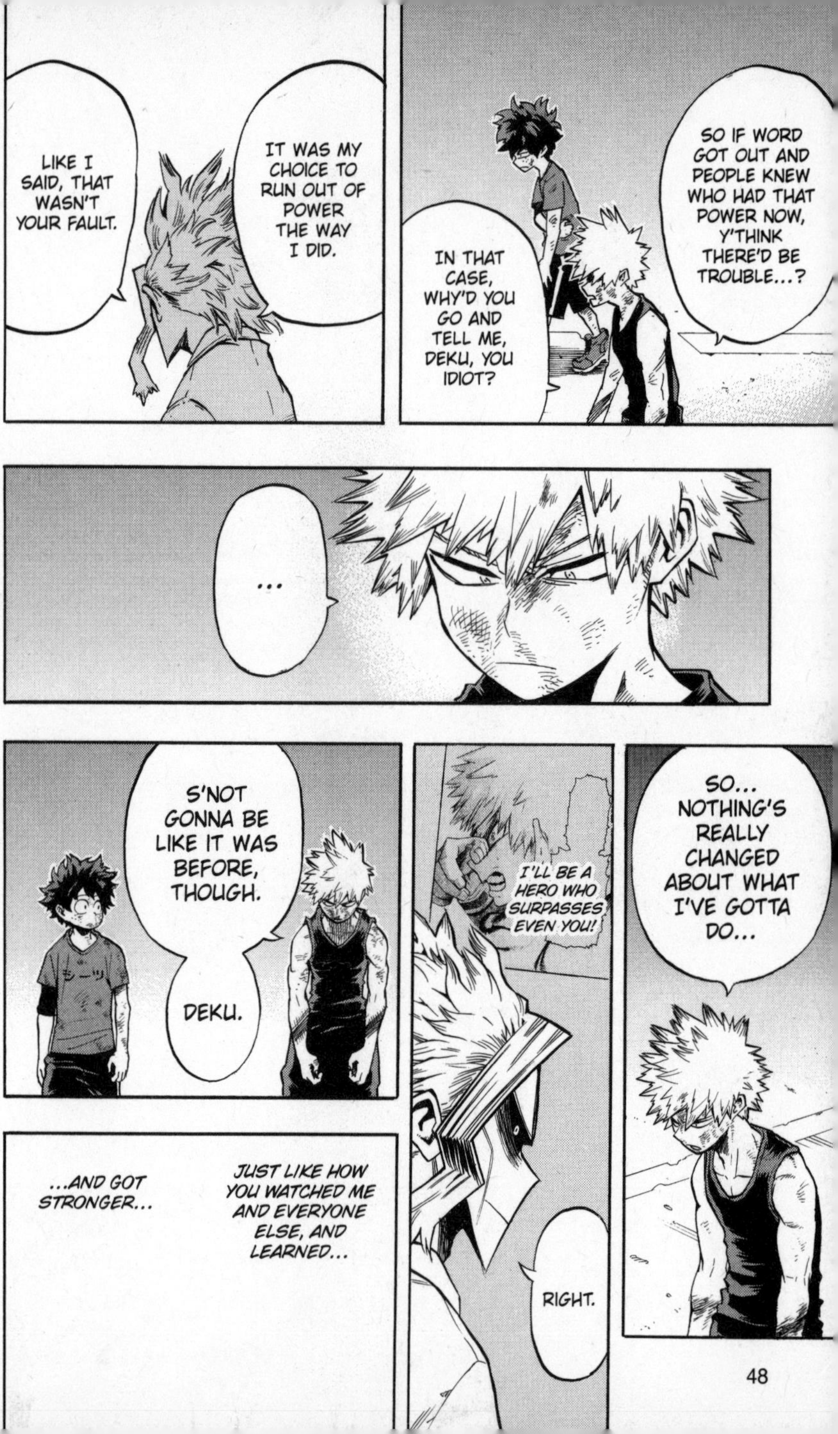
SO IF WORD GOT OUT AND PEOPLE KNEW WHO HAD THAT POWER NOW, Y'THINK THERE'D BE TROUBLE...?
IN THAT CASE, WHY'D YOU GO AND TELL ME, DEKU, YOU IDIOT?
IT WAS MY CHOICE TO RUN OUT OF POWER THE WAY I DID.
LIKE I SAID, THAT WASN'T YOUR FAULT.
...
SO... NOTHING'S REALLY CHANGED ABOUT WHAT I'VE GOTTA DO...
I'LL BE A HERO WHO SURPASSES EVEN YOU!
RIGHT.
S'NOT GONNA BE LIKE IT WAS BEFORE, THOUGH.
DEKU.
JUST LIKE HOW YOU WATCHED ME AND EVERYONE ELSE, AND LEARNED...
...AND GOT STRONGER...

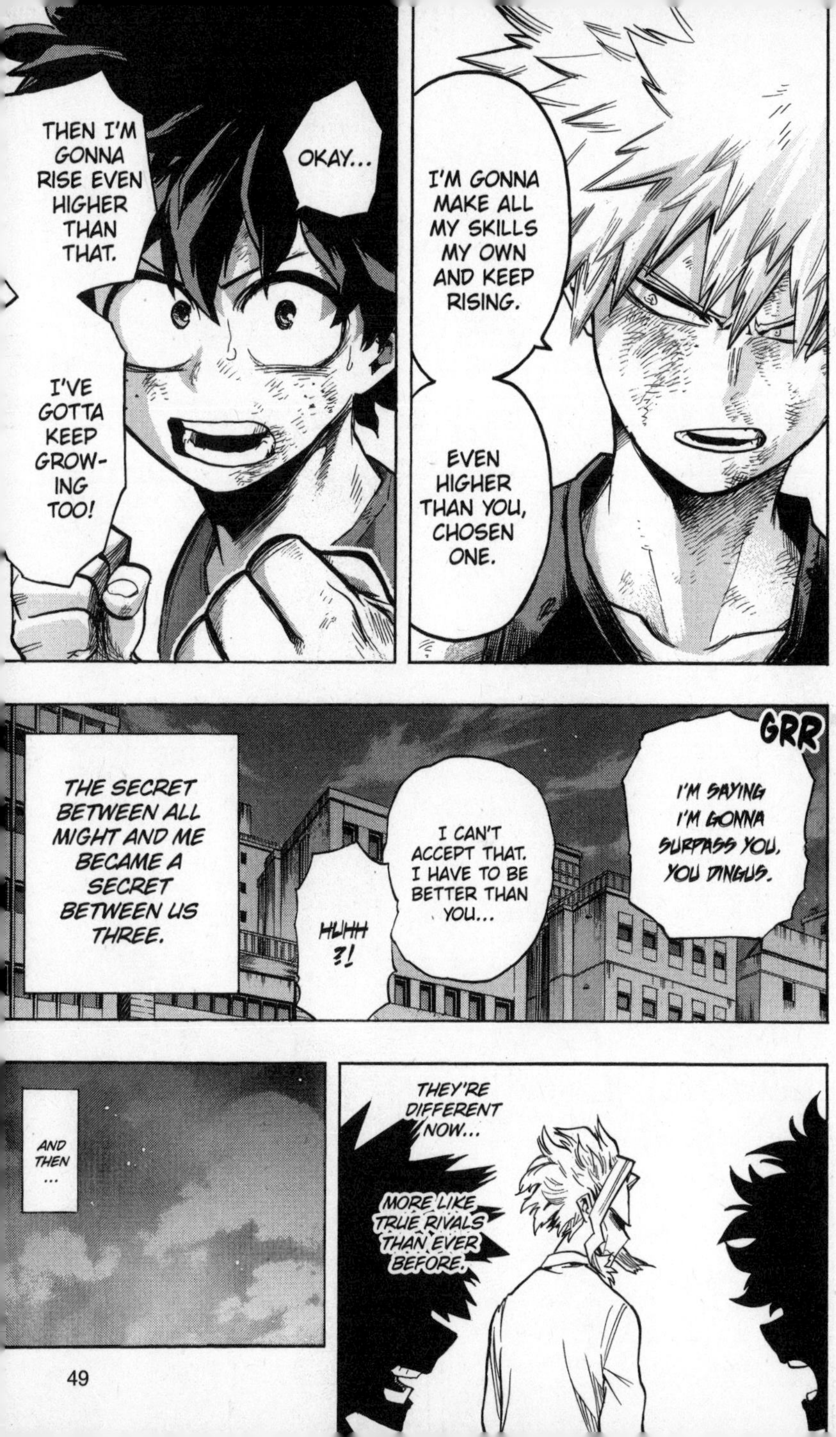
I'M GONNA MAKE ALL MY SKILLS MY OWN AND KEEP RISING.
EVEN HIGHER THAN YOU, CHOSEN ONE.
OKAY...
THEN I'M GONNA RISE EVEN HIGHER THAN THAT.
I'VE GOTTA KEEP GROW-ING TOO!
GRR
I'M SAYING I'M GONNA SURPASS YOU, YOU DINGUS.
I CAN'T ACCEPT THAT. I HAVE TO BE BETTER THAN YOU...
HUHH ?!
THE SECRET BETWEEN ALL MIGHT AND ME BECAME A SECRET BETWEEN US THREE.
THEY'RE DIFFERENT NOW...
MORE LIKE TRUE RIVALS THAN EVER BEFORE.
AND THEN ...

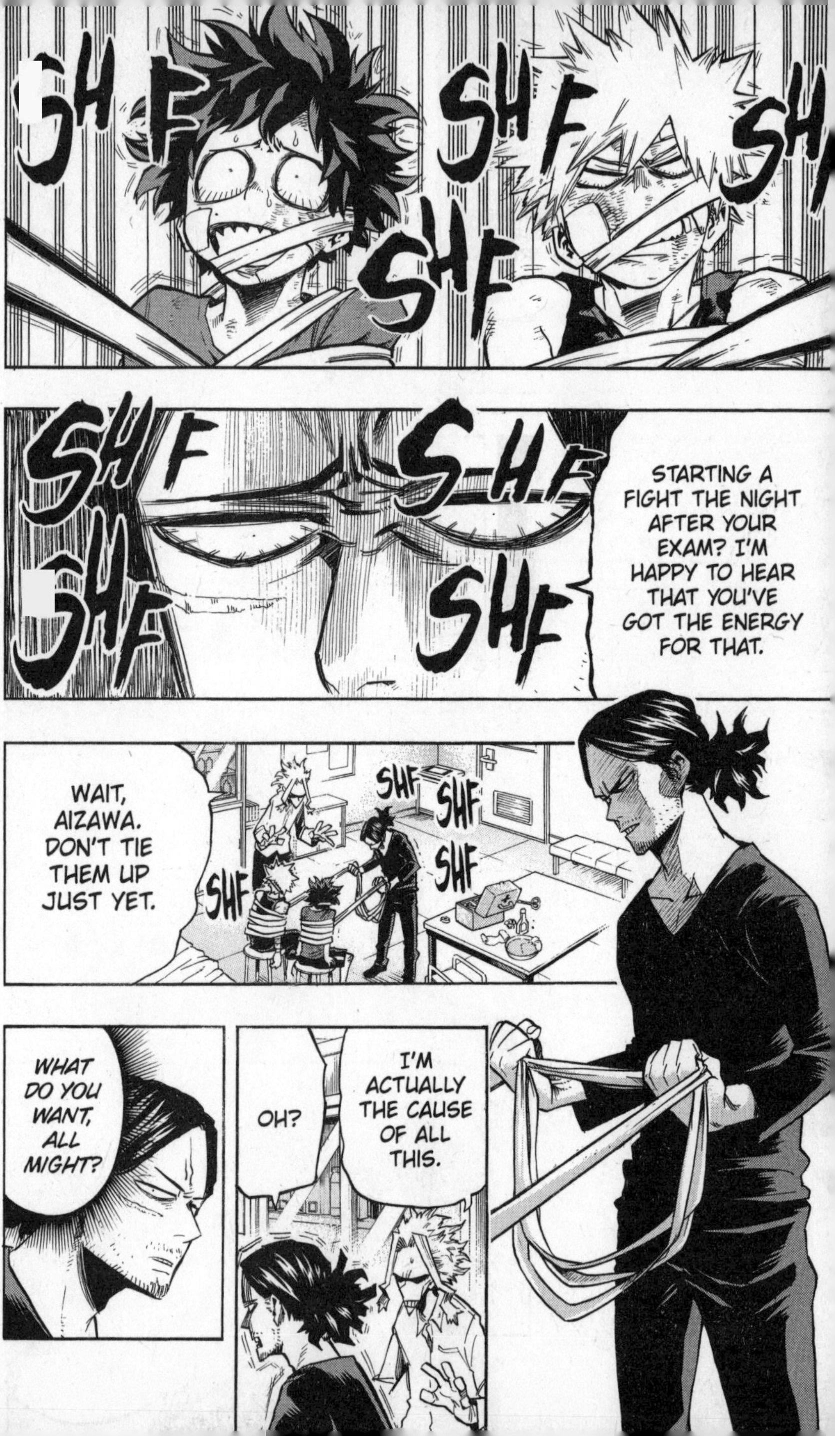
SH
SHF
SHF
SHF
STARTING A FIGHT THE NIGHT AFTER YOUR EXAM? I'M HAPPY TO HEAR THAT YOU'VE GOT THE ENERGY FOR THAT.
S-H-F
SHF
SHF
SHF
SHF
SHF
SHF
SHF
WAIT, AIZAWA. DON'T TIE THEM UP JUST YET.
I'M ACTUALLY THE CAUSE OF ALL THIS.
OH?
WHAT DO YOU WANT, ALL MIGHT?

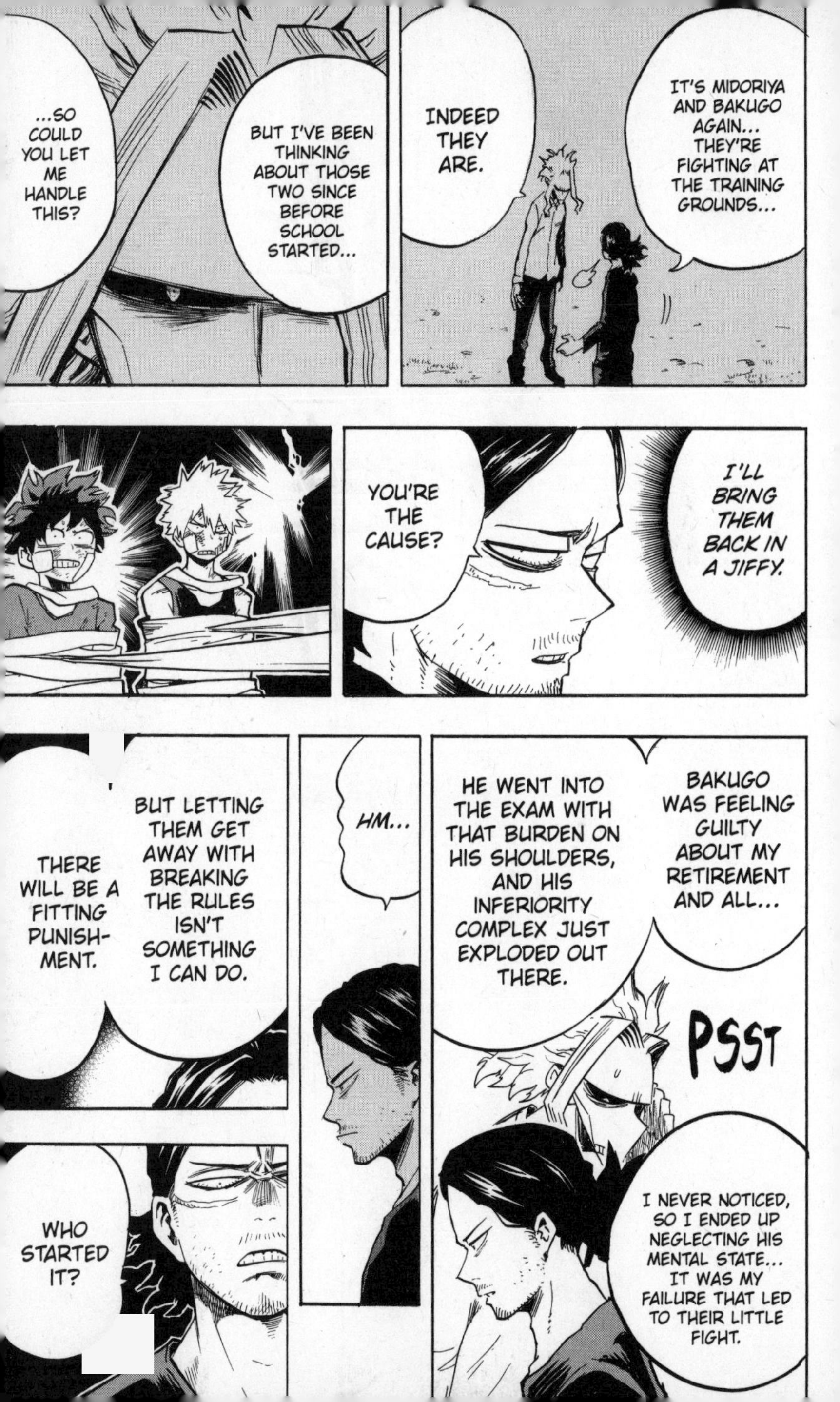
IT'S MIDORIYA AND BAKUGO AGAIN... THEY'RE FIGHTING AT THE TRAINING GROUNDS...
INDEED THEY ARE.
BUT I'VE BEEN THINKING ABOUT THOSE TWO SINCE BEFORE SCHOOL STARTED...
...SO COULD YOU LET ME HANDLE THIS?
I'LL BRING THEM BACK IN A JIFFY.
YOU'RE THE CAUSE?
BAKUGO WAS FEELING GUILTY ABOUT MY RETIREMENT AND ALL...
HE WENT INTO THE EXAM WITH THAT BURDEN ON HIS SHOULDERS, AND HIS INFERIORITY COMPLEX JUST EXPLODED OUT THERE.
PSST
I NEVER NOTICED, SO I ENDED UP NEGLECTING HIS MENTAL STATE... IT WAS MY FAILURE THAT LED TO THEIR LITTLE FIGHT.
HM...
BUT LETTING THEM GET AWAY WITH BREAKING THE RULES ISN'T SOMETHING I CAN DO.
THERE WILL BE A FITTING PUNISH-MENT.
WHO STARTED IT?

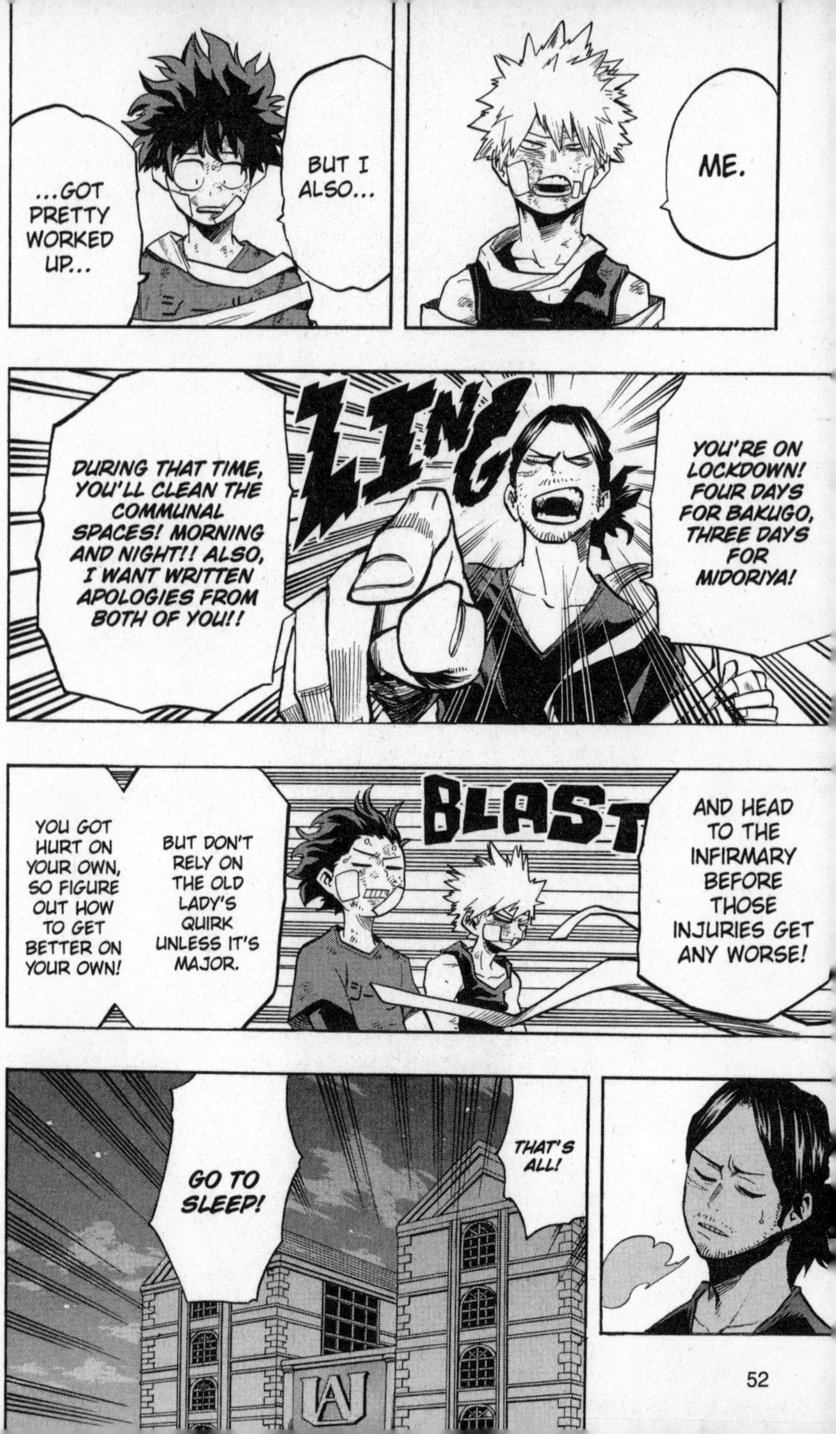
ME.
BUT I ALSO...
...GOT PRETTY WORKED UP...
YOU'RE ON LOCKDOWN! FOUR DAYS FOR BAKUGO, THREE DAYS FOR MIDORIYA!
LING
DURING THAT TIME, YOU'LL CLEAN THE COMMUNAL SPACES! MORNING AND NIGHT!! ALSO, I WANT WRITTEN APOLOGIES FROM BOTH OF YOU!!
AND HEAD TO THE INFIRMARY BEFORE THOSE INJURIES GET ANY WORSE!
BLAST
BUT DON'T RELY ON THE OLD LADY'S QUIRK UNLESS IT'S MAJOR.
YOU GOT HURT ON YOUR OWN, SO FIGURE OUT HOW TO GET BETTER ON YOUR OWN!
THAT'S ALL!
GO TO SLEEP!

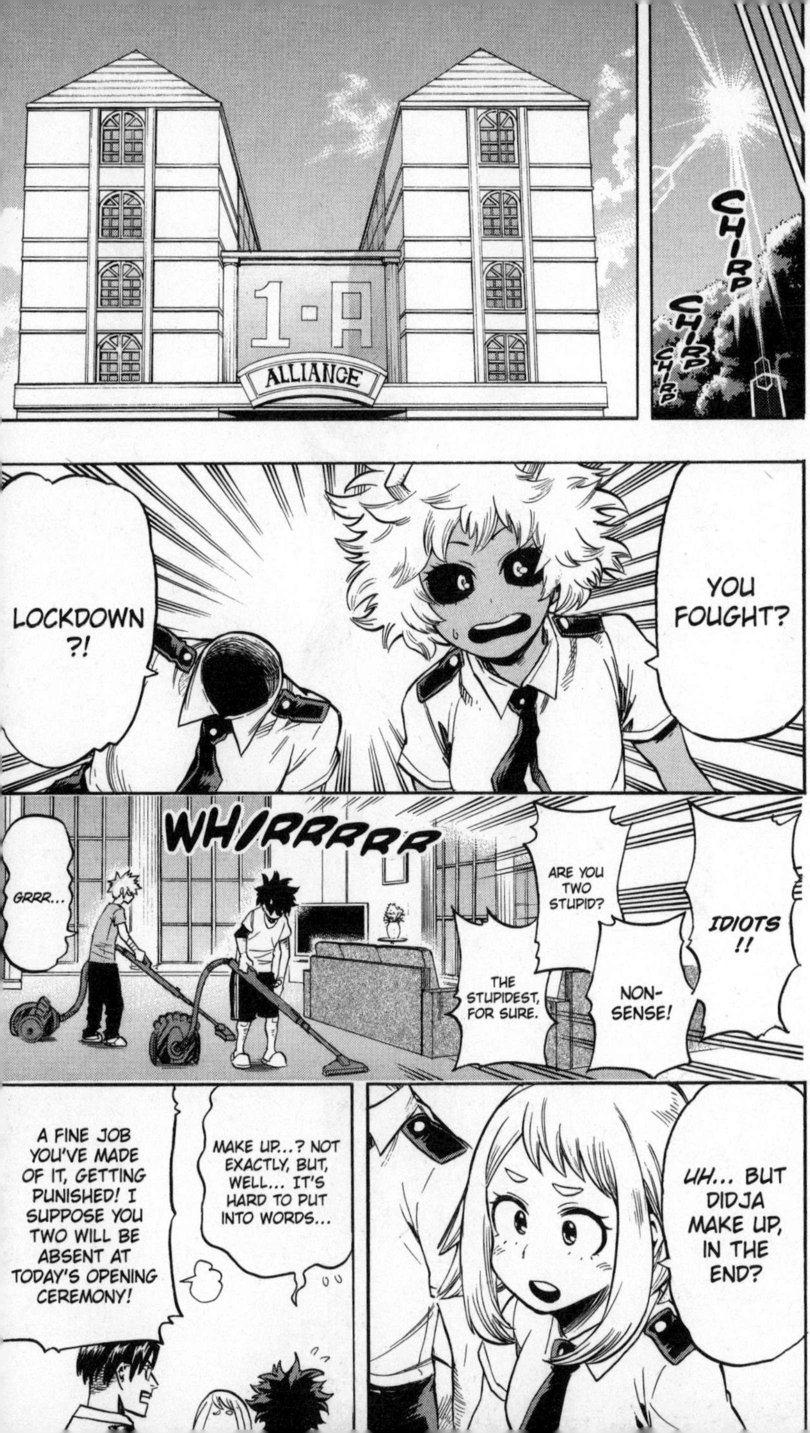
CHIRP
CHIRP
CHIRP
1-A
ALLIANCE
YOU FOUGHT?
LOCKDOWN ?!
IDIOTS !!
ARE YOU TWO STUPID?
NON-SENSE!
THE STUPIDEST, FOR SURE.
WHIRRRRR
GRRR...
UH... BUT DIDJA MAKE UP, IN THE END?
MAKE UP...? NOT EXACTLY, BUT, WELL... IT'S HARD TO PUT INTO WORDS...
A FINE JOB YOU'VE MADE OF IT, GETTING PUNISHED! I SUPPOSE YOU TWO WILL BE ABSENT AT TODAY'S OPENING CEREMONY!

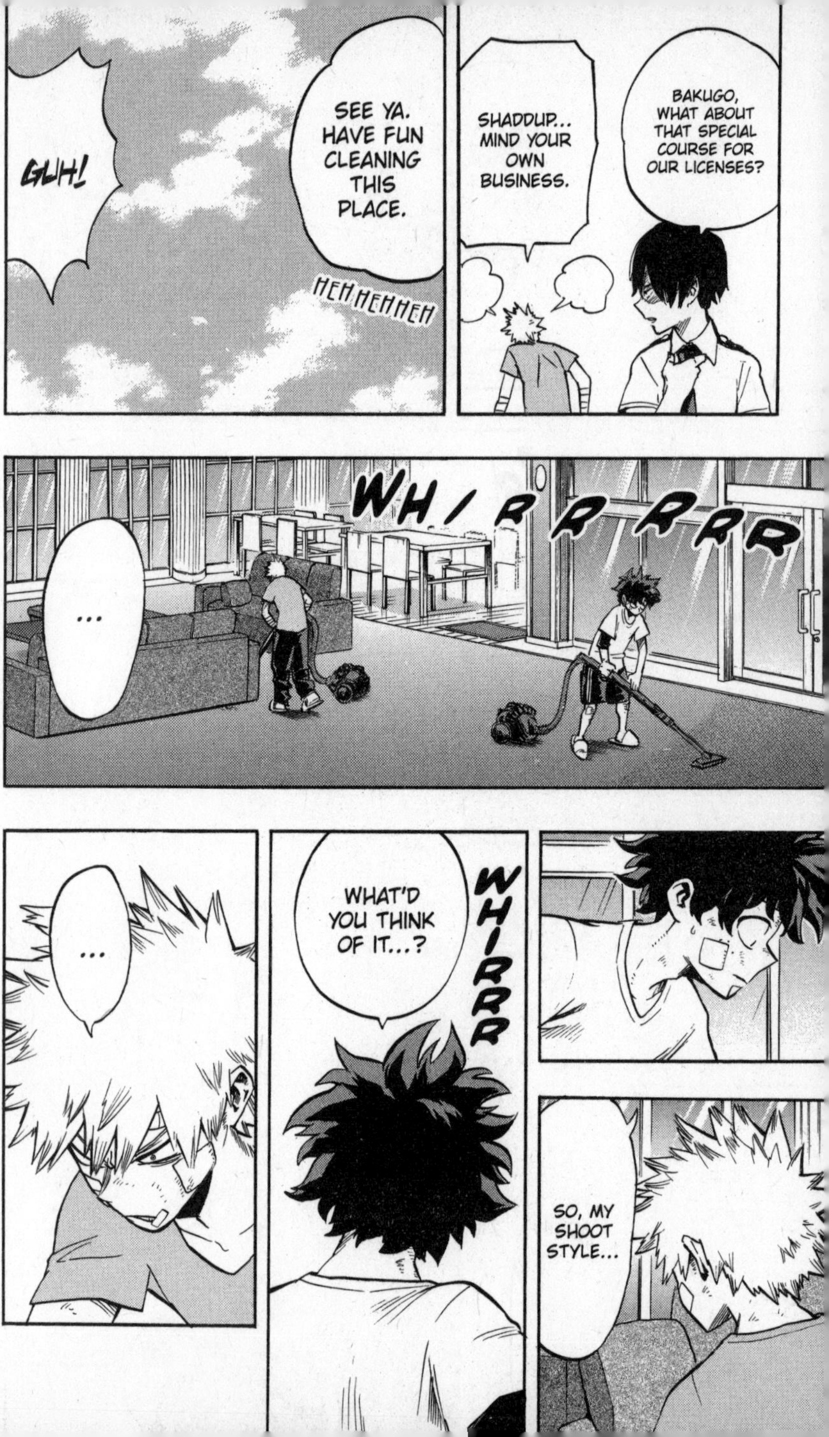
BAKUGO, WHAT ABOUT THAT SPECIAL COURSE FOR OUR LICENSES?
SHADDUP... MIND YOUR OWN BUSINESS.
SEE YA. HAVE FUN CLEANING THIS PLACE.
HEH HEH HEH
GUH!
WHIRRRRR
...
SO, MY SHOOT STYLE...
WHIRRR
WHAT'D YOU THINK OF IT...?
...

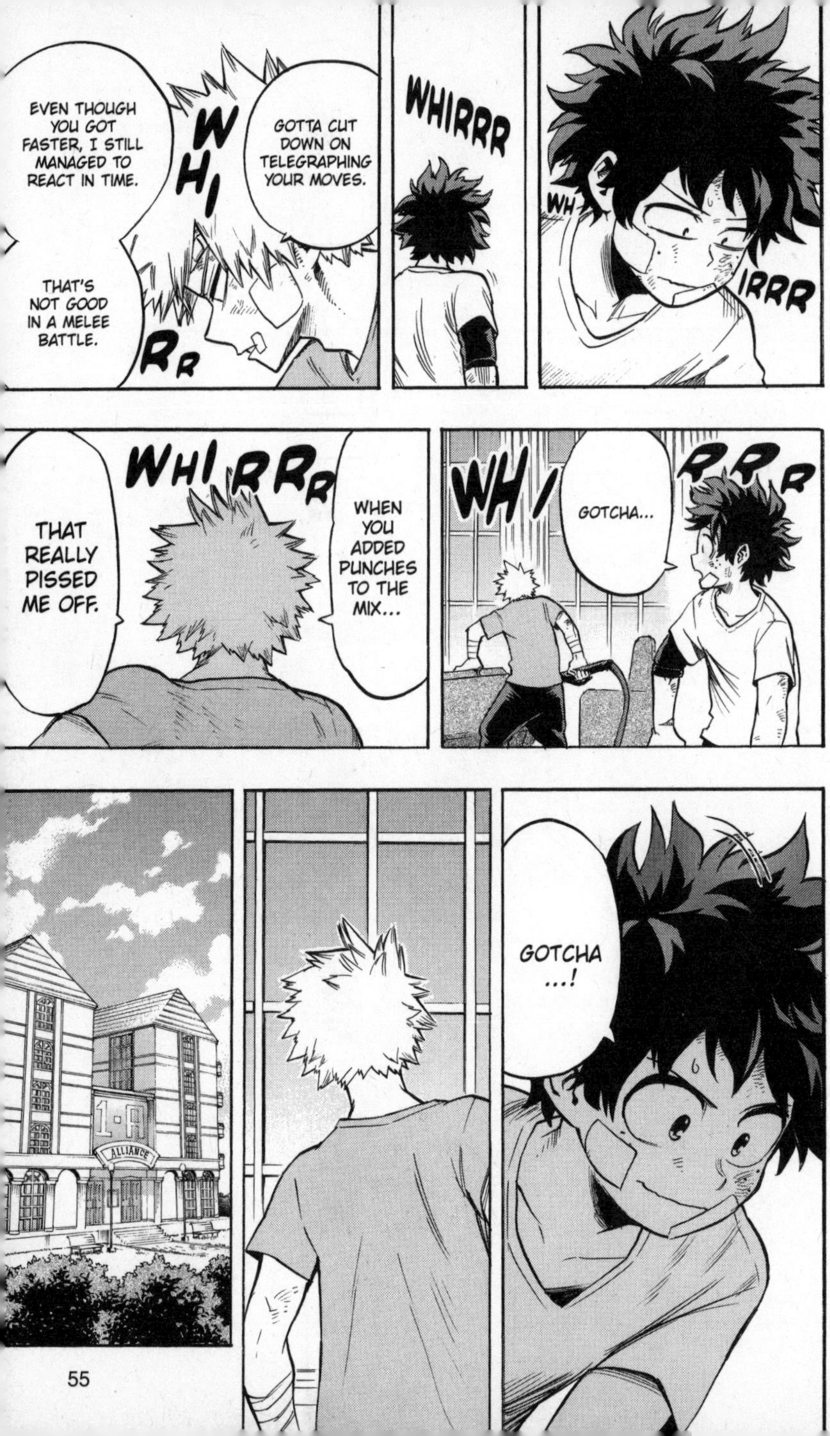
WH IRRR
WHIRRR
GOTTA CUT DOWN ON TELEGRAPHING YOUR MOVES.
WHIRR
EVEN THOUGH YOU GOT FASTER, I STILL MANAGED TO REACT IN TIME.
THAT'S NOT GOOD IN A MELEE BATTLE.
WHIRRR
GOTCHA...
WHIRRR
WHEN YOU ADDED PUNCHES TO THE MIX...
THAT REALLY PISSED ME OFF.
GOTCHA ...!
1-A
ALLIANCE

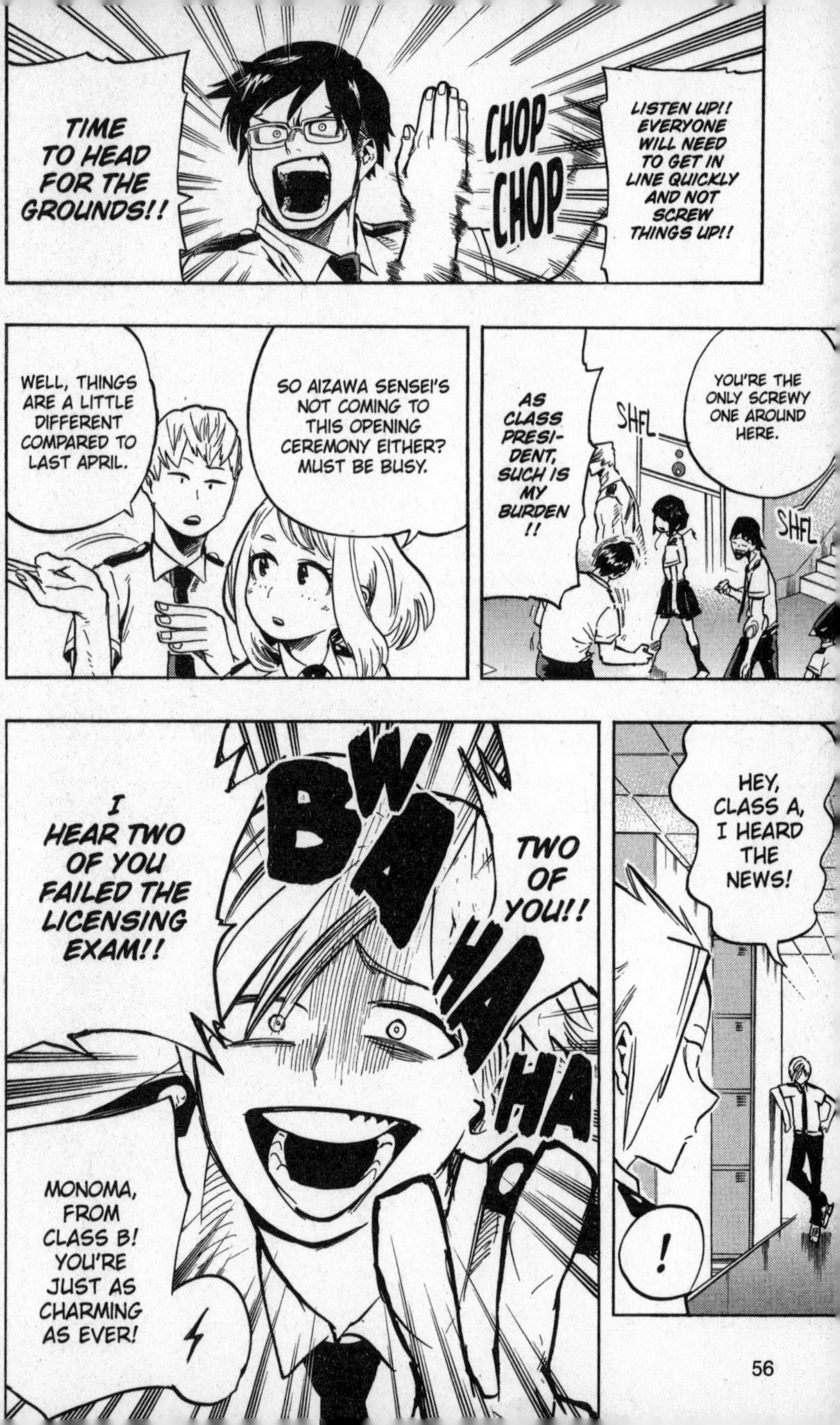
LISTEN UP!! EVERYONE WILL NEED TO GET IN LINE QUICKLY AND NOT SCREW THINGS UP!!
CHOP CHOP
TIME TO HEAD FOR THE GROUNDS!!
YOU'RE THE ONLY SCREWY ONE AROUND HERE.
SHFL
SHFL
AS CLASS PRESIDENT, SUCH IS MY BURDEN!!
SO AIZAWA SENSEI'S NOT COMING TO THIS OPENING CEREMONY EITHER? MUST BE BUSY.
WELL, THINGS ARE A LITTLE DIFFERENT COMPARED TO LAST APRIL.
HEY, CLASS A, I HEARD THE NEWS!
!
TWO OF YOU!!
BWAHAHAHA
I HEAR TWO OF YOU FAILED THE LICENSING EXAM!!
MONOMA, FROM CLASS B! YOU'RE JUST AS CHARMING AS EVER!

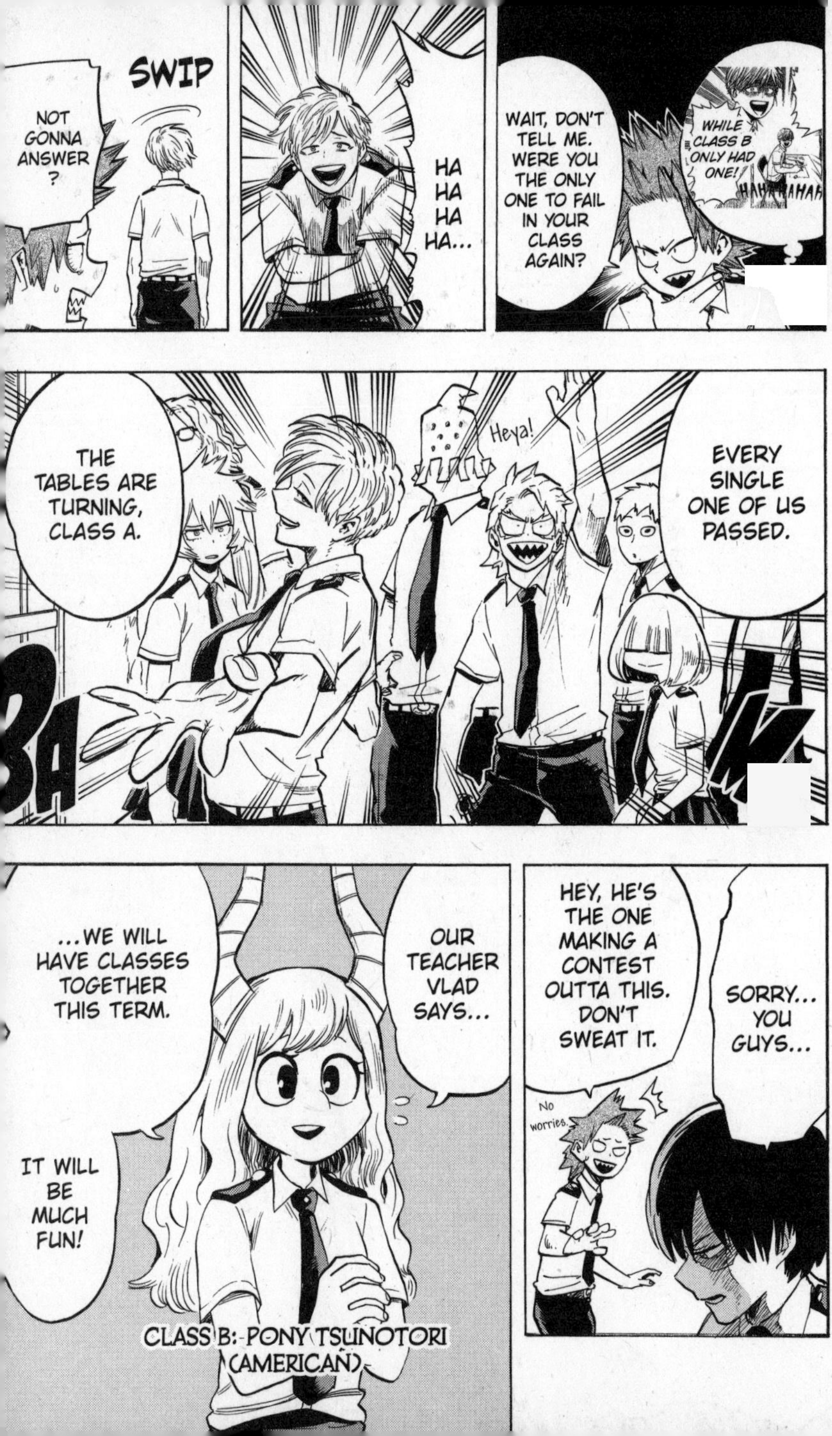
WHILE CLASS B ONLY HAD ONE!
HAHAHAHAH
WAIT, DON'T TELL ME. WERE YOU THE ONLY ONE TO FAIL IN YOUR CLASS AGAIN?
HA HA HA HA...
SWIP
NOT GONNA ANSWER?
EVERY SINGLE ONE OF US PASSED.
Heya!
THE TABLES ARE TURNING, CLASS A.
SORRY... YOU GUYS...
HEY, HE'S THE ONE MAKING A CONTEST OUTTA THIS. DON'T SWEAT IT.
No worries.
OUR TEACHER VLAD SAYS...
...WE WILL HAVE CLASSES TOGETHER THIS TERM.
IT WILL BE MUCH FUN!
CLASS B: PONY TSUNOTORI (AMERICAN)

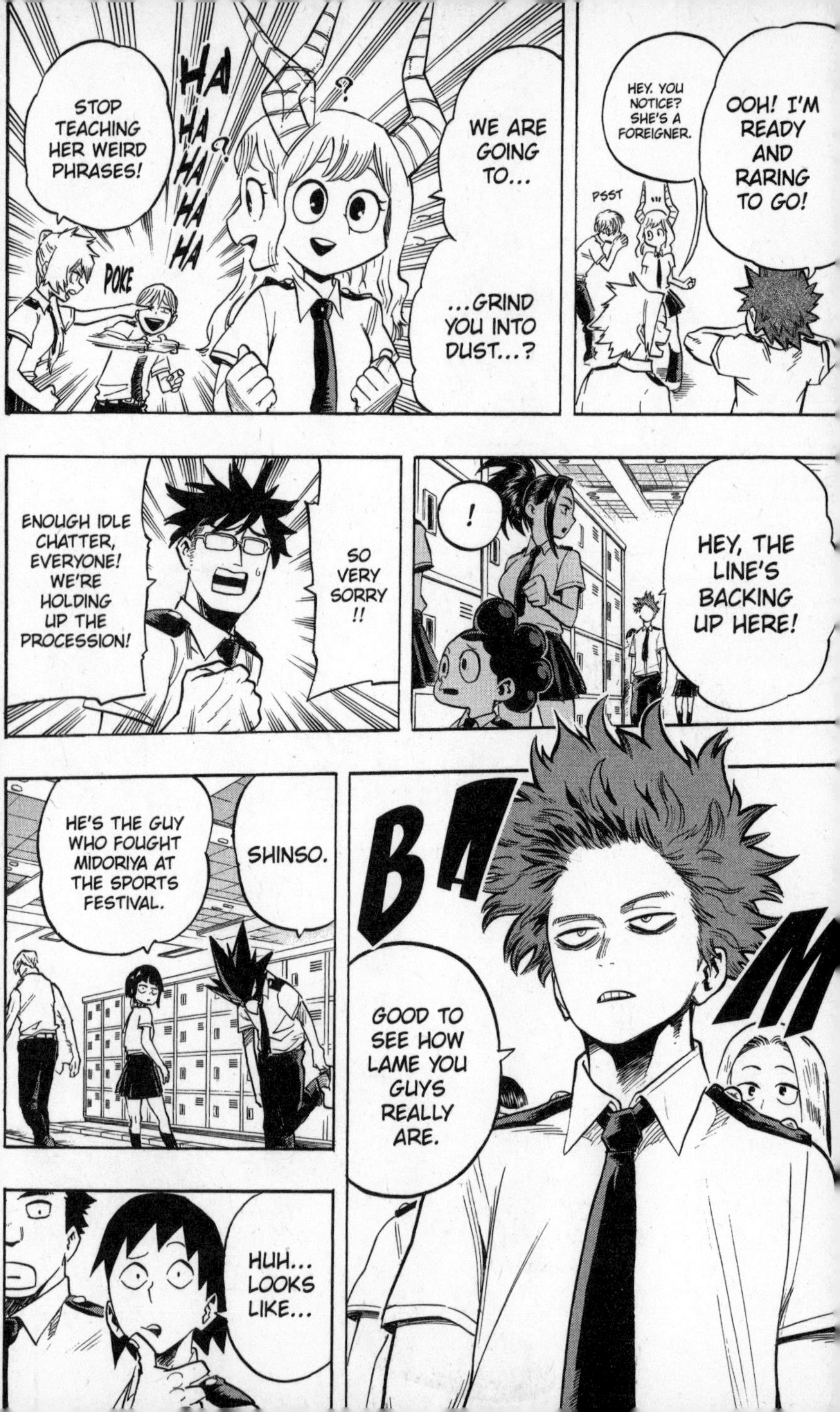
OOH! I'M READY AND RARING TO GO!
HEY. YOU NOTICE? SHE'S A FOREIGNER.
...
PSST
WE ARE GOING TO...
...GRIND YOU INTO DUST...?
HA HA HA HA HA HA
STOP TEACHING HER WEIRD PHRASES!
POKE
HEY, THE LINE'S BACKING UP HERE!
!
SO VERY SORRY!!
ENOUGH IDLE CHATTER, EVERYONE! WE'RE HOLDING UP THE PROCESSION!
BAM
GOOD TO SEE HOW LAME YOU GUYS REALLY ARE.
SHINSO.
HE'S THE GUY WHO FOUGHT MIDORIYA AT THE SPORTS FESTIVAL.
HUH... LOOKS LIKE...

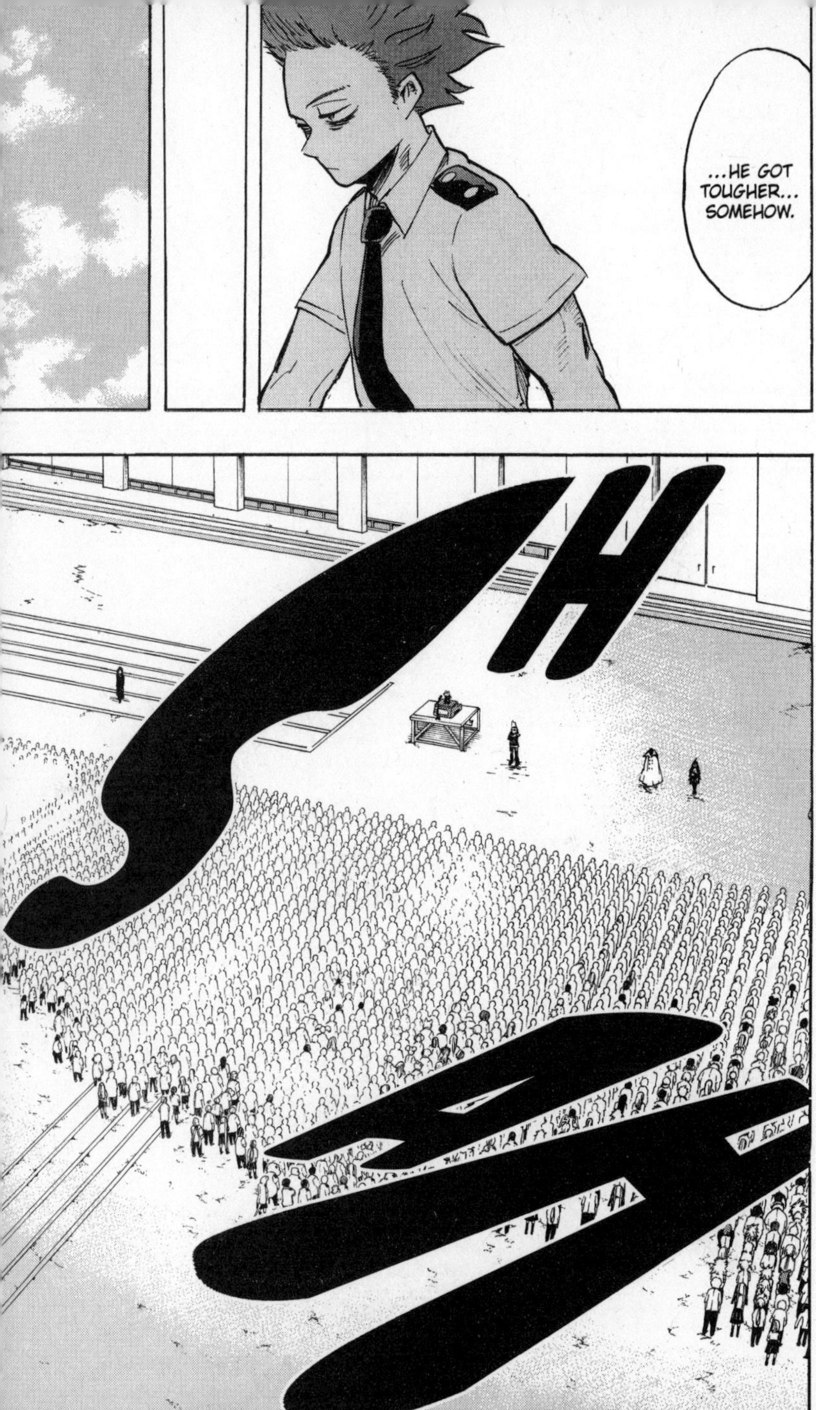
...HE GOT TOUGHER... SOMEHOW.

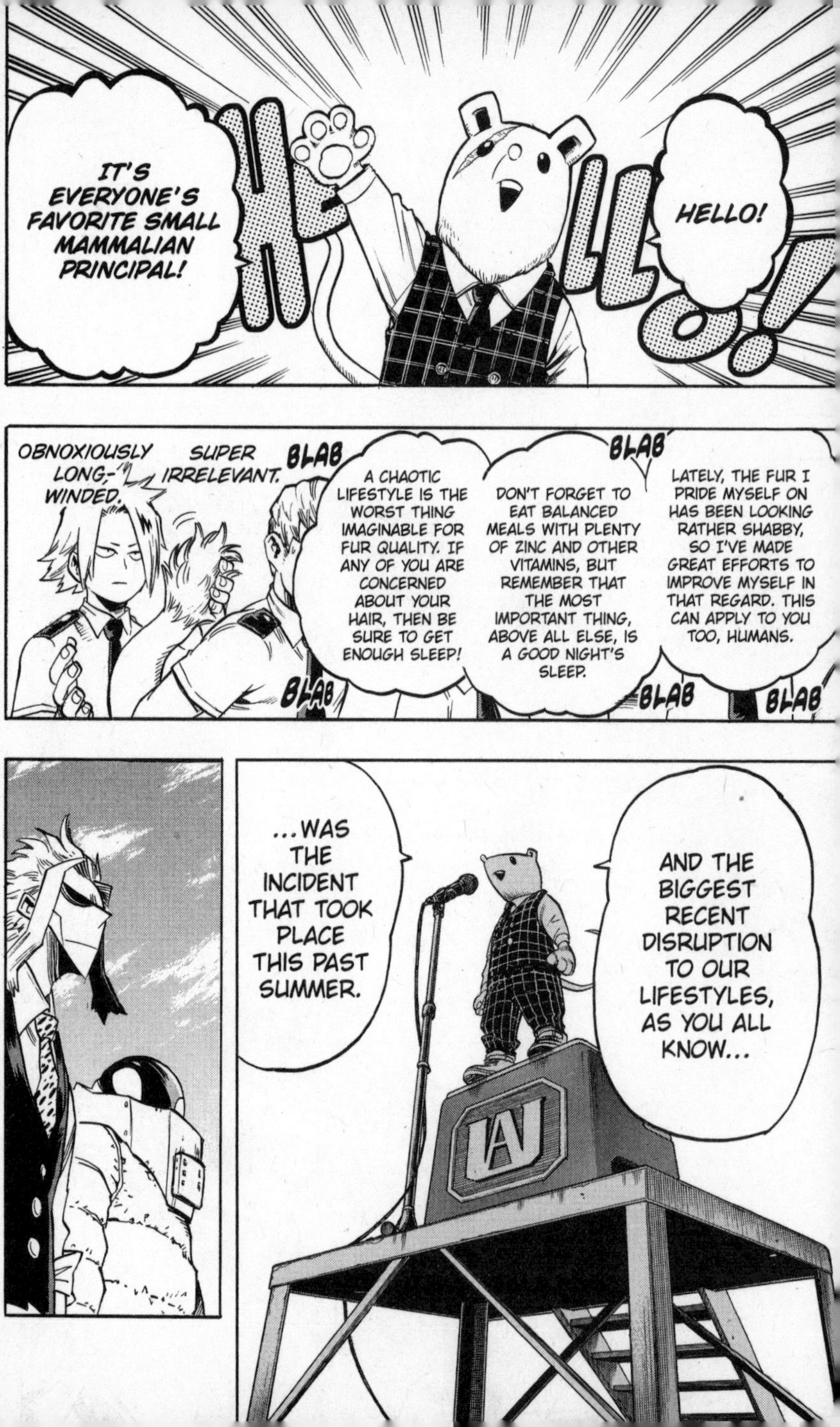
HELLO!
HELLO!
IT'S EVERYONE'S FAVORITE SMALL MAMMALIAN PRINCIPAL!
BLAB
LATELY, THE FUR I PRIDE MYSELF ON HAS BEEN LOOKING RATHER SHABBY, SO I'VE MADE GREAT EFFORTS TO IMPROVE MYSELF IN THAT REGARD. THIS CAN APPLY TO YOU TOO, HUMANS.
BLAB
BLAB
DON'T FORGET TO EAT BALANCED MEALS WITH PLENTY OF ZINC AND OTHER VITAMINS, BUT REMEMBER THAT THE MOST IMPORTANT THING, ABOVE ALL ELSE, IS A GOOD NIGHT'S SLEEP.
BLAB
BLAB
A CHAOTIC LIFESTYLE IS THE WORST THING IMAGINABLE FOR FUR QUALITY. IF ANY OF YOU ARE CONCERNED ABOUT YOUR HAIR, THEN BE SURE TO GET ENOUGH SLEEP!
BLAB
SUPER IRRELEVANT.
OBNOXIOUSLY LONG-WINDED.
AND THE BIGGEST RECENT DISRUPTION TO OUR LIFESTYLES, AS YOU ALL KNOW...
...WAS THE INCIDENT THAT TOOK PLACE THIS PAST SUMMER.

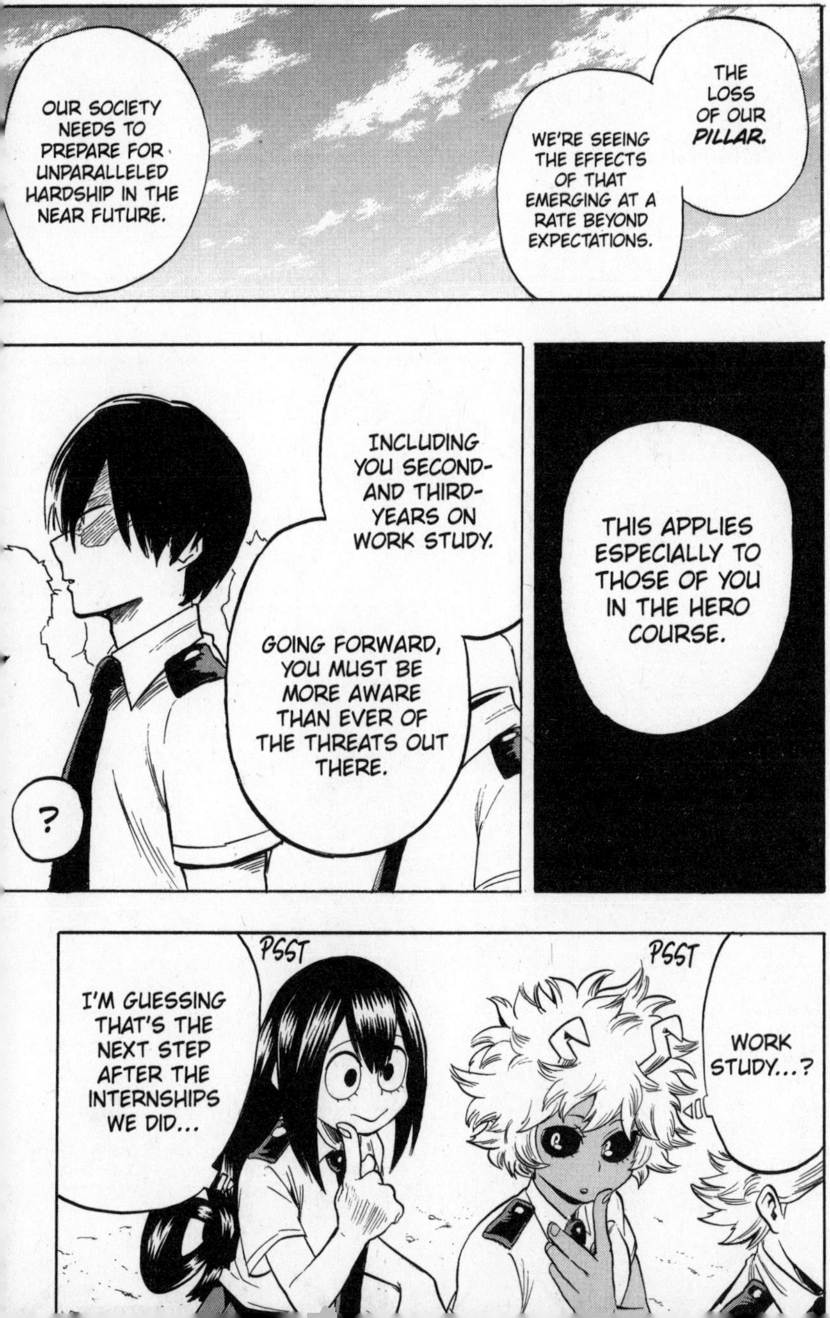
THE LOSS OF OUR PILLAR.
WE'RE SEEING THE EFFECTS OF THAT EMERGING AT A RATE BEYOND EXPECTATIONS.
OUR SOCIETY NEEDS TO PREPARE FOR UNPARALLELED HARDSHIP IN THE NEAR FUTURE.
THIS APPLIES ESPECIALLY TO THOSE OF YOU IN THE HERO COURSE.
INCLUDING YOU SECOND- AND THIRD-YEARS ON WORK STUDY.
GOING FORWARD, YOU MUST BE MORE AWARE THAN EVER OF THE THREATS OUT THERE.
?
PSST
WORK STUDY...?
PSST
I'M GUESSING THAT'S THE NEXT STEP AFTER THE INTERNSHIPS WE DID...

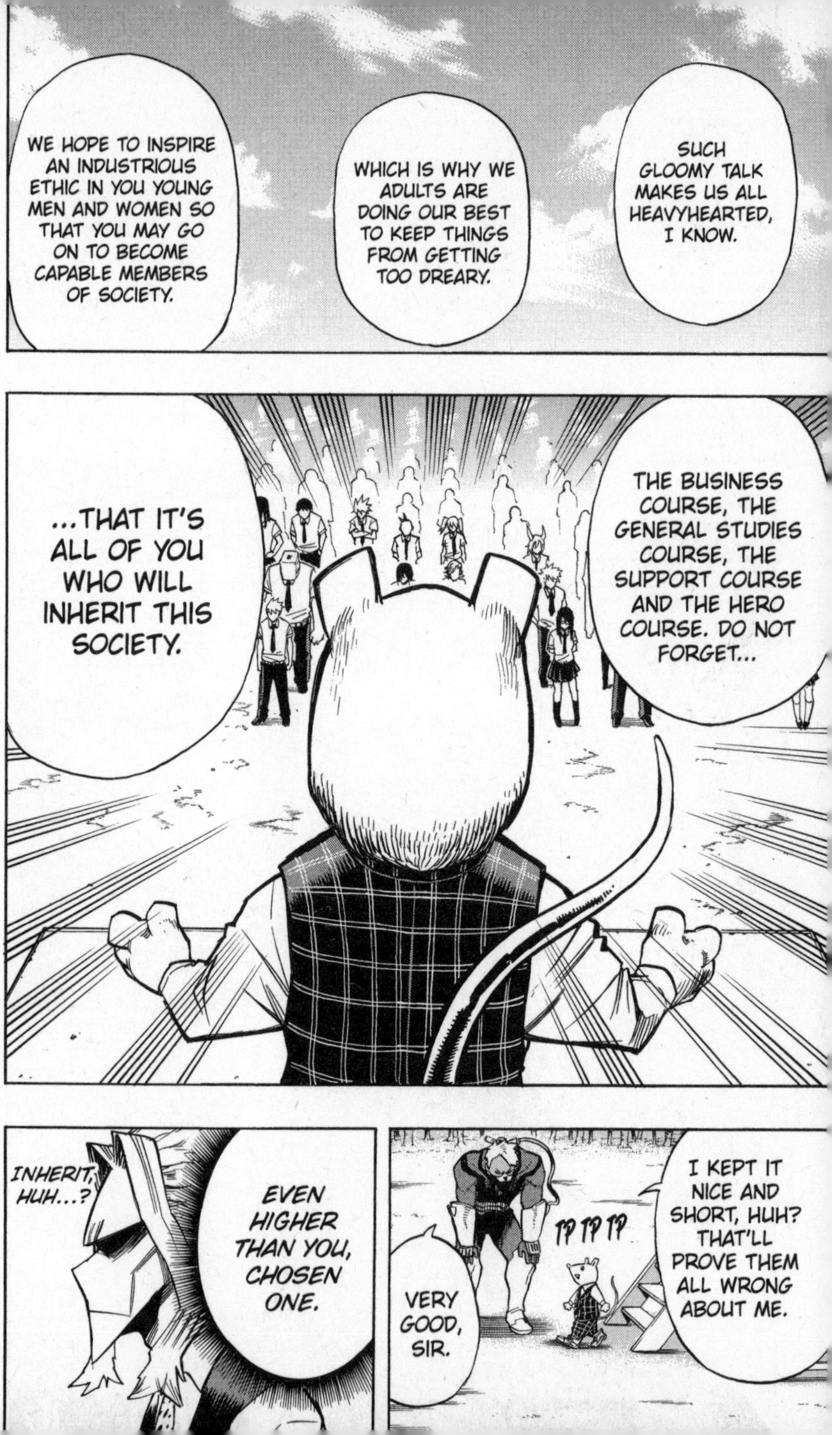
SUCH GLOOMY TALK MAKES US ALL HEAVYHEARTED, I KNOW.
WHICH IS WHY WE ADULTS ARE DOING OUR BEST TO KEEP THINGS FROM GETTING TOO DREARY.
WE HOPE TO INSPIRE AN INDUSTRIOUS ETHIC IN YOU YOUNG MEN AND WOMEN SO THAT YOU MAY GO ON TO BECOME CAPABLE MEMBERS OF SOCIETY.
THE BUSINESS COURSE, THE GENERAL STUDIES COURSE, THE SUPPORT COURSE AND THE HERO COURSE. DO NOT FORGET...
...THAT IT'S ALL OF YOU WHO WILL INHERIT THIS SOCIETY.
I KEPT IT NICE AND SHORT, HUH? THAT'LL PROVE THEM ALL WRONG ABOUT ME.
TP TP TP
VERY GOOD, SIR.
INHERIT, HUH...?
EVEN HIGHER THAN YOU, CHOSEN ONE.

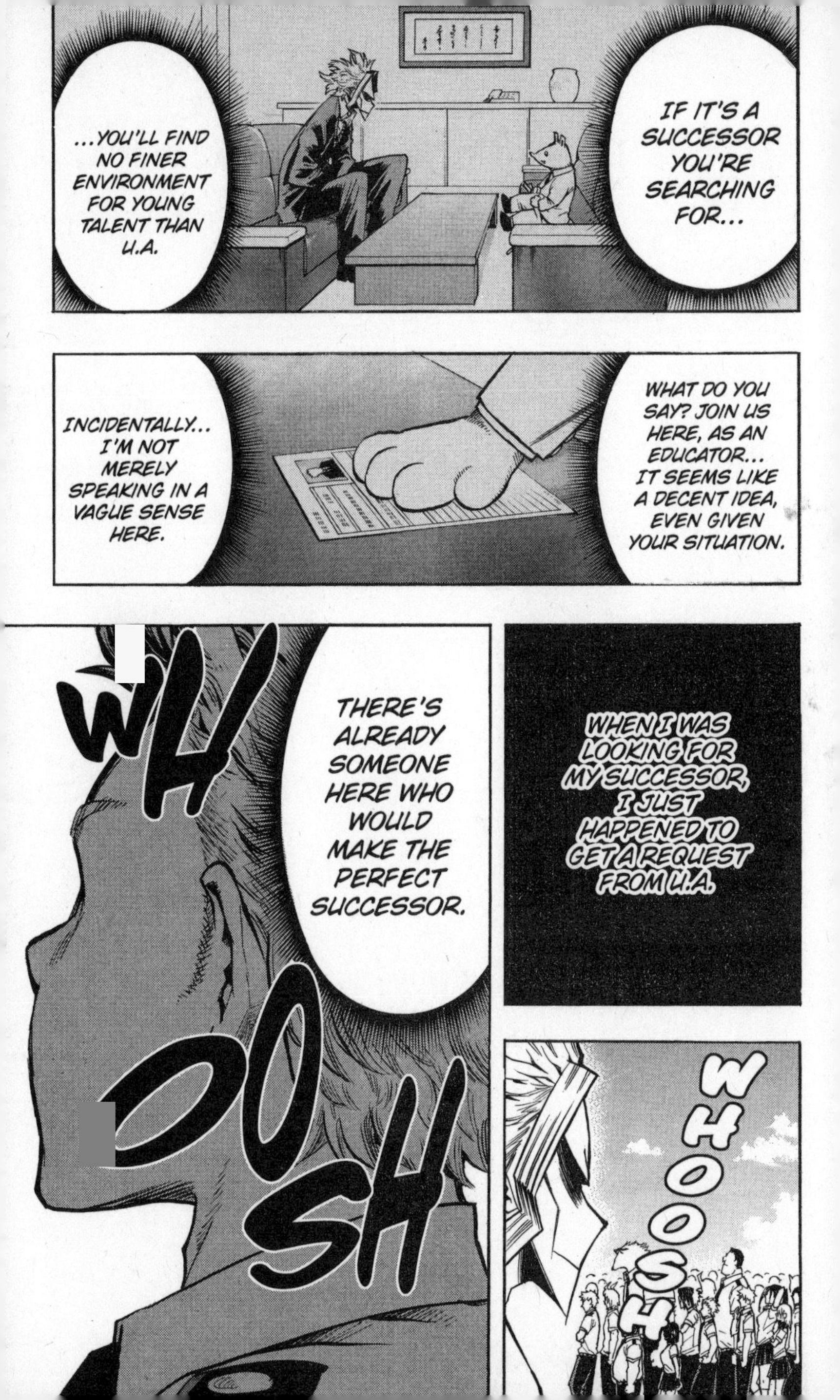
IF IT'S A SUCCESSOR YOU'RE SEARCHING FOR...
...YOU'LL FIND NO FINER ENVIRONMENT FOR YOUNG TALENT THAN U.A.
WHAT DO YOU SAY? JOIN US HERE, AS AN EDUCATOR... IT SEEMS LIKE A DECENT IDEA, EVEN GIVEN YOUR SITUATION.
INCIDENTALLY... I'M NOT MERELY SPEAKING IN A VAGUE SENSE HERE.
WHEN I WAS LOOKING FOR MY SUCCESSOR, I JUST HAPPENED TO GET A REQUEST FROM U.A.
WHOOSH
THERE'S ALREADY SOMEONE HERE WHO WOULD MAKE THE PERFECT SUCCESSOR.
WHOOSH

HERO

PONY TSUNOTORI (16)

STREET CLOTHES

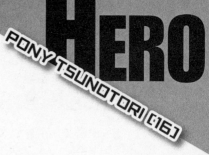

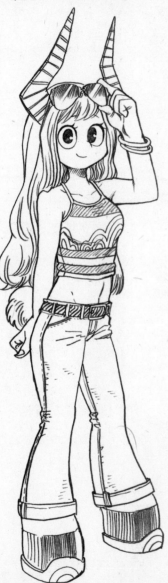

Birthday: 4/21
Height: 155 cm
Favorite Things: Apples, anime

THE SUPPLEMENT

Pony Tsunotori. She's Japanese American, and she hails from the hero capital of the world, the United States.

Her face has really changed since her debut...!!

MY HERO ACADEMIA

No. 122 - A Season for Encounters

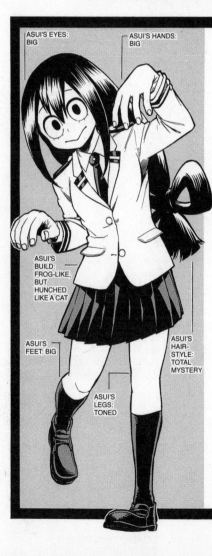

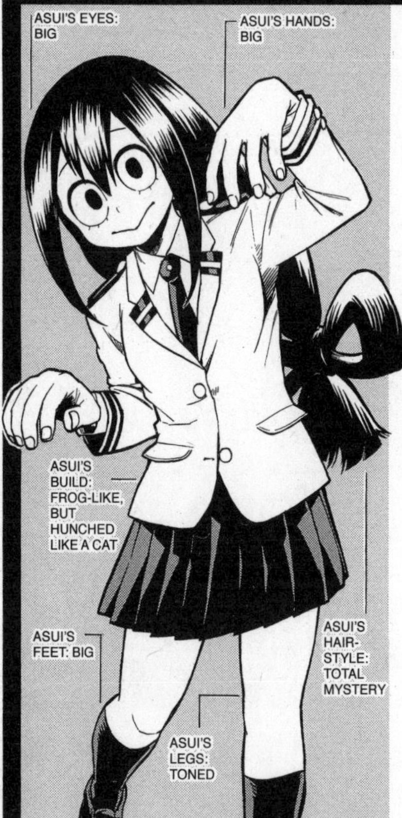
ASUI'S EYES: BIG
ASUI'S HANDS: BIG
ASUI'S BUILD: FROG-LIKE, BUT HUNCHED LIKE A CAT
ASUI'S FEET: BIG
ASUI'S HAIR-STYLE: TOTAL MYSTERY
ASUI'S LEGS: TONED

U.A. FILE.11

CLASS No.03

TSUYU ASUI

Quirk: FROG

She can basically do anything a frog can do!

She's got a stretchy tongue and can jump really, really high and far!!

With her recent camouflage ability, it kind of feels like she's almost getting too strong!

That said, she's got weaknesses!!

She becomes unable to use her quirk in cold environments, and the chill will leave her muttering, "So sleepy…"!

She's quite the sight to see in winter!!

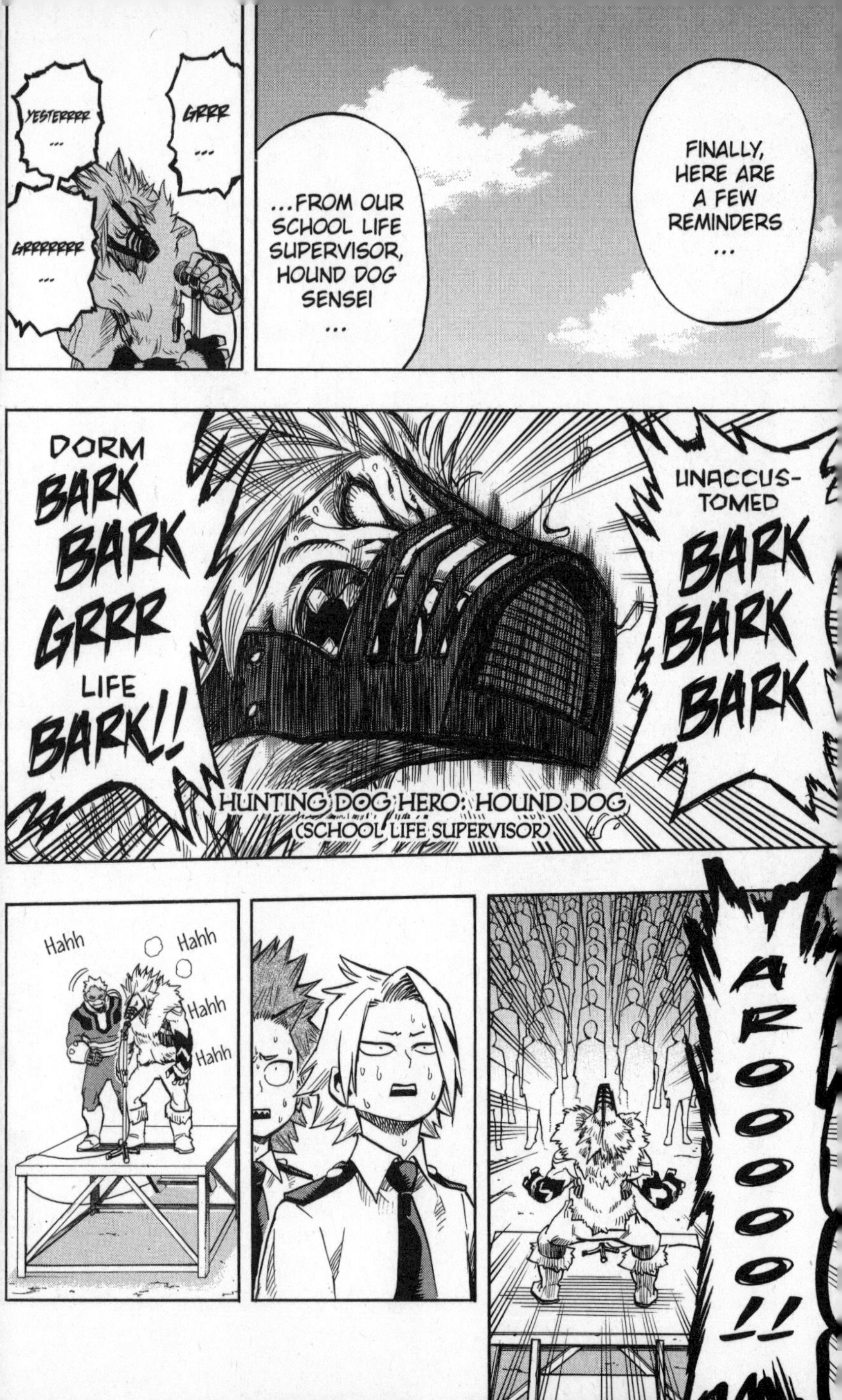
FINALLY, HERE ARE A FEW REMINDERS ...
...FROM OUR SCHOOL LIFE SUPERVISOR, HOUND DOG SENSEI ...
GRRR ...
YESTERRRR ...
GRRRRRRR ...
UNACCUS-TOMED BARK BARK BARK BARK
DORM BARK BARK GRRR LIFE BARK!!
HUNTING DOG HERO: HOUND DOG
(SCHOOL LIFE SUPERVISOR)
AROOOOOO!!
Hahh
Hahh
Hahh
Hahh

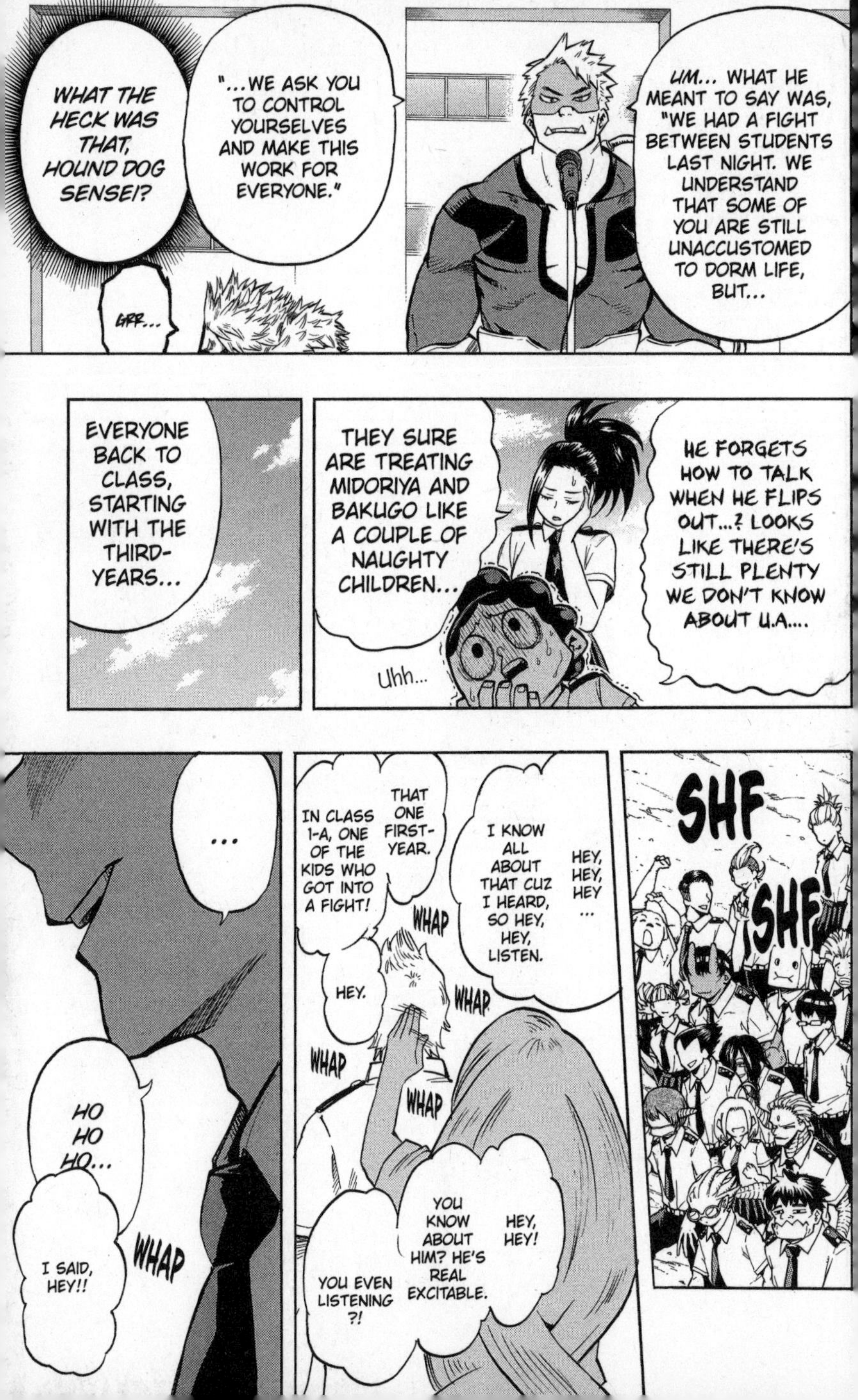
UM... WHAT HE MEANT TO SAY WAS, "WE HAD A FIGHT BETWEEN STUDENTS LAST NIGHT. WE UNDERSTAND THAT SOME OF YOU ARE STILL UNACCUSTOMED TO DORM LIFE, BUT...
"...WE ASK YOU TO CONTROL YOURSELVES AND MAKE THIS WORK FOR EVERYONE."
WHAT THE HECK WAS THAT, HOUND DOG SENSEI?
GRR...
HE FORGETS HOW TO TALK WHEN HE FLIPS OUT...? LOOKS LIKE THERE'S STILL PLENTY WE DON'T KNOW ABOUT U.A....
THEY SURE ARE TREATING MIDORIYA AND BAKUGO LIKE A COUPLE OF NAUGHTY CHILDREN...
Uhh...
EVERYONE BACK TO CLASS, STARTING WITH THE THIRD-YEARS...
SHF
SHF
HEY, HEY, HEY...
I KNOW ALL ABOUT THAT CUZ I HEARD, SO HEY, HEY, LISTEN.
THAT ONE FIRST-YEAR.
IN CLASS 1-A, ONE OF THE KIDS WHO GOT INTO A FIGHT!
WHAP
HEY.
WHAP
WHAP
WHAP
HEY, HEY!
YOU KNOW ABOUT HIM? HE'S REAL EXCITABLE.
YOU EVEN LISTENING ?!
...
HO HO HO...
WHAP
I SAID, HEY!!

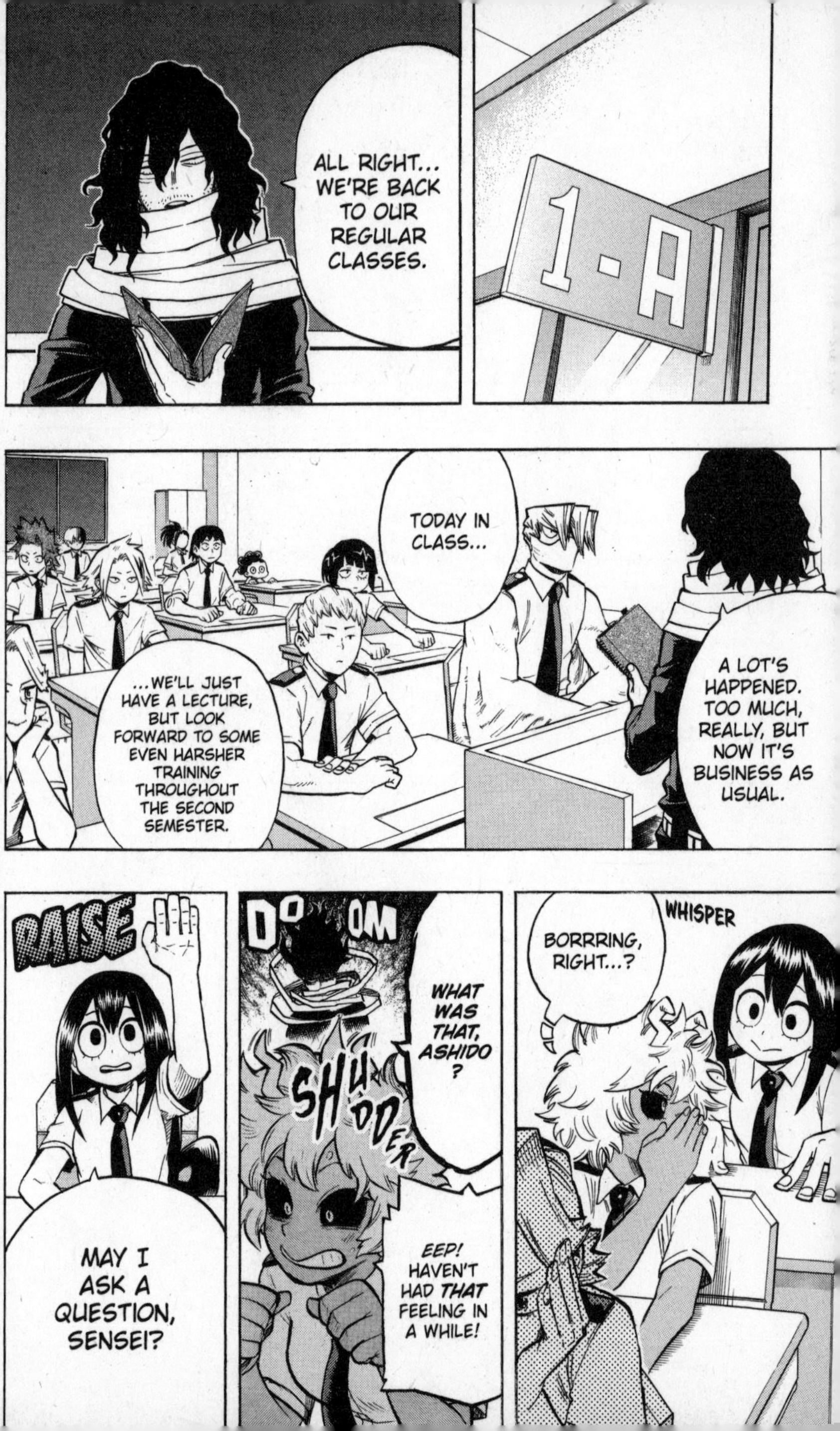
ALL RIGHT... WE'RE BACK TO OUR REGULAR CLASSES.
A LOT'S HAPPENED. TOO MUCH, REALLY, BUT NOW IT'S BUSINESS AS USUAL.
TODAY IN CLASS...
...WE'LL JUST HAVE A LECTURE, BUT LOOK FORWARD TO SOME EVEN HARSHER TRAINING THROUGHOUT THE SECOND SEMESTER.
WHISPER
BORRRING, RIGHT...?
DOOM
WHAT WAS THAT, ASHIDO?
SHUDDER
EEP! HAVEN'T HAD THAT FEELING IN A WHILE!
RAISE
MAY I ASK A QUESTION, SENSEI?

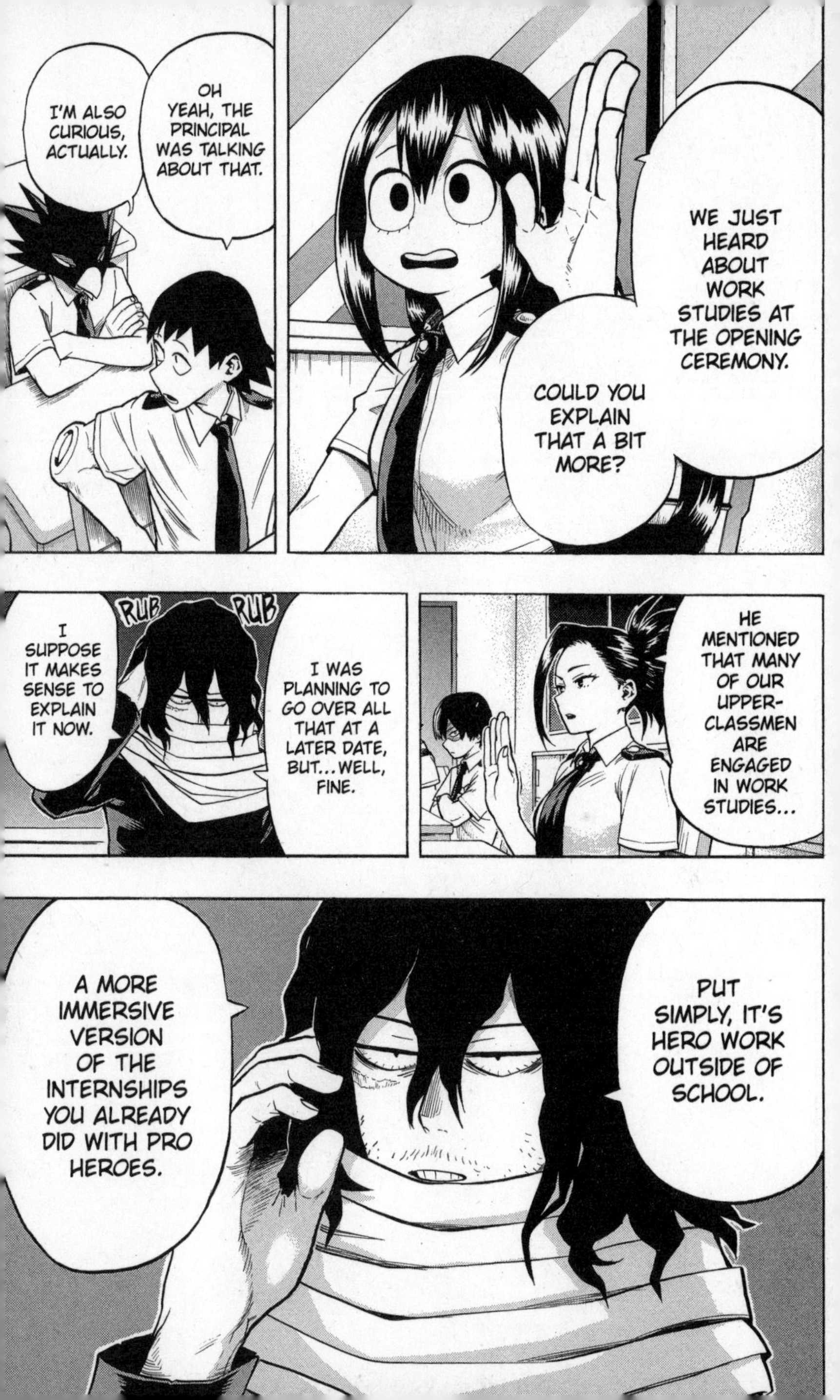
WE JUST HEARD ABOUT WORK STUDIES AT THE OPENING CEREMONY.
COULD YOU EXPLAIN THAT A BIT MORE?
OH YEAH, THE PRINCIPAL WAS TALKING ABOUT THAT.
I'M ALSO CURIOUS, ACTUALLY.
HE MENTIONED THAT MANY OF OUR UPPER-CLASSMEN ARE ENGAGED IN WORK STUDIES...
RUB RUB
I WAS PLANNING TO GO OVER ALL THAT AT A LATER DATE, BUT...WELL, FINE.
I SUPPOSE IT MAKES SENSE TO EXPLAIN IT NOW.
PUT SIMPLY, IT'S HERO WORK OUTSIDE OF SCHOOL.
A MORE IMMERSIVE VERSION OF THE INTERNSHIPS YOU ALREADY DID WITH PRO HEROES.

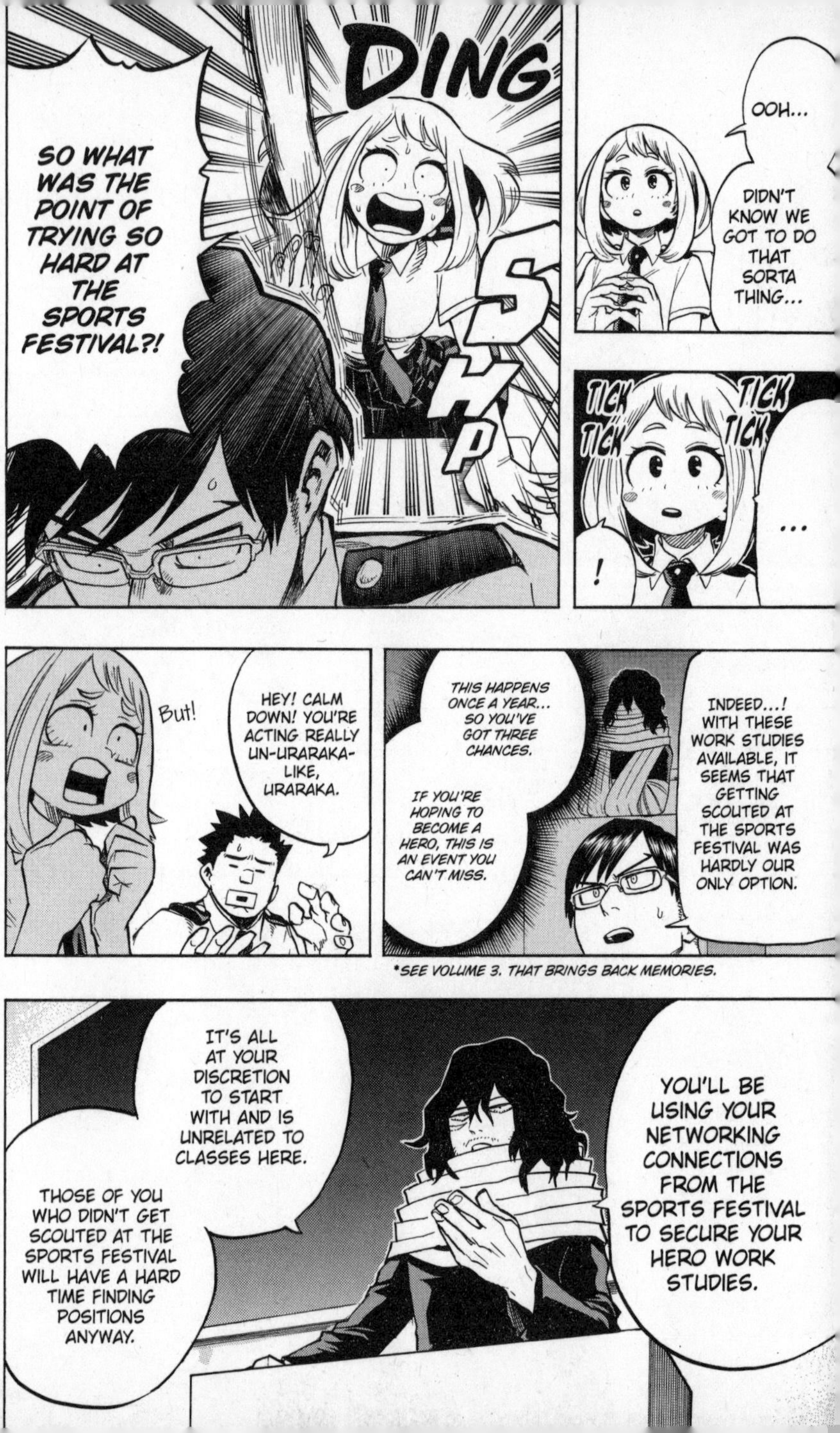
OOH...
DIDN'T KNOW WE GOT TO DO THAT SORTA THING...
TICK TICK
TICK TICK
...
!
DING
SO WHAT WAS THE POINT OF TRYING SO HARD AT THE SPORTS FESTIVAL?!
SHP
INDEED...! WITH THESE WORK STUDIES AVAILABLE, IT SEEMS THAT GETTING SCOUTED AT THE SPORTS FESTIVAL WAS HARDLY OUR ONLY OPTION.
THIS HAPPENS ONCE A YEAR... SO YOU'VE GOT THREE CHANCES.
IF YOU'RE HOPING TO BECOME A HERO, THIS IS AN EVENT YOU CAN'T MISS.
HEY! CALM DOWN! YOU'RE ACTING REALLY UN-URARAKA-LIKE, URARAKA.
But!
YOU'LL BE USING YOUR NETWORKING CONNECTIONS FROM THE SPORTS FESTIVAL TO SECURE YOUR HERO WORK STUDIES.
IT'S ALL AT YOUR DISCRETION TO START WITH AND IS UNRELATED TO CLASSES HERE.
THOSE OF YOU WHO DIDN'T GET SCOUTED AT THE SPORTS FESTIVAL WILL HAVE A HARD TIME FINDING POSITIONS ANYWAY.

*SEE VOLUME 3. THAT BRINGS BACK MEMORIES.

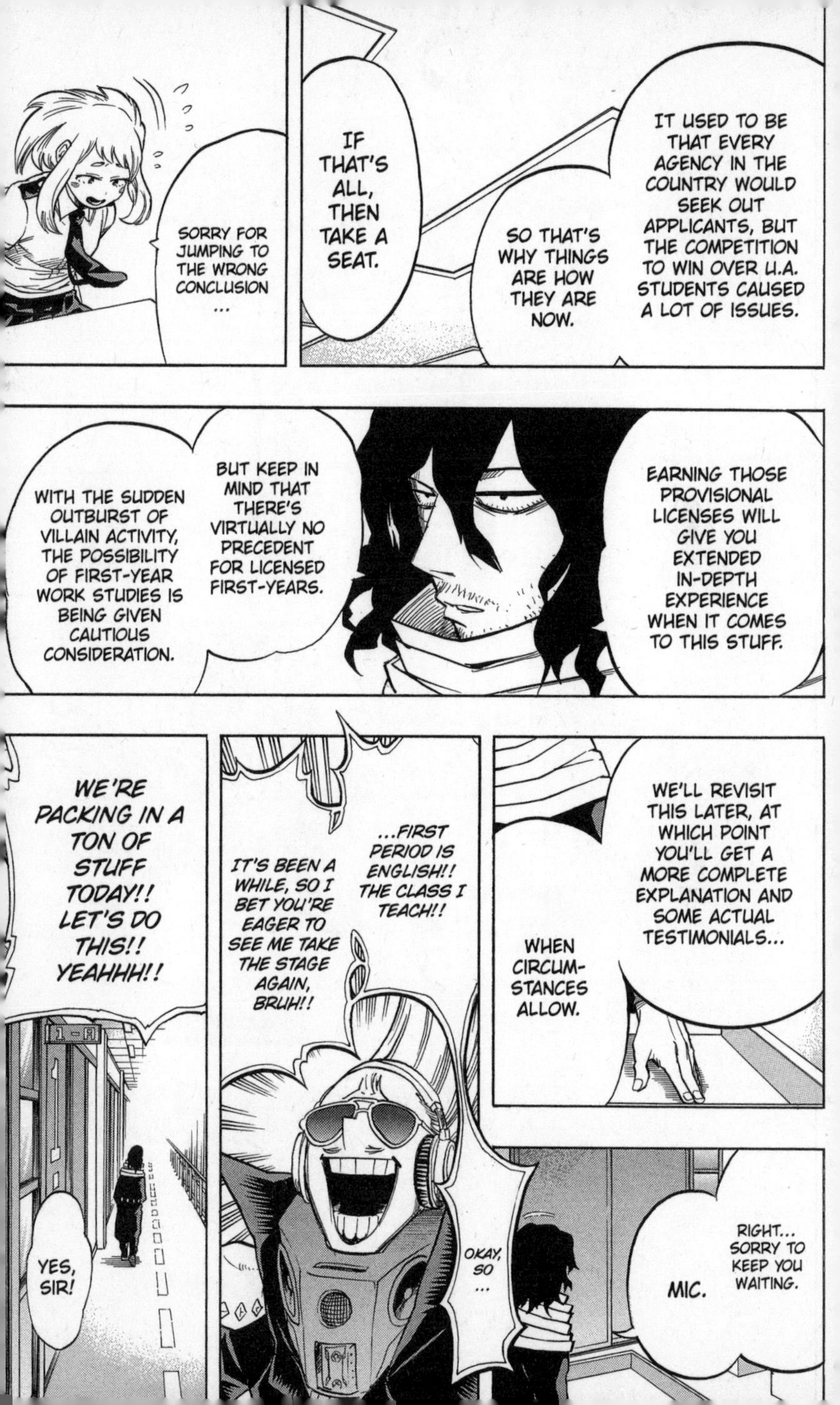
IT USED TO BE THAT EVERY AGENCY IN THE COUNTRY WOULD SEEK OUT APPLICANTS, BUT THE COMPETITION TO WIN OVER U.A. STUDENTS CAUSED A LOT OF ISSUES.
SO THAT'S WHY THINGS ARE HOW THEY ARE NOW.
IF THAT'S ALL, THEN TAKE A SEAT.
SORRY FOR JUMPING TO THE WRONG CONCLUSION...
EARNING THOSE PROVISIONAL LICENSES WILL GIVE YOU EXTENDED IN-DEPTH EXPERIENCE WHEN IT COMES TO THIS STUFF.
BUT KEEP IN MIND THAT THERE'S VIRTUALLY NO PRECEDENT FOR LICENSED FIRST-YEARS.
WITH THE SUDDEN OUTBURST OF VILLAIN ACTIVITY, THE POSSIBILITY OF FIRST-YEAR WORK STUDIES IS BEING GIVEN CAUTIOUS CONSIDERATION.
WE'LL REVISIT THIS LATER, AT WHICH POINT YOU'LL GET A MORE COMPLETE EXPLANATION AND SOME ACTUAL TESTIMONIALS...
WHEN CIRCUM-STANCES ALLOW.
RIGHT... SORRY TO KEEP YOU WAITING.
MIC.
OKAY, SO...
...FIRST PERIOD IS ENGLISH!! THE CLASS I TEACH!!
IT'S BEEN A WHILE, SO I BET YOU'RE EAGER TO SEE ME TAKE THE STAGE AGAIN, BRUH!!
WE'RE PACKING IN A TON OF STUFF TODAY!! LET'S DO THIS!! YEAHHH!!
1-A
YES, SIR!

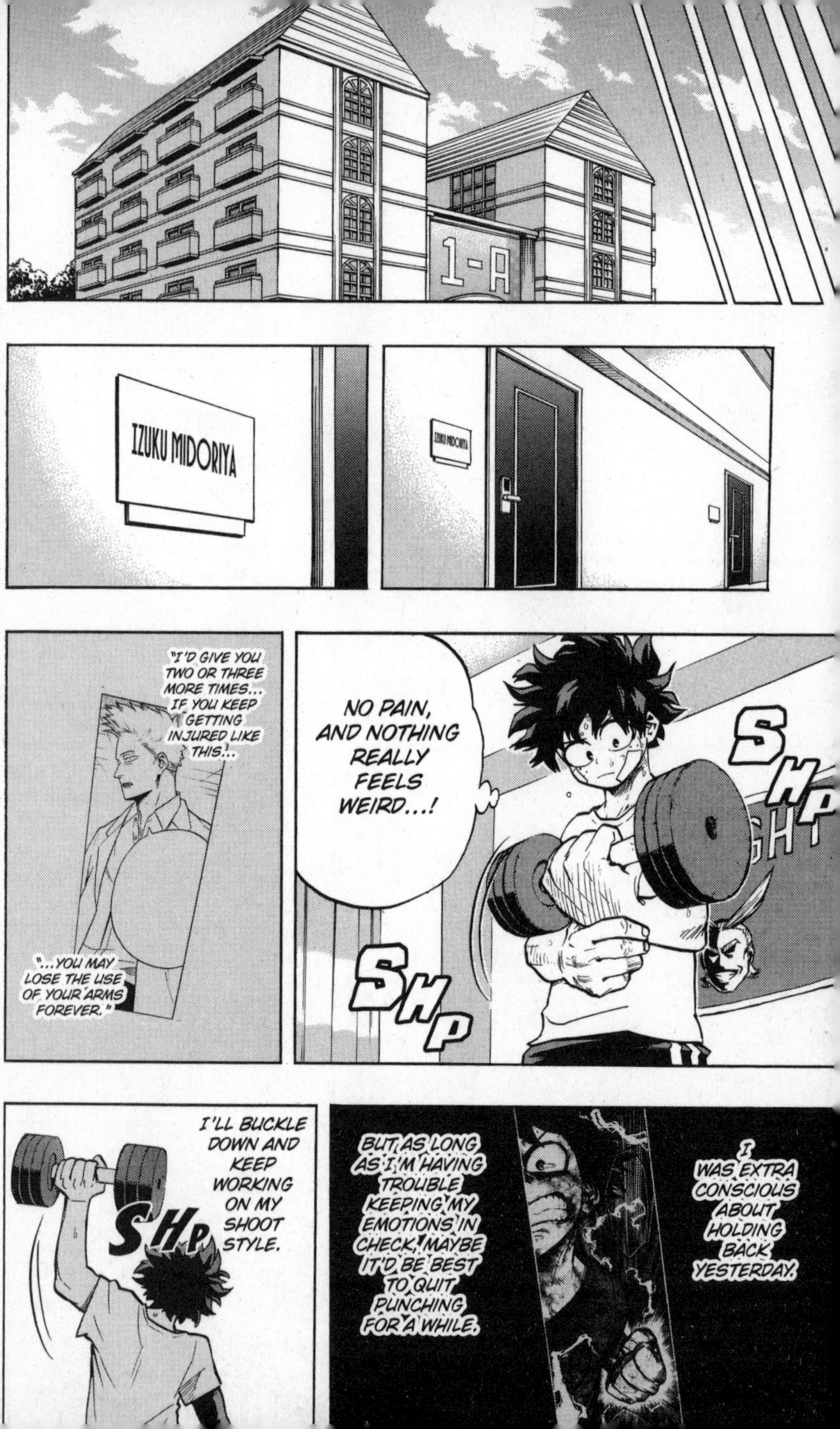
1-A
IZUKU MIDORIYA
IZUKU MIDORIYA
SHP
NO PAIN, AND NOTHING REALLY FEELS WEIRD...!
SHP
"I'D GIVE YOU TWO OR THREE MORE TIMES... IF YOU KEEP GETTING INJURED LIKE THIS...
"...YOU MAY LOSE THE USE OF YOUR ARMS FOREVER."
I WAS EXTRA CONSCIOUS ABOUT HOLDING BACK YESTERDAY.
BUT AS LONG AS I'M HAVING TROUBLE KEEPING MY EMOTIONS IN CHECK, MAYBE IT'D BE BEST TO QUIT PUNCHING FOR A WHILE.
I'LL BUCKLE DOWN AND KEEP WORKING ON MY SHOOT STYLE.
SHP

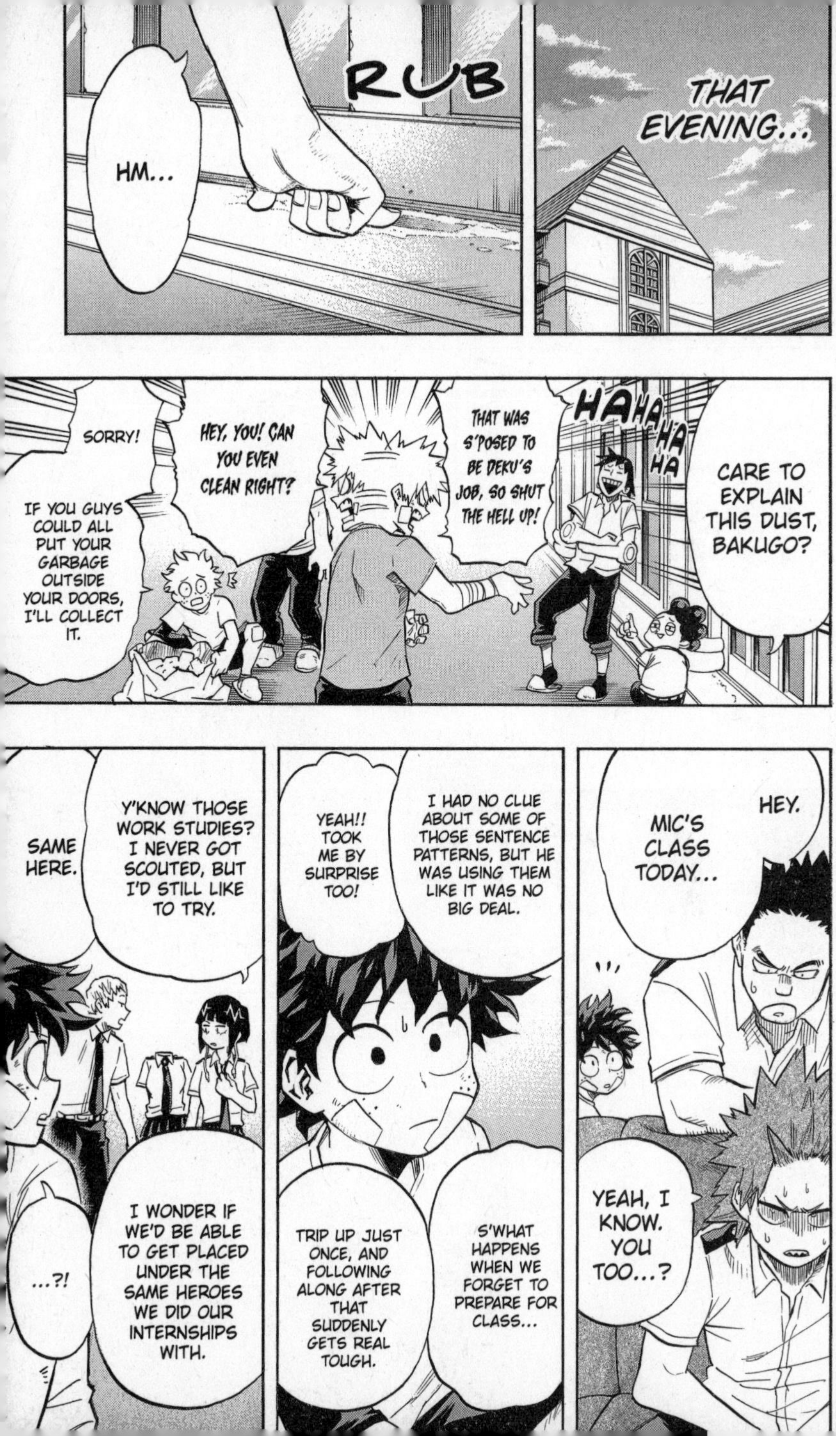
THAT EVENING...
RUB
HM...
CARE TO EXPLAIN THIS DUST, BAKUGO?
HAHA HA HA
THAT WAS S'POSED TO BE DEKU'S JOB, SO SHUT THE HELL UP!
HEY, YOU! CAN YOU EVEN CLEAN RIGHT?
SORRY!
IF YOU GUYS COULD ALL PUT YOUR GARBAGE OUTSIDE YOUR DOORS, I'LL COLLECT IT.
HEY.
MIC'S CLASS TODAY...
YEAH, I KNOW. YOU TOO...?
I HAD NO CLUE ABOUT SOME OF THOSE SENTENCE PATTERNS, BUT HE WAS USING THEM LIKE IT WAS NO BIG DEAL.
YEAH!! TOOK ME BY SURPRISE TOO!
S'WHAT HAPPENS WHEN WE FORGET TO PREPARE FOR CLASS...
TRIP UP JUST ONCE, AND FOLLOWING ALONG AFTER THAT SUDDENLY GETS REAL TOUGH.
Y'KNOW THOSE WORK STUDIES? I NEVER GOT SCOUTED, BUT I'D STILL LIKE TO TRY.
SAME HERE.
I WONDER IF WE'D BE ABLE TO GET PLACED UNDER THE SAME HEROES WE DID OUR INTERNSHIPS WITH.
...?!

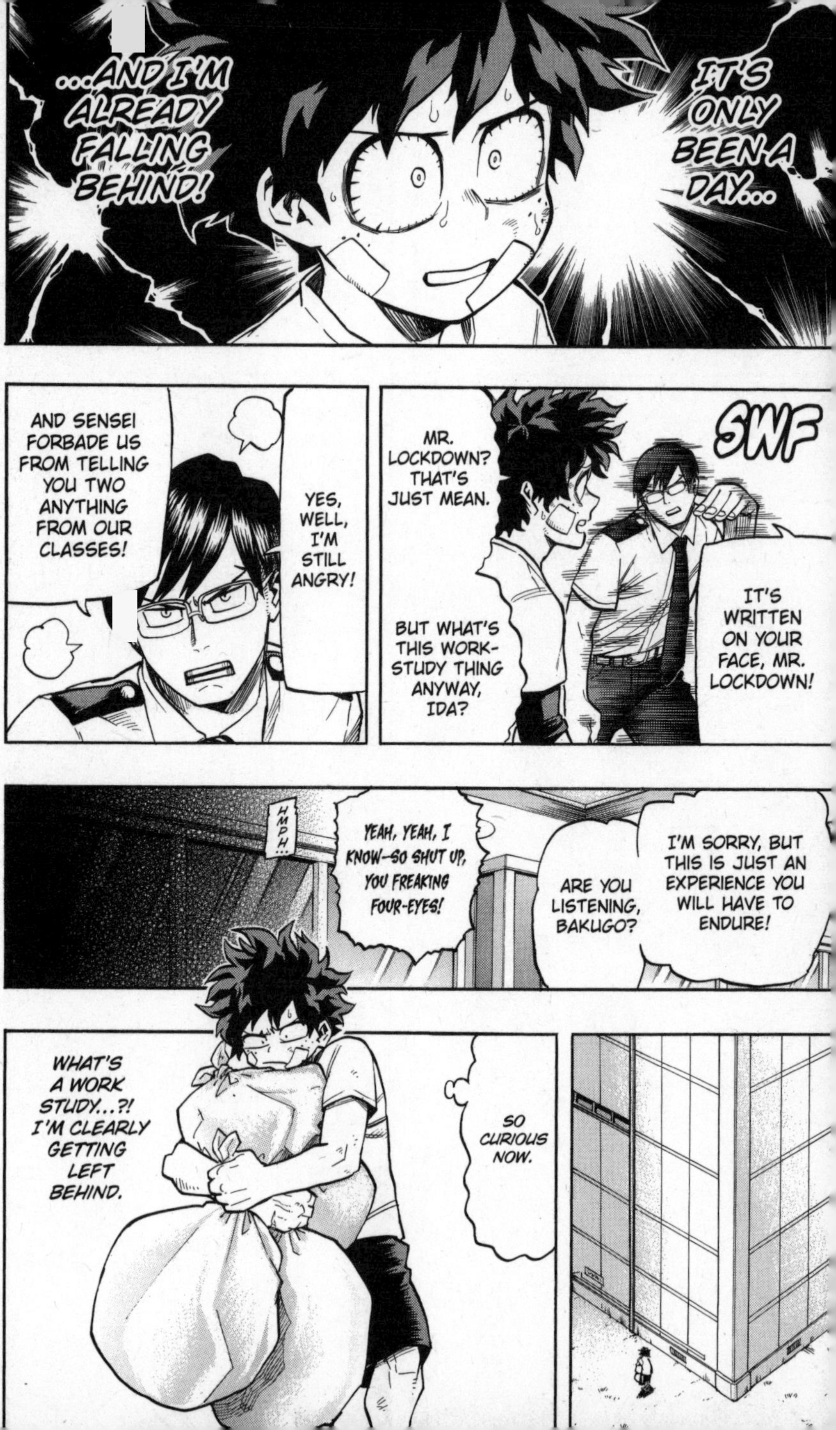
IT'S ONLY BEEN A DAY...
...AND I'M ALREADY FALLING BEHIND!
SWF
IT'S WRITTEN ON YOUR FACE, MR. LOCKDOWN!
MR. LOCKDOWN? THAT'S JUST MEAN.
BUT WHAT'S THIS WORK-STUDY THING ANYWAY, IDA?
YES, WELL, I'M STILL ANGRY!
AND SENSEI FORBADE US FROM TELLING YOU TWO ANYTHING FROM OUR CLASSES!
I'M SORRY, BUT THIS IS JUST AN EXPERIENCE YOU WILL HAVE TO ENDURE!
ARE YOU LISTENING, BAKUGO?
YEAH, YEAH, I KNOW—SO SHUT UP, YOU FREAKING FOUR-EYES!
HMPH...
SO CURIOUS NOW.
WHAT'S A WORK STUDY...?! I'M CLEARLY GETTING LEFT BEHIND.

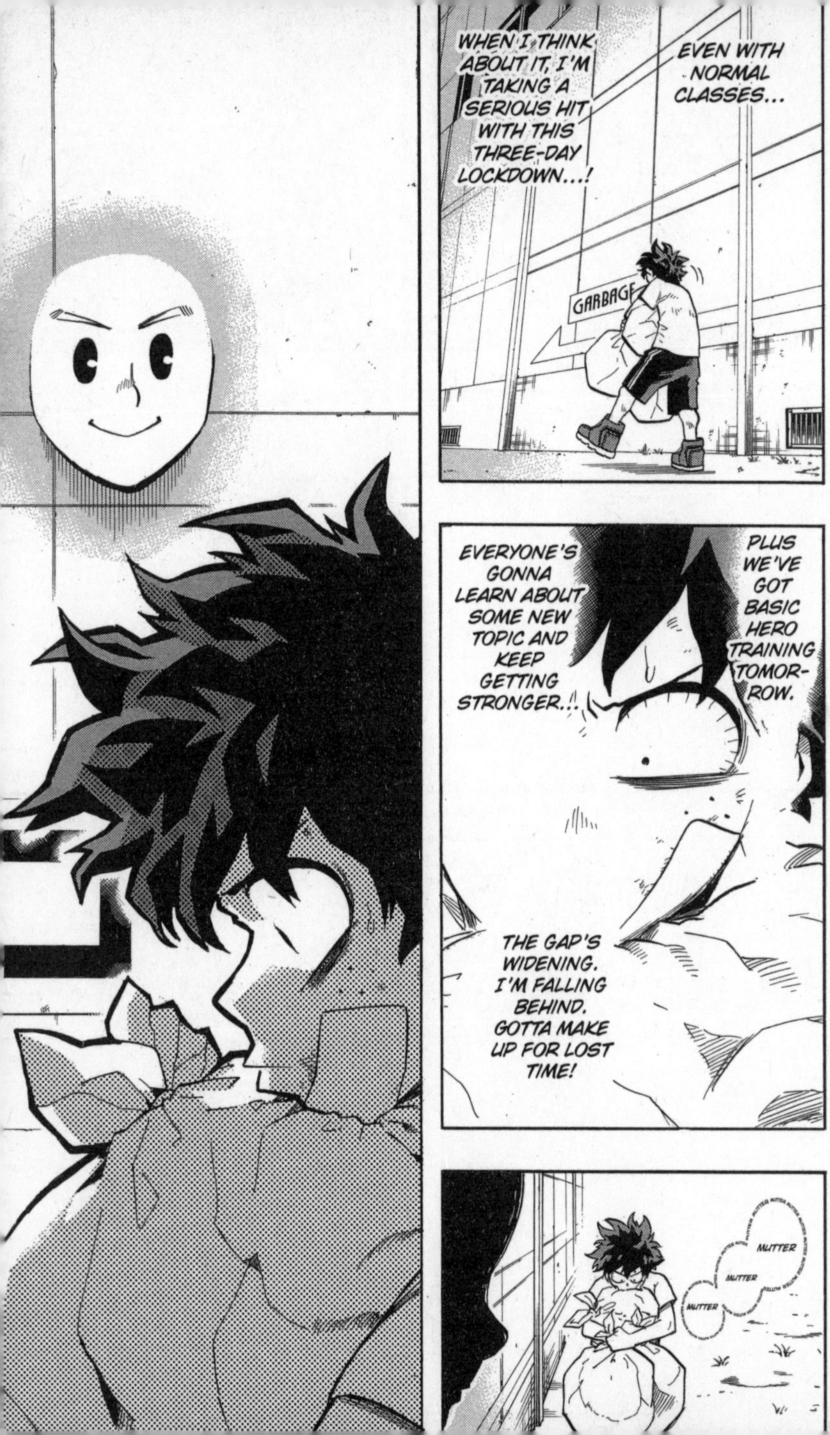

EVEN WITH NORMAL CLASSES...
WHEN I THINK ABOUT IT, I'M TAKING A SERIOUS HIT WITH THIS THREE-DAY LOCKDOWN...!
GARBAGE
PLUS WE'VE GOT BASIC HERO TRAINING TOMORROW.
EVERYONE'S GONNA LEARN ABOUT SOME NEW TOPIC AND KEEP GETTING STRONGER...!
THE GAP'S WIDENING. I'M FALLING BEHIND. GOTTA MAKE UP FOR LOST TIME!
MUTTER
MUTTER
MUTTER

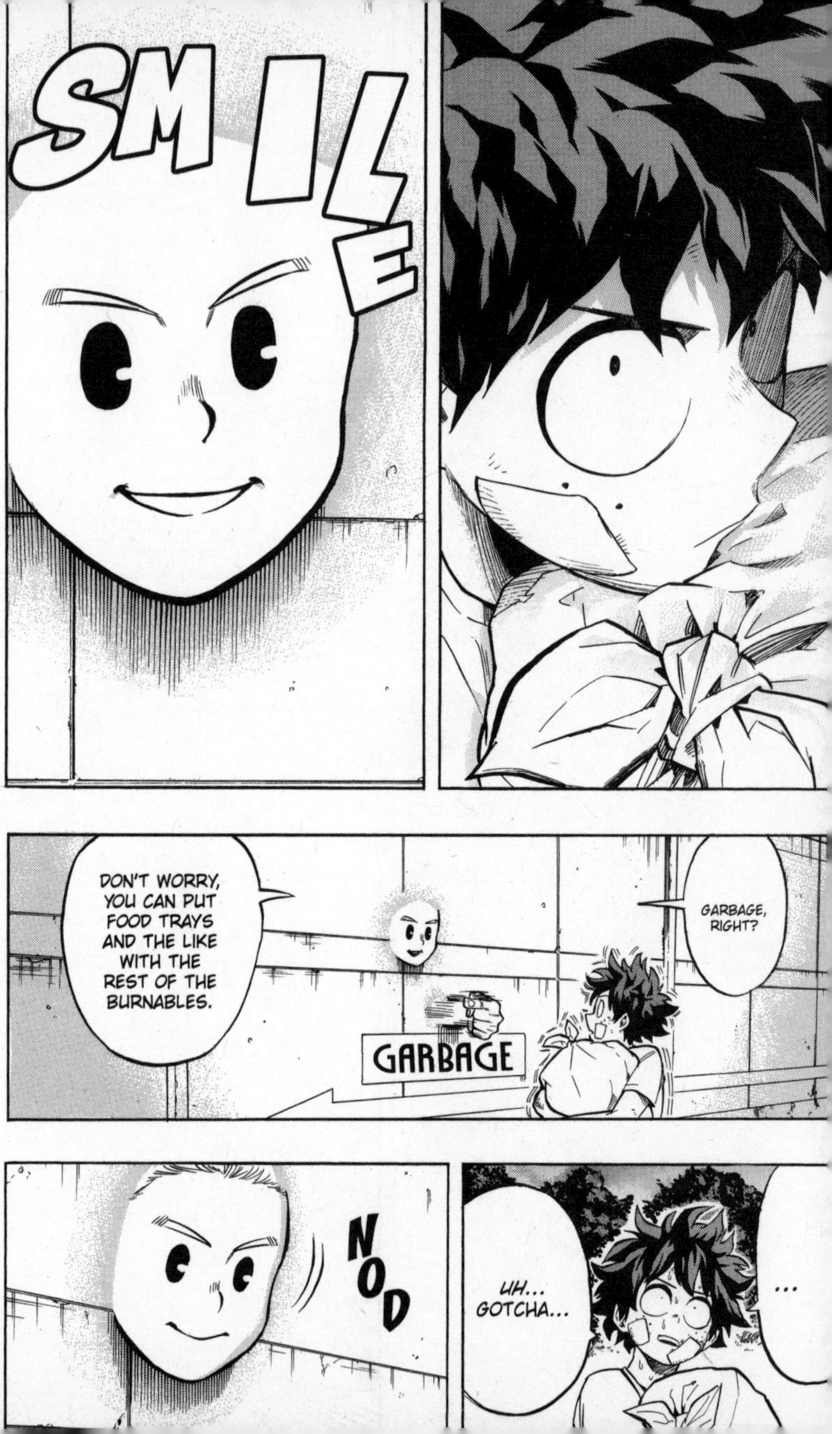
SMILE
GARBAGE, RIGHT?
GARBAGE
DON'T WORRY, YOU CAN PUT FOOD TRAYS AND THE LIKE WITH THE REST OF THE BURNABLES.
...
UH... GOTCHA...
NOD

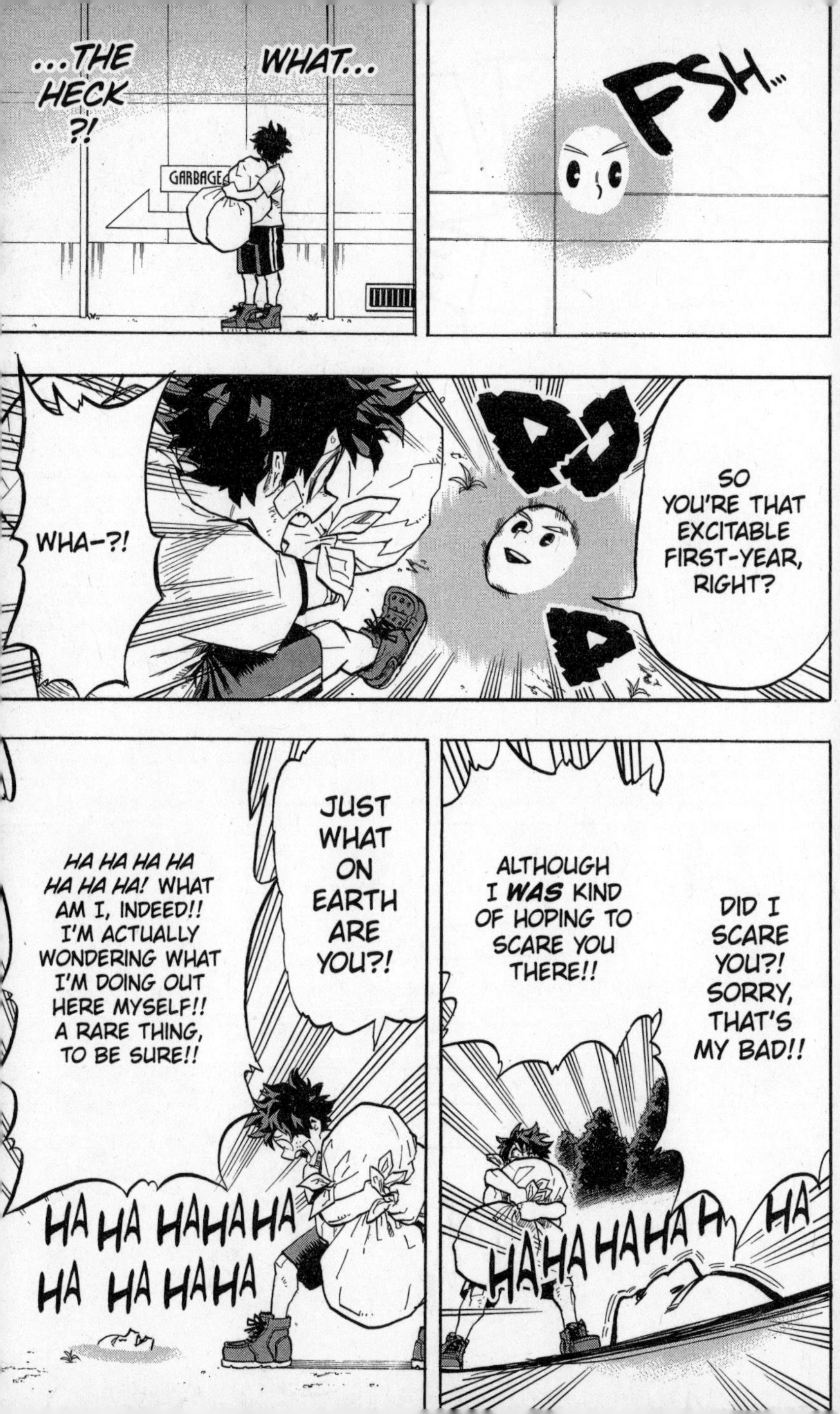
FSH...
WHAT...
...THE HECK ?!
GARBAGE
SO YOU'RE THAT EXCITABLE FIRST-YEAR, RIGHT?
WHA-?!
DID I SCARE YOU?! SORRY, THAT'S MY BAD!!
ALTHOUGH I WAS KIND OF HOPING TO SCARE YOU THERE!!
HA HA HA HA HA H HA
JUST WHAT ON EARTH ARE YOU?!
HA HA HA HA HA HA HA HA! WHAT AM I, INDEED!! I'M ACTUALLY WONDERING WHAT I'M DOING OUT HERE MYSELF!! A RARE THING, TO BE SURE!!
HA HA HAHAHA HA HA HAHAHA

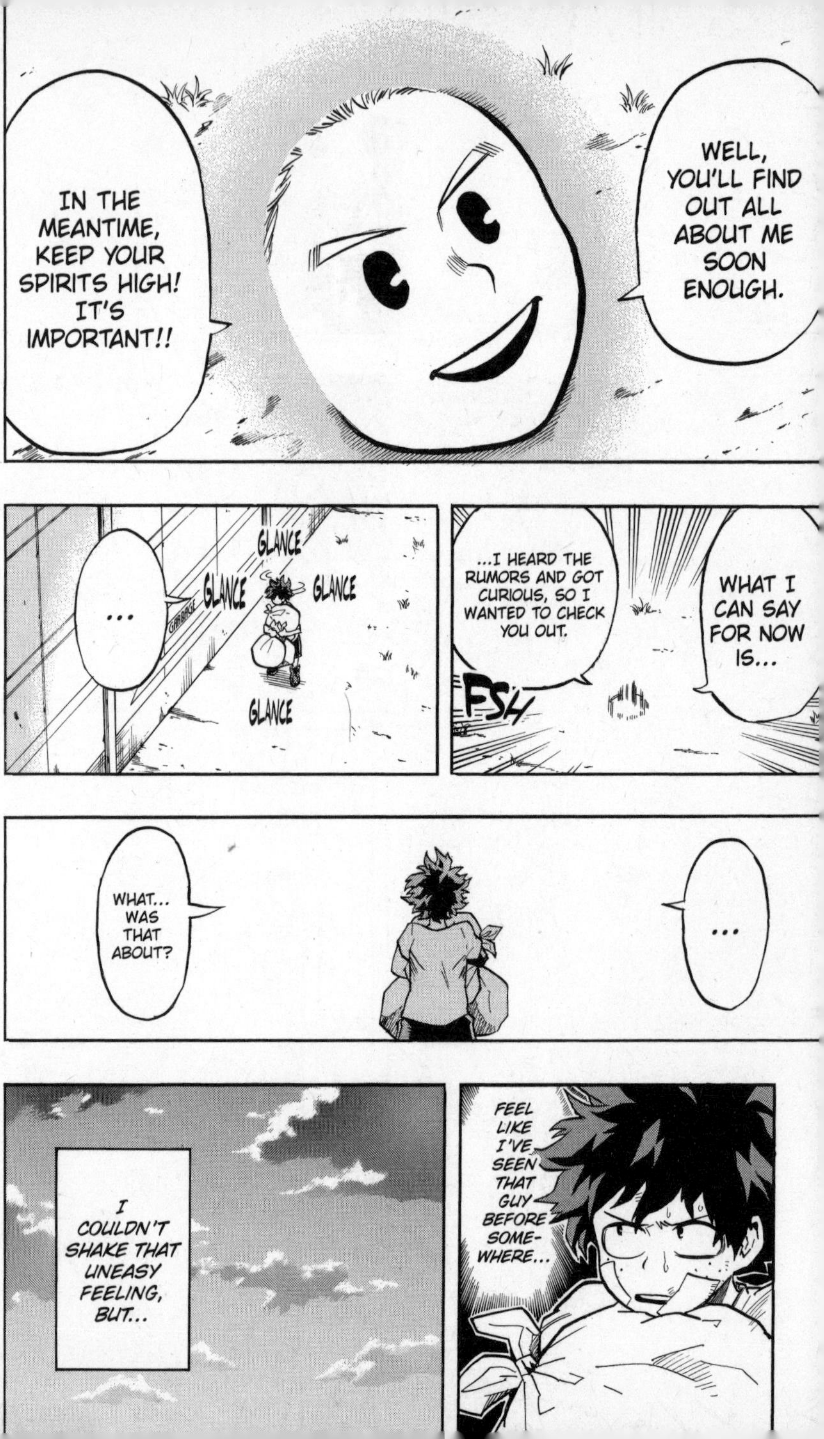
WELL, YOU'LL FIND OUT ALL ABOUT ME SOON ENOUGH.
IN THE MEANTIME, KEEP YOUR SPIRITS HIGH! IT'S IMPORTANT!!
WHAT I CAN SAY FOR NOW IS...
...I HEARD THE RUMORS AND GOT CURIOUS, SO I WANTED TO CHECK YOU OUT.
FSH
...
GLANCE
GLANCE
GLANCE
GARBAGE
GLANCE
...
WHAT... WAS THAT ABOUT?
FEEL LIKE I'VE SEEN THAT GUY BEFORE SOME-WHERE...
I COULDN'T SHAKE THAT UNEASY FEELING, BUT...

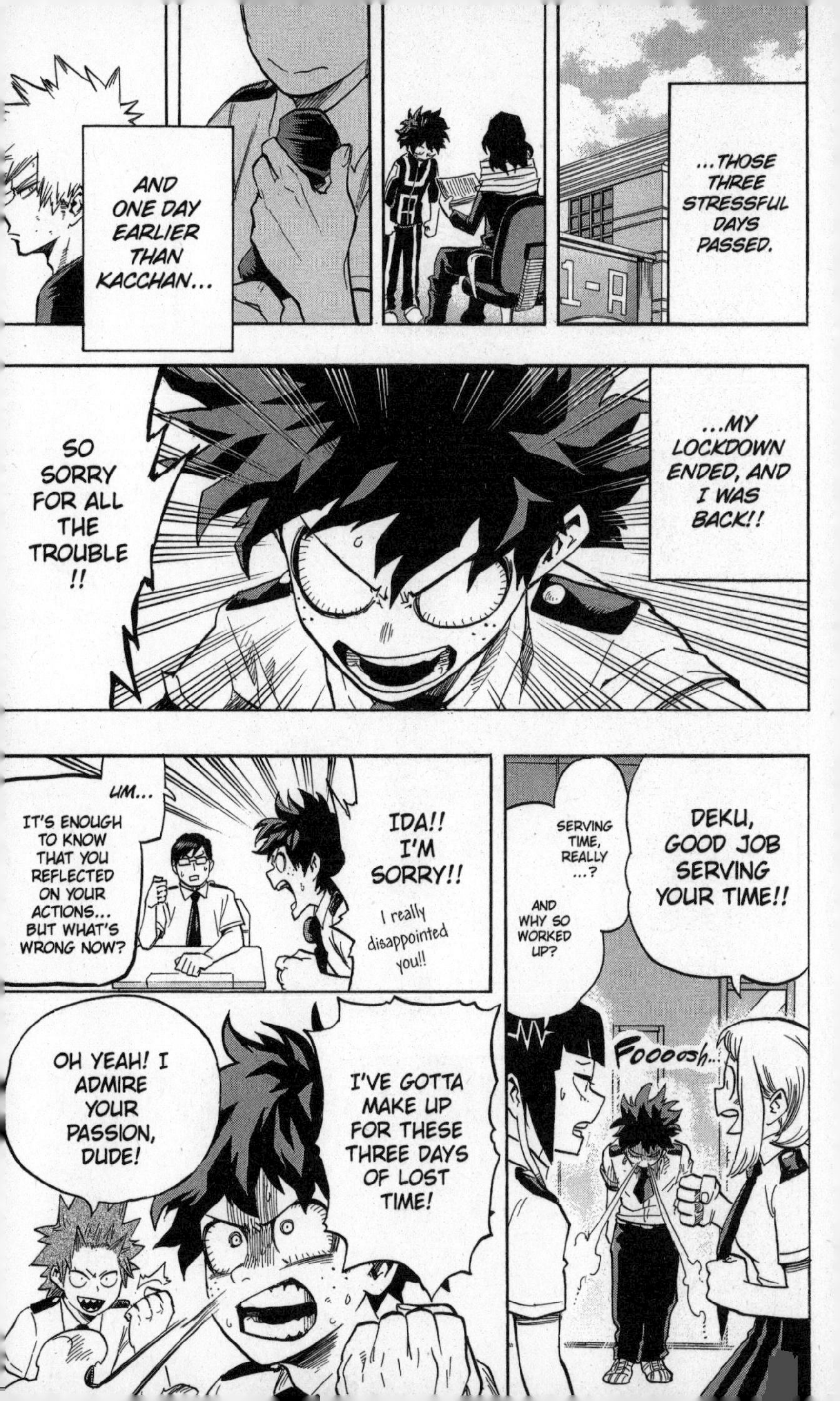
...THOSE THREE STRESSFUL DAYS PASSED.
AND ONE DAY EARLIER THAN KACCHAN...
...MY LOCKDOWN ENDED, AND I WAS BACK!!
SO SORRY FOR ALL THE TROUBLE!!
DEKU, GOOD JOB SERVING YOUR TIME!!
SERVING TIME, REALLY...?
AND WHY SO WORKED UP?
Foooosh...
IDA!! I'M SORRY!!
I really disappointed you!!
UM...
IT'S ENOUGH TO KNOW THAT YOU REFLECTED ON YOUR ACTIONS... BUT WHAT'S WRONG NOW?
I'VE GOTTA MAKE UP FOR THESE THREE DAYS OF LOST TIME!
OH YEAH! I ADMIRE YOUR PASSION, DUDE!

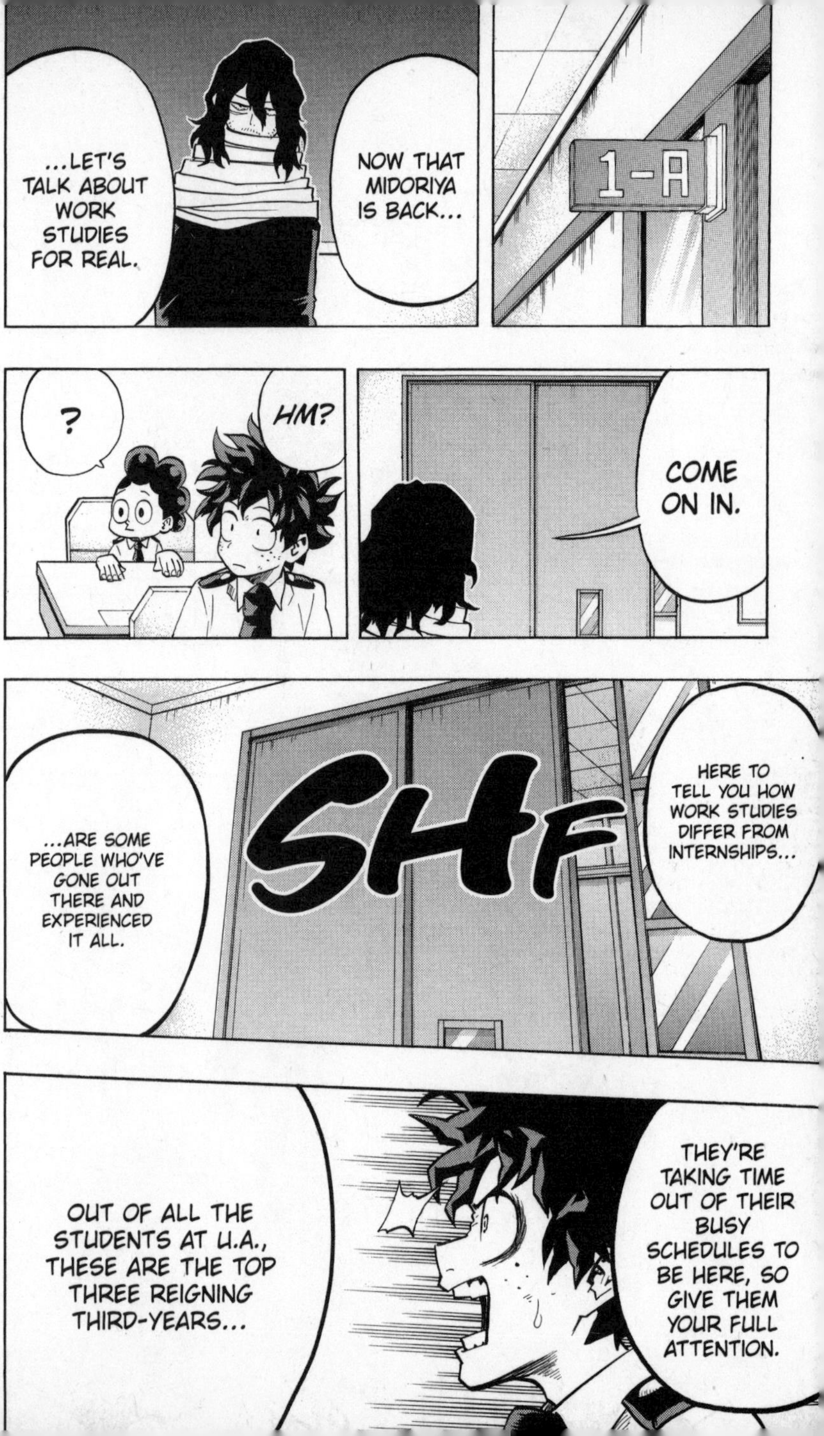
1-A
NOW THAT MIDORIYA IS BACK...
...LET'S TALK ABOUT WORK STUDIES FOR REAL.
COME ON IN.
HM?
?
HERE TO TELL YOU HOW WORK STUDIES DIFFER FROM INTERNSHIPS...
SHF
...ARE SOME PEOPLE WHO'VE GONE OUT THERE AND EXPERIENCED IT ALL.
THEY'RE TAKING TIME OUT OF THEIR BUSY SCHEDULES TO BE HERE, SO GIVE THEM YOUR FULL ATTENTION.
OUT OF ALL THE STUDENTS AT U.A., THESE ARE THE TOP THREE REIGNING THIRD-YEARS...

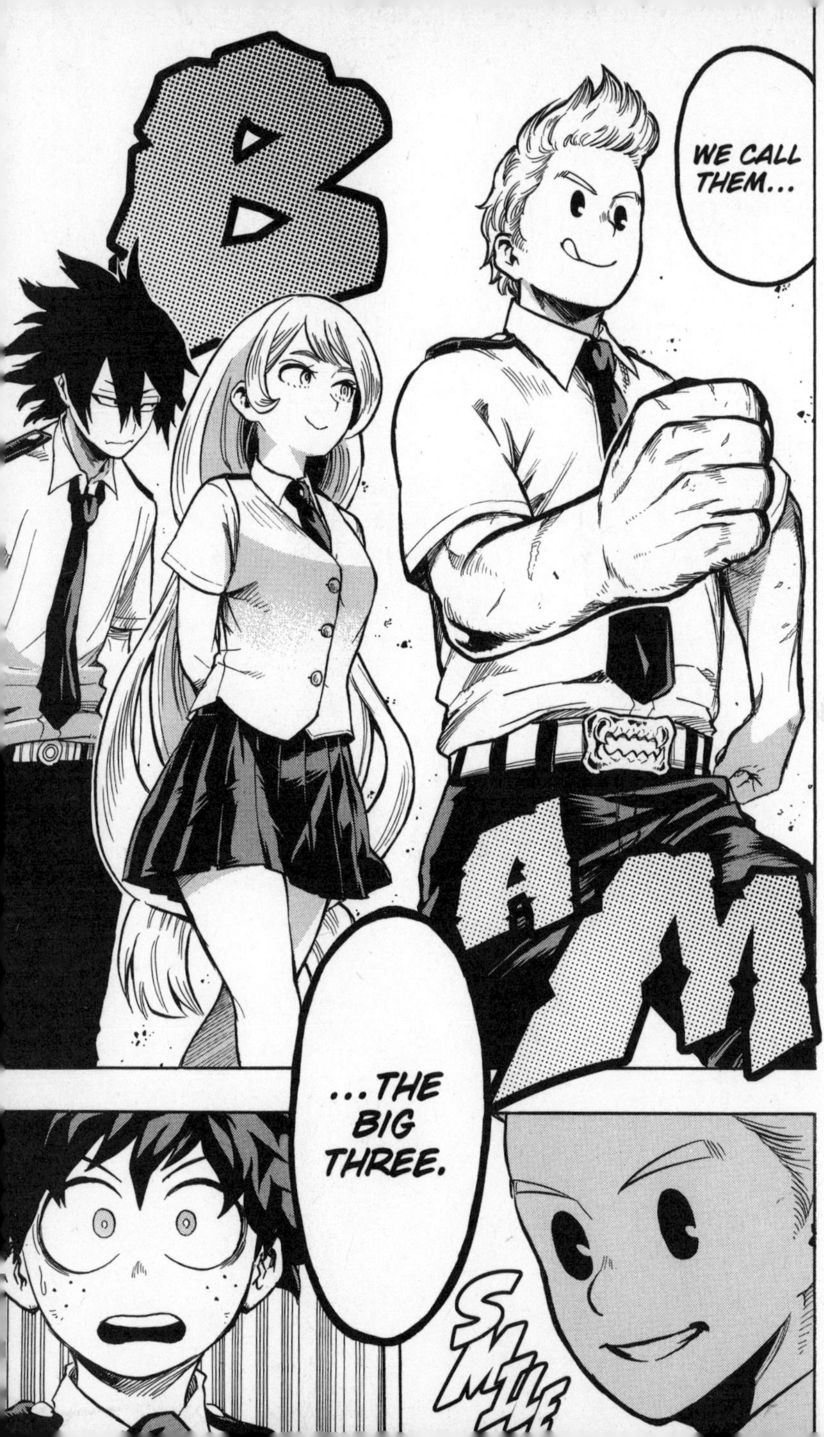
WE CALL THEM...
BAM
...THE BIG THREE.
SMILE

STREET CLOTHES

Birthday: 11/15
Height: 196 cm
Favorite Things: Drinks with dinner, soccer

THE SENSEI
U.A. students are generally terrified of him. He embraces that role. Smart guy. Gets along with Vlad King.

His Quirk is just "Dog." No relation to Chief Tsuragamae, though.

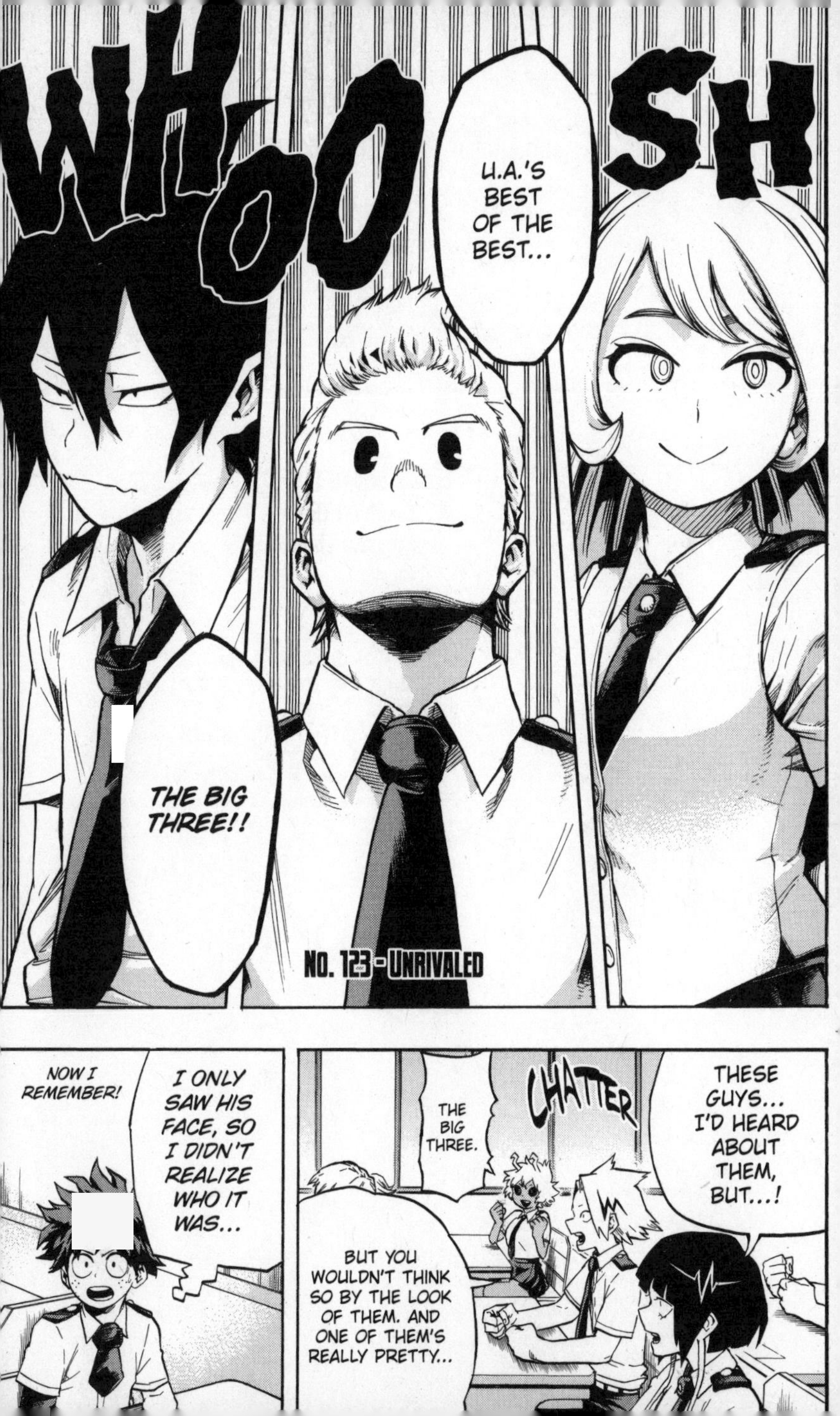
WHOOOSH
U.A.'S BEST OF THE BEST...
THE BIG THREE!!
NO. 123 - UNRIVALED
THESE GUYS... I'D HEARD ABOUT THEM, BUT...!
CHATTER
THE BIG THREE.
BUT YOU WOULDN'T THINK SO BY THE LOOK OF THEM. AND ONE OF THEM'S REALLY PRETTY...
I ONLY SAW HIS FACE, SO I DIDN'T REALIZE WHO IT WAS...
NOW I REMEMBER!

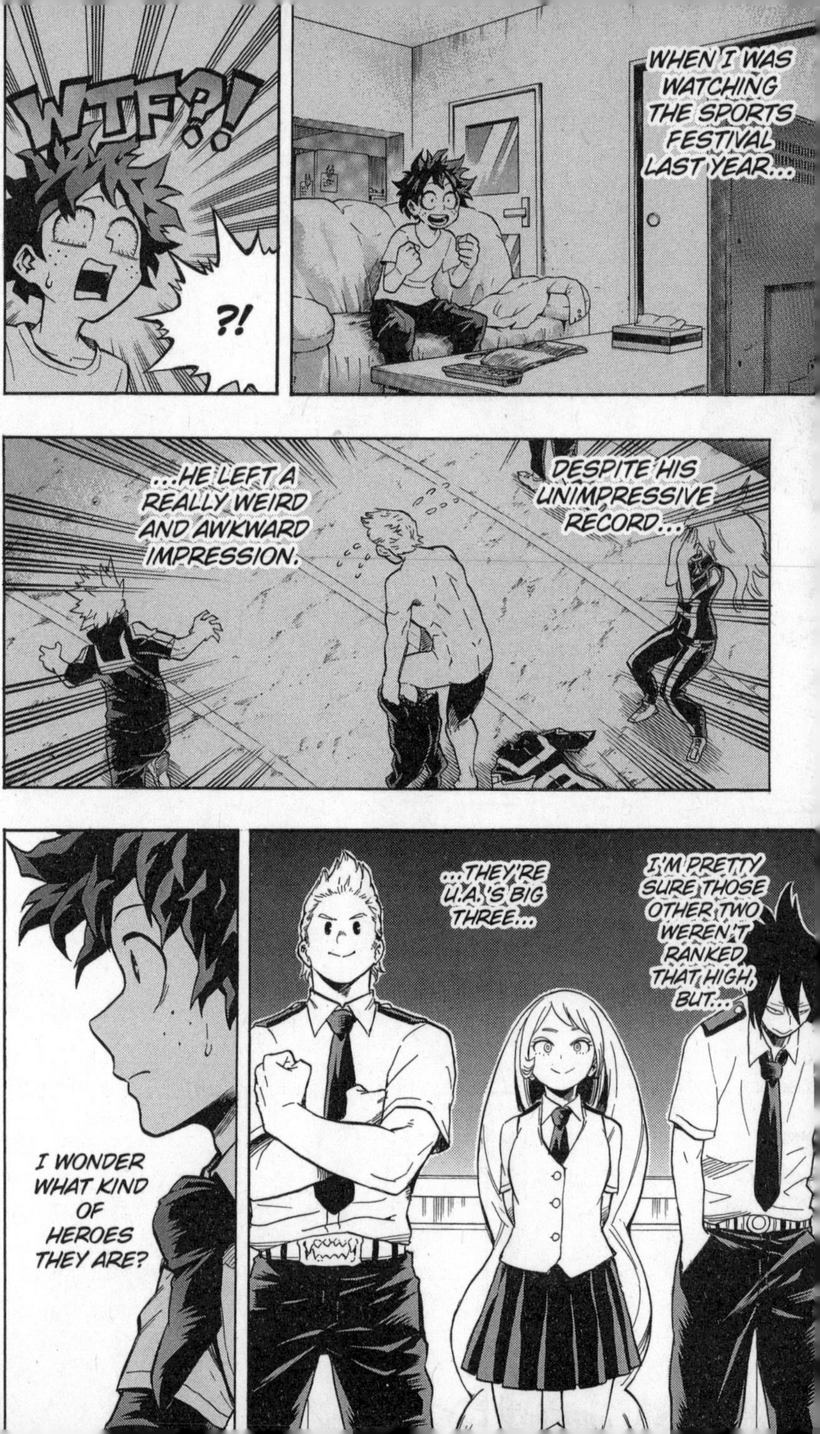
WHEN I WAS WATCHING THE SPORTS FESTIVAL LAST YEAR...
WTF?!
?!
DESPITE HIS UNIMPRESSIVE RECORD...
...HE LEFT A REALLY WEIRD AND AWKWARD IMPRESSION.
I'M PRETTY SURE THOSE OTHER TWO WEREN'T RANKED THAT HIGH, BUT...
...THEY'RE U.A.'S BIG THREE...
I WONDER WHAT KIND OF HEROES THEY ARE?

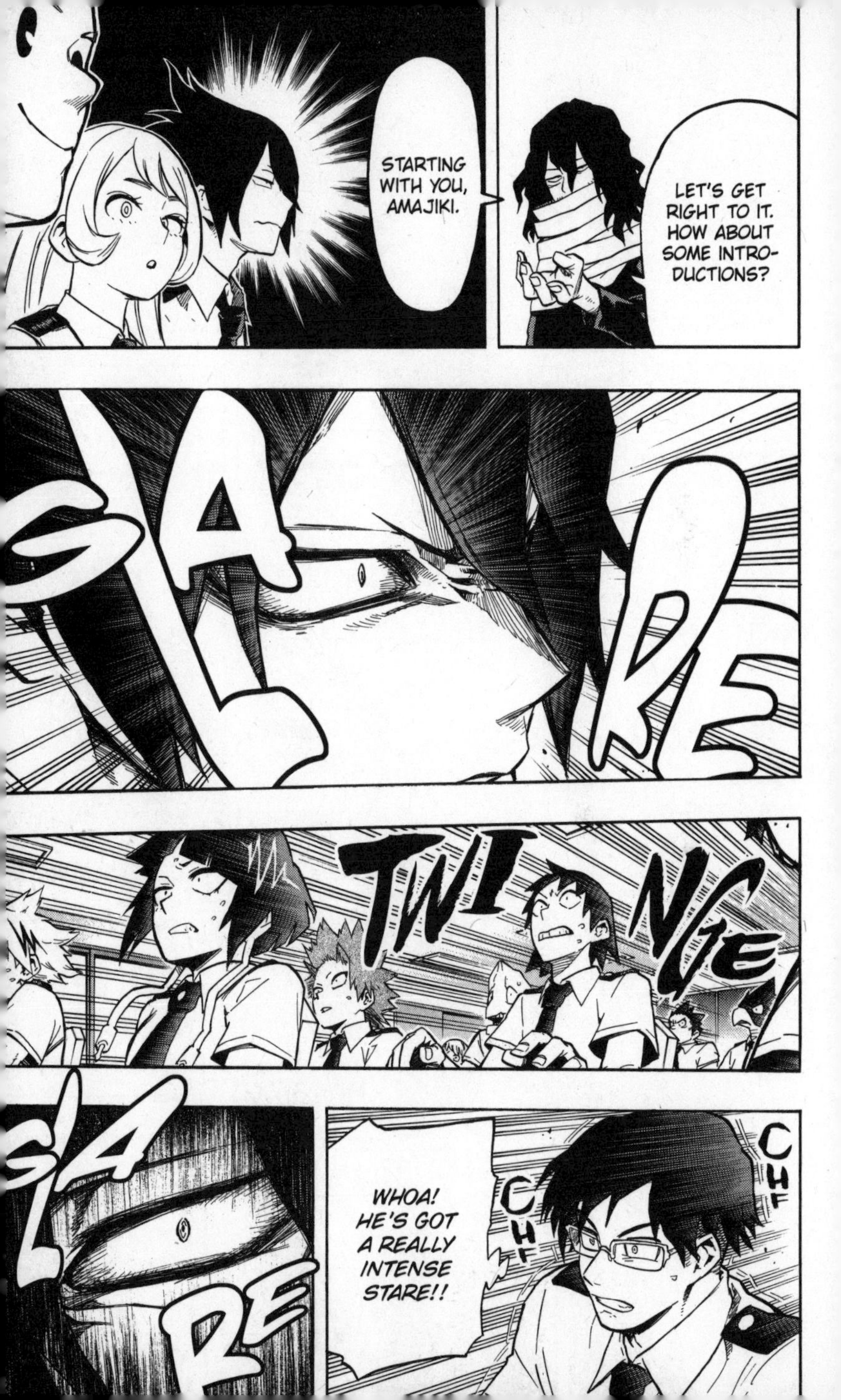
LET'S GET RIGHT TO IT. HOW ABOUT SOME INTRODUCTIONS?
STARTING WITH YOU, AMAJIKI.
GLARE
TWINGE
CHF CHF
WHOA! HE'S GOT A REALLY INTENSE STARE!!
GLARE

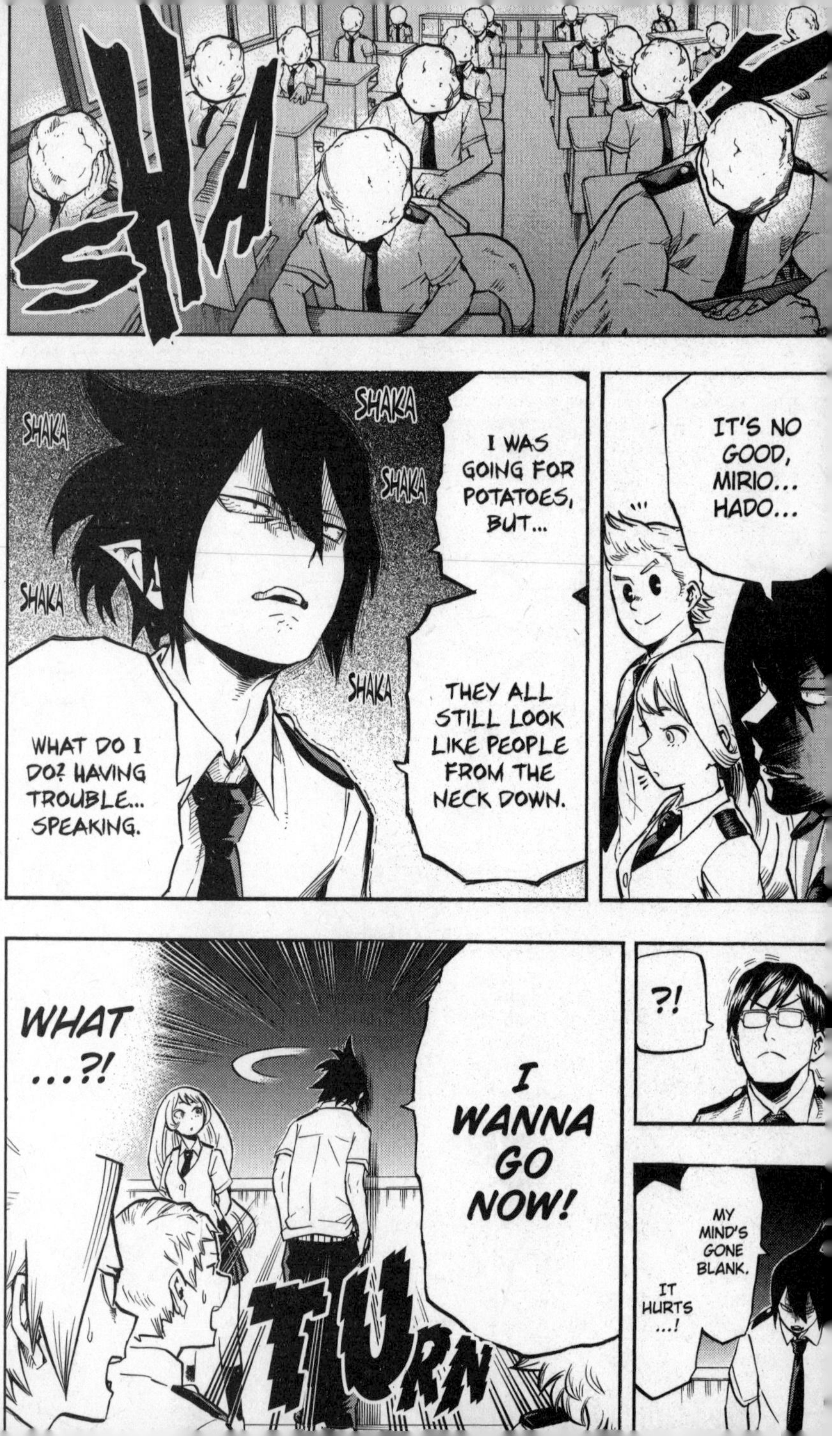
SHA
KA
IT'S NO GOOD, MIRIO... HADO...
...
I WAS GOING FOR POTATOES, BUT...
THEY ALL STILL LOOK LIKE PEOPLE FROM THE NECK DOWN.
SHAKA
SHAKA
SHAKA
SHAKA
SHAKA
WHAT DO I DO? HAVING TROUBLE... SPEAKING.
?!
MY MIND'S GONE BLANK.
IT HURTS ...!
I WANNA GO NOW!
WHAT ...?!
TURN

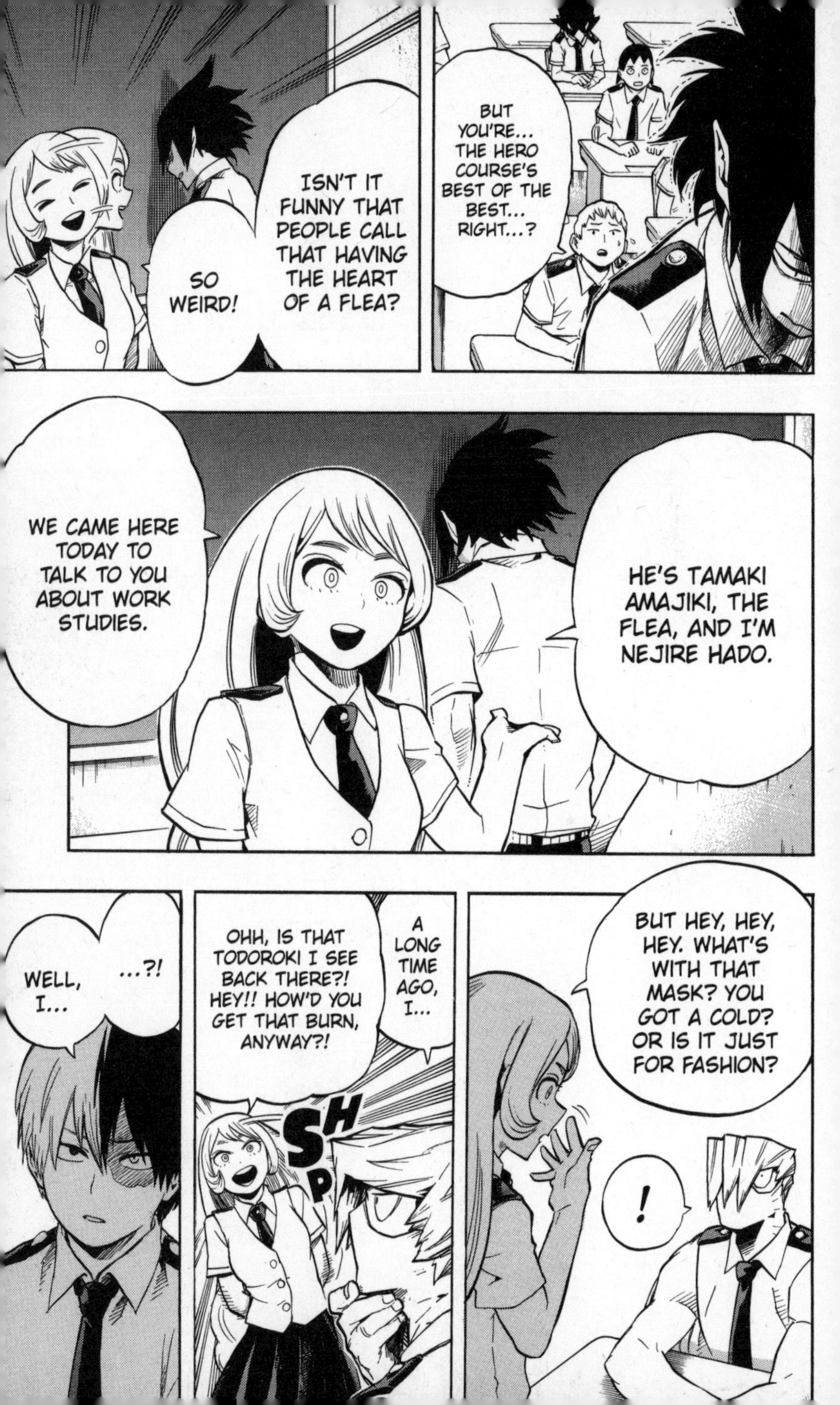

BUT YOU'RE... THE HERO COURSE'S BEST OF THE BEST... RIGHT...?
ISN'T IT FUNNY THAT PEOPLE CALL THAT HAVING THE HEART OF A FLEA?
SO WEIRD!
HE'S TAMAKI AMAJIKI, THE FLEA, AND I'M NEJIRE HADO.
WE CAME HERE TODAY TO TALK TO YOU ABOUT WORK STUDIES.
BUT HEY, HEY, HEY. WHAT'S WITH THAT MASK? YOU GOT A COLD? OR IS IT JUST FOR FASHION?
!
A LONG TIME AGO, I...
OHH, IS THAT TODOROKI I SEE BACK THERE?! HEY!! HOW'D YOU GET THAT BURN, ANYWAY?!
SHP
...?!
WELL, I...

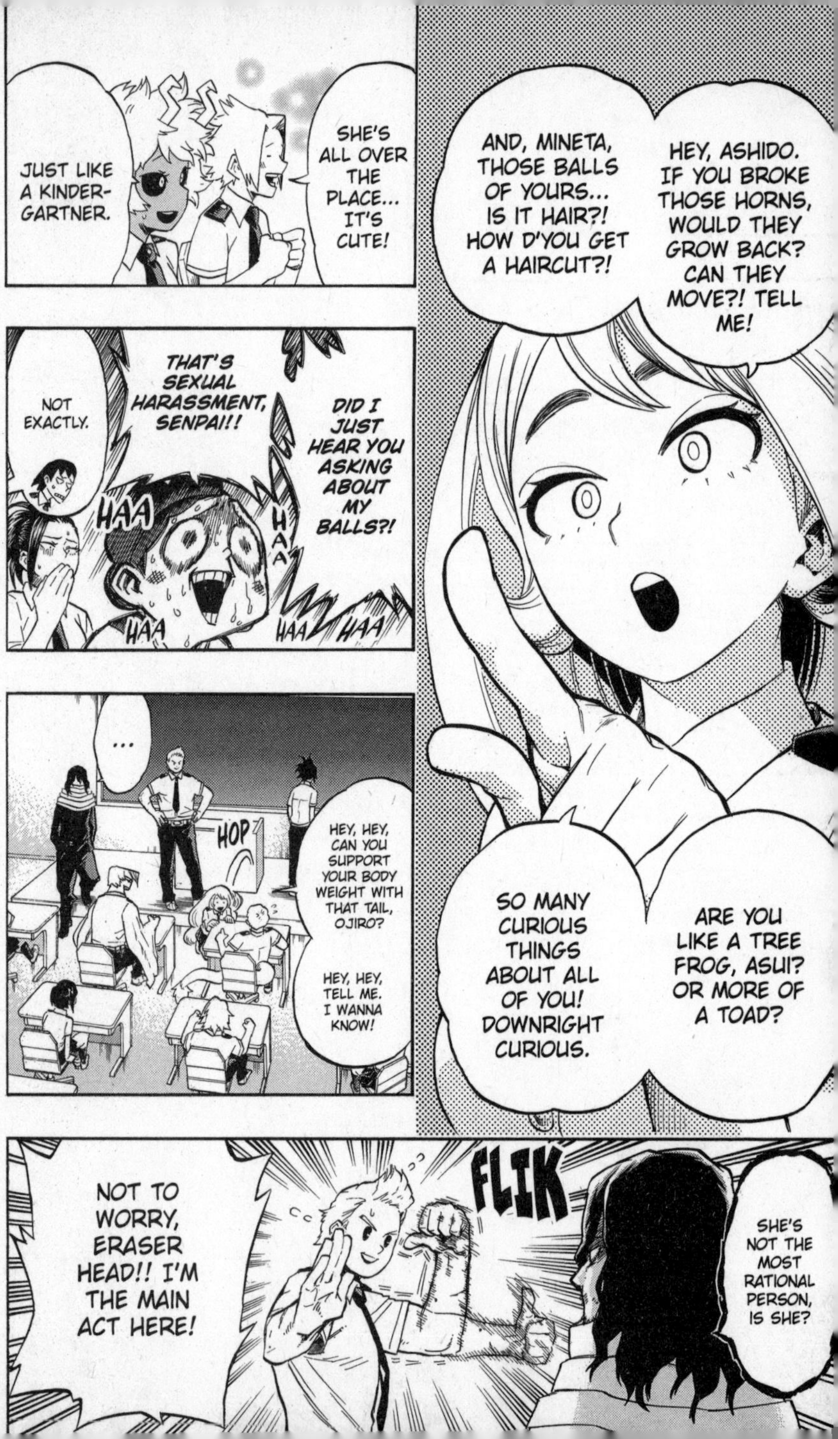
HEY, ASHIDO. IF YOU BROKE THOSE HORNS, WOULD THEY GROW BACK? CAN THEY MOVE?! TELL ME!
AND, MINETA, THOSE BALLS OF YOURS... IS IT HAIR?! HOW D'YOU GET A HAIRCUT?!
ARE YOU LIKE A TREE FROG, ASUI? OR MORE OF A TOAD?
SO MANY CURIOUS THINGS ABOUT ALL OF YOU! DOWNRIGHT CURIOUS.
SHE'S ALL OVER THE PLACE... IT'S CUTE!
JUST LIKE A KINDER-GARTNER.
DID I JUST HEAR YOU ASKING ABOUT MY BALLS?!
HAA
THAT'S SEXUAL HARASSMENT, SENPAI!!
NOT EXACTLY.
HAA
HAA
HAA HAA
HEY, HEY, CAN YOU SUPPORT YOUR BODY WEIGHT WITH THAT TAIL, OJIRO?
HEY, HEY, TELL ME. I WANNA KNOW!
HOP
...
SHE'S NOT THE MOST RATIONAL PERSON, IS SHE?
FLIK
NOT TO WORRY, ERASER HEAD!! I'M THE MAIN ACT HERE!

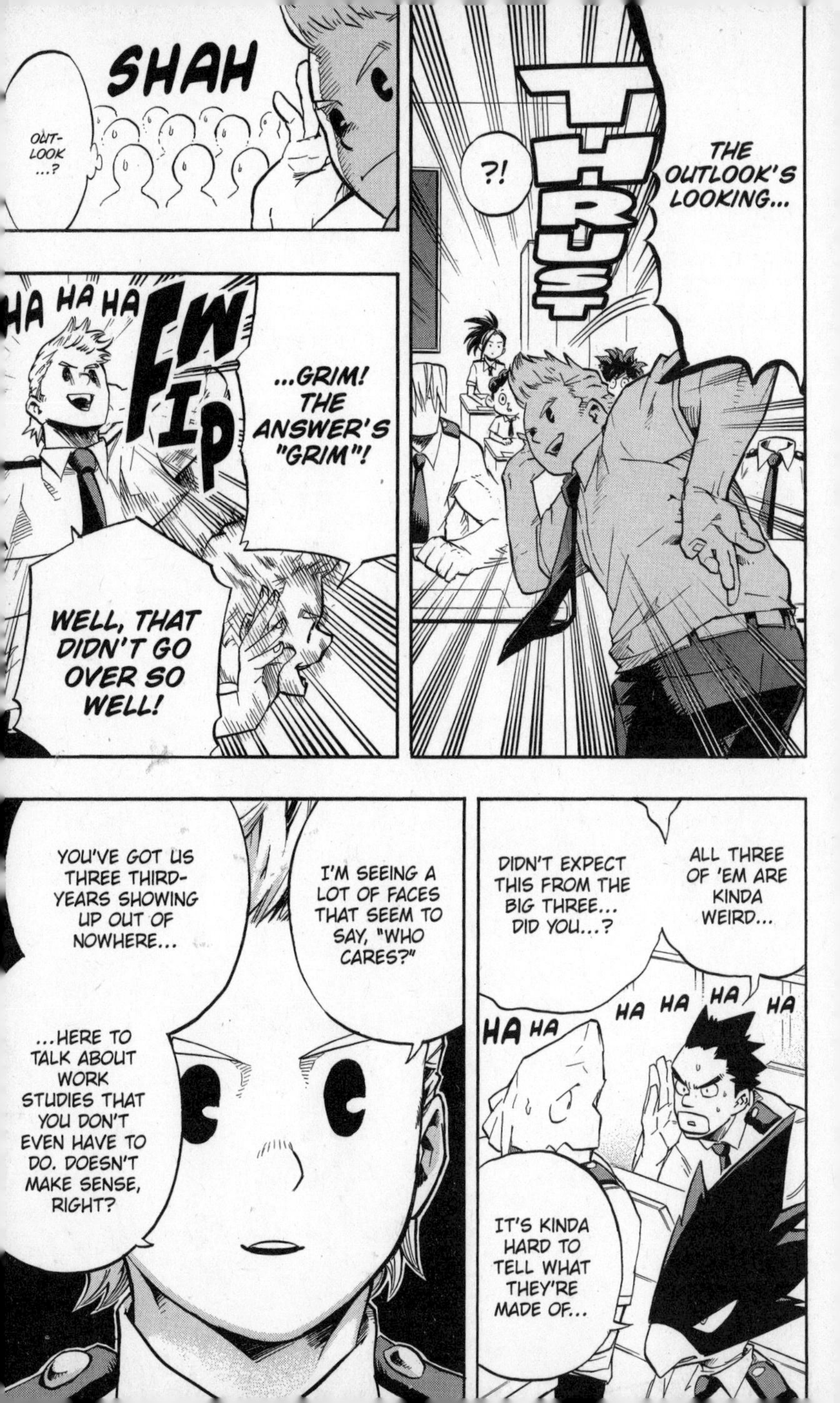
THE OUTLOOK'S LOOKING...
THRUST
?!
SHAH
OUT-LOOK ...?
HA HA HA
FWIP
...GRIM! THE ANSWER'S "GRIM"!
WELL, THAT DIDN'T GO OVER SO WELL!
ALL THREE OF 'EM ARE KINDA WEIRD...
DIDN'T EXPECT THIS FROM THE BIG THREE... DID YOU...?
HA HA HA HA HA HA
IT'S KINDA HARD TO TELL WHAT THEY'RE MADE OF...
I'M SEEING A LOT OF FACES THAT SEEM TO SAY, "WHO CARES?"
YOU'VE GOT US THREE THIRD-YEARS SHOWING UP OUT OF NOWHERE...
...HERE TO TALK ABOUT WORK STUDIES THAT YOU DON'T EVEN HAVE TO DO. DOESN'T MAKE SENSE, RIGHT?

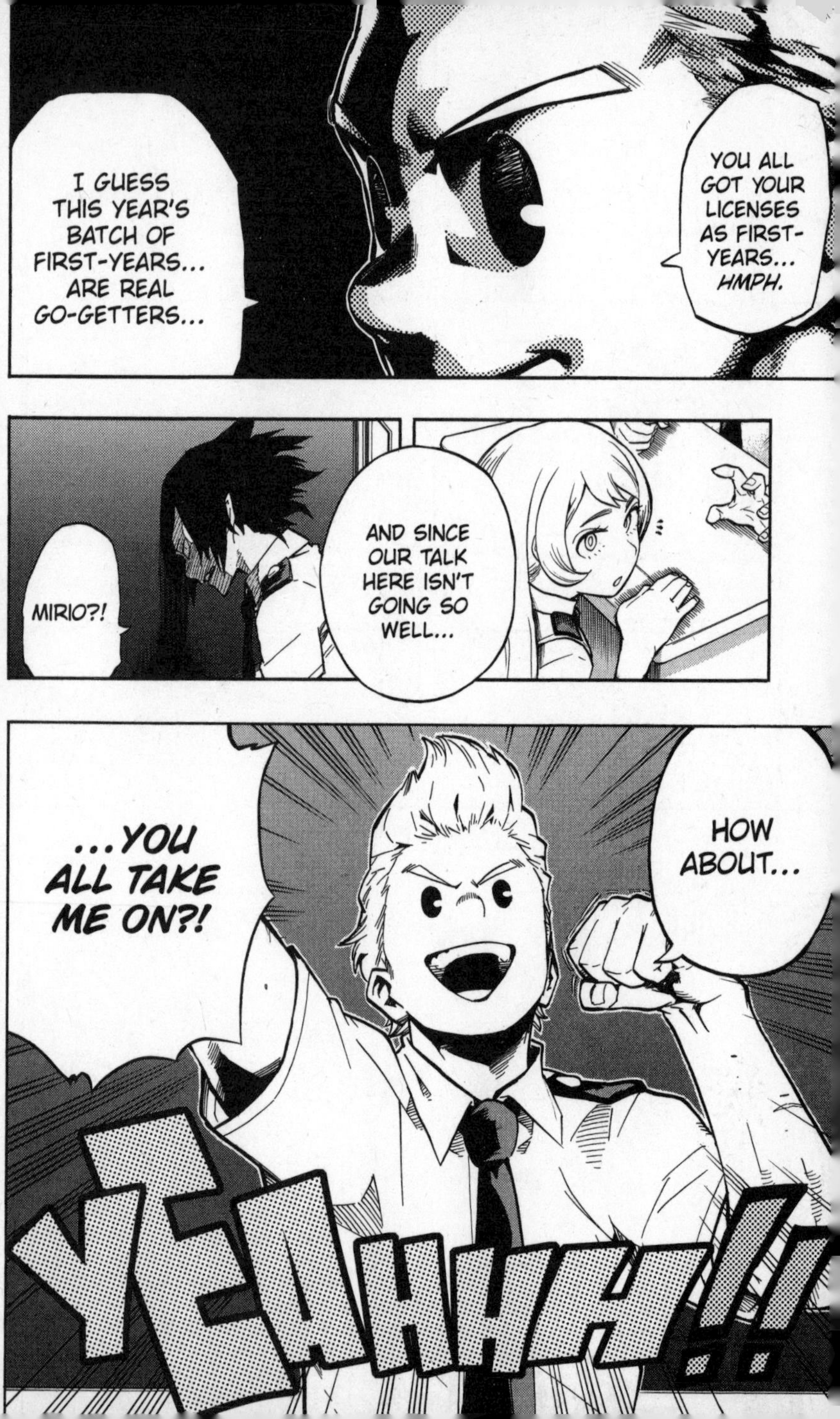
YOU ALL GOT YOUR LICENSES AS FIRST-YEARS... HMPH.
I GUESS THIS YEAR'S BATCH OF FIRST-YEARS... ARE REAL GO-GETTERS...
AND SINCE OUR TALK HERE ISN'T GOING SO WELL...
MIRIO?!
HOW ABOUT...
...YOU ALL TAKE ME ON?!
YEAHHH!!

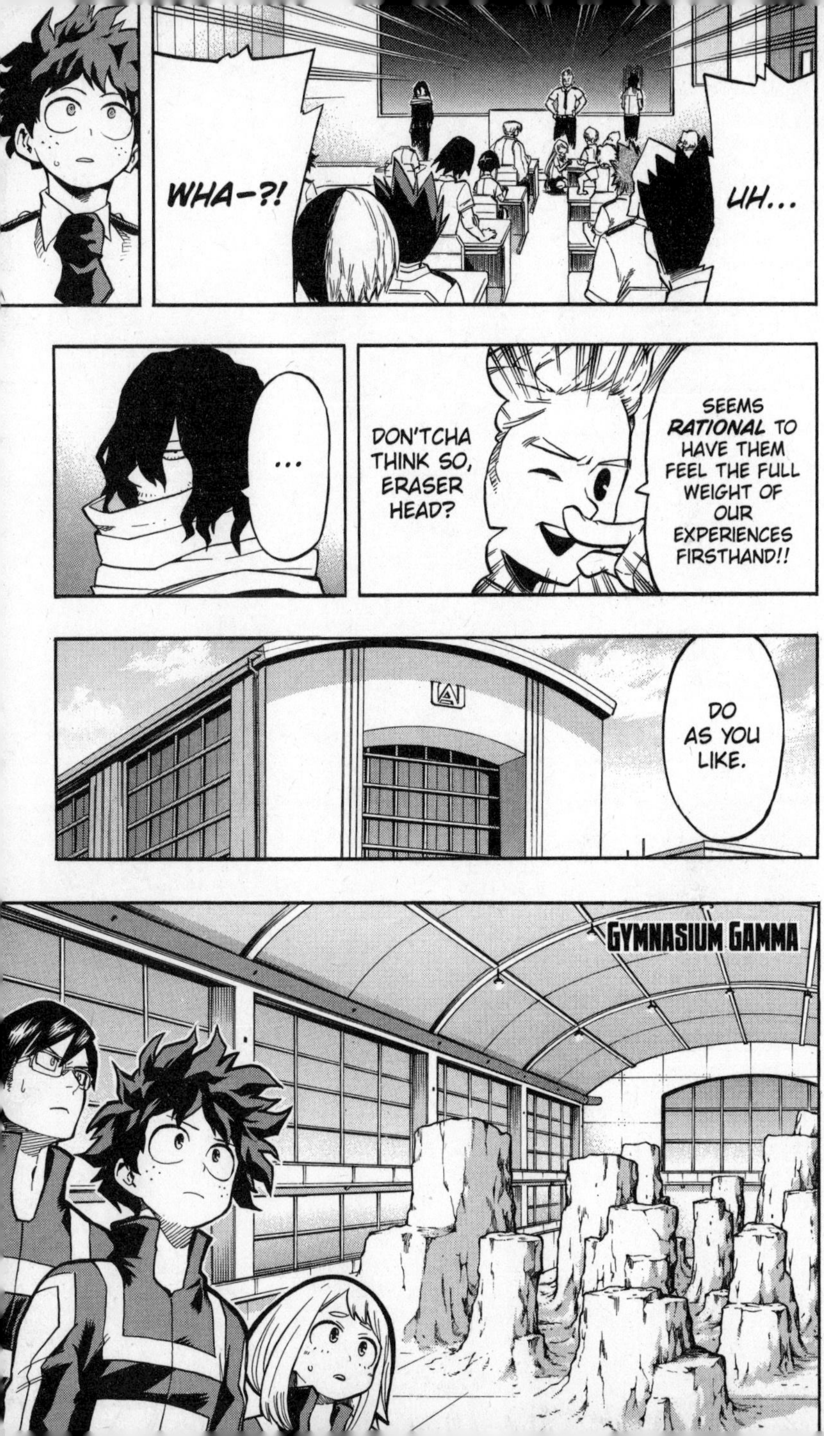
UH...
WHA-?!
SEEMS RATIONAL TO HAVE THEM FEEL THE FULL WEIGHT OF OUR EXPERIENCES FIRSTHAND!!
DON'TCHA THINK SO, ERASER HEAD?
...
DO AS YOU LIKE.
GYMNASIUM GAMMA

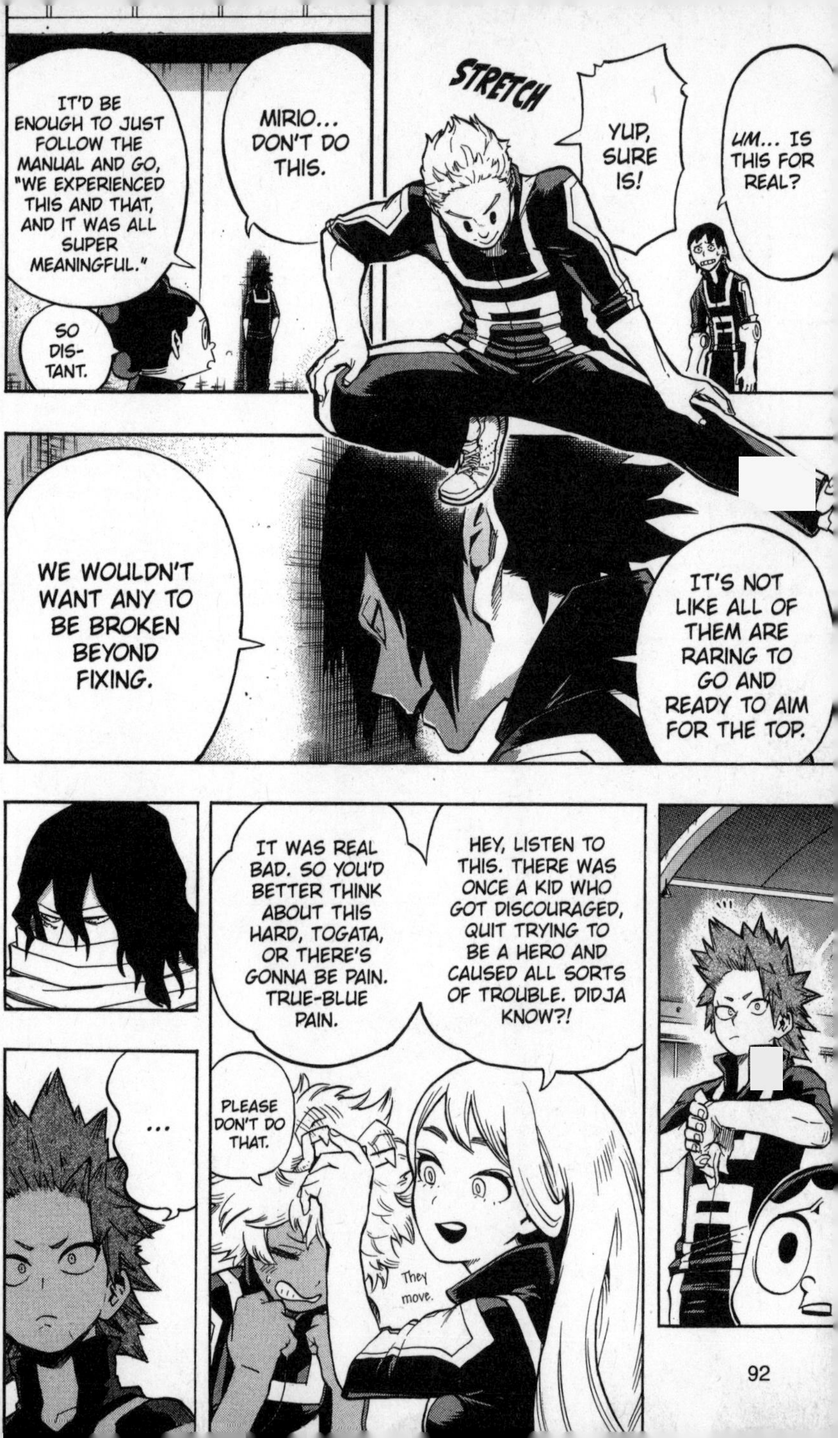
UM... IS THIS FOR REAL?
YUP, SURE IS!
STRETCH
MIRIO... DON'T DO THIS.
IT'D BE ENOUGH TO JUST FOLLOW THE MANUAL AND GO, "WE EXPERIENCED THIS AND THAT, AND IT WAS ALL SUPER MEANINGFUL."
SO DIS-TANT.
IT'S NOT LIKE ALL OF THEM ARE RARING TO GO AND READY TO AIM FOR THE TOP.
WE WOULDN'T WANT ANY TO BE BROKEN BEYOND FIXING.
HEY, LISTEN TO THIS. THERE WAS ONCE A KID WHO GOT DISCOURAGED, QUIT TRYING TO BE A HERO AND CAUSED ALL SORTS OF TROUBLE. DIDJA KNOW?!
IT WAS REAL BAD. SO YOU'D BETTER THINK ABOUT THIS HARD, TOGATA, OR THERE'S GONNA BE PAIN. TRUE-BLUE PAIN.
PLEASE DON'T DO THAT.
They move.
...

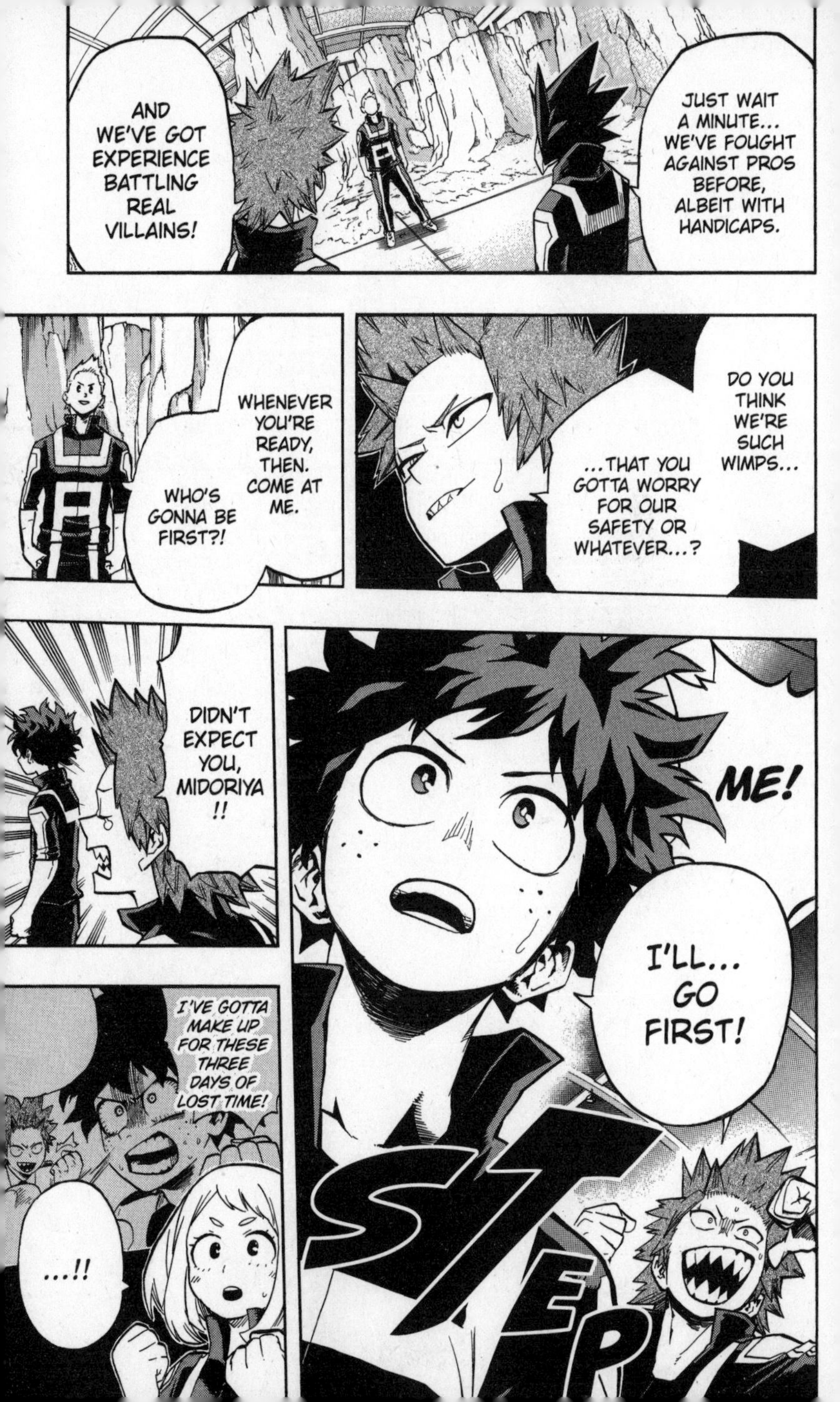

JUST WAIT A MINUTE... WE'VE FOUGHT AGAINST PROS BEFORE, ALBEIT WITH HANDICAPS.
AND WE'VE GOT EXPERIENCE BATTLING REAL VILLAINS!
DO YOU THINK WE'RE SUCH WIMPS...
...THAT YOU GOTTA WORRY FOR OUR SAFETY OR WHATEVER...?
WHENEVER YOU'RE READY, THEN. COME AT ME.
WHO'S GONNA BE FIRST?!
ME!
I'LL... GO FIRST!
STEP
DIDN'T EXPECT YOU, MIDORIYA!!
I'VE GOTTA MAKE UP FOR THESE THREE DAYS OF LOST TIME!
...!!

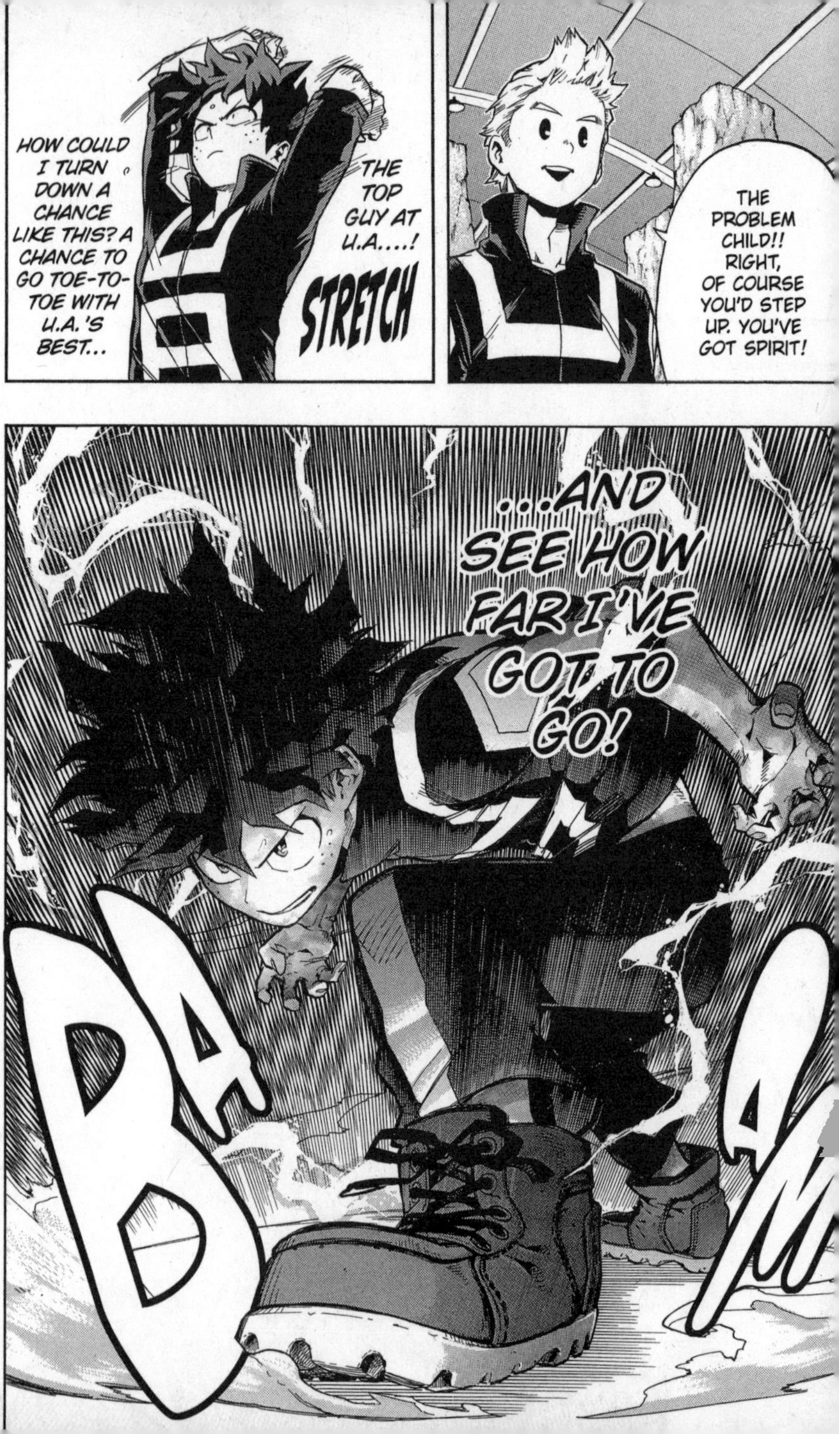
THE PROBLEM CHILD!! RIGHT, OF COURSE YOU'D STEP UP. YOU'VE GOT SPIRIT!
HOW COULD I TURN DOWN A CHANCE LIKE THIS? A CHANCE TO GO TOE-TO-TOE WITH U.A.'S BEST...
THE TOP GUY AT U.A....!
STRETCH
...AND SEE HOW FAR I'VE GOT TO GO!
BA
AM

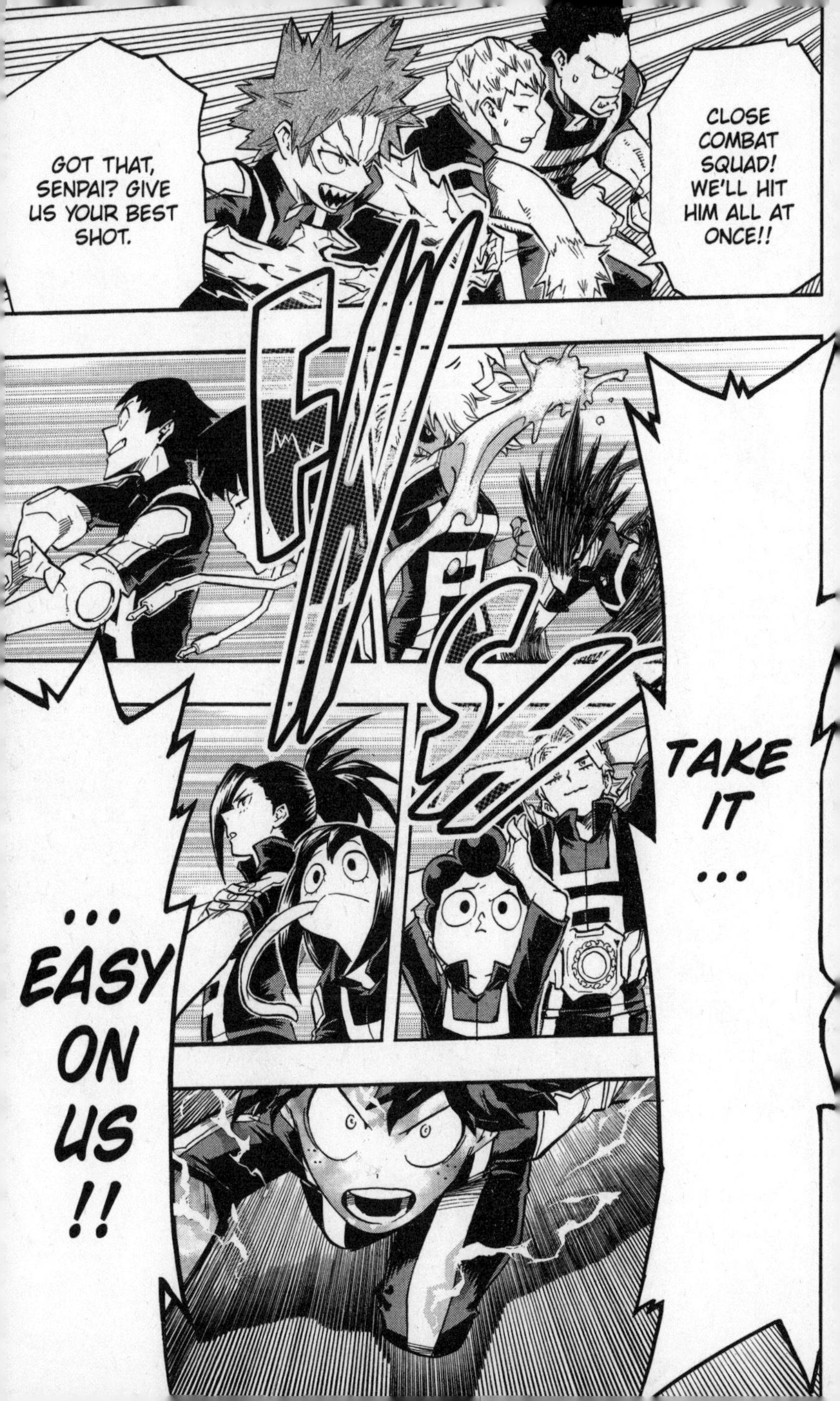
CLOSE COMBAT SQUAD! WE'LL HIT HIM ALL AT ONCE!!
GOT THAT, SENPAI? GIVE US YOUR BEST SHOT.
TAKE IT...
...EASY ON US!!

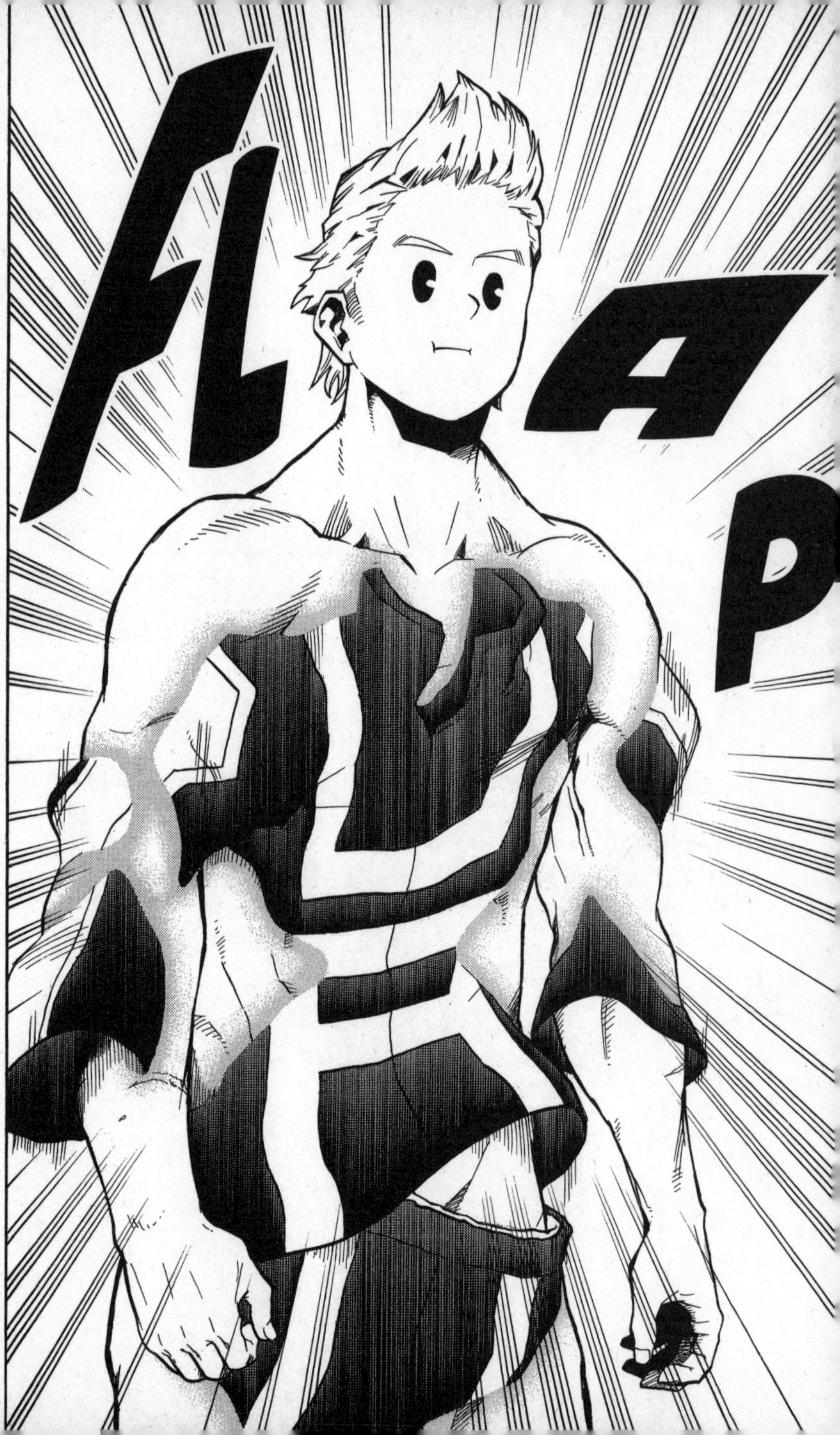
FLAP

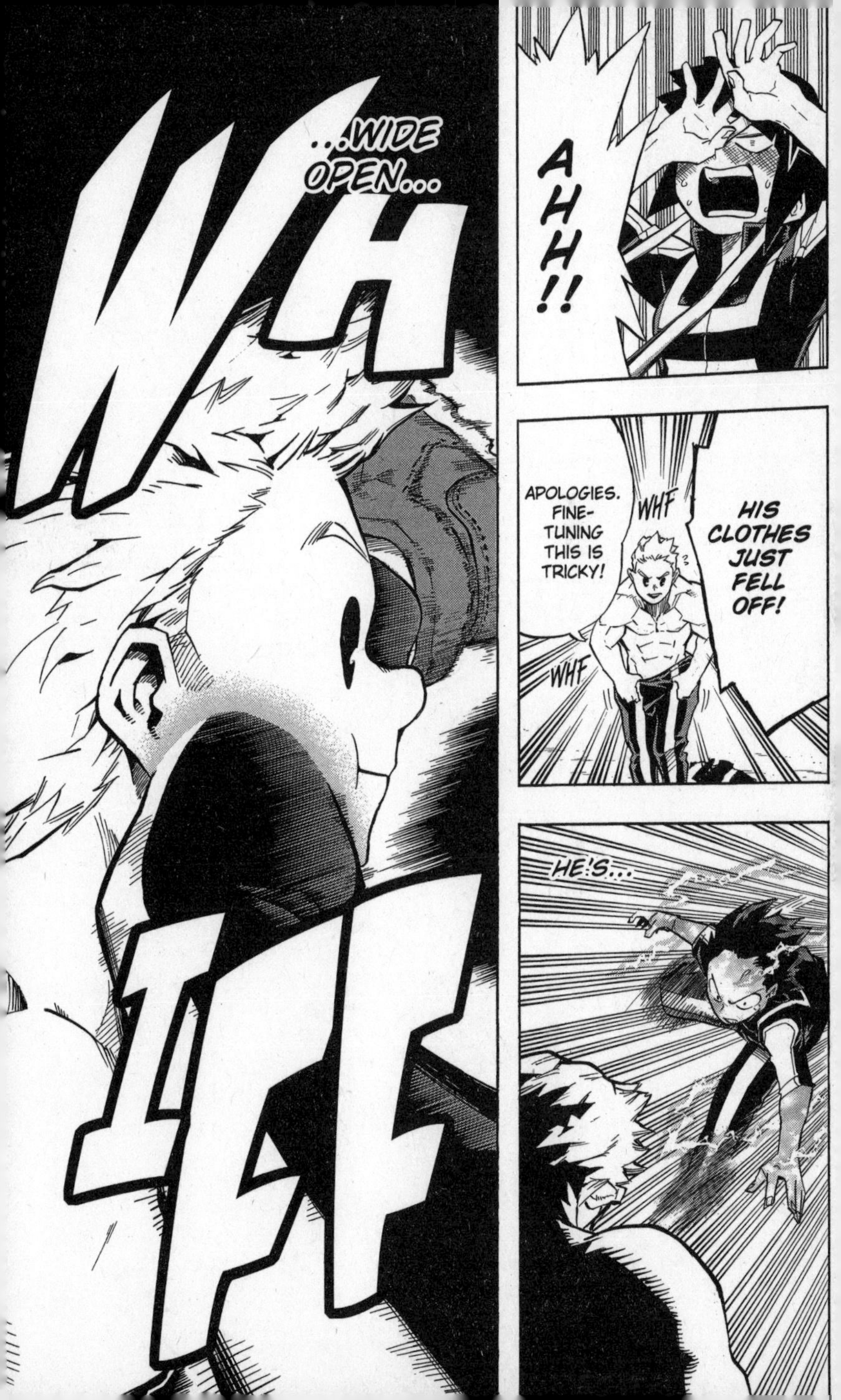
AHH!!
HIS CLOTHES JUST FELL OFF!
APOLOGIES. FINE-TUNING THIS IS TRICKY!
WHF
WHF
HE'S...
...WIDE OPEN...

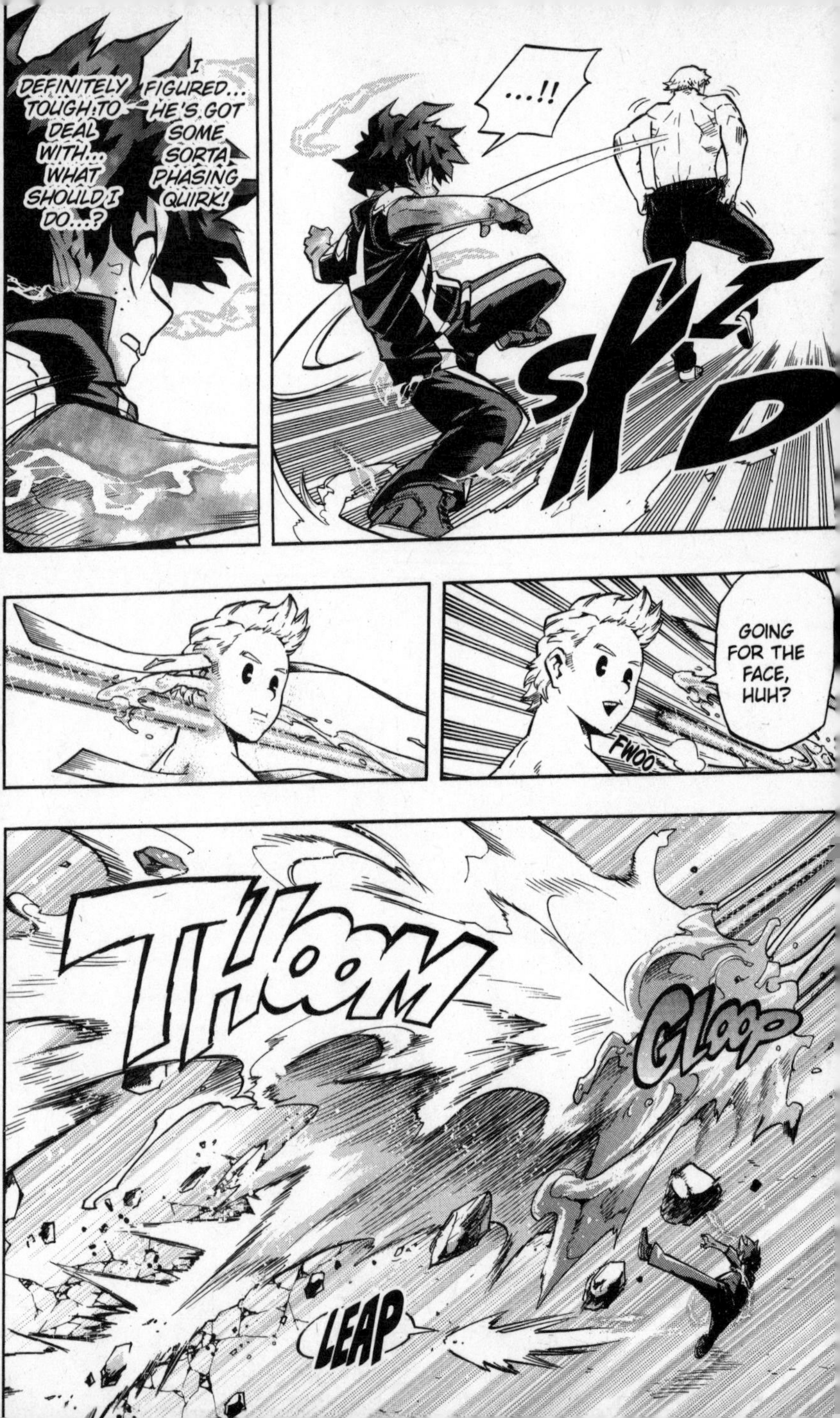

...!!
SKID
I FIGURED... HE'S GOT SOME SORTA PHASING QUIRK!
DEFINITELY TOUGH TO DEAL WITH... WHAT SHOULD I DO...?
GOING FOR THE FACE, HUH?
FWOO
THOOM
GLOOP
LEAP

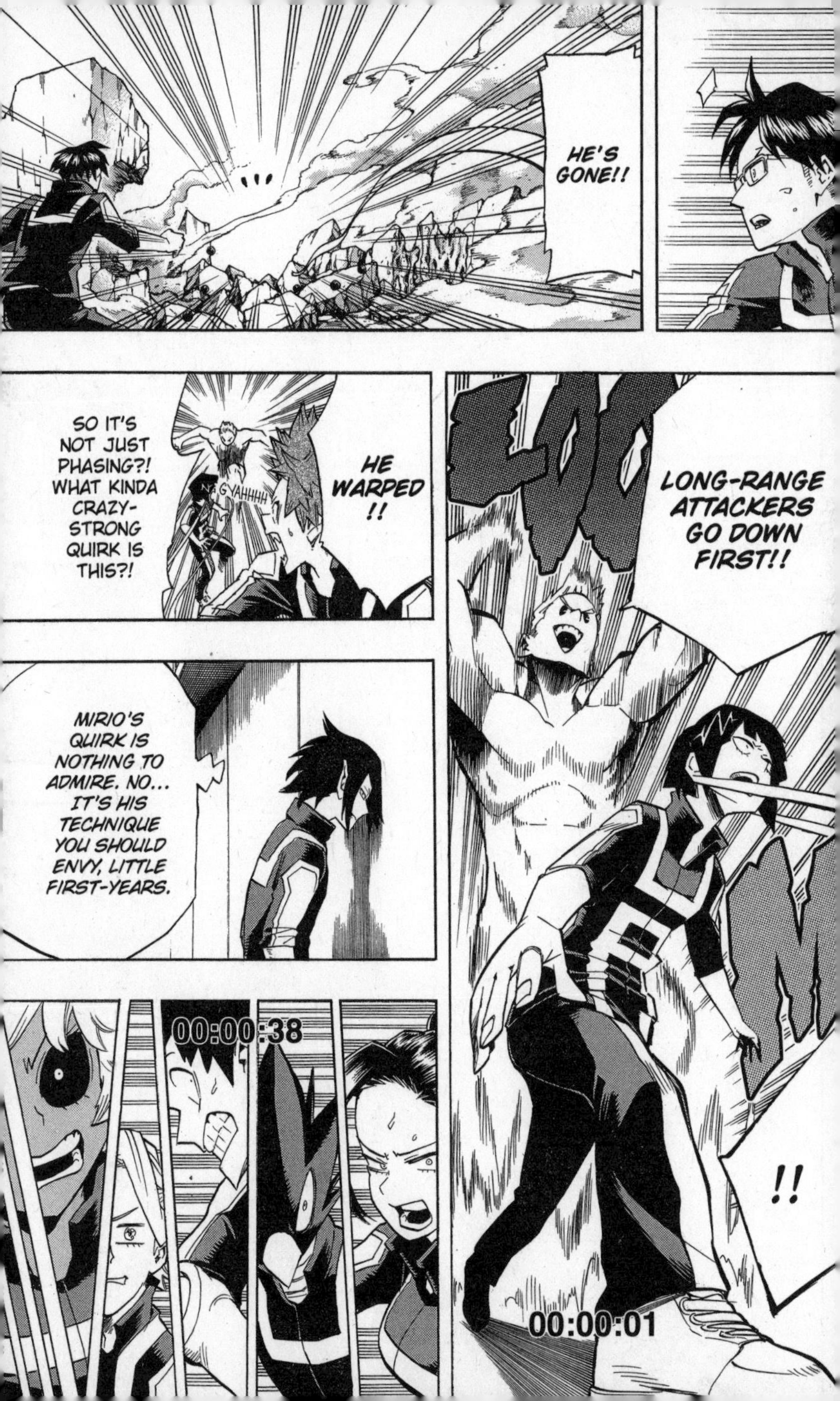
HE'S GONE!!
LONG-RANGE ATTACKERS GO DOWN FIRST!!
!!
00:00:01
HE WARPED!!
SO IT'S NOT JUST PHASING?! WHAT KINDA CRAZY-STRONG QUIRK IS THIS?!
GYAHHHH
MIRIO'S QUIRK IS NOTHING TO ADMIRE. NO... IT'S HIS TECHNIQUE YOU SHOULD ENVY, LITTLE FIRST-YEARS.
00:00:38

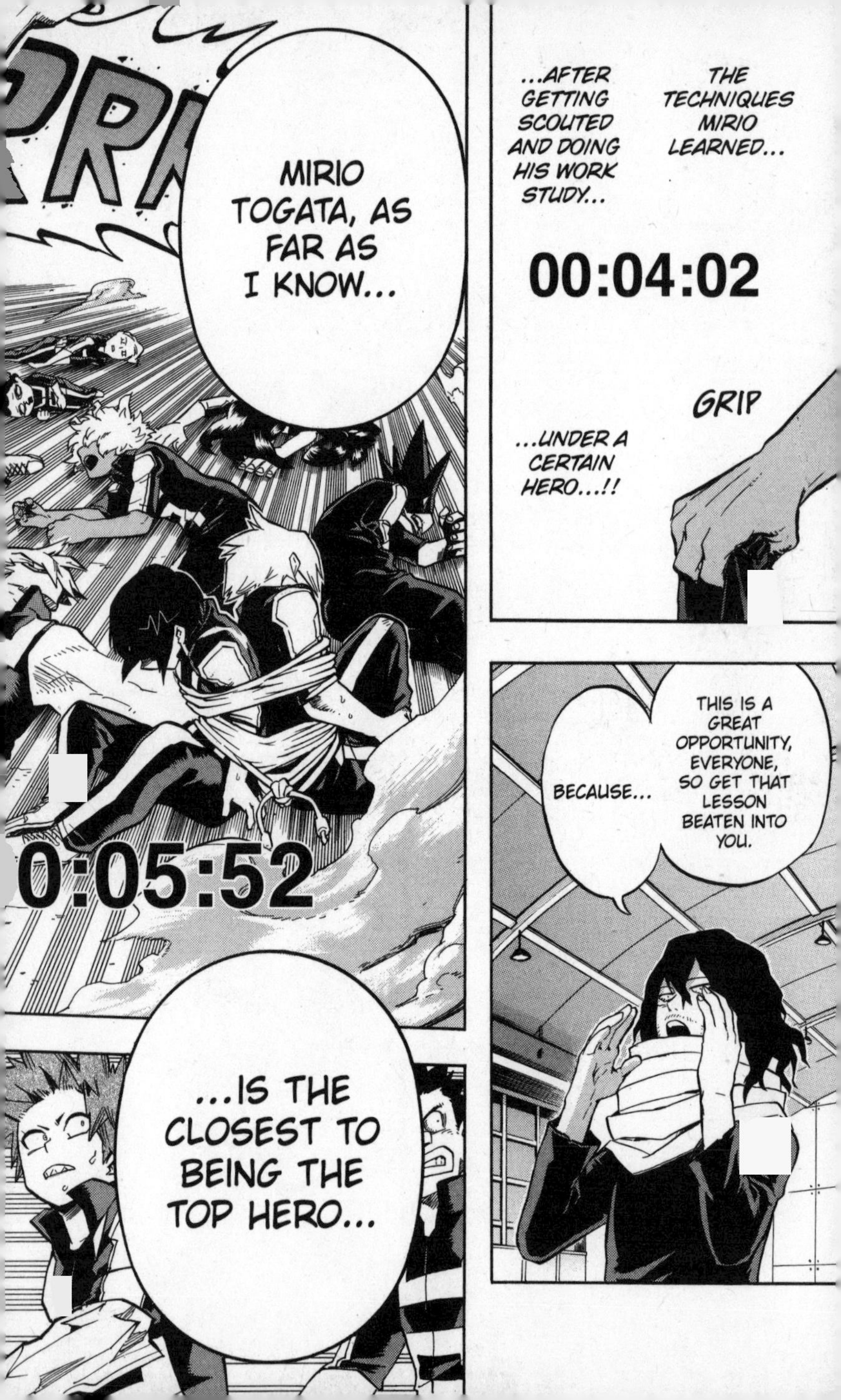
THE TECHNIQUES MIRIO LEARNED...
...AFTER GETTING SCOUTED AND DOING HIS WORK STUDY...
00:04:02
GRIP
...UNDER A CERTAIN HERO...!!
THIS IS A GREAT OPPORTUNITY, EVERYONE, SO GET THAT LESSON BEATEN INTO YOU.
BECAUSE...
MIRIO TOGATA, AS FAR AS I KNOW...
0:05:52
...IS THE CLOSEST TO BEING THE TOP HERO...

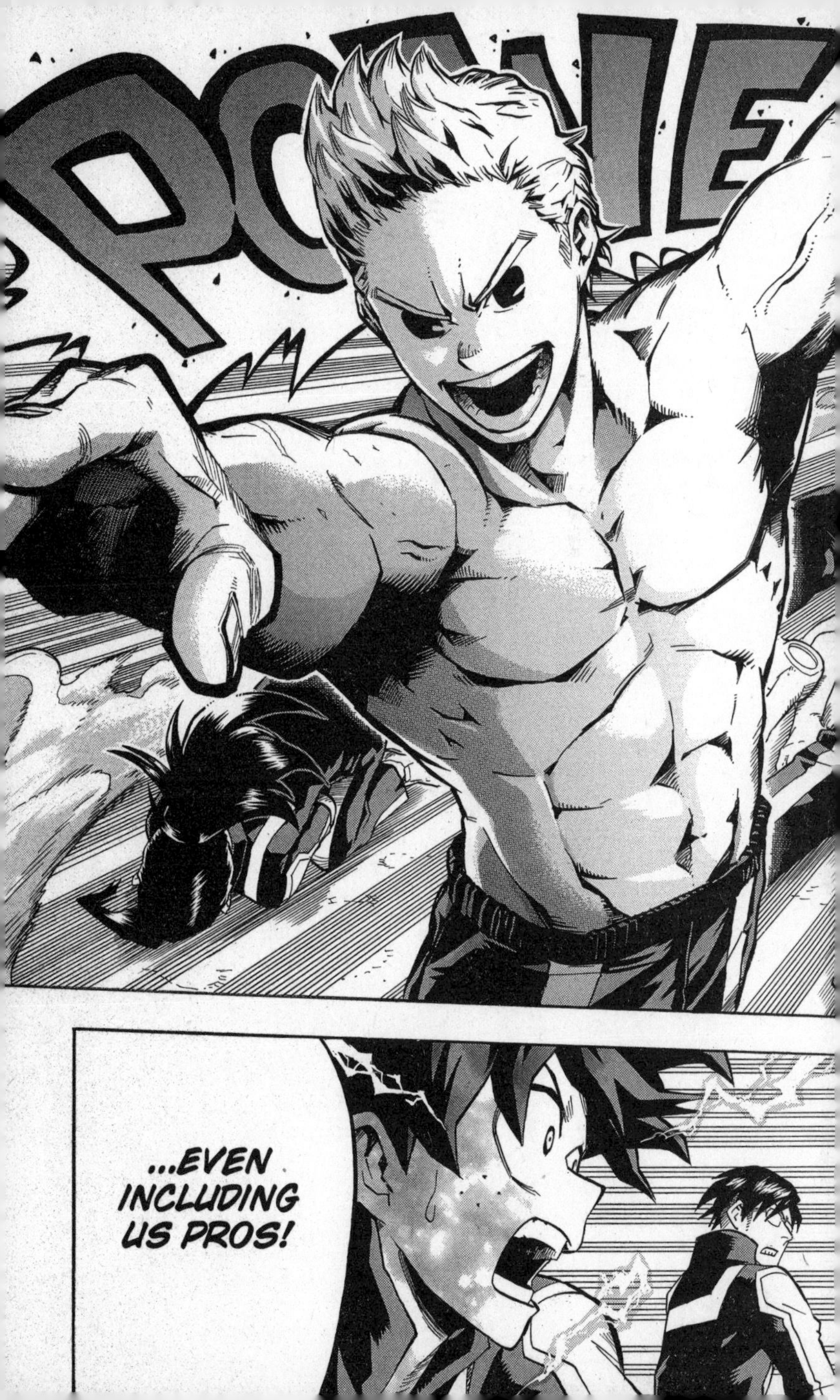
...EVEN INCLUDING US PROS!

HERO

MIRIO TOGATA [18]

STREET CLOTHES

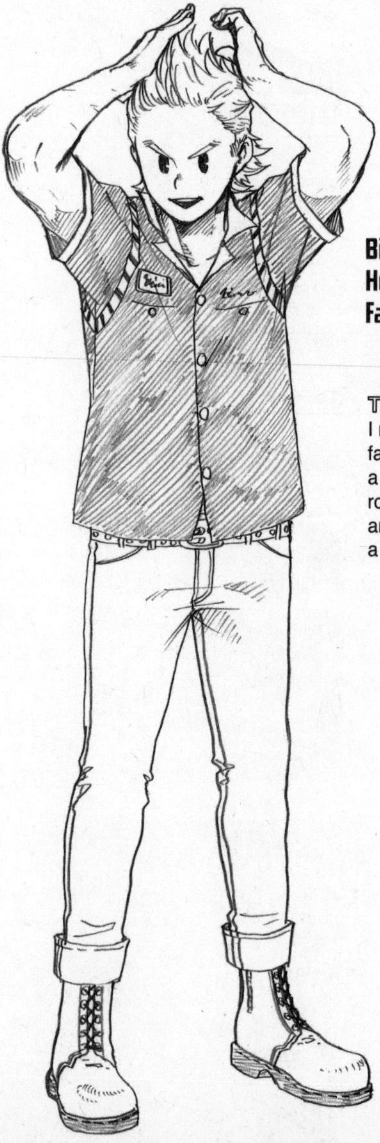

Birthday: 7/15
Height: 181 cm
Favorite Things: Ramen, comedy

THE SUPPLEMENT

I really went all in with that face, huh? I wanted to debut a character to fill this sort of role much earlier, but here we are, at volume 14. His face is a good one. Easy to draw.

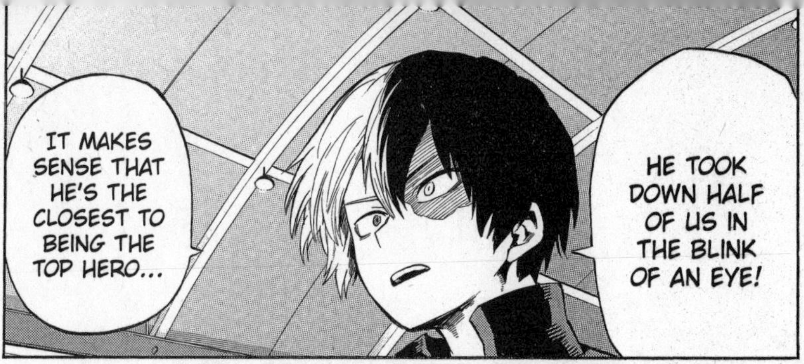
HE TOOK DOWN HALF OF US IN THE BLINK OF AN EYE!
IT MAKES SENSE THAT HE'S THE CLOSEST TO BEING THE TOP HERO...

No. 124 - Trouble Ahead!! Episode: Work Studies

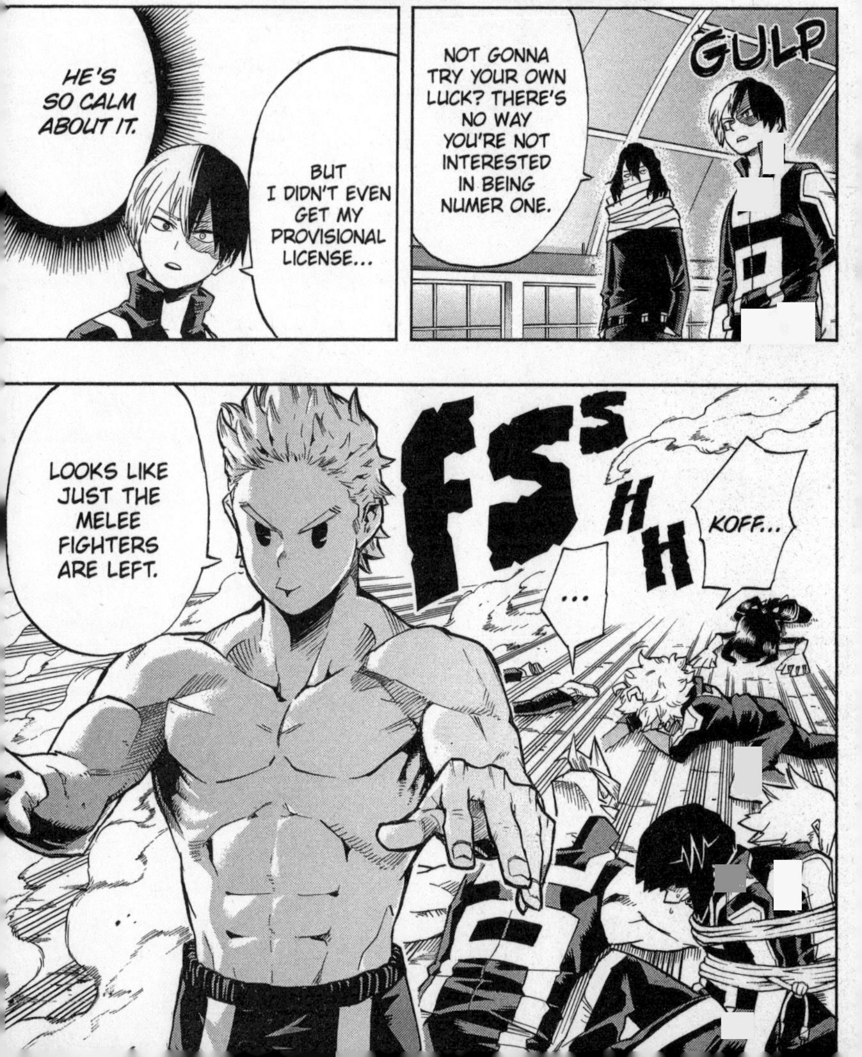
GULP
NOT GONNA TRY YOUR OWN LUCK? THERE'S NO WAY YOU'RE NOT INTERESTED IN BEING NUMER ONE.
BUT I DIDN'T EVEN GET MY PROVISIONAL LICENSE...
HE'S SO CALM ABOUT IT.
KOFF...
FSSHH
...
LOOKS LIKE JUST THE MELEE FIGHTERS ARE LEFT.

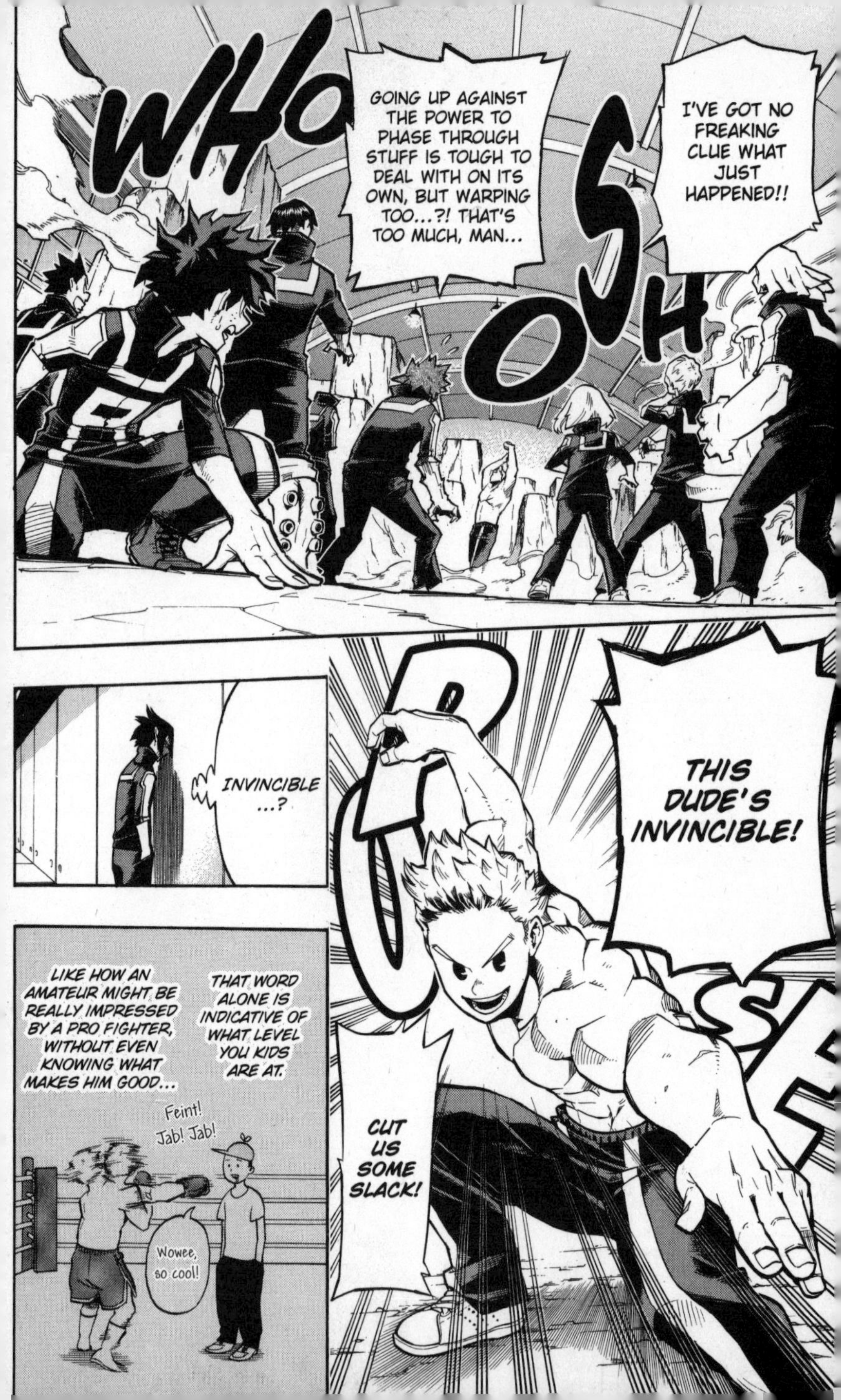
WHOOSH
I'VE GOT NO FREAKING CLUE WHAT JUST HAPPENED!!
GOING UP AGAINST THE POWER TO PHASE THROUGH STUFF IS TOUGH TO DEAL WITH ON ITS OWN, BUT WARPING TOO...?! THAT'S TOO MUCH, MAN...
THIS DUDE'S INVINCIBLE!
CUT US SOME SLACK!
INVINCIBLE ...?
THAT WORD ALONE IS INDICATIVE OF WHAT LEVEL YOU KIDS ARE AT.
LIKE HOW AN AMATEUR MIGHT BE REALLY IMPRESSED BY A PRO FIGHTER, WITHOUT EVEN KNOWING WHAT MAKES HIM GOOD...
Feint! Jab! Jab!
Wowee, so cool!

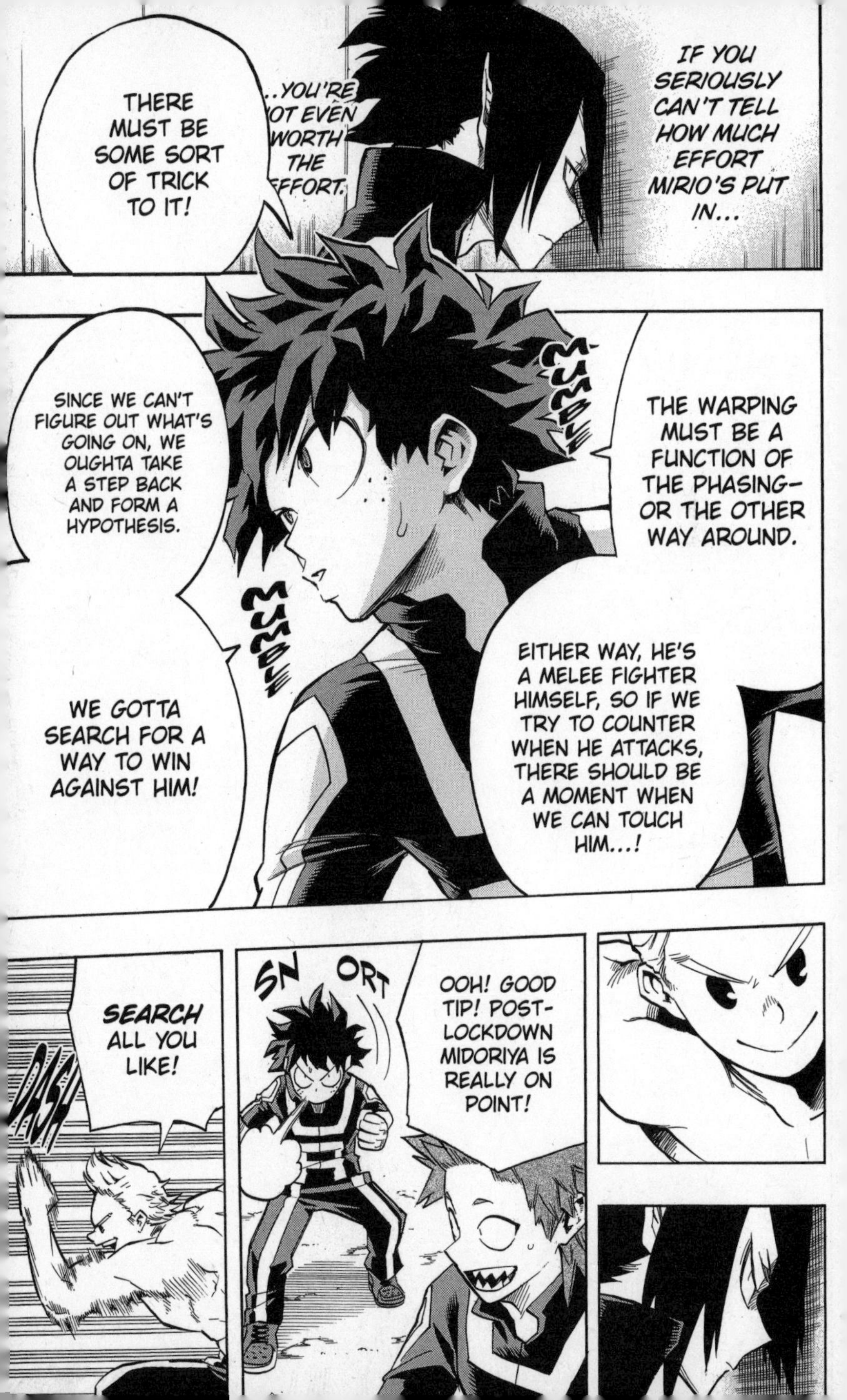
IF YOU SERIOUSLY CAN'T TELL HOW MUCH EFFORT MIRIO'S PUT IN...
...YOU'RE OT EVEN WORTH THE FFORT.
THERE MUST BE SOME SORT OF TRICK TO IT!
THE WARPING MUST BE A FUNCTION OF THE PHASING-OR THE OTHER WAY AROUND.
MUMBLE
SINCE WE CAN'T FIGURE OUT WHAT'S GOING ON, WE OUGHTA TAKE A STEP BACK AND FORM A HYPOTHESIS.
MUMBLE
EITHER WAY, HE'S A MELEE FIGHTER HIMSELF, SO IF WE TRY TO COUNTER WHEN HE ATTACKS, THERE SHOULD BE A MOMENT WHEN WE CAN TOUCH HIM...!
WE GOTTA SEARCH FOR A WAY TO WIN AGAINST HIM!
SNORT
OOH! GOOD TIP! POST-LOCKDOWN MIDORIYA IS REALLY ON POINT!
SEARCH ALL YOU LIKE!
DASH

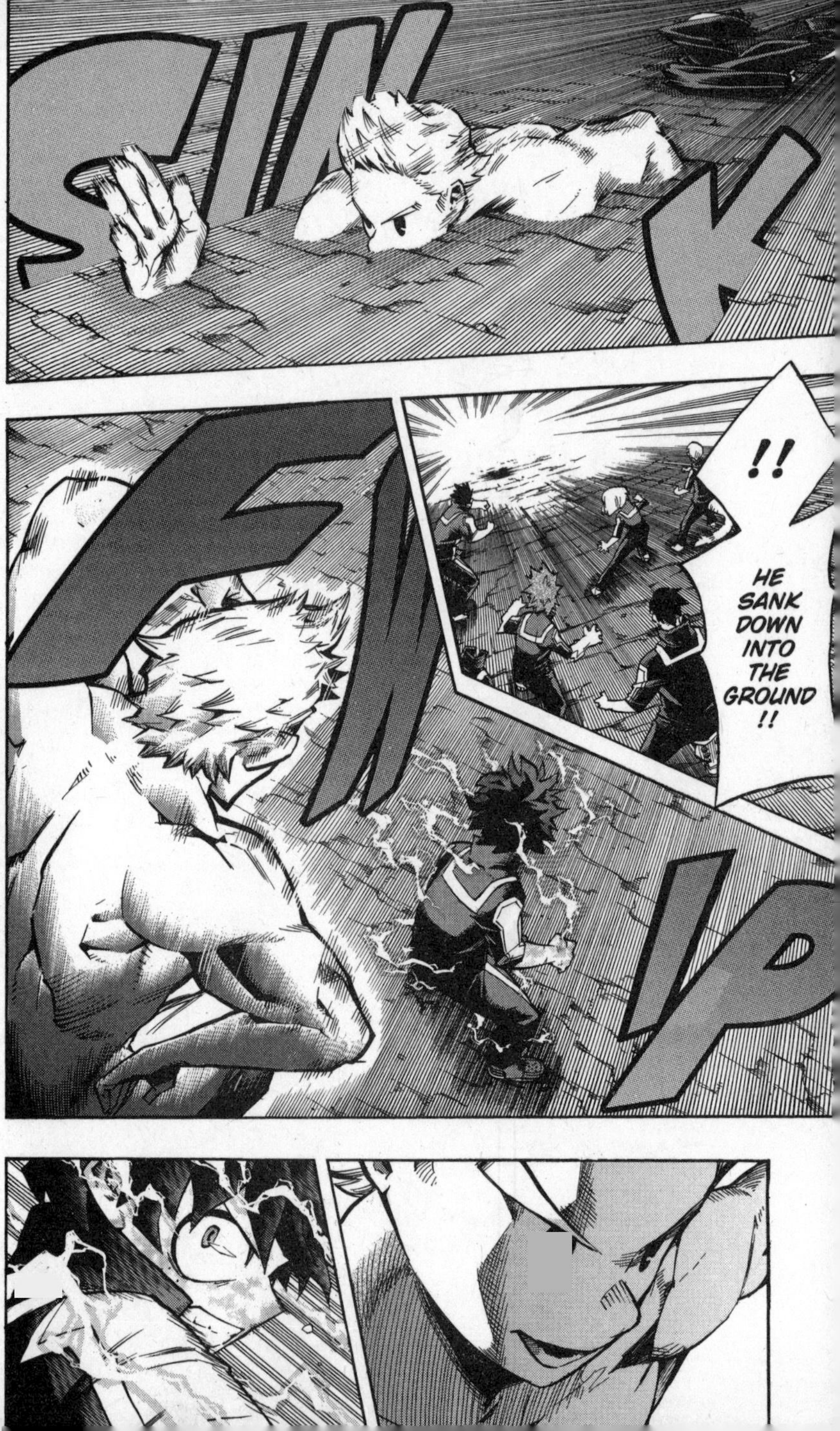
!!
HE SANK DOWN INTO THE GROUND !!

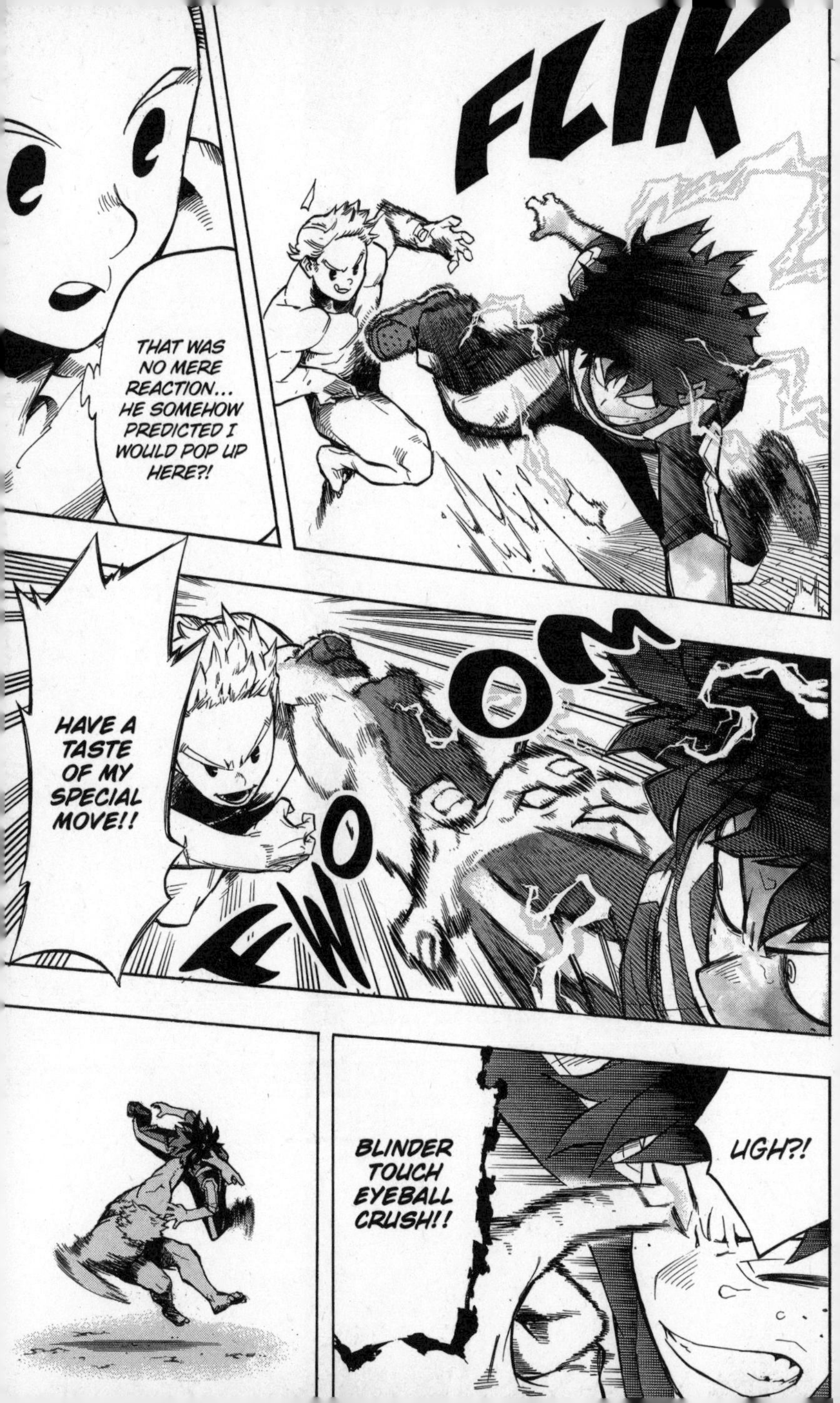
FLIK
THAT WAS NO MERE REACTION... HE SOMEHOW PREDICTED I WOULD POP UP HERE?!
FWOOM
HAVE A TASTE OF MY SPECIAL MOVE!!
UGH?!
BLINDER TOUCH EYEBALL CRUSH!!

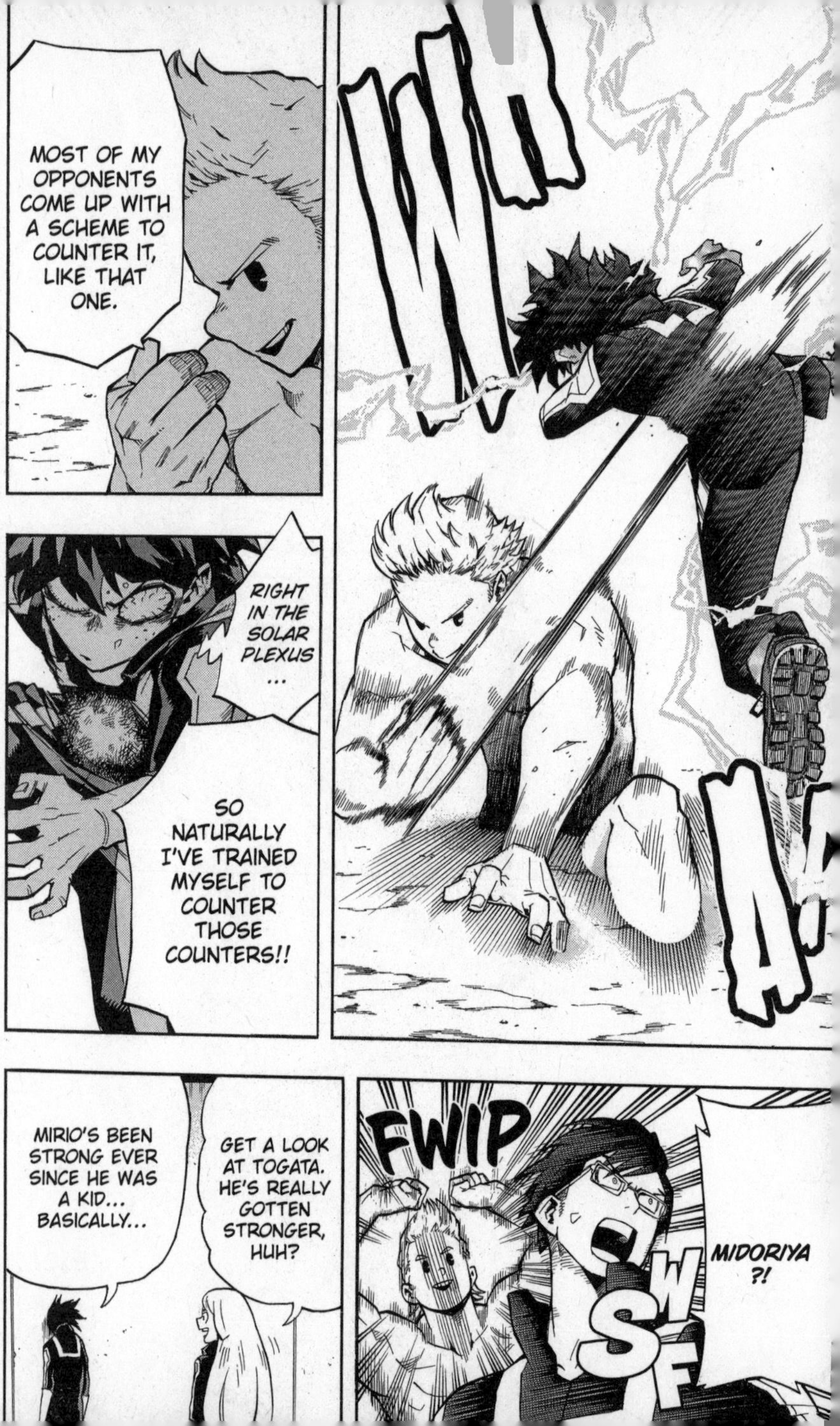
MOST OF MY OPPONENTS COME UP WITH A SCHEME TO COUNTER IT, LIKE THAT ONE.
RIGHT IN THE SOLAR PLEXUS...
SO NATURALLY I'VE TRAINED MYSELF TO COUNTER THOSE COUNTERS!!
MIDORIYA ?!
FWIP
GET A LOOK AT TOGATA. HE'S REALLY GOTTEN STRONGER, HUH?
MIRIO'S BEEN STRONG EVER SINCE HE WAS A KID... BASICALLY...

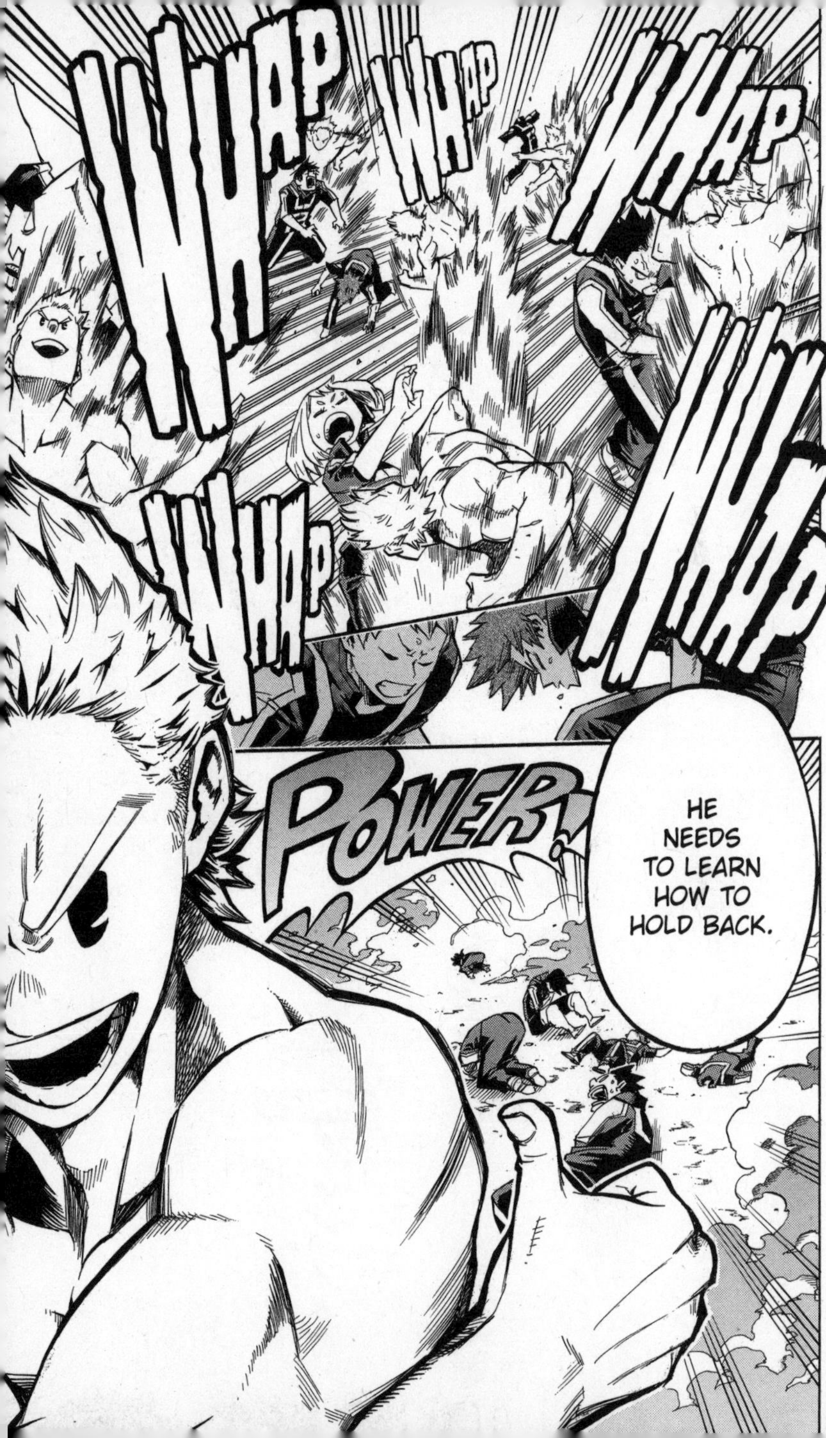
WHAP
WHAP
WHAP
WHAP
WHAP
HE NEEDS TO LEARN HOW TO HOLD BACK.
POWER!

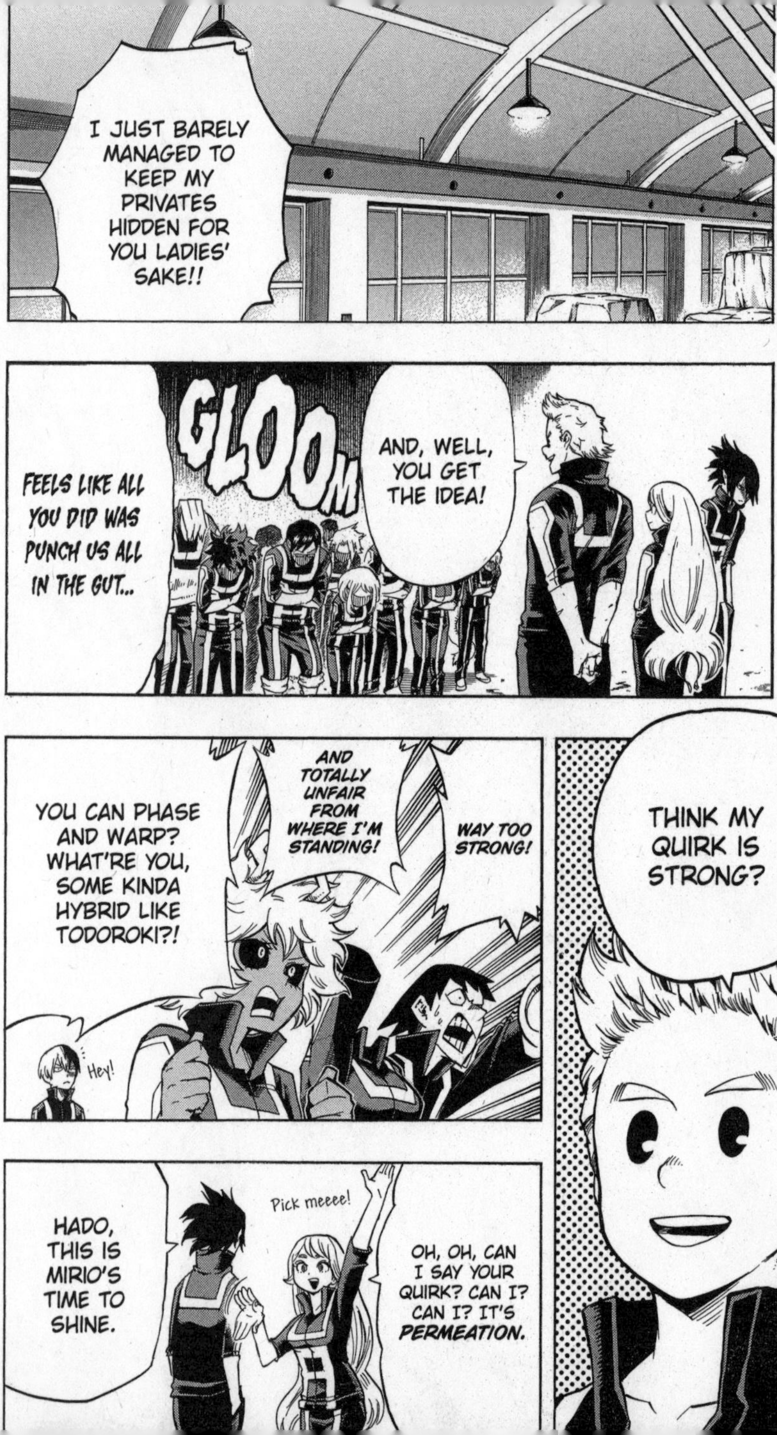

I JUST BARELY MANAGED TO KEEP MY PRIVATES HIDDEN FOR YOU LADIES' SAKE!!
AND, WELL, YOU GET THE IDEA!
GLOOM
FEELS LIKE ALL YOU DID WAS PUNCH US ALL IN THE GUT...
THINK MY QUIRK IS STRONG?
WAY TOO STRONG!
AND TOTALLY UNFAIR FROM WHERE I'M STANDING!
YOU CAN PHASE AND WARP? WHAT'RE YOU, SOME KINDA HYBRID LIKE TODOROKI?!
Hey!
Pick meeee!
OH, OH, CAN I SAY YOUR QUIRK? CAN I? CAN I? IT'S PERMEATION.
HADO, THIS IS MIRIO'S TIME TO SHINE.

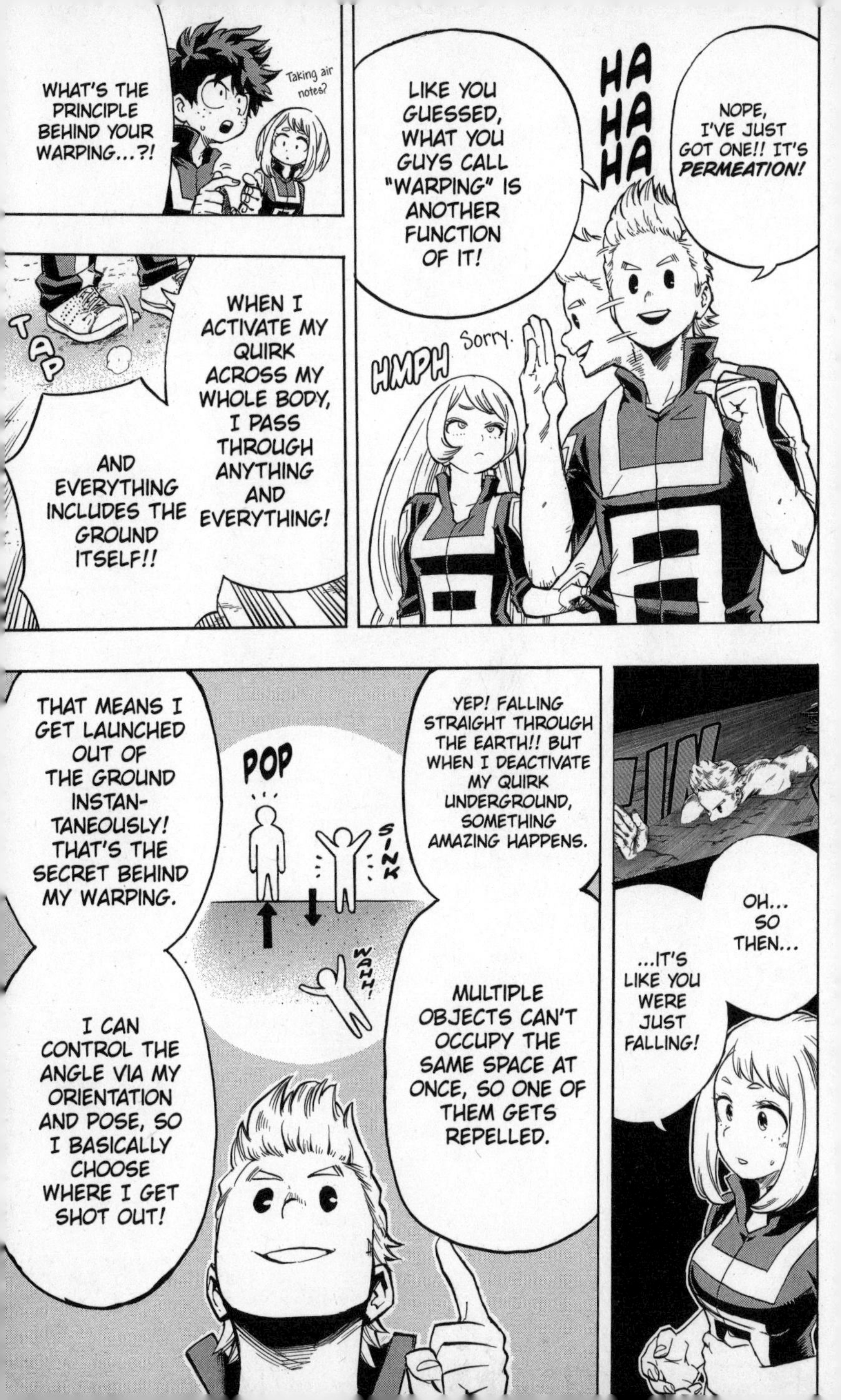
NOPE, I'VE JUST GOT ONE!! IT'S *PERMEATION!*
HA HA HA
LIKE YOU GUESSED, WHAT YOU GUYS CALL "WARPING" IS ANOTHER FUNCTION OF IT!
Sorry.
HMPH
Taking air notes?
WHAT'S THE PRINCIPLE BEHIND YOUR WARPING...?!
WHEN I ACTIVATE MY QUIRK ACROSS MY WHOLE BODY, I PASS THROUGH ANYTHING AND EVERYTHING!
TAP
AND EVERYTHING INCLUDES THE GROUND ITSELF!!
OH... SO THEN...
...IT'S LIKE YOU WERE JUST FALLING!
YEP! FALLING STRAIGHT THROUGH THE EARTH!! BUT WHEN I DEACTIVATE MY QUIRK UNDERGROUND, SOMETHING AMAZING HAPPENS.
MULTIPLE OBJECTS CAN'T OCCUPY THE SAME SPACE AT ONCE, SO ONE OF THEM GETS REPELLED.
THAT MEANS I GET LAUNCHED OUT OF THE GROUND INSTAN-TANEOUSLY! THAT'S THE SECRET BEHIND MY WARPING.
POP
SINK
WAHH!
I CAN CONTROL THE ANGLE VIA MY ORIENTATION AND POSE, SO I BASICALLY CHOOSE WHERE I GET SHOT OUT!

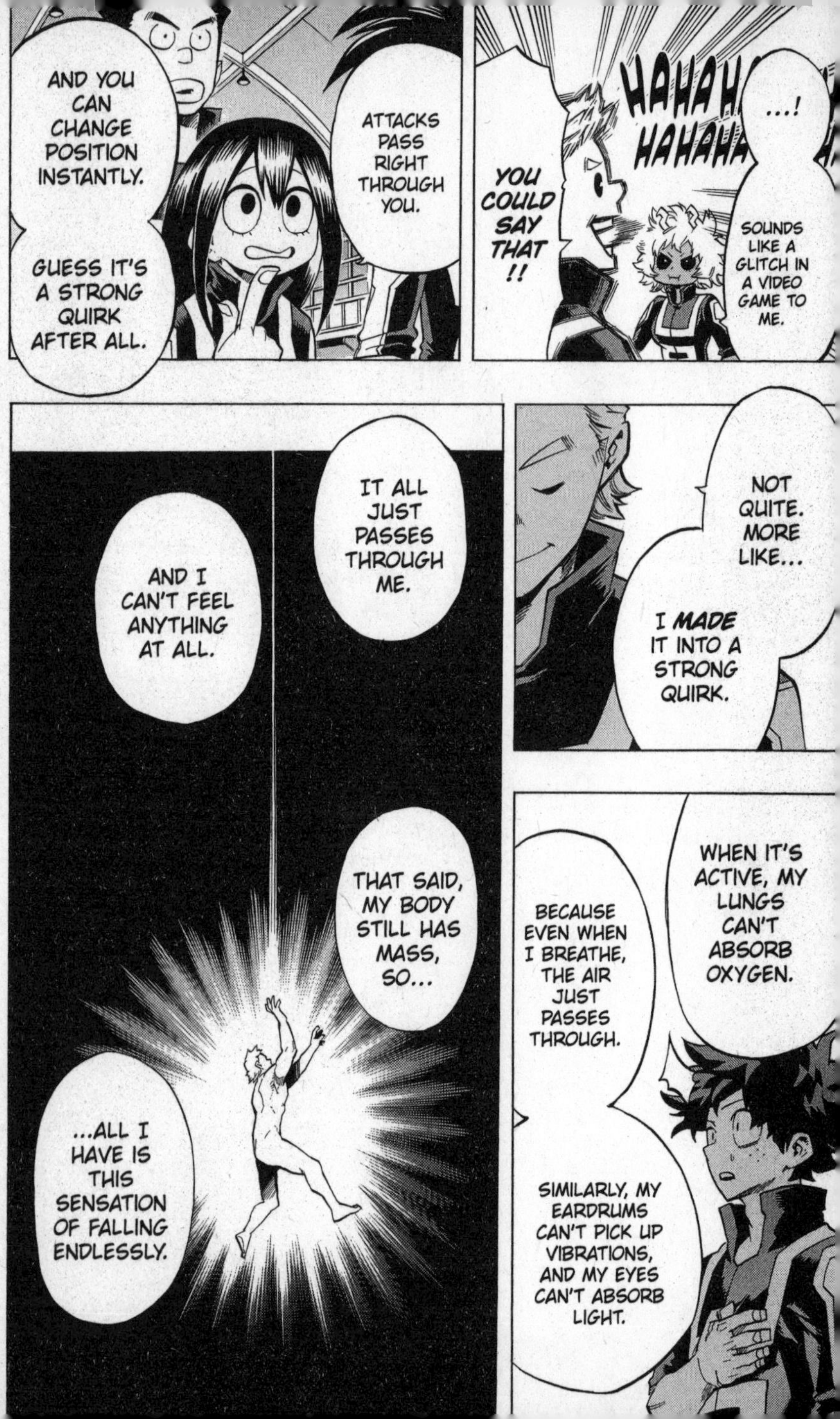
...!
HAHAHA HAHAHA
SOUNDS LIKE A GLITCH IN A VIDEO GAME TO ME.
YOU COULD SAY THAT!!
ATTACKS PASS RIGHT THROUGH YOU.
AND YOU CAN CHANGE POSITION INSTANTLY.
GUESS IT'S A STRONG QUIRK AFTER ALL.
NOT QUITE. MORE LIKE...
I *MADE* IT INTO A STRONG QUIRK.
WHEN IT'S ACTIVE, MY LUNGS CAN'T ABSORB OXYGEN.
BECAUSE EVEN WHEN I BREATHE, THE AIR JUST PASSES THROUGH.
SIMILARLY, MY EARDRUMS CAN'T PICK UP VIBRATIONS, AND MY EYES CAN'T ABSORB LIGHT.
IT ALL JUST PASSES THROUGH ME.
AND I CAN'T FEEL ANYTHING AT ALL.
THAT SAID, MY BODY STILL HAS MASS, SO...
...ALL I HAVE IS THIS SENSATION OF FALLING ENDLESSLY.

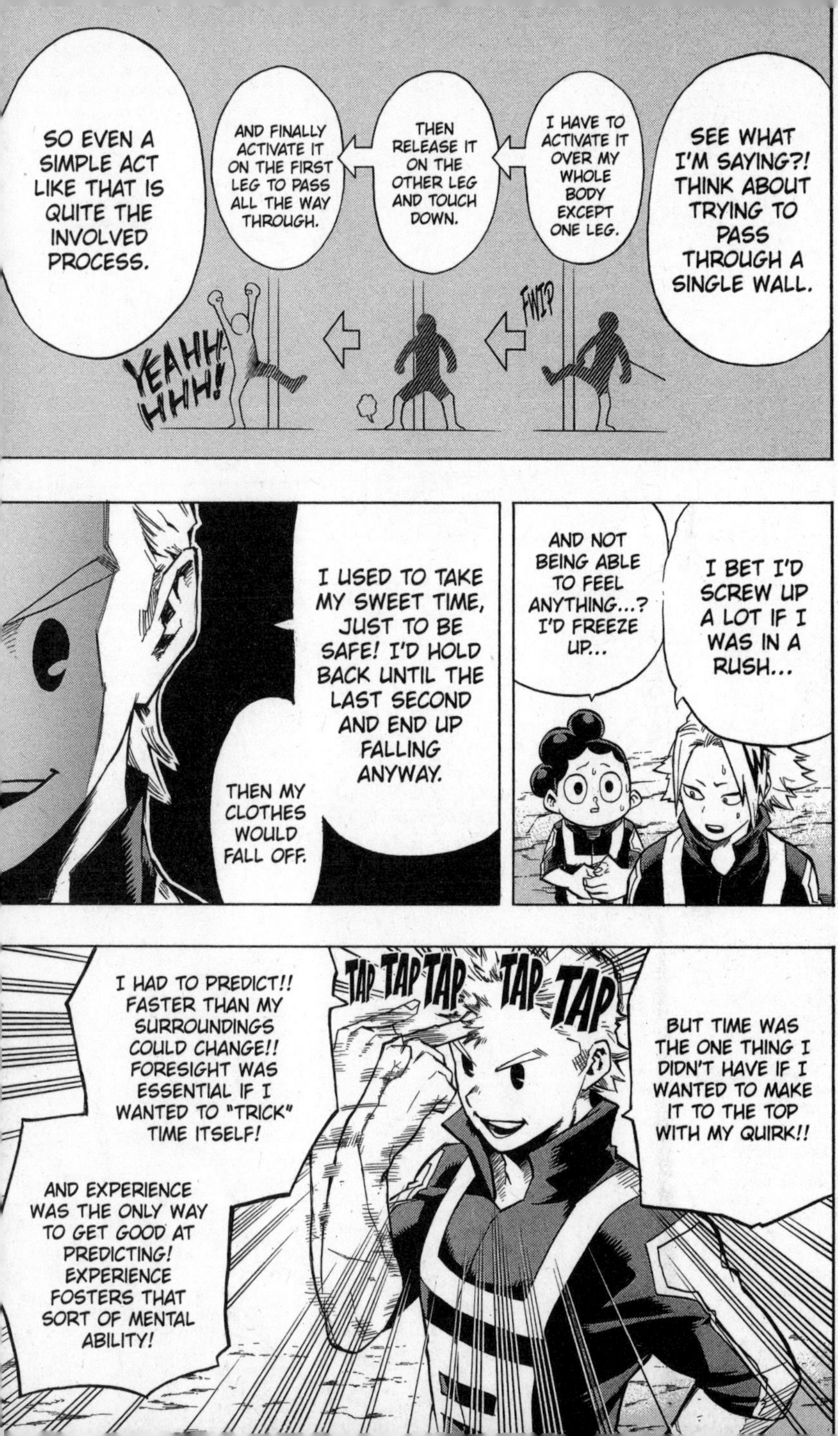
SEE WHAT I'M SAYING?! THINK ABOUT TRYING TO PASS THROUGH A SINGLE WALL.
I HAVE TO ACTIVATE IT OVER MY WHOLE BODY EXCEPT ONE LEG.
FWIP
THEN RELEASE IT ON THE OTHER LEG AND TOUCH DOWN.
AND FINALLY ACTIVATE IT ON THE FIRST LEG TO PASS ALL THE WAY THROUGH.
YEAHHHHH!
SO EVEN A SIMPLE ACT LIKE THAT IS QUITE THE INVOLVED PROCESS.
I BET I'D SCREW UP A LOT IF I WAS IN A RUSH...
AND NOT BEING ABLE TO FEEL ANYTHING...? I'D FREEZE UP...
I USED TO TAKE MY SWEET TIME, JUST TO BE SAFE! I'D HOLD BACK UNTIL THE LAST SECOND AND END UP FALLING ANYWAY.
THEN MY CLOTHES WOULD FALL OFF.
TAP TAP TAP TAP TAP
BUT TIME WAS THE ONE THING I DIDN'T HAVE IF I WANTED TO MAKE IT TO THE TOP WITH MY QUIRK!!
I HAD TO PREDICT!! FASTER THAN MY SURROUNDINGS COULD CHANGE!! FORESIGHT WAS ESSENTIAL IF I WANTED TO "TRICK" TIME ITSELF!
AND EXPERIENCE WAS THE ONLY WAY TO GET GOOD AT PREDICTING! EXPERIENCE FOSTERS THAT SORT OF MENTAL ABILITY!

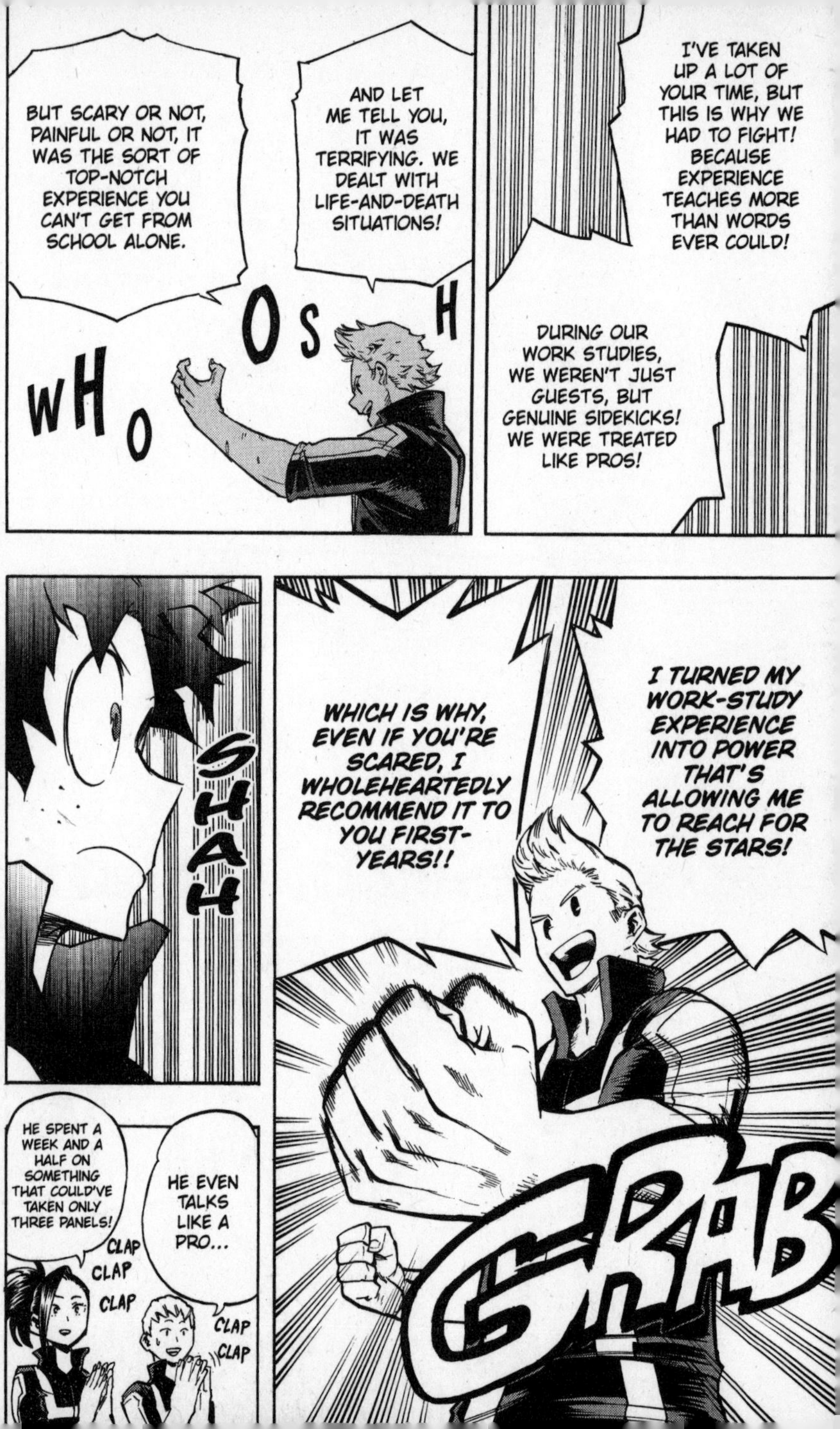
I'VE TAKEN UP A LOT OF YOUR TIME, BUT THIS IS WHY WE HAD TO FIGHT! BECAUSE EXPERIENCE TEACHES MORE THAN WORDS EVER COULD!
DURING OUR WORK STUDIES, WE WEREN'T JUST GUESTS, BUT GENUINE SIDEKICKS! WE WERE TREATED LIKE PROS!
AND LET ME TELL YOU, IT WAS TERRIFYING. WE DEALT WITH LIFE-AND-DEATH SITUATIONS!
BUT SCARY OR NOT, PAINFUL OR NOT, IT WAS THE SORT OF TOP-NOTCH EXPERIENCE YOU CAN'T GET FROM SCHOOL ALONE.
WHOOSH
I TURNED MY WORK-STUDY EXPERIENCE INTO POWER THAT'S ALLOWING ME TO REACH FOR THE STARS!
WHICH IS WHY, EVEN IF YOU'RE SCARED, I WHOLEHEARTEDLY RECOMMEND IT TO YOU FIRST-YEARS!!
GRAB
SHAH
HE EVEN TALKS LIKE A PRO...
HE SPENT A WEEK AND A HALF ON SOMETHING THAT COULD'VE TAKEN ONLY THREE PANELS!
CLAP CLAP
CLAP CLAP CLAP

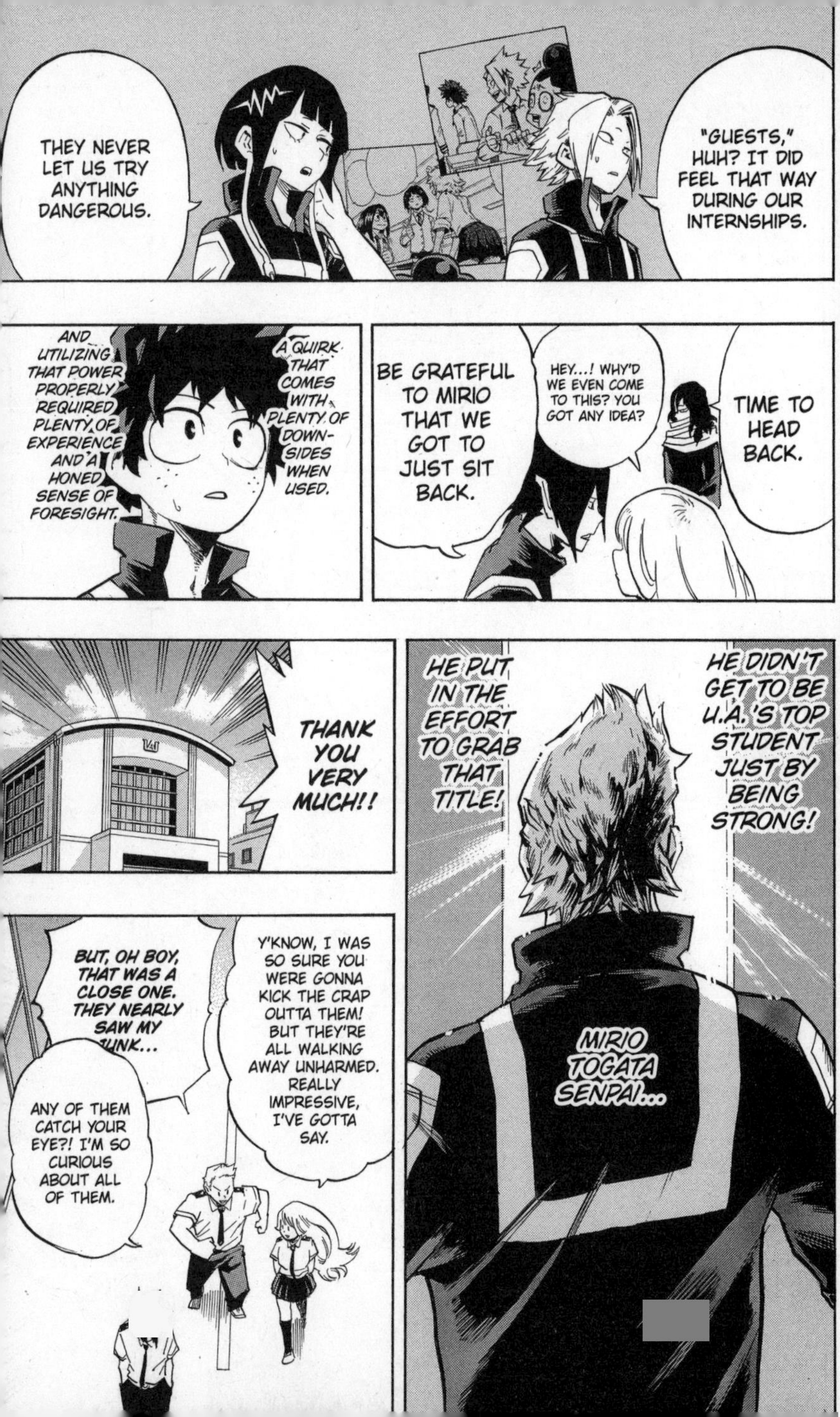
"GUESTS," HUH? IT DID FEEL THAT WAY DURING OUR INTERNSHIPS.
THEY NEVER LET US TRY ANYTHING DANGEROUS.
TIME TO HEAD BACK.
HEY...! WHY'D WE EVEN COME TO THIS? YOU GOT ANY IDEA?
BE GRATEFUL TO MIRIO THAT WE GOT TO JUST SIT BACK.
A QUIRK THAT COMES WITH PLENTY OF DOWNSIDES WHEN USED.
AND UTILIZING THAT POWER PROPERLY REQUIRED PLENTY OF EXPERIENCE AND A HONED SENSE OF FORESIGHT.
HE DIDN'T GET TO BE U.A.'S TOP STUDENT JUST BY BEING STRONG!
HE PUT IN THE EFFORT TO GRAB THAT TITLE!
MIRIO TOGATA SENPAI...
THANK YOU VERY MUCH!!
Y'KNOW, I WAS SO SURE YOU WERE GONNA KICK THE CRAP OUTTA THEM! BUT THEY'RE ALL WALKING AWAY UNHARMED. REALLY IMPRESSIVE, I'VE GOTTA SAY.
BUT, OH BOY, THAT WAS A CLOSE ONE. THEY NEARLY SAW MY JUNK...
ANY OF THEM CATCH YOUR EYE?! I'M SO CURIOUS ABOUT ALL OF THEM.

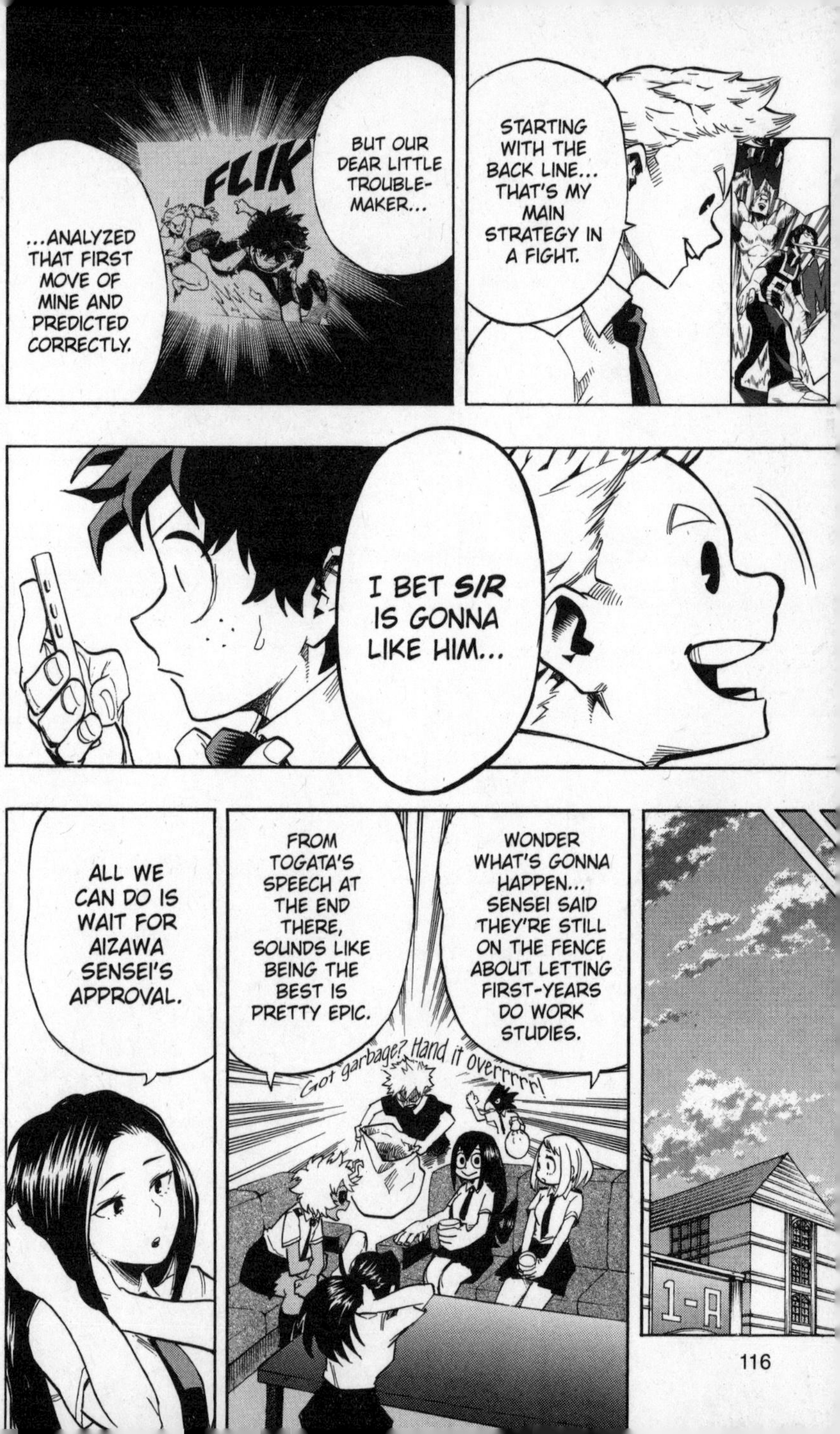

STARTING WITH THE BACK LINE... THAT'S MY MAIN STRATEGY IN A FIGHT.
BUT OUR DEAR LITTLE TROUBLE-MAKER...
FLIK
...ANALYZED THAT FIRST MOVE OF MINE AND PREDICTED CORRECTLY.
I BET SIR IS GONNA LIKE HIM...
WONDER WHAT'S GONNA HAPPEN... SENSEI SAID THEY'RE STILL ON THE FENCE ABOUT LETTING FIRST-YEARS DO WORK STUDIES.
FROM TOGATA'S SPEECH AT THE END THERE, SOUNDS LIKE BEING THE BEST IS PRETTY EPIC.
Got garbage? Hand it overrrrrr!
1-A
ALL WE CAN DO IS WAIT FOR AIZAWA SENSEI'S APPROVAL.

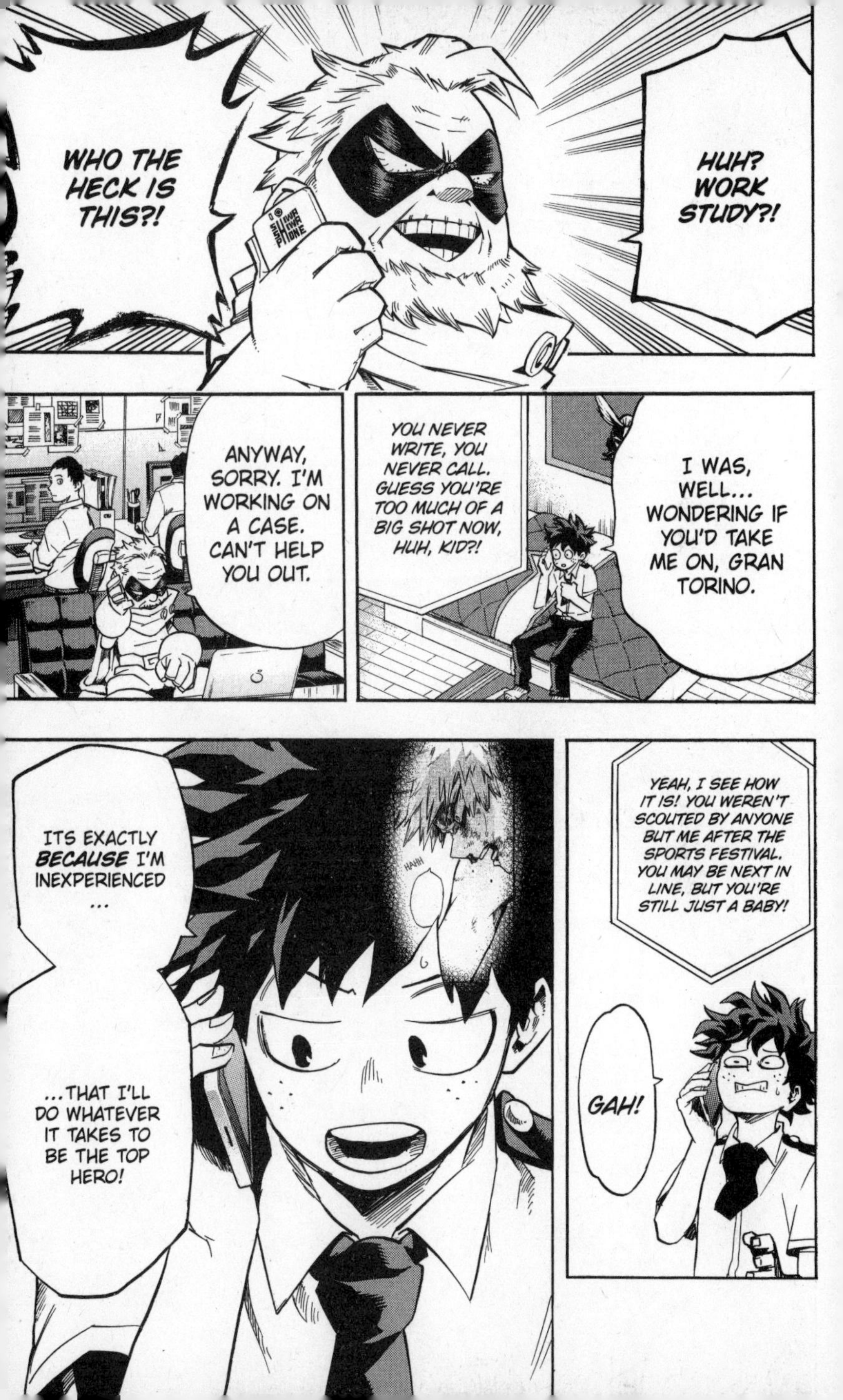
HUH? WORK STUDY?!
WHO THE HECK IS THIS?!
I WAS, WELL... WONDERING IF YOU'D TAKE ME ON, GRAN TORINO.
YOU NEVER WRITE, YOU NEVER CALL. GUESS YOU'RE TOO MUCH OF A BIG SHOT NOW, HUH, KID?!
ANYWAY, SORRY. I'M WORKING ON A CASE. CAN'T HELP YOU OUT.
YEAH, I SEE HOW IT IS! YOU WEREN'T SCOUTED BY ANYONE BUT ME AFTER THE SPORTS FESTIVAL. YOU MAY BE NEXT IN LINE, BUT YOU'RE STILL JUST A BABY!
GAH!
ITS EXACTLY *BECAUSE* I'M INEXPERIENCED ...
HAHH
...THAT I'LL DO WHATEVER IT TAKES TO BE THE TOP HERO!

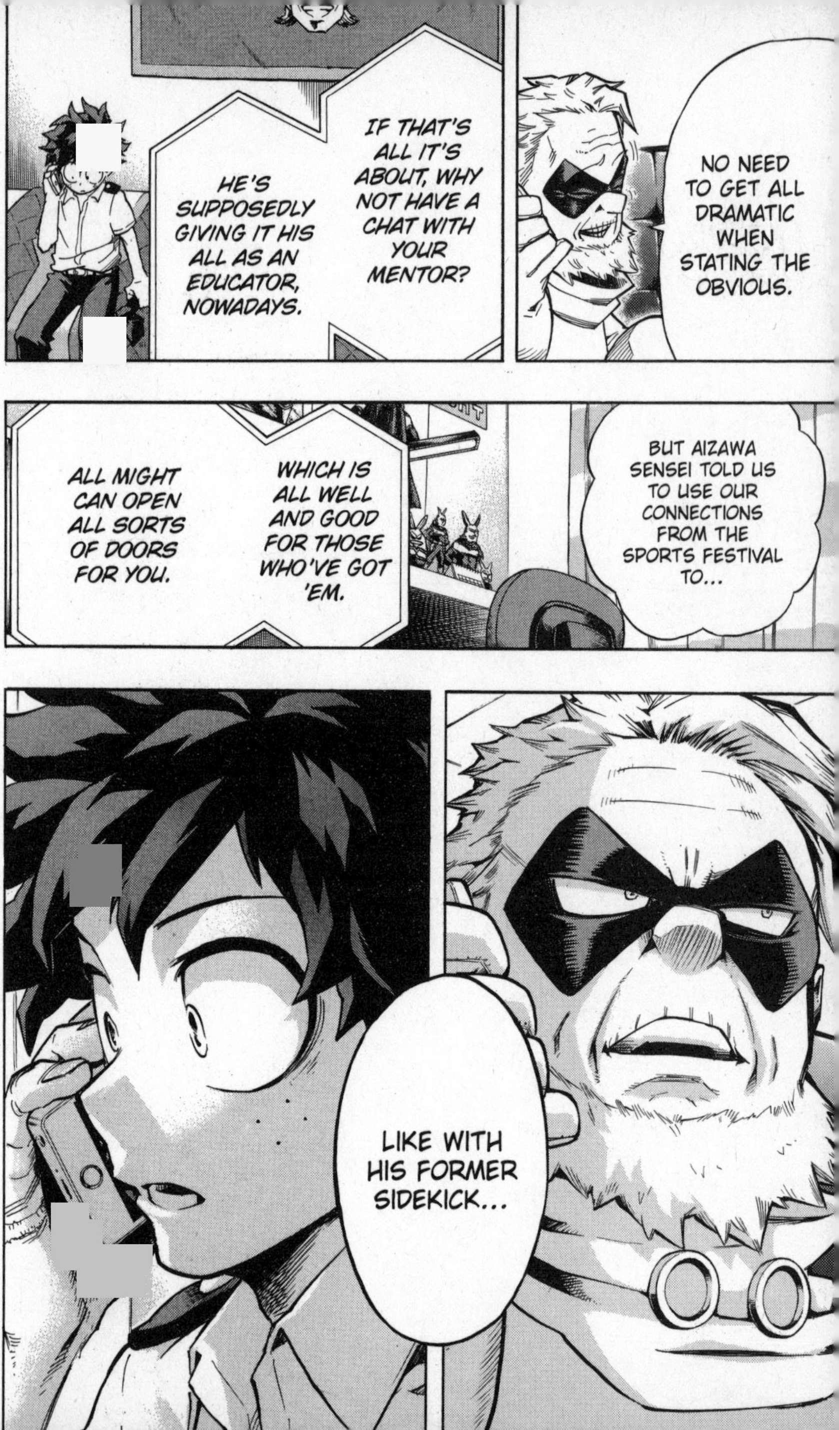
NO NEED TO GET ALL DRAMATIC WHEN STATING THE OBVIOUS.
IF THAT'S ALL IT'S ABOUT, WHY NOT HAVE A CHAT WITH YOUR MENTOR?
HE'S SUPPOSEDLY GIVING IT HIS ALL AS AN EDUCATOR, NOWADAYS.
BUT AIZAWA SENSEI TOLD US TO USE OUR CONNECTIONS FROM THE SPORTS FESTIVAL TO...
WHICH IS ALL WELL AND GOOD FOR THOSE WHO'VE GOT 'EM.
ALL MIGHT CAN OPEN ALL SORTS OF DOORS FOR YOU.
LIKE WITH HIS FORMER SIDEKICK...

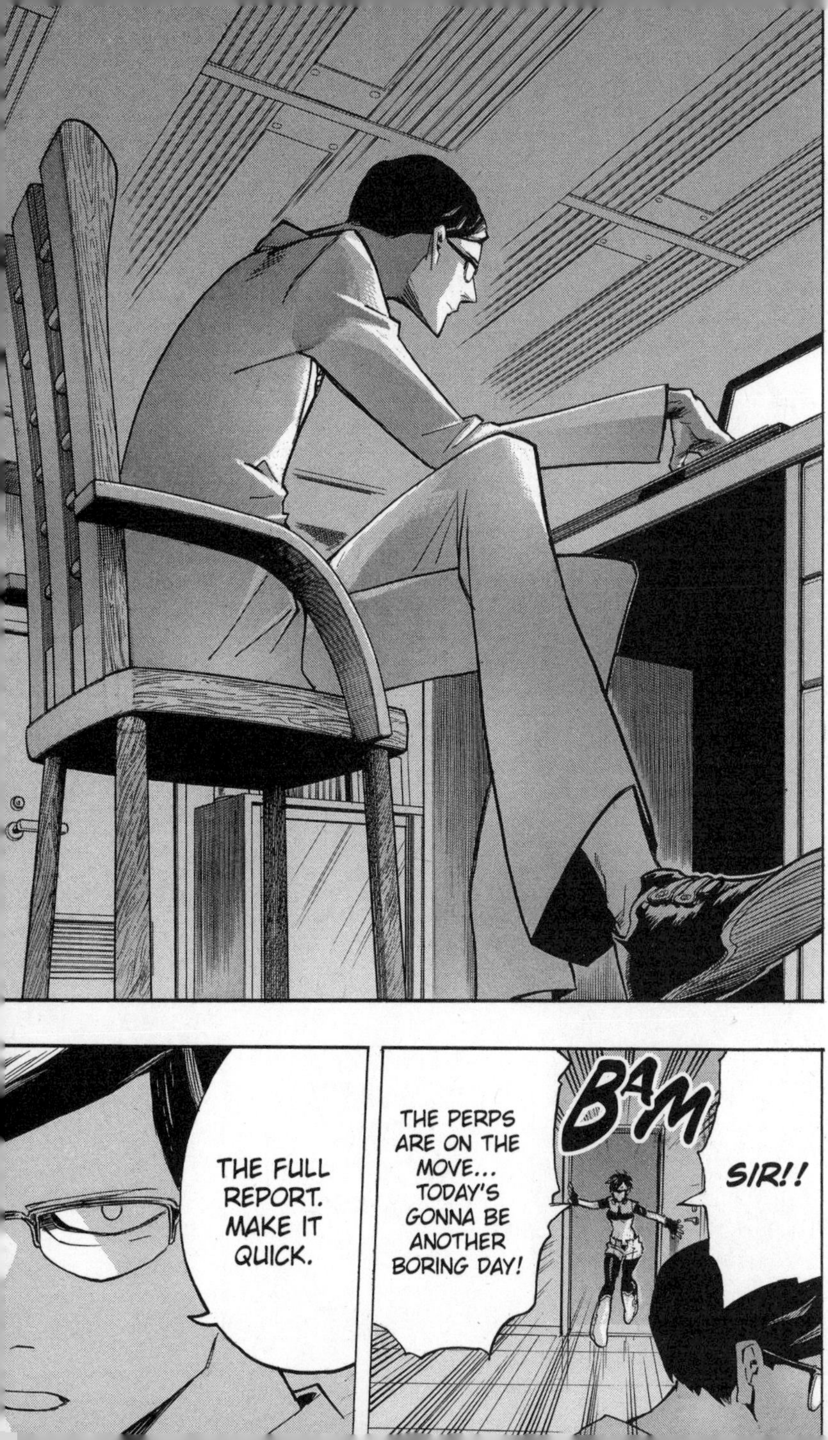
BAM
SIR!!
THE PERPS ARE ON THE MOVE... TODAY'S GONNA BE ANOTHER BORING DAY!
THE FULL REPORT. MAKE IT QUICK.

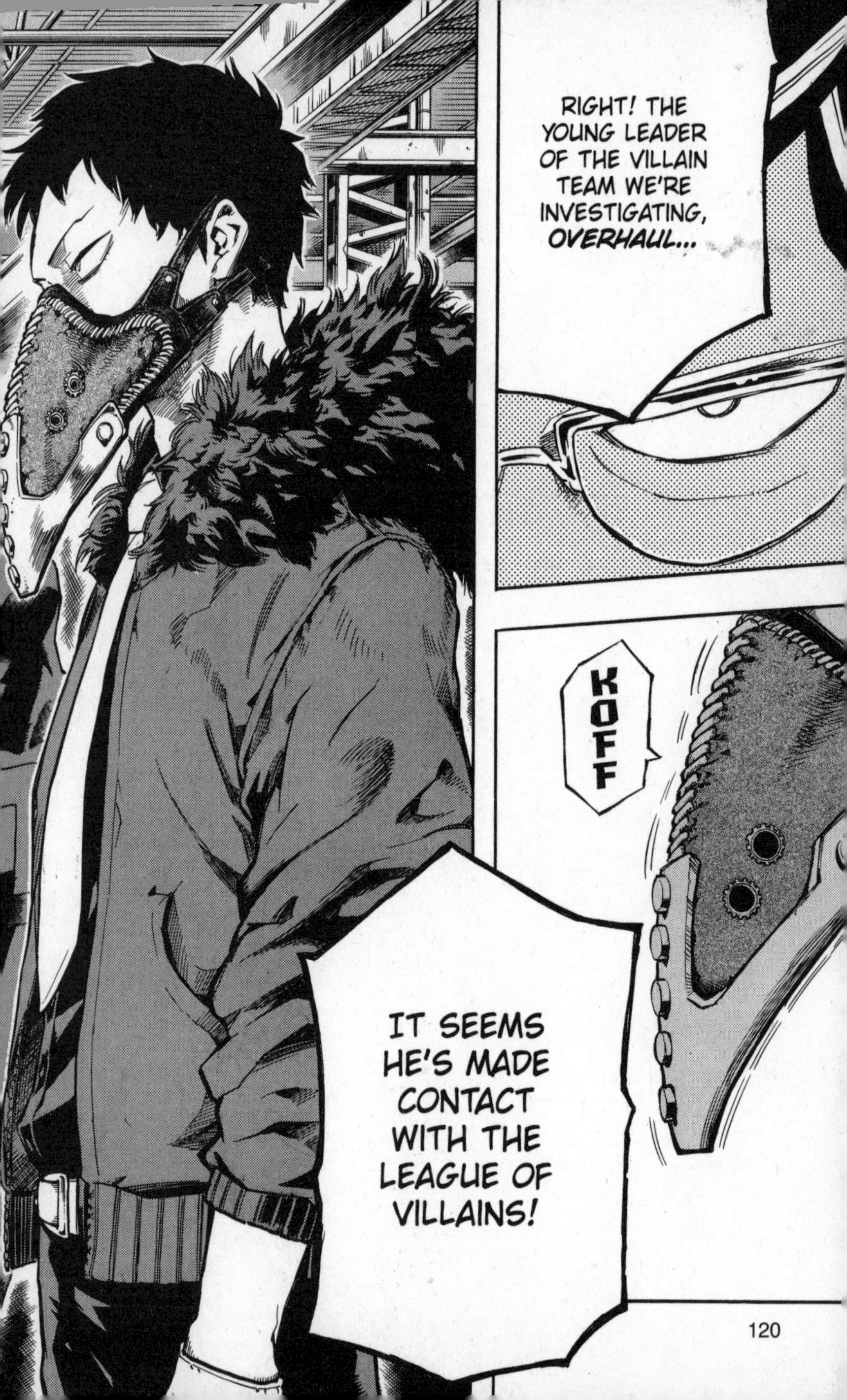
RIGHT! THE YOUNG LEADER OF THE VILLAIN TEAM WE'RE INVESTIGATING, *OVERHAUL*...
KOFF
IT SEEMS HE'S MADE CONTACT WITH THE LEAGUE OF VILLAINS!

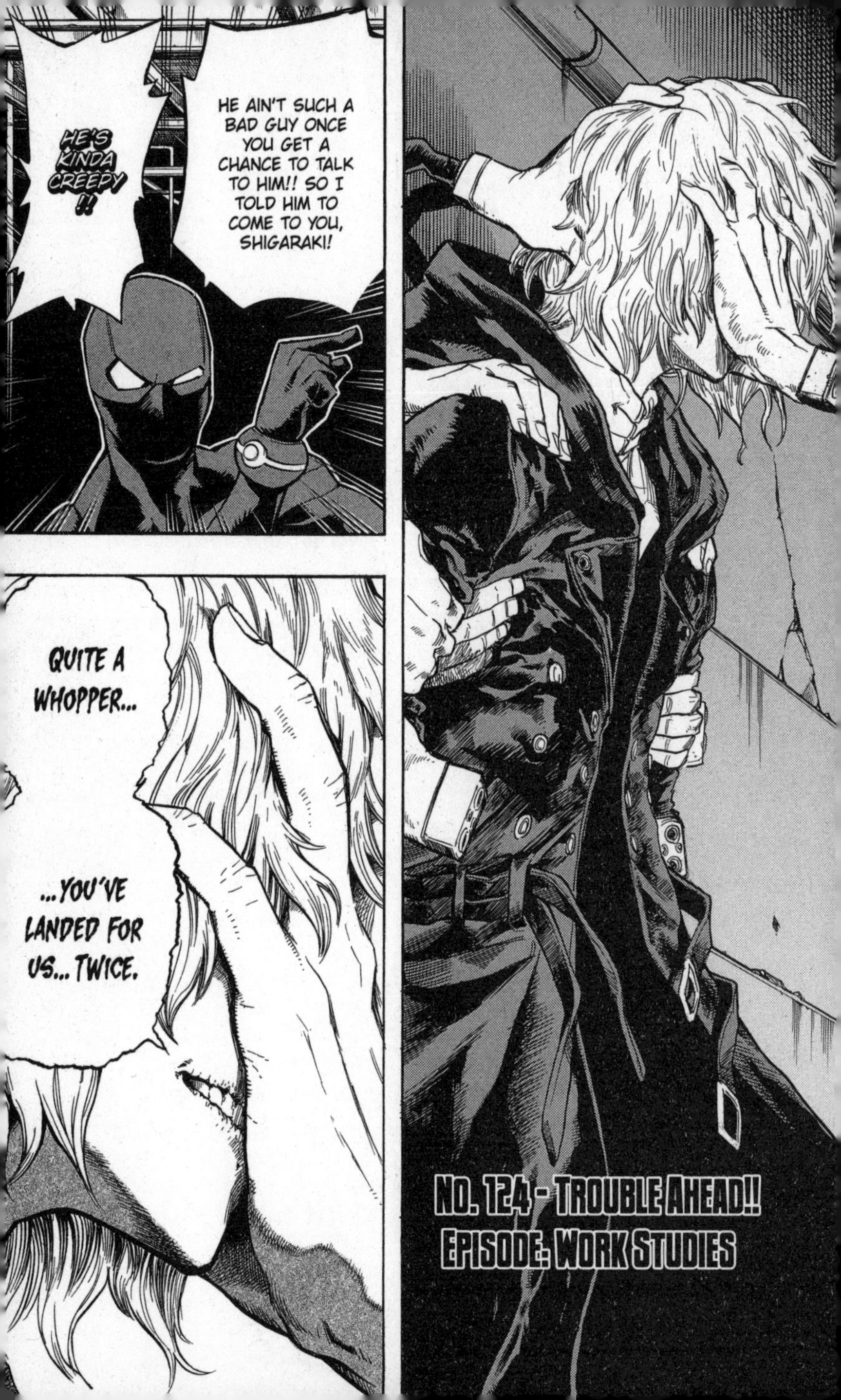
No. 124 - Trouble Ahead!! Episode: Work Studies
HE AIN'T SUCH A BAD GUY ONCE YOU GET A CHANCE TO TALK TO HIM!! SO I TOLD HIM TO COME TO YOU, SHIGARAKI!
HE'S KINDA CREEPY!!
QUITE A WHOPPER...
...YOU'VE LANDED FOR US... TWICE.

HERO

TAMAKI AMAJIKI (17)

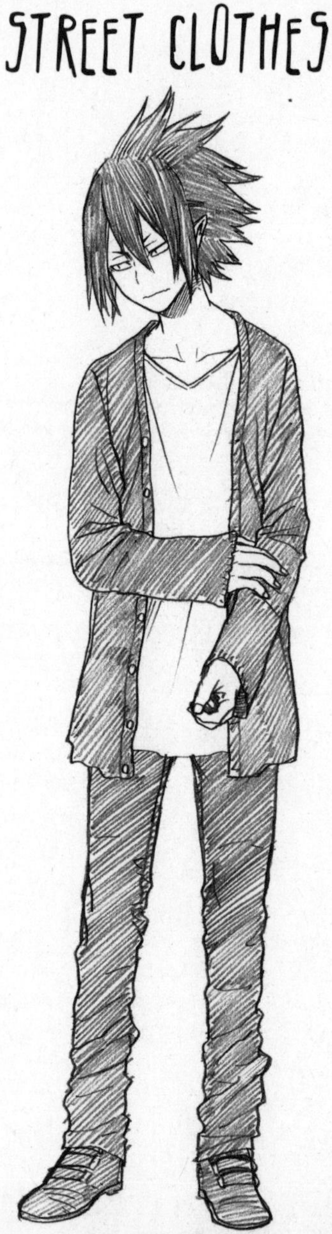
STREET CLOTHES

Birthday: 3/4
Height: 177 cm
Favorite Thing: Butterflies

THE PERSONAL SIDE

It was a little bit before he showed up in the story, I think, that I had the amazing experience of speaking onstage at Jump Festa. The nerves and anxiety I felt then really helped me write convincing dialogue for him, I think.

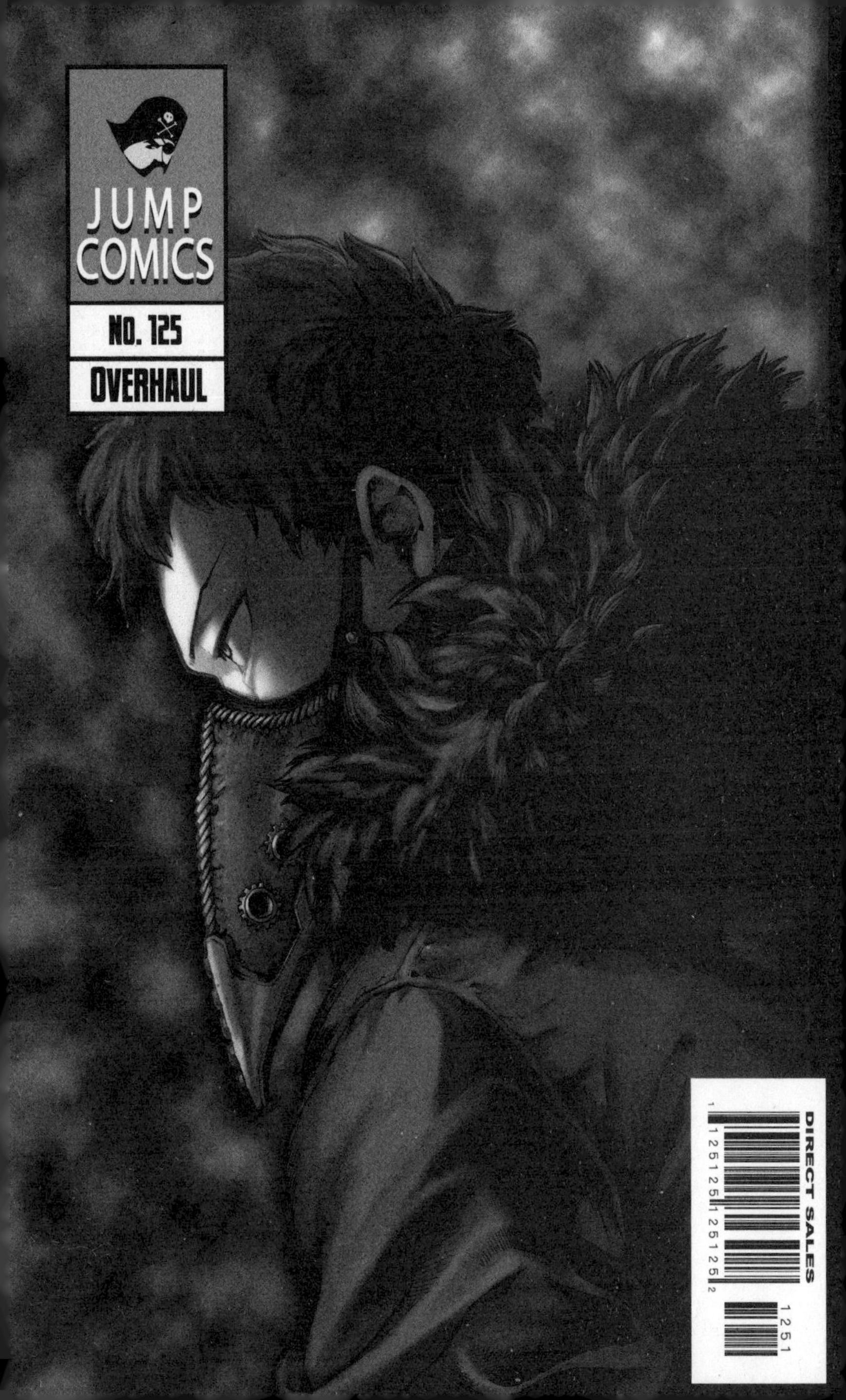
JUMP COMICS
No. 125
OVERHAUL
DIRECT SALES

MY HERO ACADEMIA

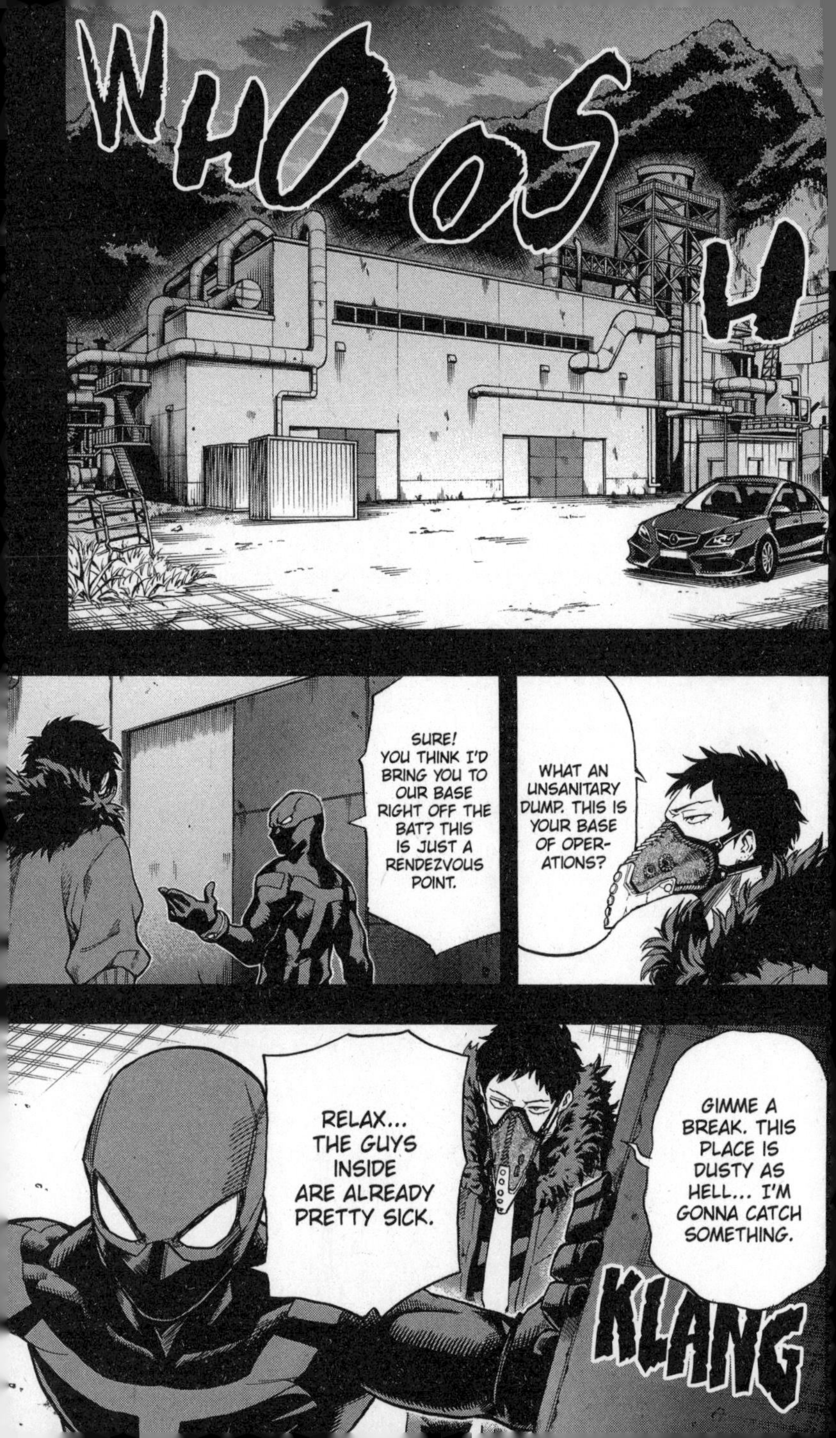
WHOOSH
WHAT AN UNSANITARY DUMP. THIS IS YOUR BASE OF OPER- ATIONS?
SURE! YOU THINK I'D BRING YOU TO OUR BASE RIGHT OFF THE BAT? THIS IS JUST A RENDEZVOUS POINT.
GIMME A BREAK. THIS PLACE IS DUSTY AS HELL... I'M GONNA CATCH SOMETHING.
RELAX... THE GUYS INSIDE ARE ALREADY PRETTY SICK.
KLANG

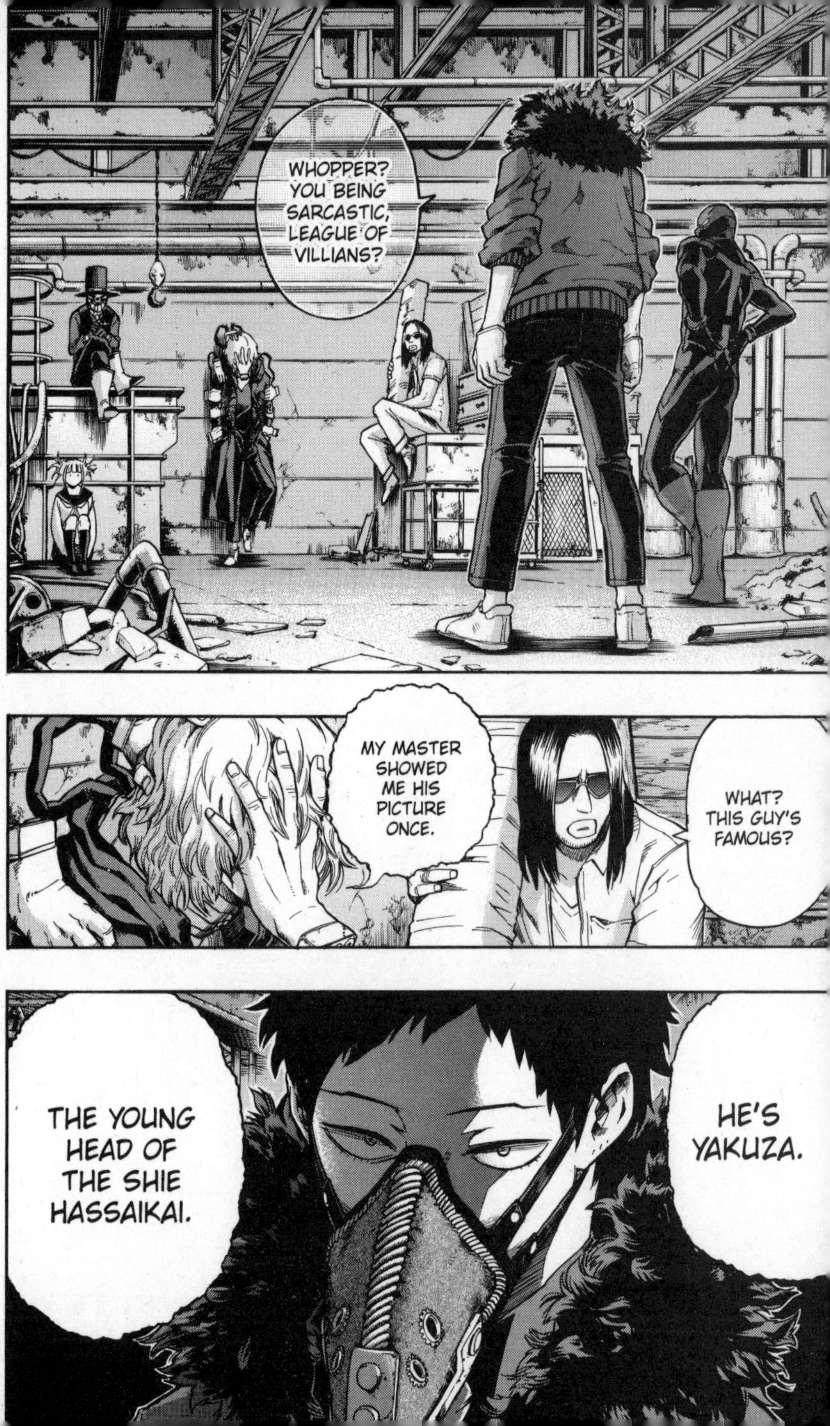
WHOPPER? YOU BEING SARCASTIC, LEAGUE OF VILLIANS?
WHAT? THIS GUY'S FAMOUS?
MY MASTER SHOWED ME HIS PICTURE ONCE.
HE'S YAKUZA.
THE YOUNG HEAD OF THE SHIE HASSAIKAI.

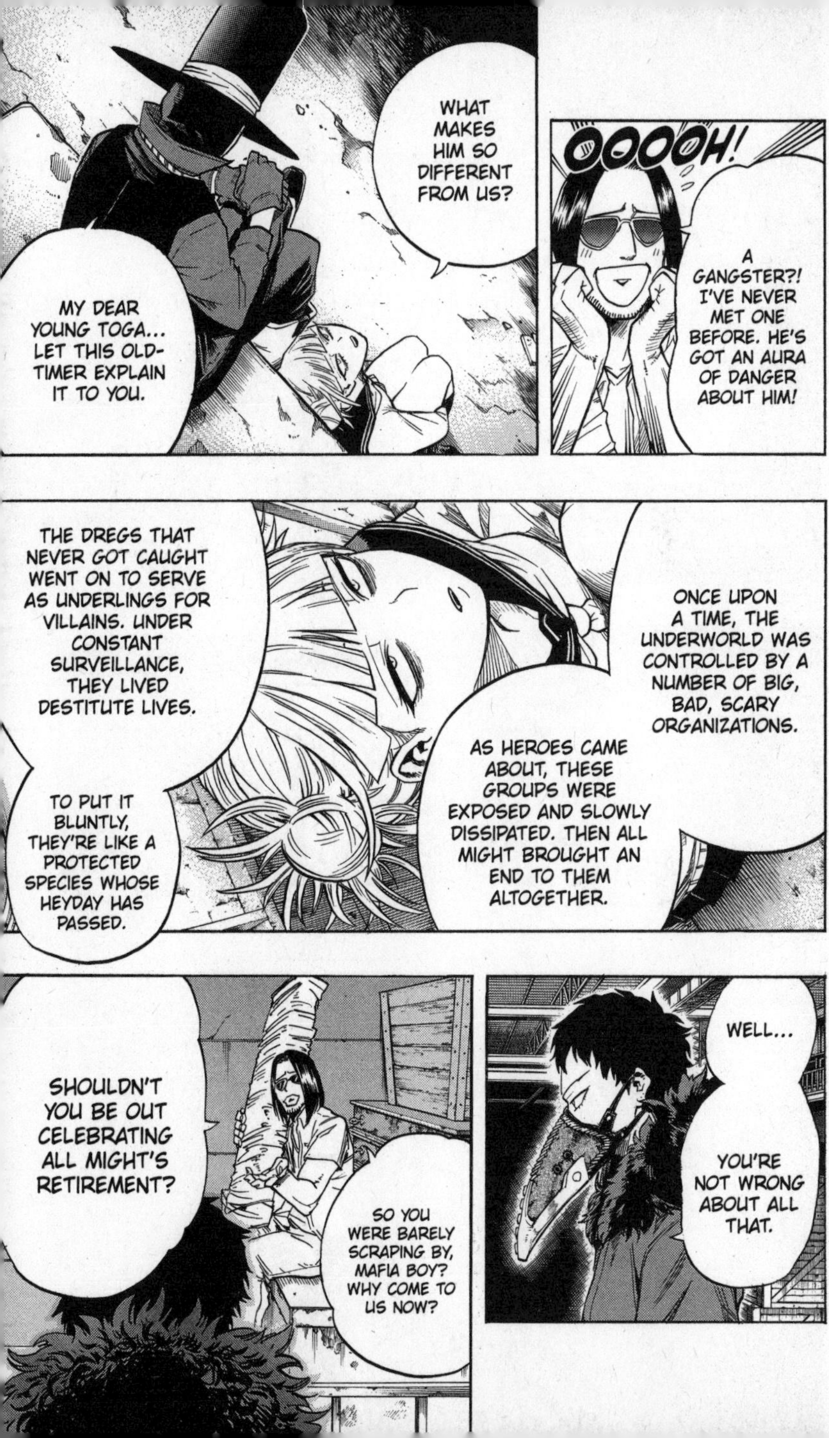
OOOOH!
A GANGSTER?! I'VE NEVER MET ONE BEFORE. HE'S GOT AN AURA OF DANGER ABOUT HIM!
WHAT MAKES HIM SO DIFFERENT FROM US?
MY DEAR YOUNG TOGA... LET THIS OLD-TIMER EXPLAIN IT TO YOU.
ONCE UPON A TIME, THE UNDERWORLD WAS CONTROLLED BY A NUMBER OF BIG, BAD, SCARY ORGANIZATIONS.
AS HEROES CAME ABOUT, THESE GROUPS WERE EXPOSED AND SLOWLY DISSIPATED. THEN ALL MIGHT BROUGHT AN END TO THEM ALTOGETHER.
THE DREGS THAT NEVER GOT CAUGHT WENT ON TO SERVE AS UNDERLINGS FOR VILLAINS. UNDER CONSTANT SURVEILLANCE, THEY LIVED DESTITUTE LIVES.
TO PUT IT BLUNTLY, THEY'RE LIKE A PROTECTED SPECIES WHOSE HEYDAY HAS PASSED.
WELL...
YOU'RE NOT WRONG ABOUT ALL THAT.
SO YOU WERE BARELY SCRAPING BY, MAFIA BOY? WHY COME TO US NOW?
SHOULDN'T YOU BE OUT CELEBRATING ALL MIGHT'S RETIREMENT?

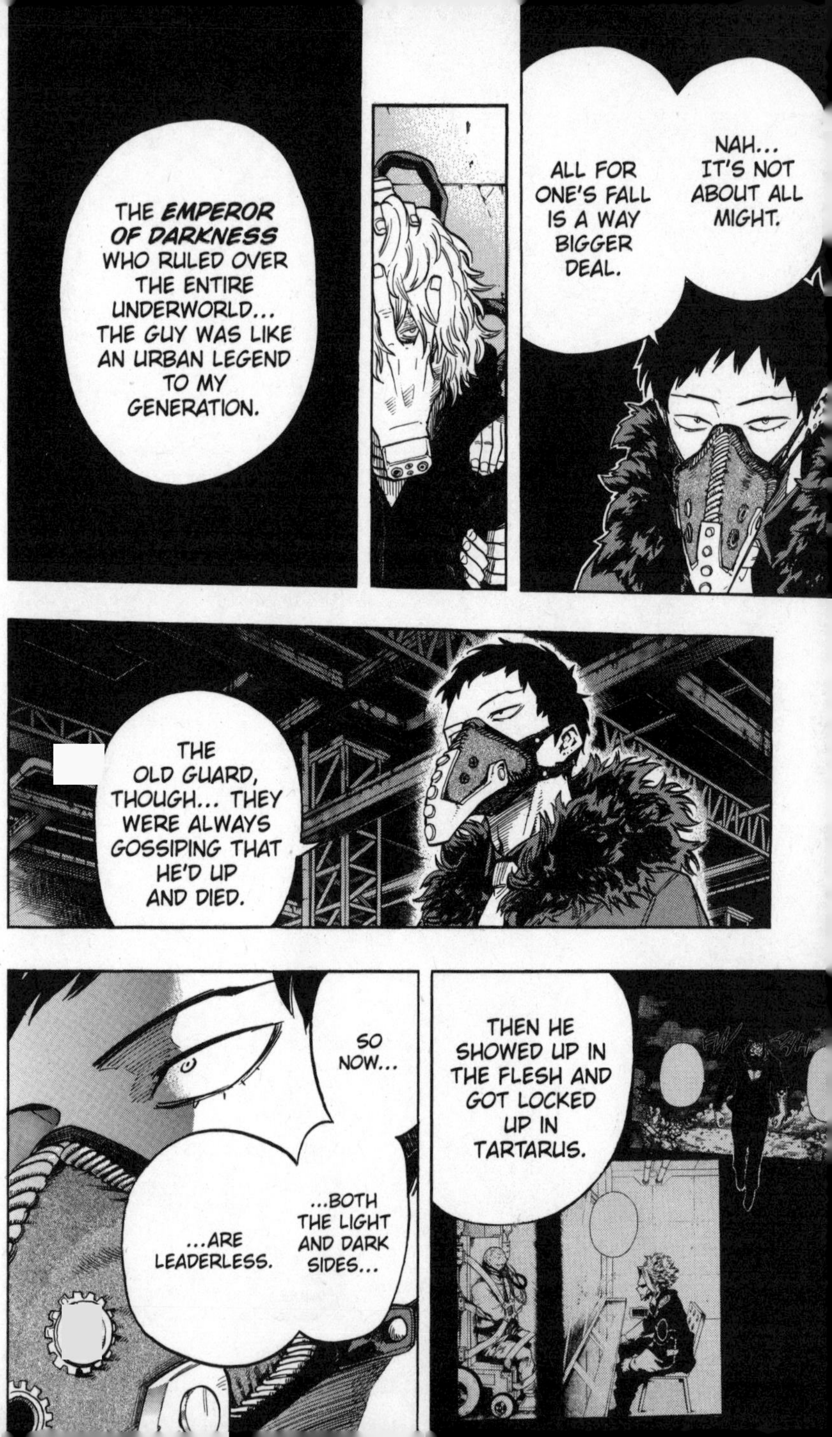
NAH... IT'S NOT ABOUT ALL MIGHT.
ALL FOR ONE'S FALL IS A WAY BIGGER DEAL.
THE *EMPEROR OF DARKNESS* WHO RULED OVER THE ENTIRE UNDERWORLD... THE GUY WAS LIKE AN URBAN LEGEND TO MY GENERATION.
THE OLD GUARD, THOUGH... THEY WERE ALWAYS GOSSIPING THAT HE'D UP AND DIED.
THEN HE SHOWED UP IN THE FLESH AND GOT LOCKED UP IN TARTARUS.
SO NOW...
...BOTH THE LIGHT AND DARK SIDES...
...ARE LEADERLESS.

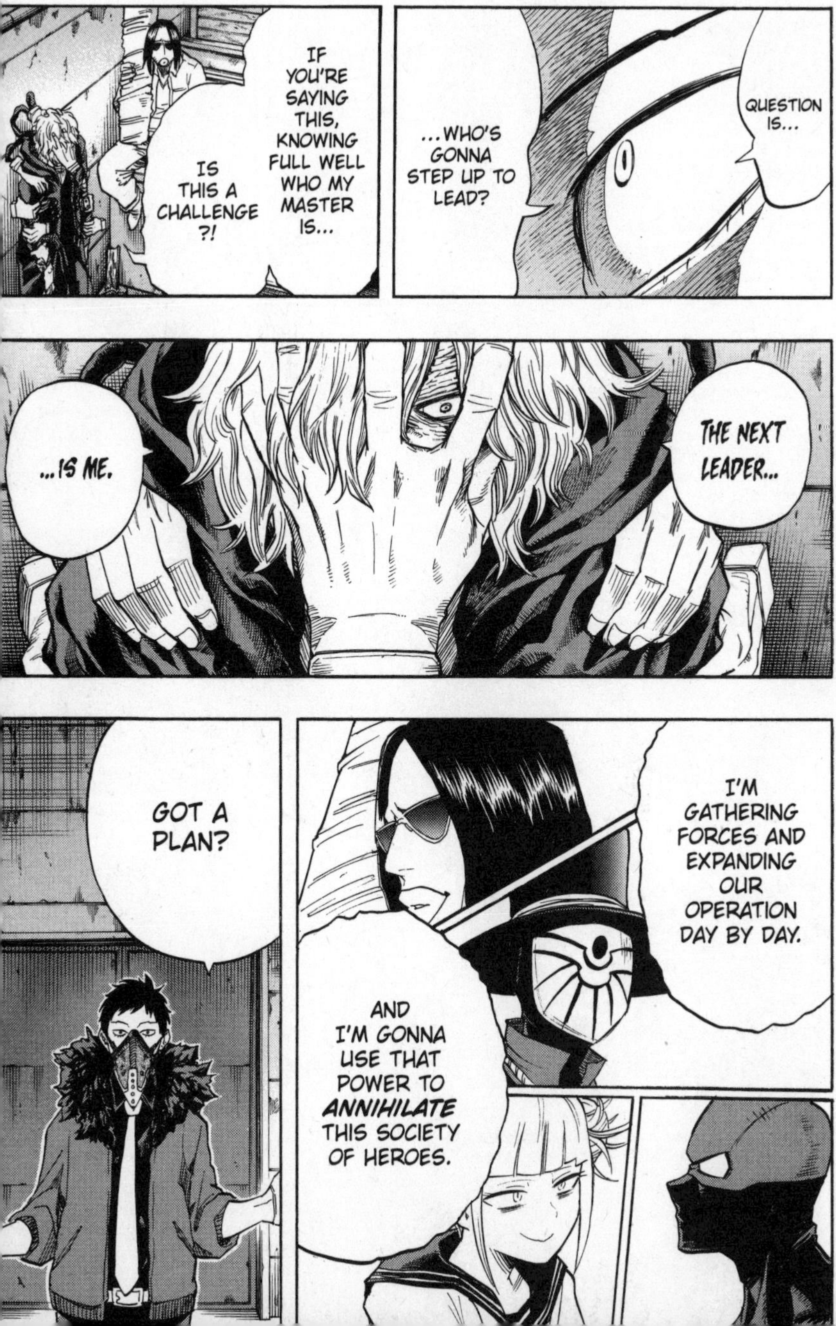
QUESTION IS...
...WHO'S GONNA STEP UP TO LEAD?
IF YOU'RE SAYING THIS, KNOWING FULL WELL WHO MY MASTER IS...
IS THIS A CHALLENGE ?!
THE NEXT LEADER...
...IS ME.
I'M GATHERING FORCES AND EXPANDING OUR OPERATION DAY BY DAY.
AND I'M GONNA USE THAT POWER TO ANNIHILATE THIS SOCIETY OF HEROES.
GOT A PLAN?

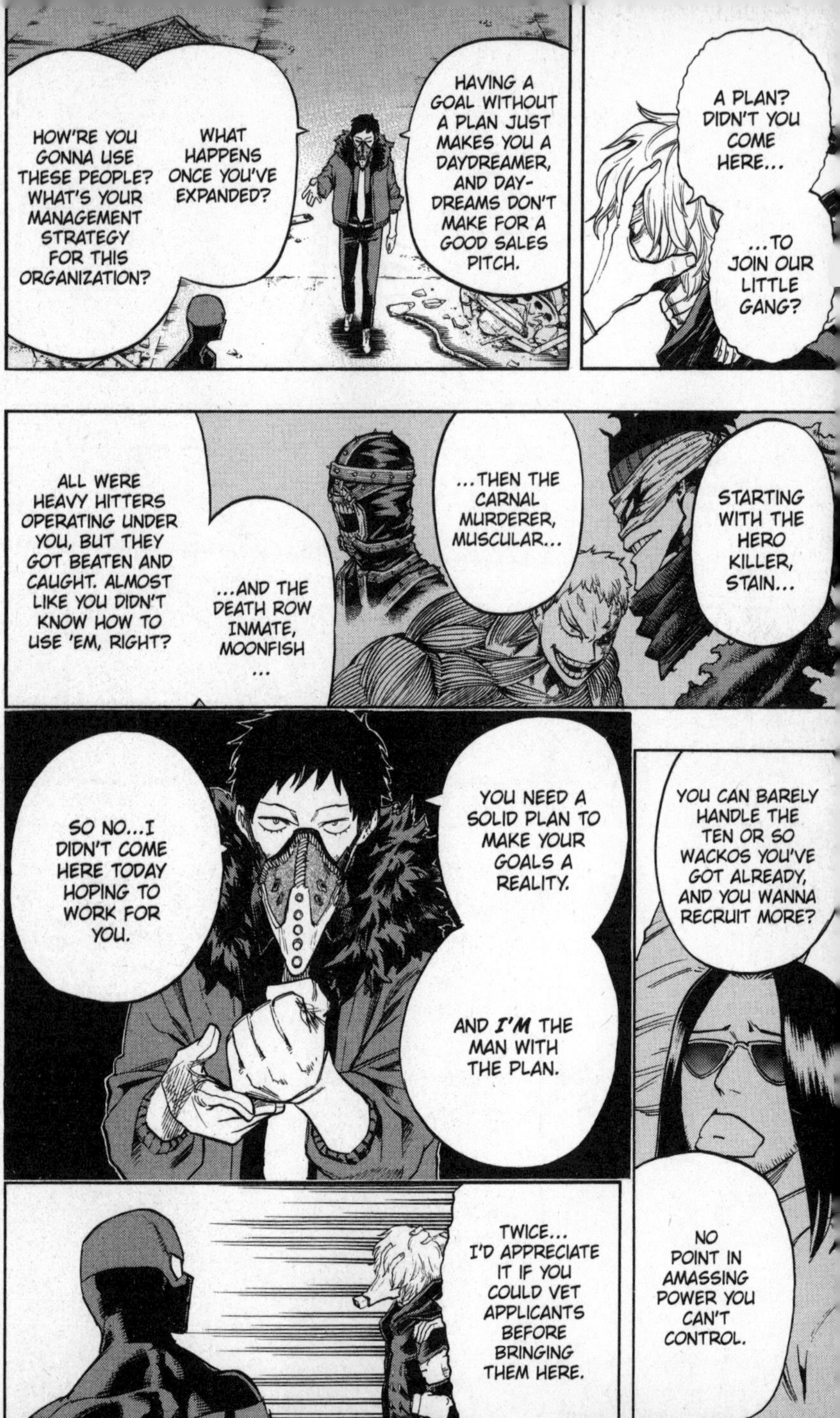
A PLAN? DIDN'T YOU COME HERE...
...TO JOIN OUR LITTLE GANG?
HAVING A GOAL WITHOUT A PLAN JUST MAKES YOU A DAYDREAMER, AND DAY-DREAMS DON'T MAKE FOR A GOOD SALES PITCH.
WHAT HAPPENS ONCE YOU'VE EXPANDED?
HOW'RE YOU GONNA USE THESE PEOPLE? WHAT'S YOUR MANAGEMENT STRATEGY FOR THIS ORGANIZATION?
STARTING WITH THE HERO KILLER, STAIN...
...THEN THE CARNAL MURDERER, MUSCULAR...
...AND THE DEATH ROW INMATE, MOONFISH ...
ALL WERE HEAVY HITTERS OPERATING UNDER YOU, BUT THEY GOT BEATEN AND CAUGHT. ALMOST LIKE YOU DIDN'T KNOW HOW TO USE 'EM, RIGHT?
YOU CAN BARELY HANDLE THE TEN OR SO WACKOS YOU'VE GOT ALREADY, AND YOU WANNA RECRUIT MORE?
NO POINT IN AMASSING POWER YOU CAN'T CONTROL.
YOU NEED A SOLID PLAN TO MAKE YOUR GOALS A REALITY.
AND *I'M* THE MAN WITH THE PLAN.
SO NO...I DIDN'T COME HERE TODAY HOPING TO WORK FOR YOU.
TWICE... I'D APPRECIATE IT IF YOU COULD VET APPLICANTS BEFORE BRINGING THEM HERE.

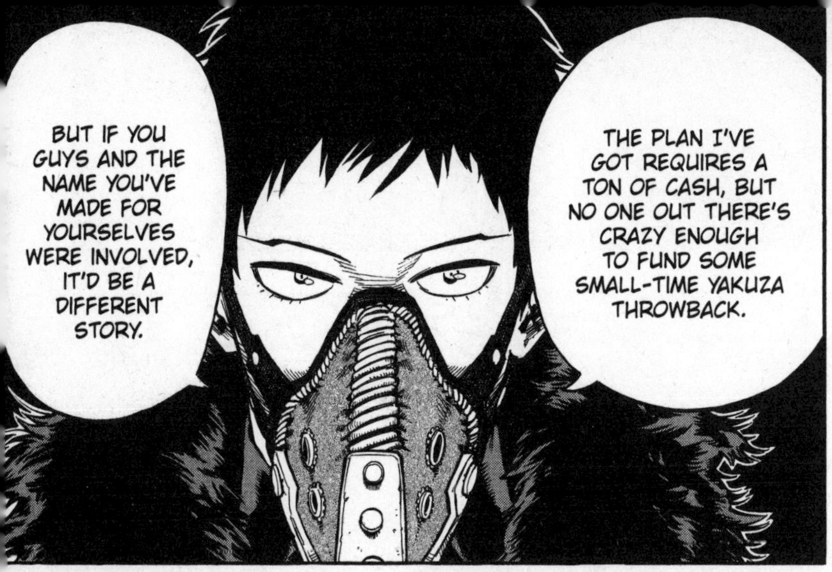
THE PLAN I'VE GOT REQUIRES A TON OF CASH, BUT NO ONE OUT THERE'S CRAZY ENOUGH TO FUND SOME SMALL-TIME YAKUZA THROWBACK.
BUT IF YOU GUYS AND THE NAME YOU'VE MADE FOR YOURSELVES WERE INVOLVED, IT'D BE A DIFFERENT STORY.
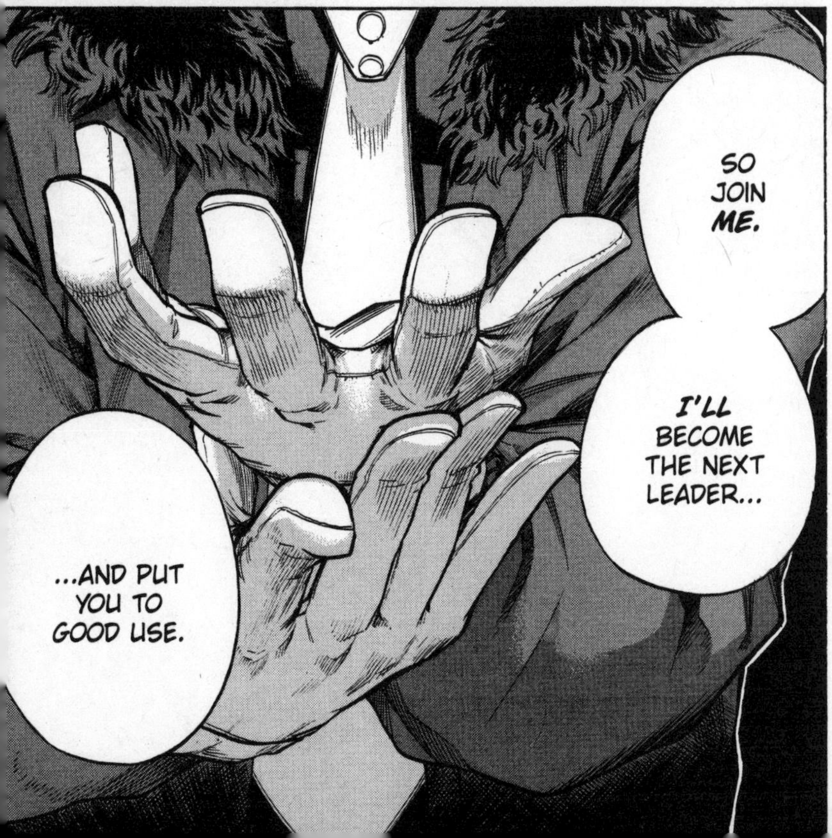
SO JOIN *ME.*
I'LL BECOME THE NEXT LEADER...
...AND PUT YOU TO GOOD USE.

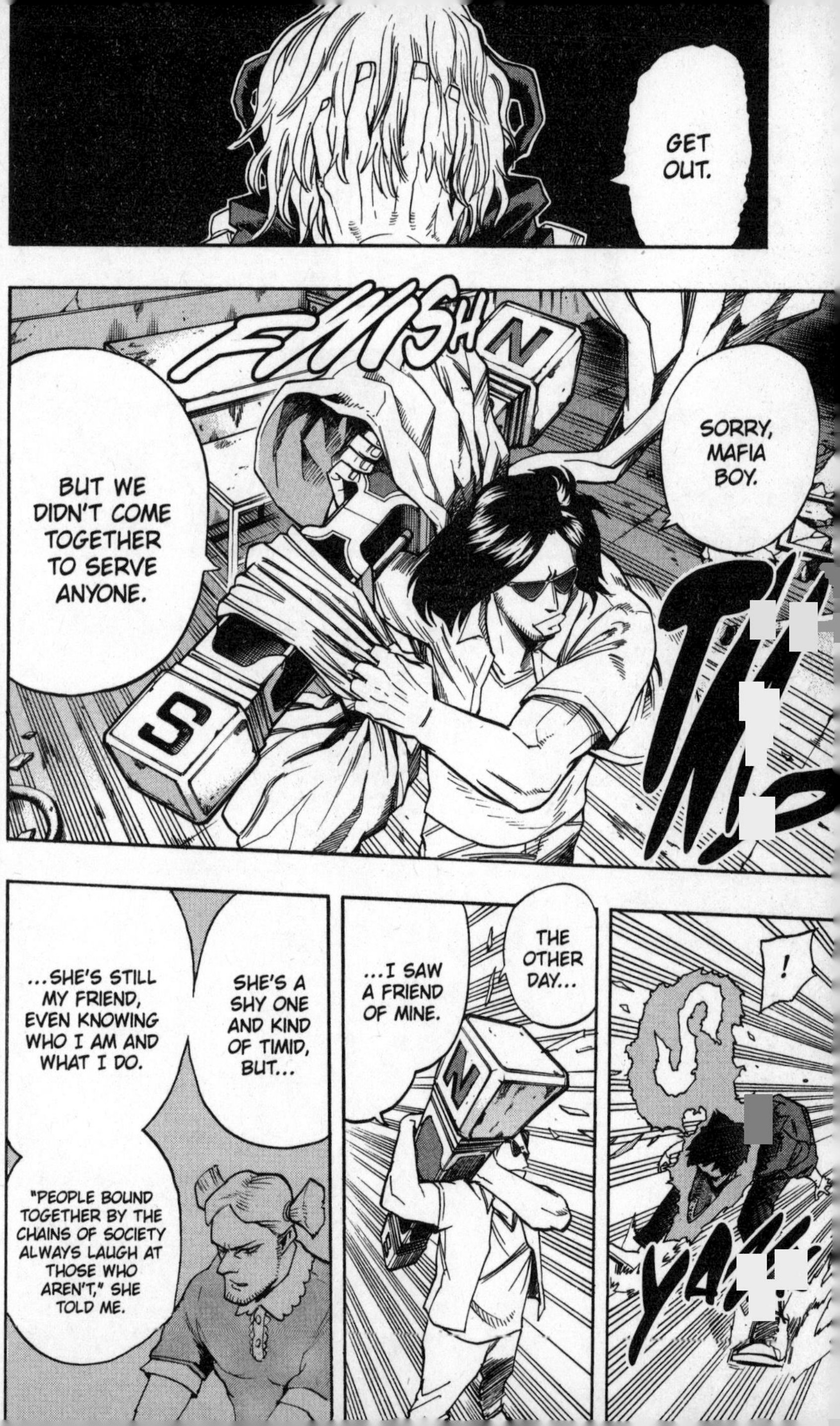
GET OUT.
SORRY, MAFIA BOY.
BUT WE DIDN'T COME TOGETHER TO SERVE ANYONE.
!
THE OTHER DAY...
...I SAW A FRIEND OF MINE.
SHE'S A SHY ONE AND KIND OF TIMID, BUT...
...SHE'S STILL MY FRIEND, EVEN KNOWING WHO I AM AND WHAT I DO.
"PEOPLE BOUND TOGETHER BY THE CHAINS OF SOCIETY ALWAYS LAUGH AT THOSE WHO AREN'T," SHE TOLD ME.

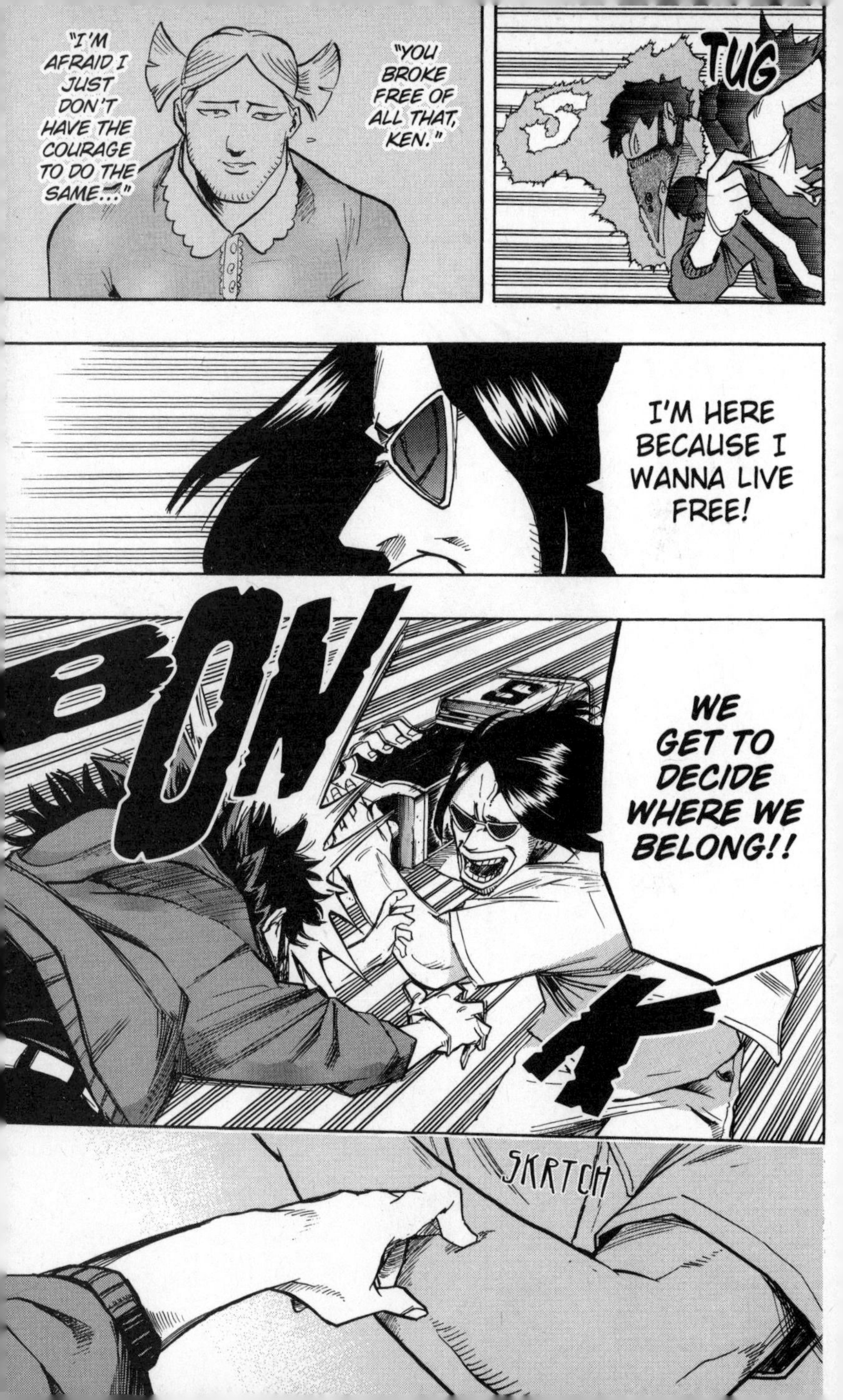

TUG
"YOU BROKE FREE OF ALL THAT, KEN."
"I'M AFRAID I JUST DON'T HAVE THE COURAGE TO DO THE SAME..."
I'M HERE BECAUSE I WANNA LIVE FREE!
WE GET TO DECIDE WHERE WE BELONG!!
BONK
SKRTCH

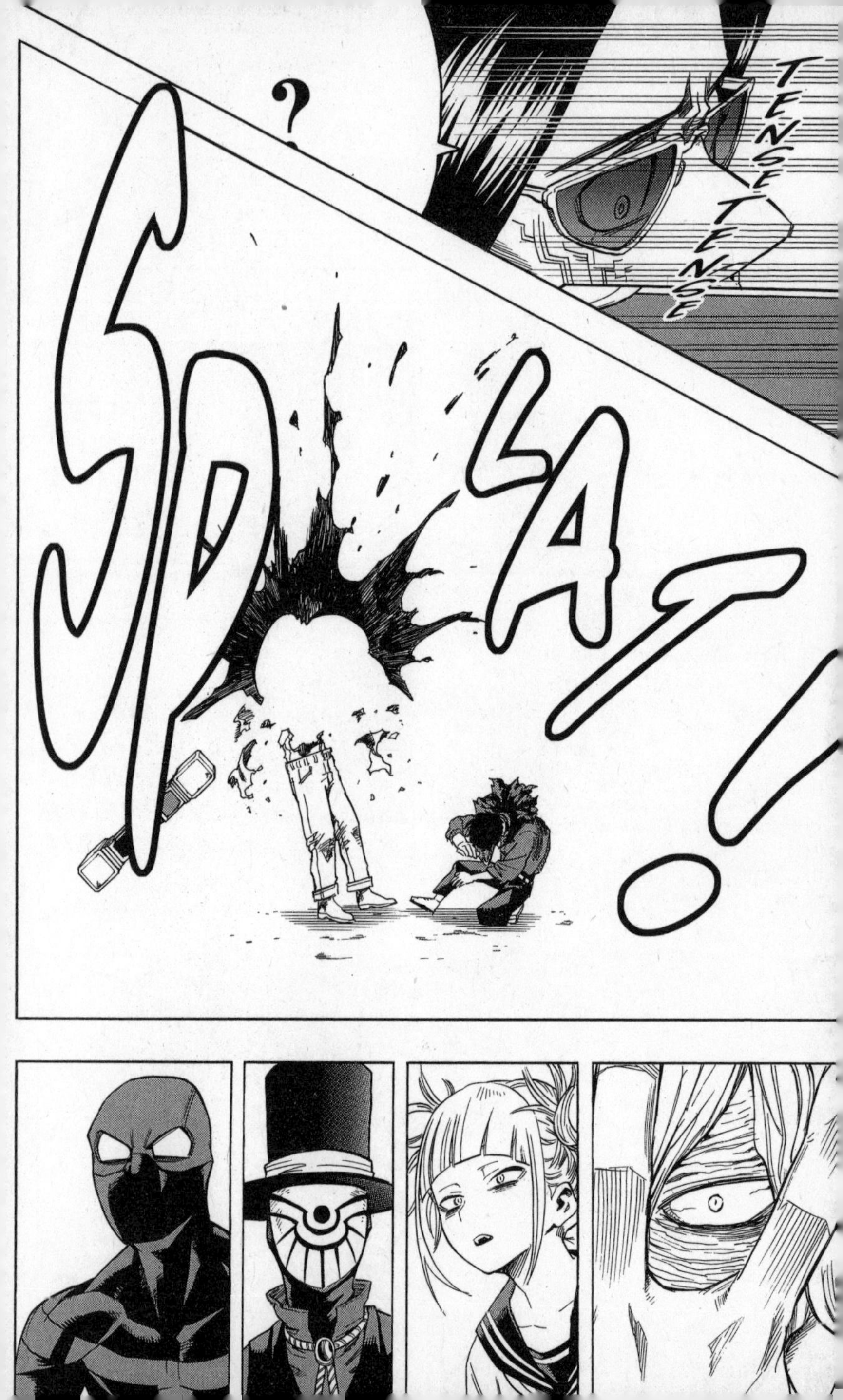
TENSE TENSE TENSE
?
SPLAT!

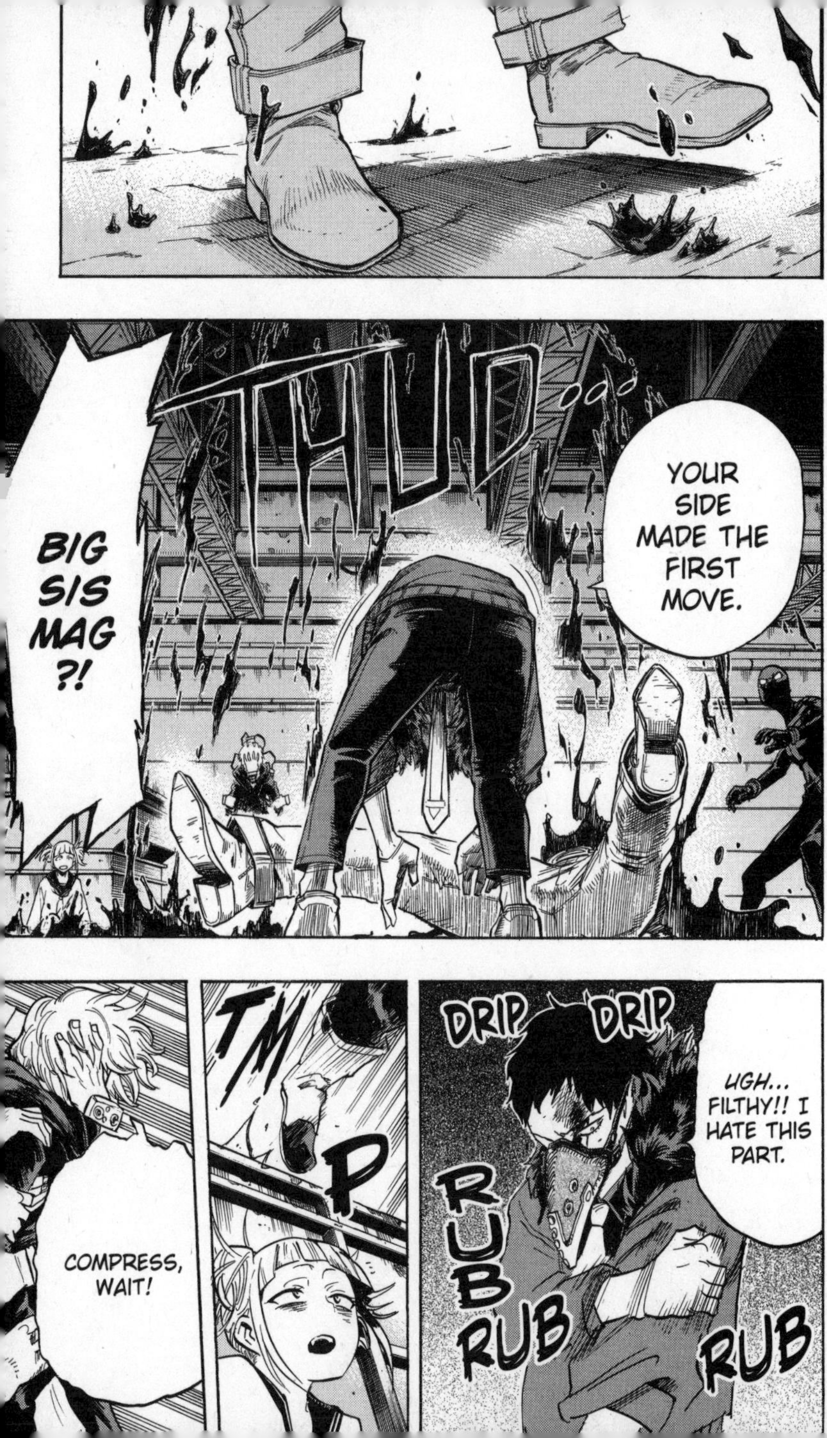
YOUR SIDE MADE THE FIRST MOVE.
THUD
BIG SIS MAG?!
DRIP DRIP
UGH... FILTHY!! I HATE THIS PART.
RUB RUB
RUB RUB
TMP
COMPRESS, WAIT!

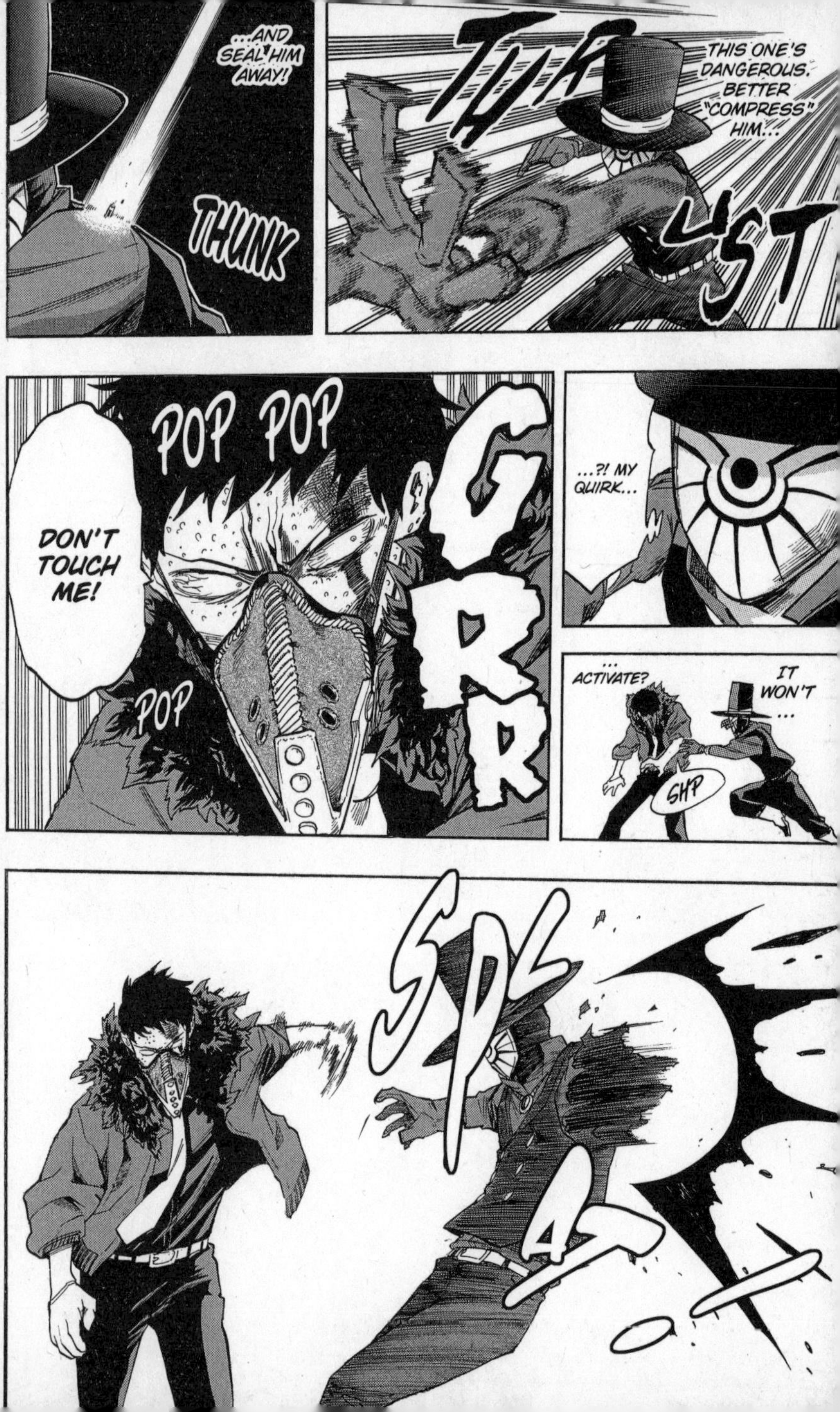
THIS ONE'S DANGEROUS. BETTER "COMPRESS" HIM...
...AND SEAL HIM AWAY!
THUNK
...?! MY QUIRK...
IT WON'T ...
... ACTIVATE?
SHP
GRR
POP POP
POP
DON'T TOUCH ME!

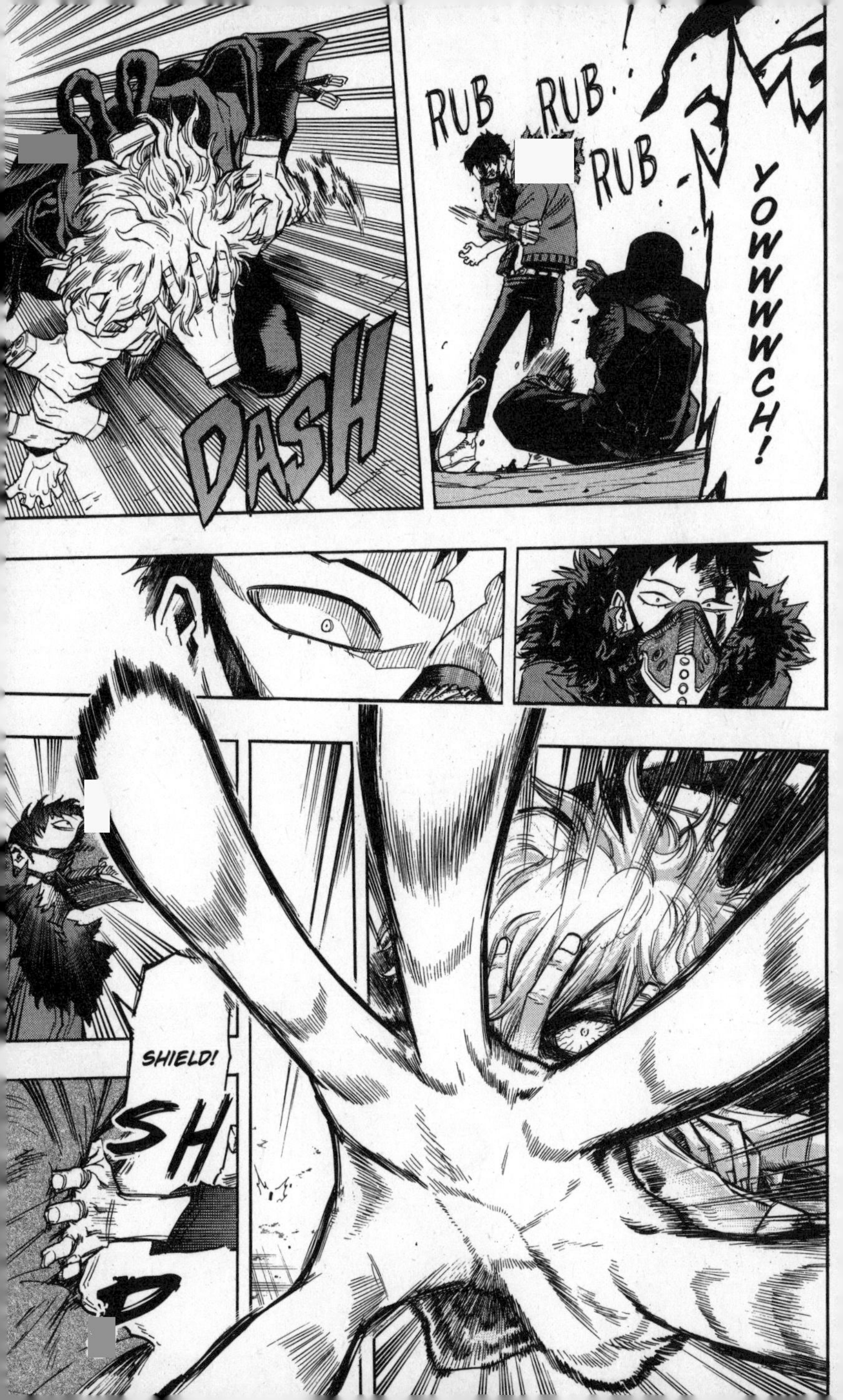
RUB RUB RUB
YOWWWWCH!
DASH
SHIELD!
SH

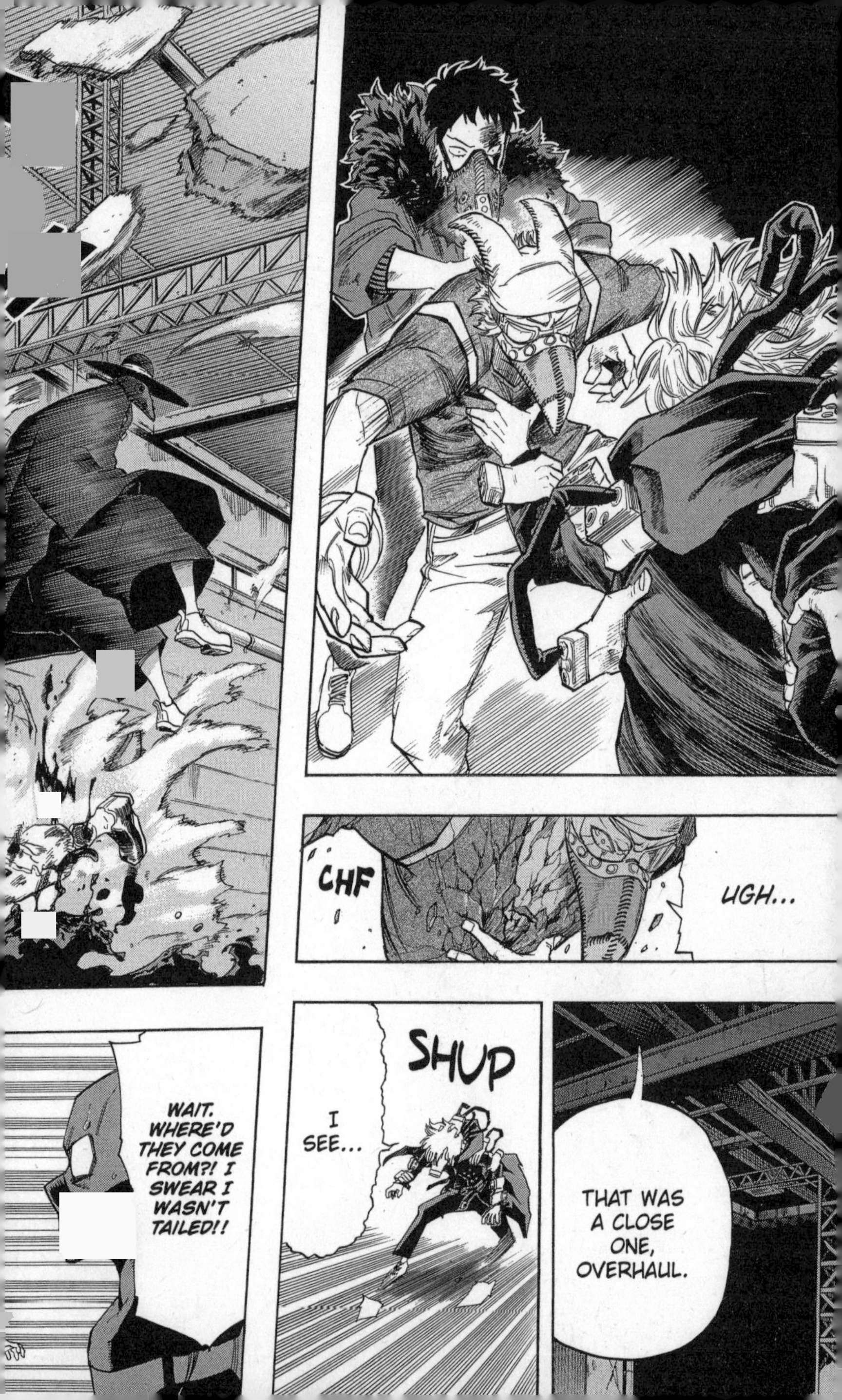

UGH...
CHF
THAT WAS A CLOSE ONE, OVERHAUL.
SHUP
I SEE...
WAIT. WHERE'D THEY COME FROM?! I SWEAR I WASN'T TAILED!!

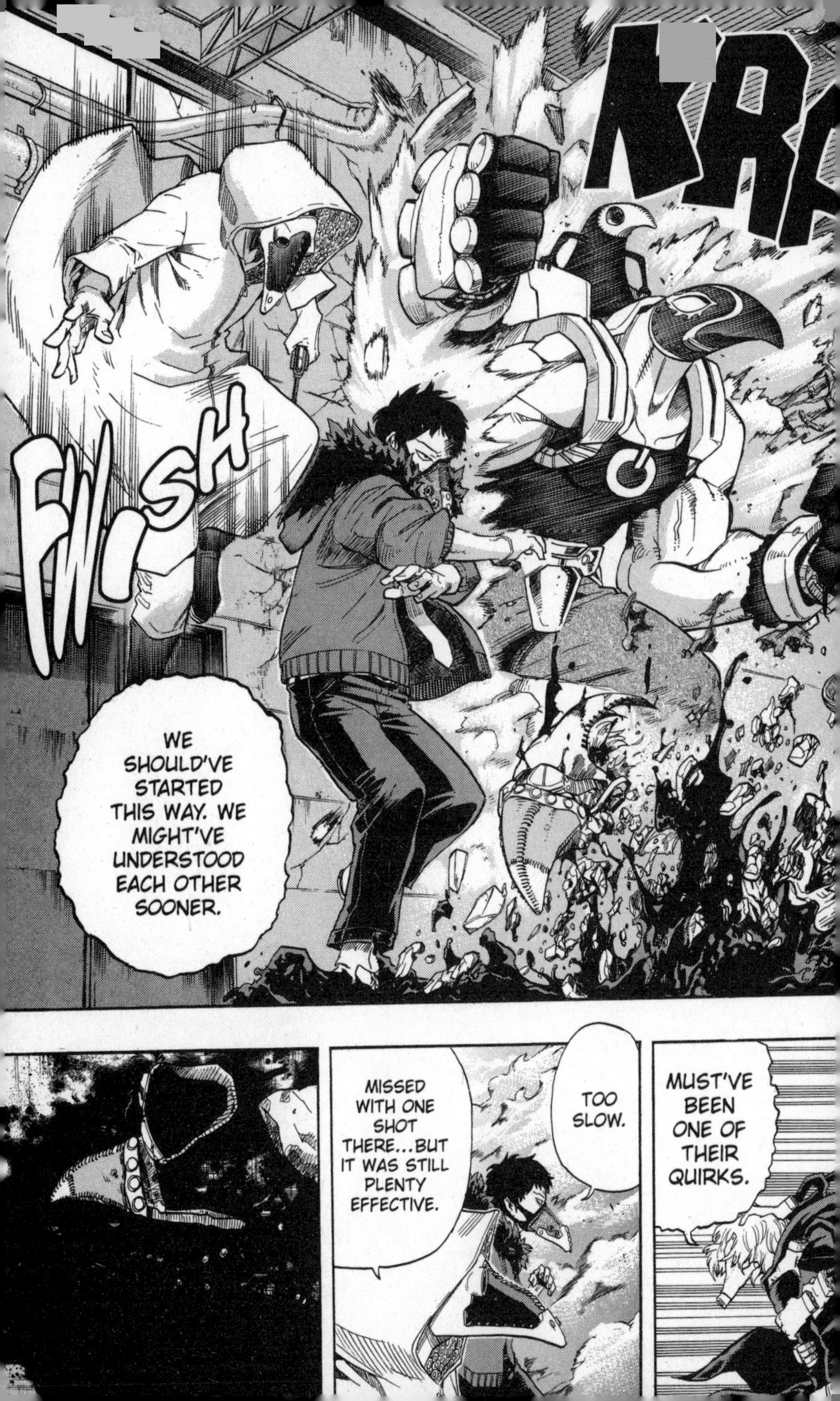
KRA
FWISH
WE SHOULD'VE STARTED THIS WAY. WE MIGHT'VE UNDERSTOOD EACH OTHER SOONER.
MUST'VE BEEN ONE OF THEIR QUIRKS.
TOO SLOW.
MISSED WITH ONE SHOT THERE...BUT IT WAS STILL PLENTY EFFECTIVE.

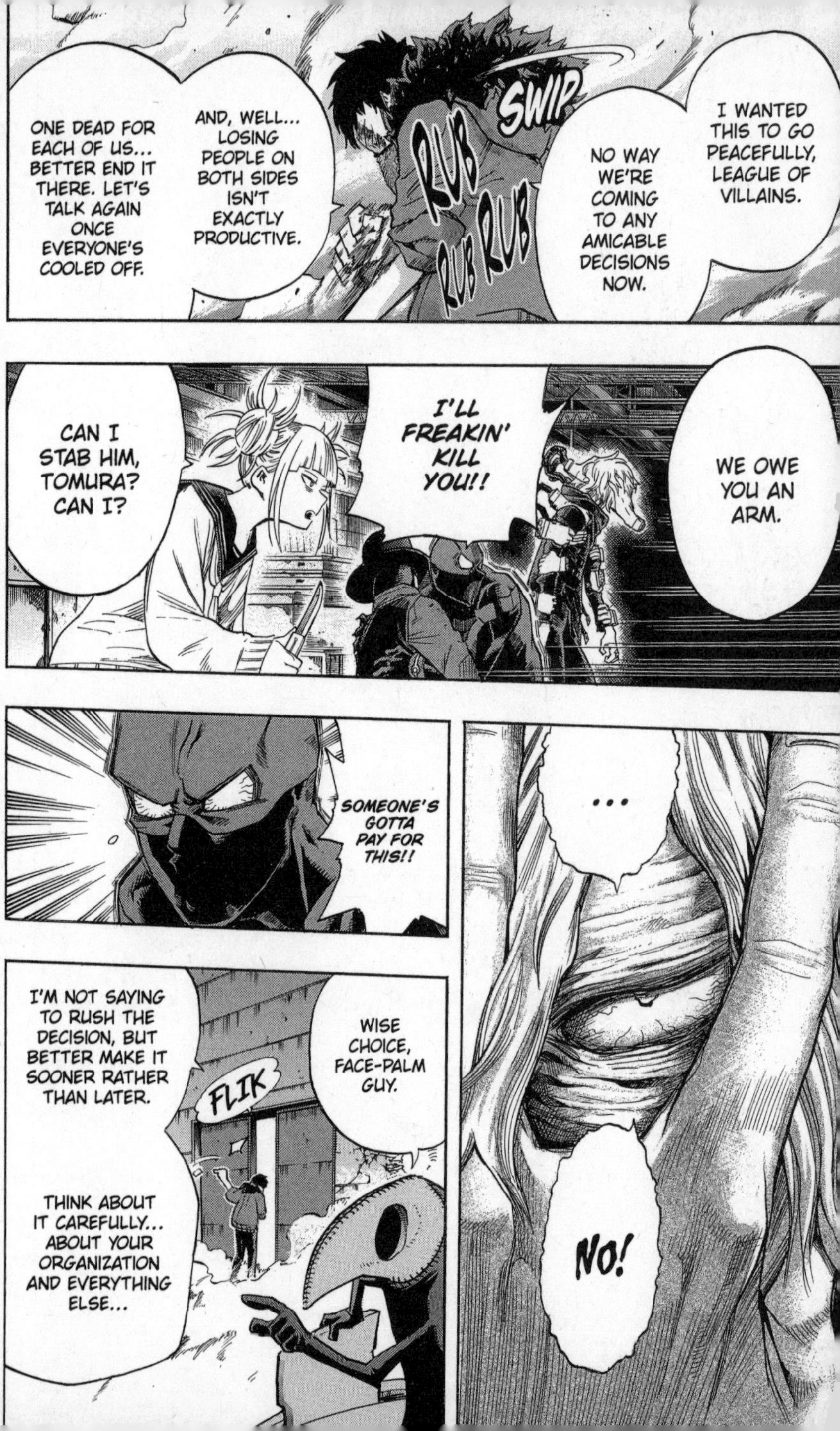
I WANTED THIS TO GO PEACEFULLY, LEAGUE OF VILLAINS.
NO WAY WE'RE COMING TO ANY AMICABLE DECISIONS NOW.
SWIP
RUB RUB RUB
AND, WELL... LOSING PEOPLE ON BOTH SIDES ISN'T EXACTLY PRODUCTIVE.
ONE DEAD FOR EACH OF US... BETTER END IT THERE. LET'S TALK AGAIN ONCE EVERYONE'S COOLED OFF.
WE OWE YOU AN ARM.
I'LL FREAKIN' KILL YOU!!
CAN I STAB HIM, TOMURA? CAN I?
...
NO!
SOMEONE'S GOTTA PAY FOR THIS!!
WISE CHOICE, FACE-PALM GUY.
FLIK
I'M NOT SAYING TO RUSH THE DECISION, BUT BETTER MAKE IT SOONER RATHER THAN LATER.
THINK ABOUT IT CAREFULLY... ABOUT YOUR ORGANIZATION AND EVERYTHING ELSE...

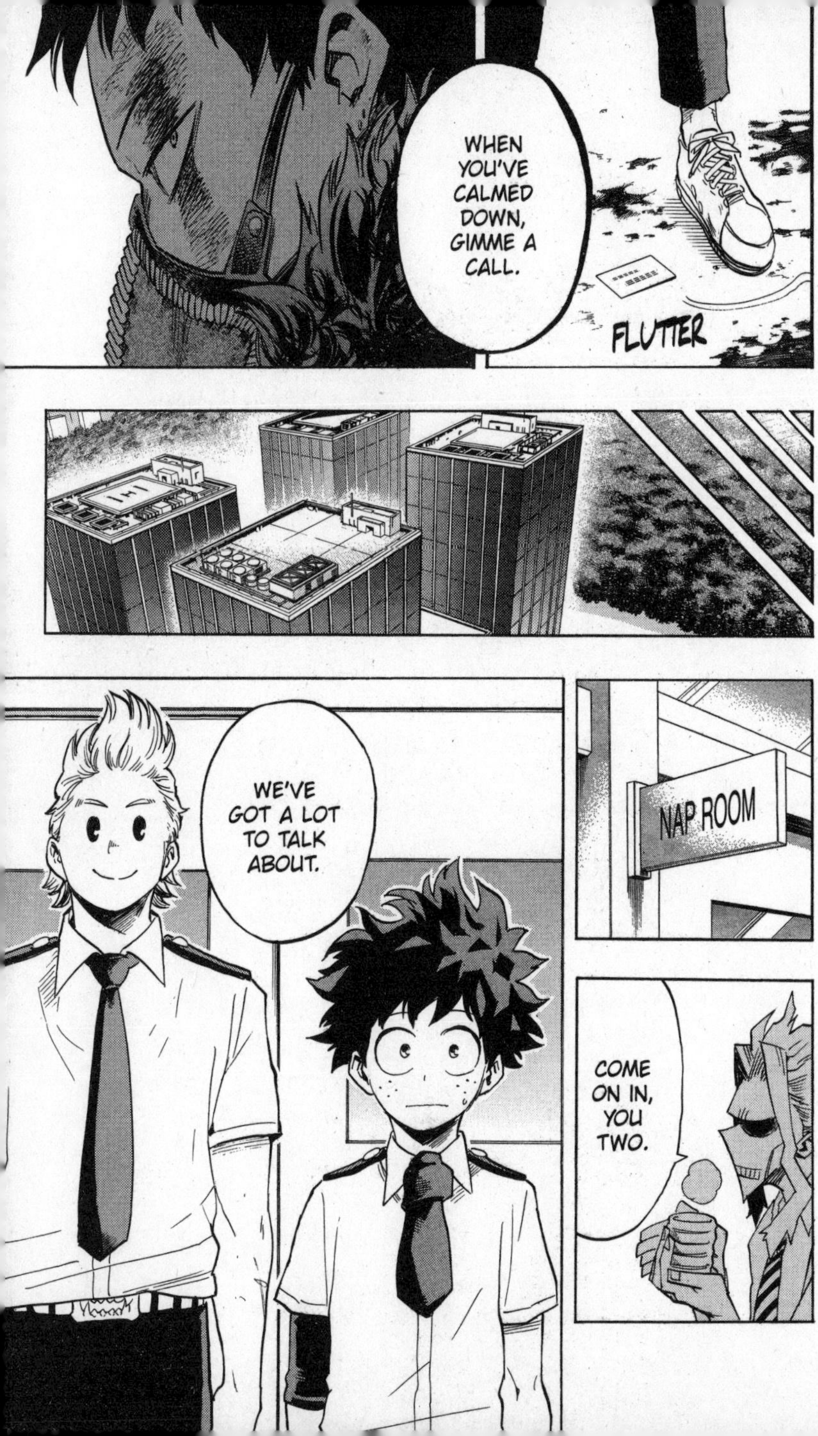
FLUTTER
WHEN YOU'VE CALMED DOWN, GIMME A CALL.
NAP ROOM
COME ON IN, YOU TWO.
WE'VE GOT A LOT TO TALK ABOUT.

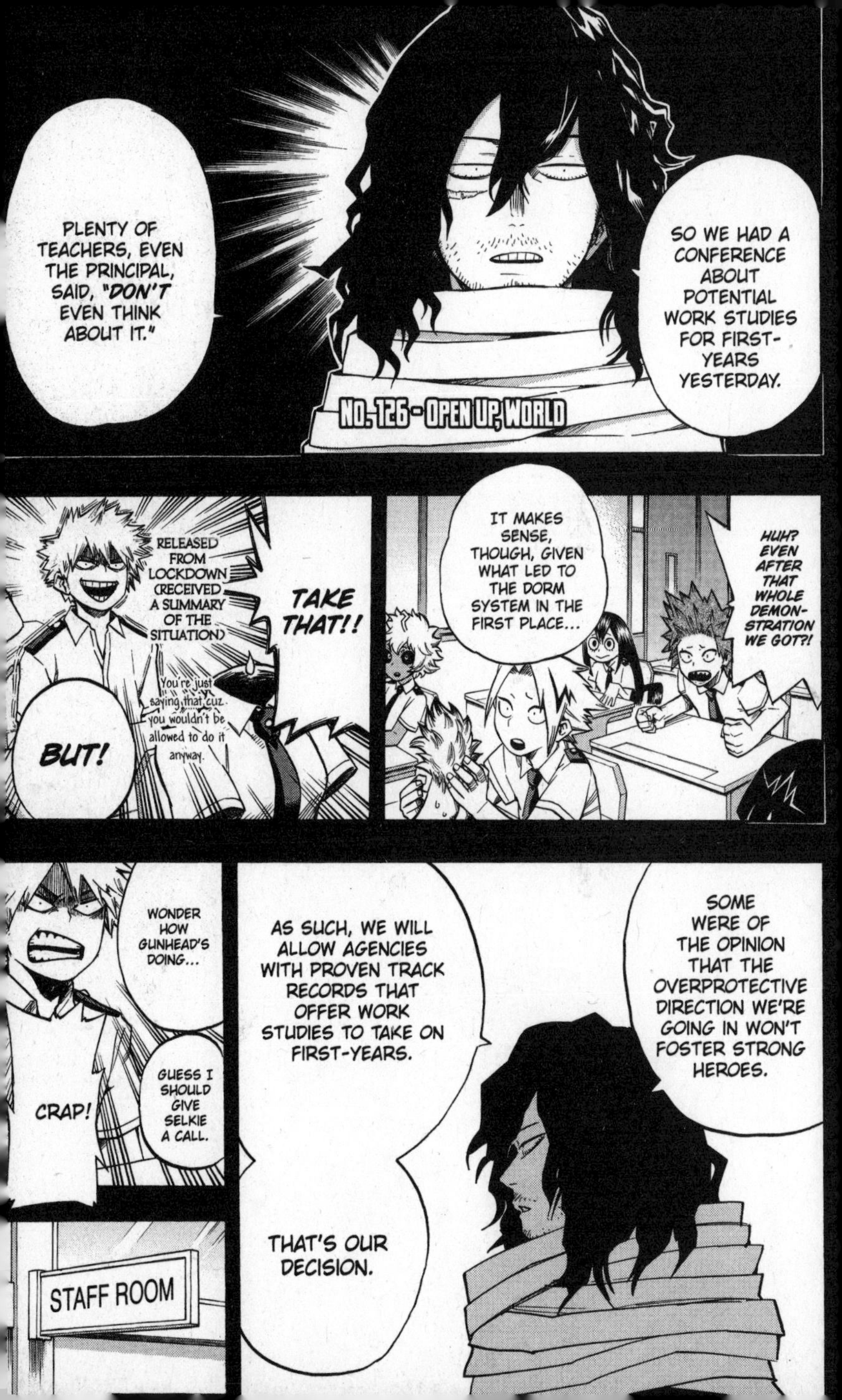

SO WE HAD A CONFERENCE ABOUT POTENTIAL WORK STUDIES FOR FIRST-YEARS YESTERDAY.
No. 126 - Open Up, World
PLENTY OF TEACHERS, EVEN THE PRINCIPAL, SAID, "DON'T EVEN THINK ABOUT IT."
HUH? EVEN AFTER THAT WHOLE DEMON-STRATION WE GOT?!
IT MAKES SENSE, THOUGH, GIVEN WHAT LED TO THE DORM SYSTEM IN THE FIRST PLACE...
TAKE THAT!!
RELEASED FROM LOCKDOWN (RECEIVED A SUMMARY OF THE SITUATION)
You're just saying that cuz you wouldn't be allowed to do it anyway.
BUT!
SOME WERE OF THE OPINION THAT THE OVERPROTECTIVE DIRECTION WE'RE GOING IN WON'T FOSTER STRONG HEROES.
AS SUCH, WE WILL ALLOW AGENCIES WITH PROVEN TRACK RECORDS THAT OFFER WORK STUDIES TO TAKE ON FIRST-YEARS.
THAT'S OUR DECISION.
WONDER HOW GUNHEAD'S DOING...
GUESS I SHOULD GIVE SELKIE A CALL.
CRAP!
STAFF ROOM

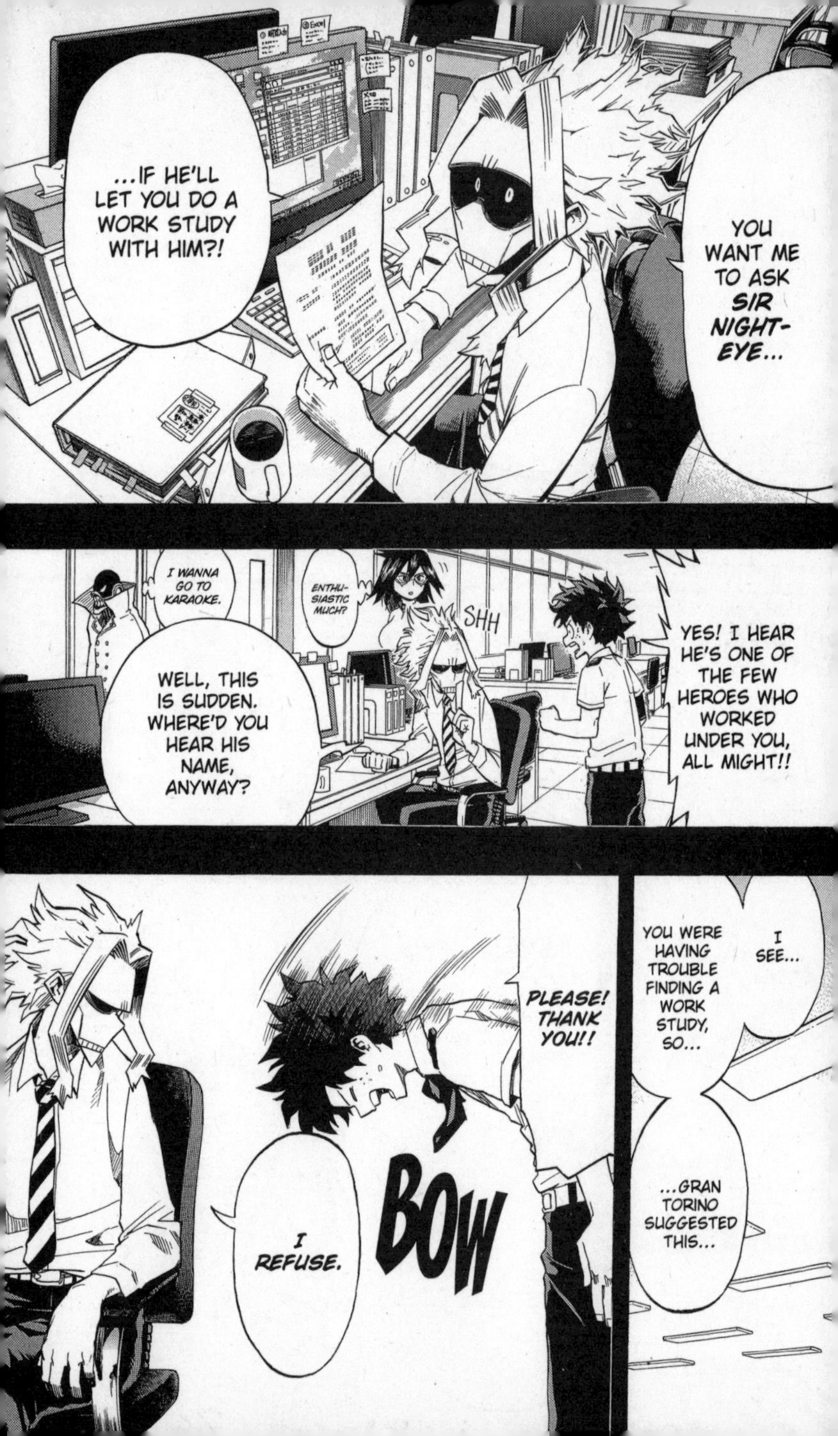
YOU WANT ME TO ASK SIR NIGHT-EYE...
...IF HE'LL LET YOU DO A WORK STUDY WITH HIM?!
YES! I HEAR HE'S ONE OF THE FEW HEROES WHO WORKED UNDER YOU, ALL MIGHT!!
SHH
ENTHUSIASTIC MUCH?
I WANNA GO TO KARAOKE.
WELL, THIS IS SUDDEN. WHERE'D YOU HEAR HIS NAME, ANYWAY?
I SEE...
YOU WERE HAVING TROUBLE FINDING A WORK STUDY, SO...
...GRAN TORINO SUGGESTED THIS...
PLEASE! THANK YOU!!
BOW
I REFUSE.

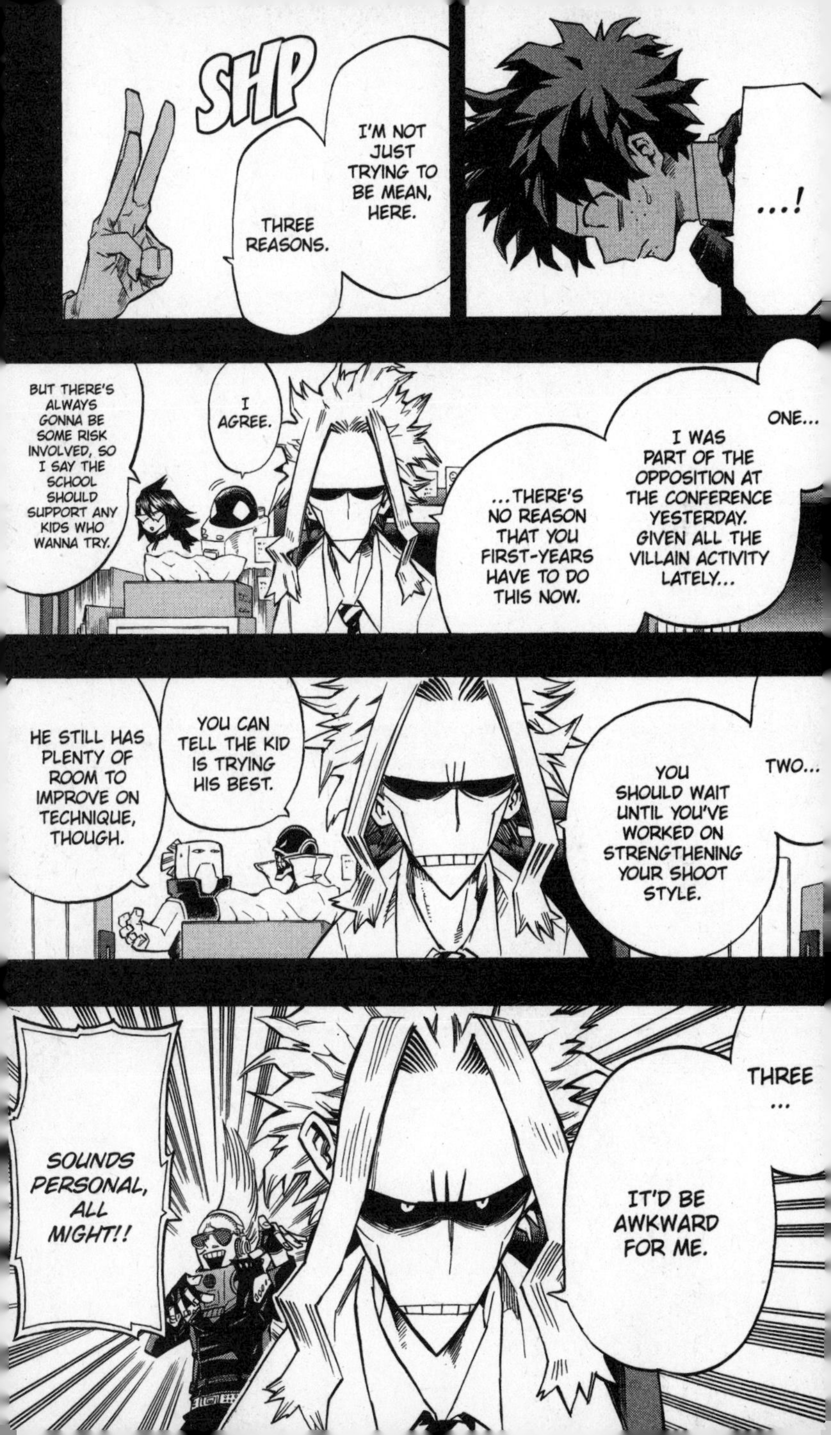
...!
I'M NOT JUST TRYING TO BE MEAN, HERE.
THREE REASONS.
SHP
ONE...
I WAS PART OF THE OPPOSITION AT THE CONFERENCE YESTERDAY. GIVEN ALL THE VILLAIN ACTIVITY LATELY...
...THERE'S NO REASON THAT YOU FIRST-YEARS HAVE TO DO THIS NOW.
I AGREE.
BUT THERE'S ALWAYS GONNA BE SOME RISK INVOLVED, SO I SAY THE SCHOOL SHOULD SUPPORT ANY KIDS WHO WANNA TRY.
TWO...
YOU SHOULD WAIT UNTIL YOU'VE WORKED ON STRENGTHENING YOUR SHOOT STYLE.
YOU CAN TELL THE KID IS TRYING HIS BEST.
HE STILL HAS PLENTY OF ROOM TO IMPROVE ON TECHNIQUE, THOUGH.
THREE ...
IT'D BE AWKWARD FOR ME.
SOUNDS PERSONAL, ALL MIGHT!!

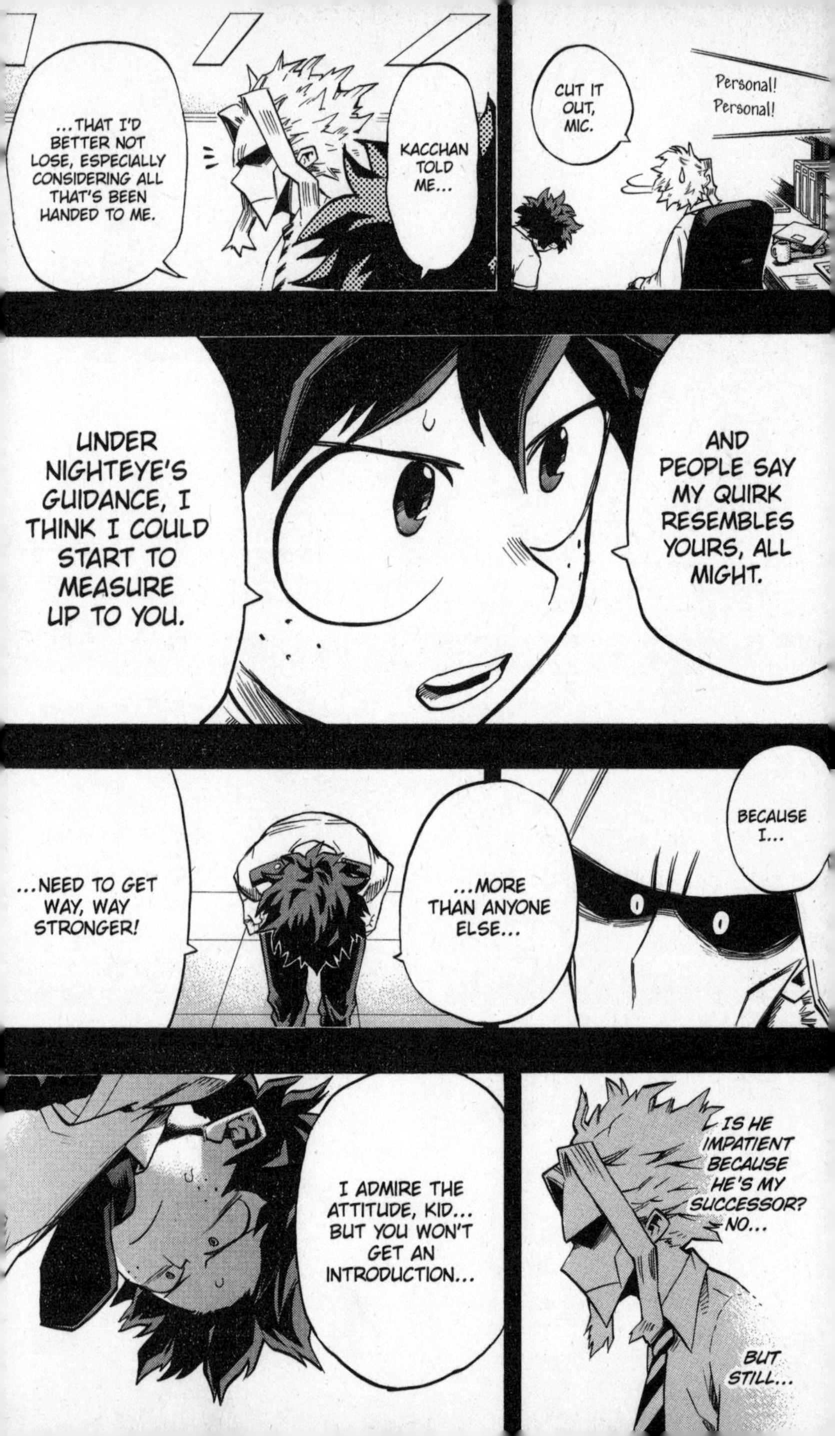
Personal! Personal!
CUT IT OUT, MIC.
KACCHAN TOLD ME...
...THAT I'D BETTER NOT LOSE, ESPECIALLY CONSIDERING ALL THAT'S BEEN HANDED TO ME.
AND PEOPLE SAY MY QUIRK RESEMBLES YOURS, ALL MIGHT.
UNDER NIGHTEYE'S GUIDANCE, I THINK I COULD START TO MEASURE UP TO YOU.
BECAUSE I...
...MORE THAN ANYONE ELSE...
...NEED TO GET WAY, WAY STRONGER!
IS HE IMPATIENT BECAUSE HE'S MY SUCCESSOR? NO...
BUT STILL...
I ADMIRE THE ATTITUDE, KID... BUT YOU WON'T GET AN INTRODUCTION...

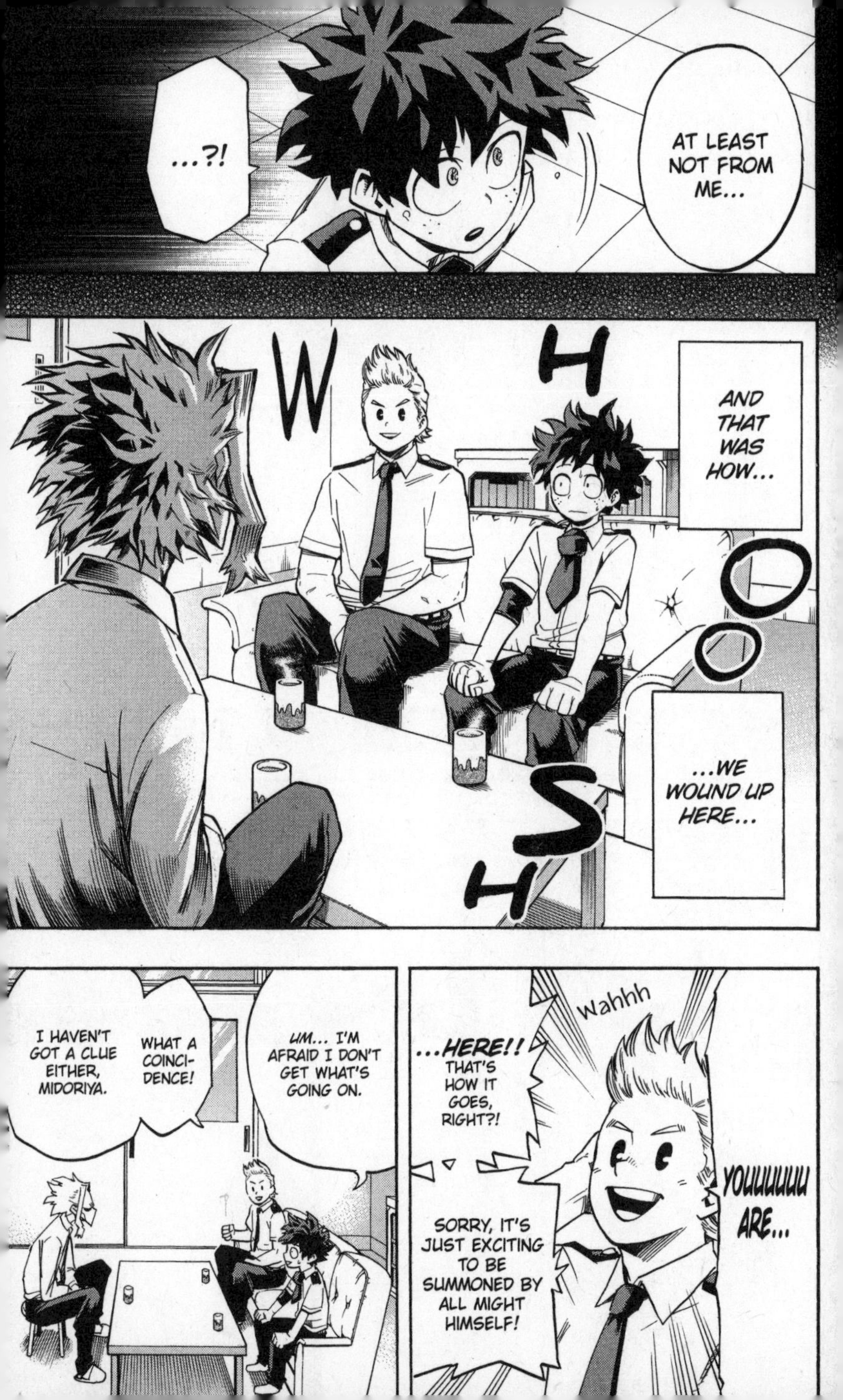
AT LEAST NOT FROM ME...
...?!
AND THAT WAS HOW...
W H O O S H
...WE WOUND UP HERE...
YOUUUUUU ARE...
Wahhh
...HERE!! THAT'S HOW IT GOES, RIGHT?!
SORRY, IT'S JUST EXCITING TO BE SUMMONED BY ALL MIGHT HIMSELF!
UM... I'M AFRAID I DON'T GET WHAT'S GOING ON.
WHAT A COINCI-DENCE!
I HAVEN'T GOT A CLUE EITHER, MIDORIYA.

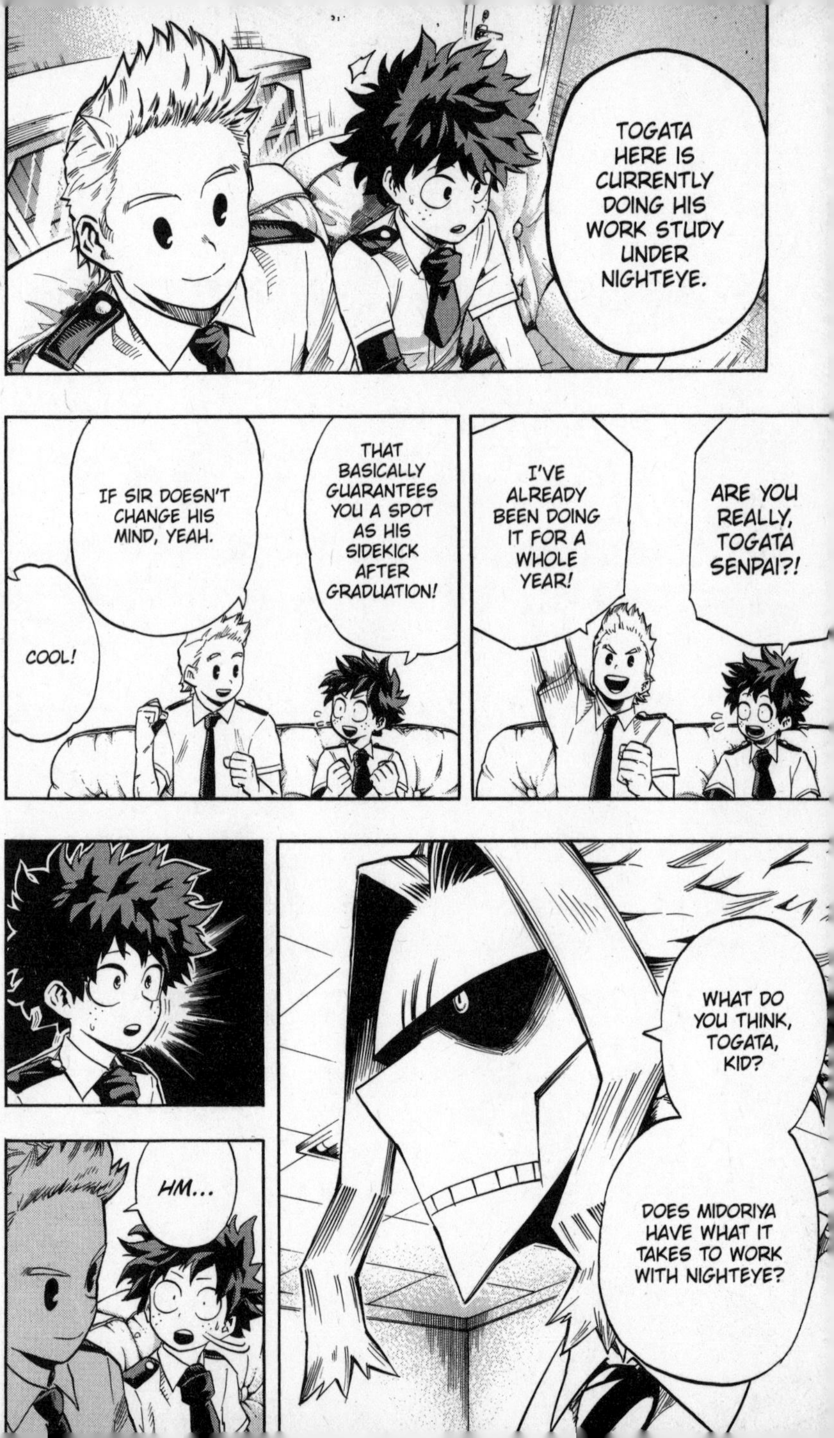
TOGATA HERE IS CURRENTLY DOING HIS WORK STUDY UNDER NIGHTEYE.
ARE YOU REALLY, TOGATA SENPAI?!
I'VE ALREADY BEEN DOING IT FOR A WHOLE YEAR!
THAT BASICALLY GUARANTEES YOU A SPOT AS HIS SIDEKICK AFTER GRADUATION!
IF SIR DOESN'T CHANGE HIS MIND, YEAH.
COOL!
WHAT DO YOU THINK, TOGATA, KID?
DOES MIDORIYA HAVE WHAT IT TAKES TO WORK WITH NIGHTEYE?
HM...

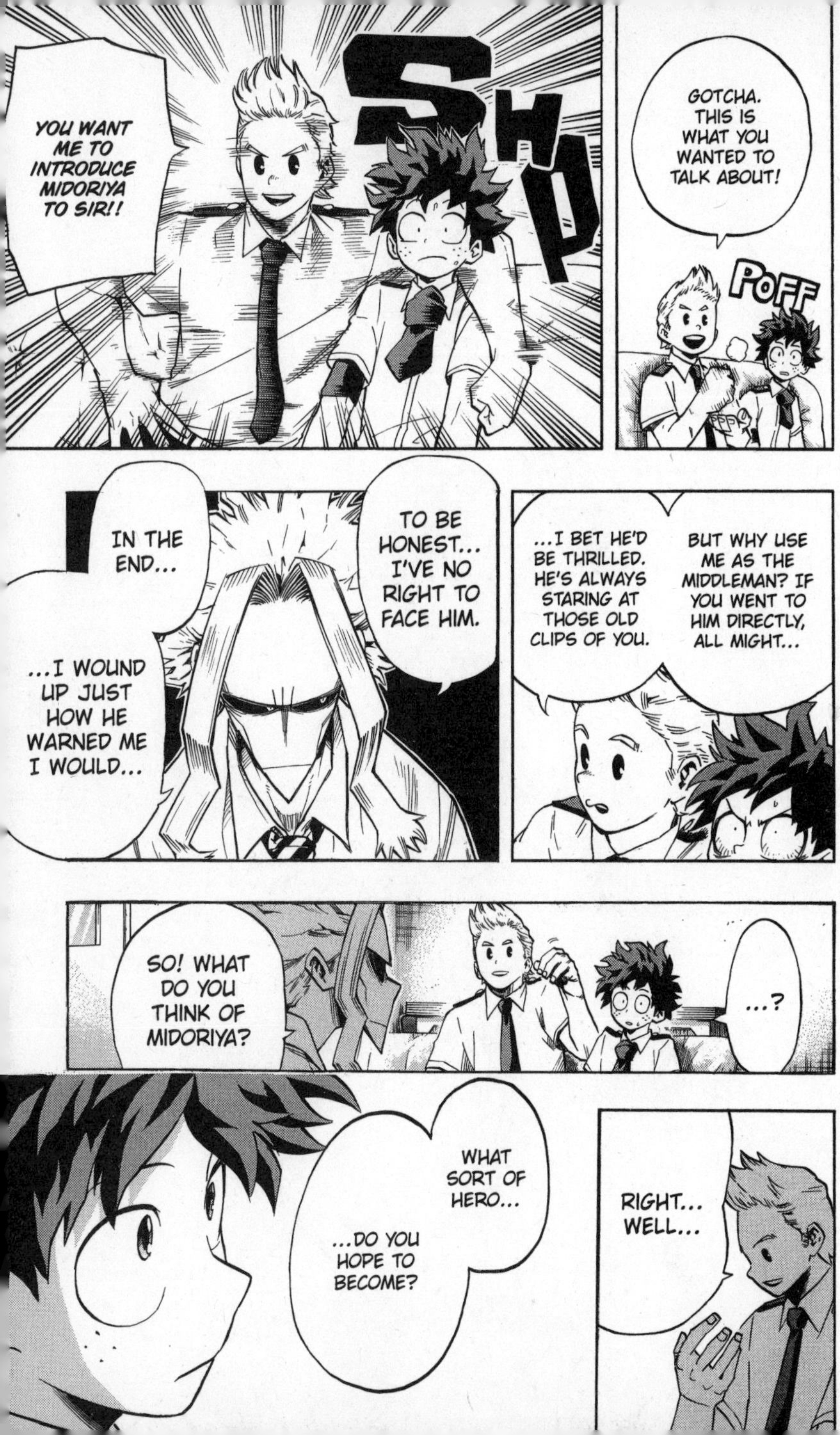
GOTCHA. THIS IS WHAT YOU WANTED TO TALK ABOUT!
POFF
SHP
YOU WANT ME TO INTRODUCE MIDORIYA TO SIR!!
BUT WHY USE ME AS THE MIDDLEMAN? IF YOU WENT TO HIM DIRECTLY, ALL MIGHT...
...I BET HE'D BE THRILLED. HE'S ALWAYS STARING AT THOSE OLD CLIPS OF YOU.
TO BE HONEST... I'VE NO RIGHT TO FACE HIM.
IN THE END...
...I WOUND UP JUST HOW HE WARNED ME I WOULD...
...?
SO! WHAT DO YOU THINK OF MIDORIYA?
RIGHT... WELL...
WHAT SORT OF HERO...
...DO YOU HOPE TO BECOME?

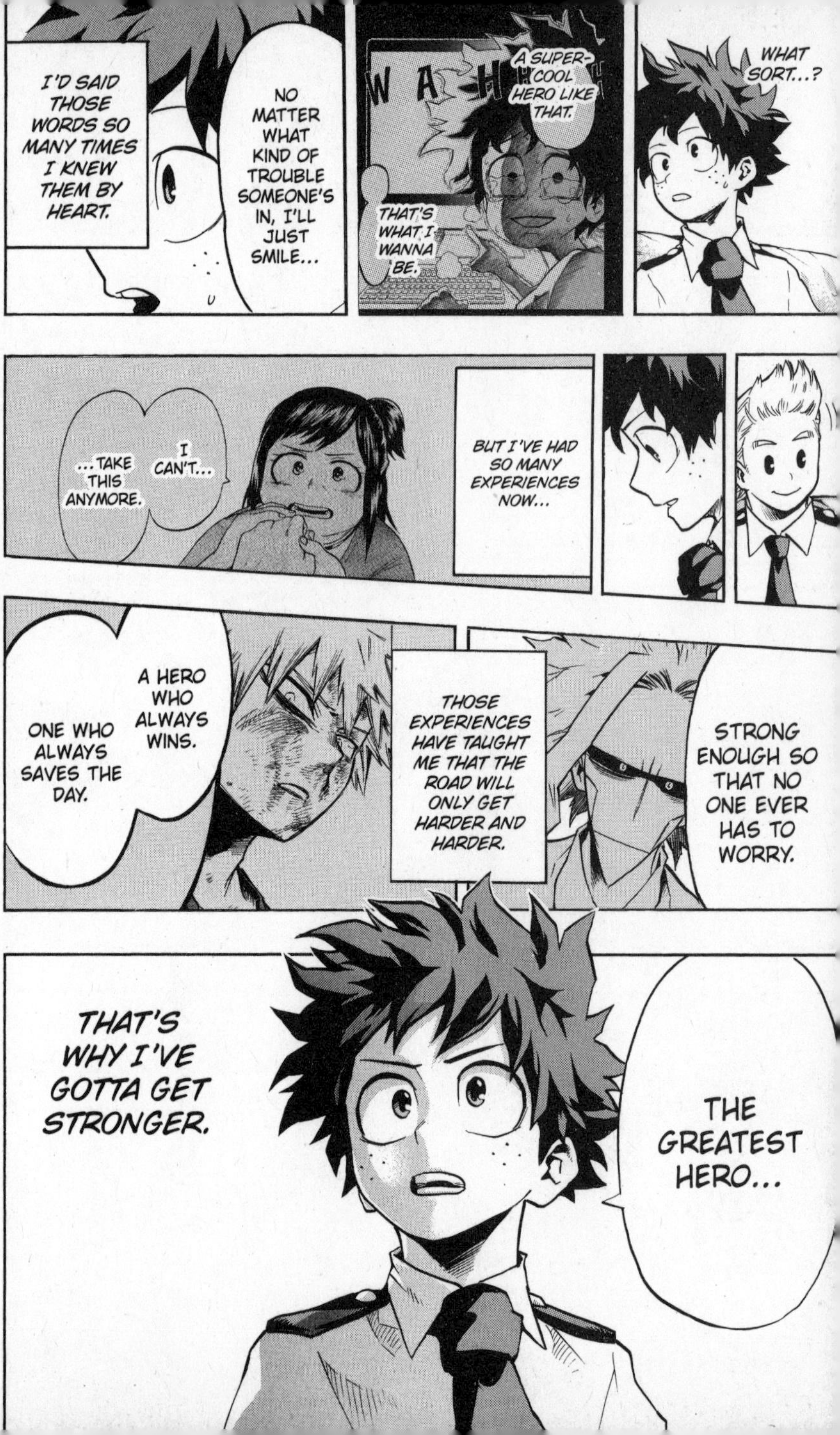
WHAT SORT...?
A SUPER-COOL HERO LIKE THAT.
THAT'S WHAT I WANNA BE.
NO MATTER WHAT KIND OF TROUBLE SOMEONE'S IN, I'LL JUST SMILE...
I'D SAID THOSE WORDS SO MANY TIMES I KNEW THEM BY HEART.
BUT I'VE HAD SO MANY EXPERIENCES NOW...
I CAN'T...
...TAKE THIS ANYMORE.
STRONG ENOUGH SO THAT NO ONE EVER HAS TO WORRY.
THOSE EXPERIENCES HAVE TAUGHT ME THAT THE ROAD WILL ONLY GET HARDER AND HARDER.
A HERO WHO ALWAYS WINS.
ONE WHO ALWAYS SAVES THE DAY.
THE GREATEST HERO...
THAT'S WHY I'VE GOTTA GET STRONGER.

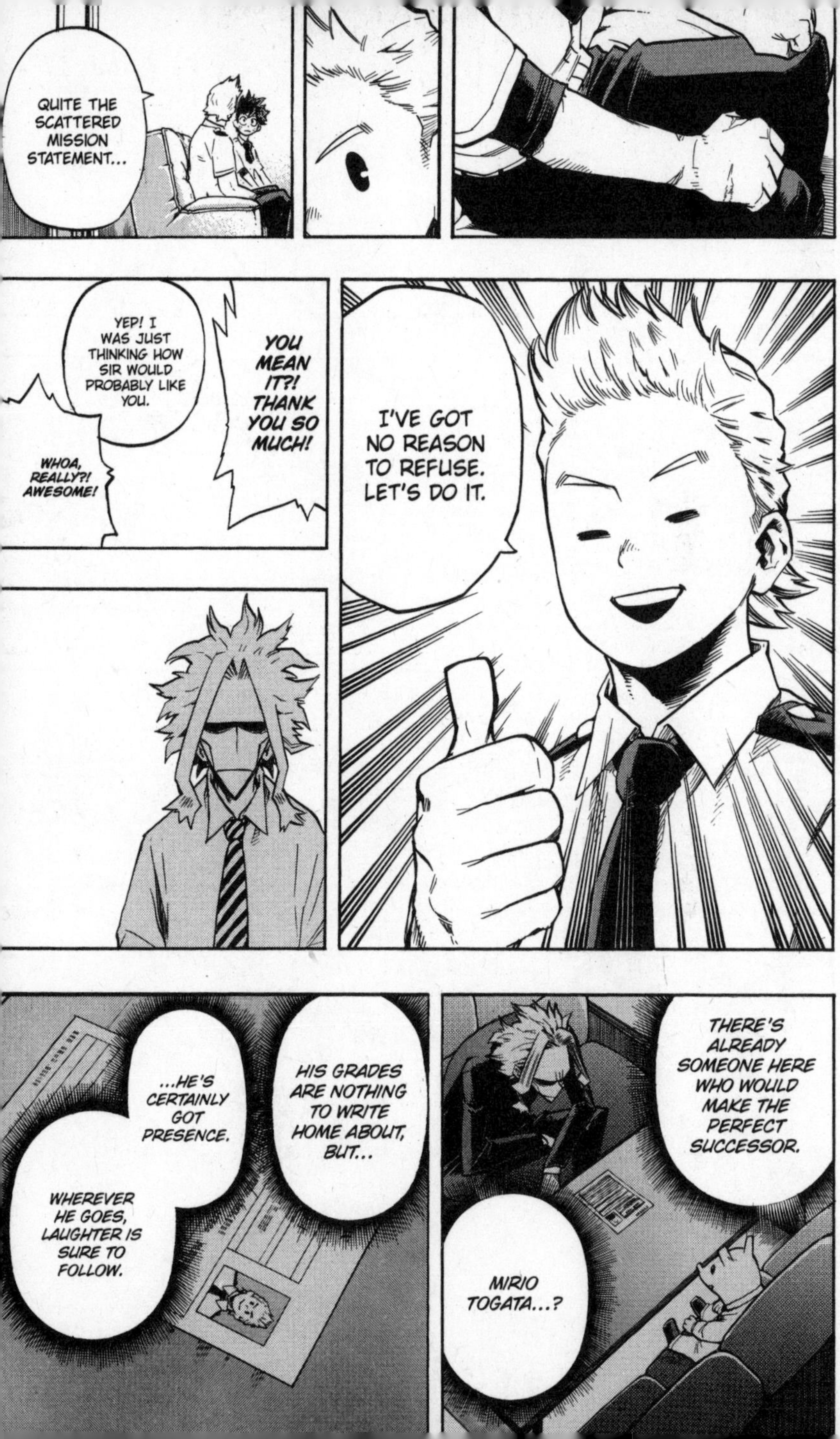
QUITE THE SCATTERED MISSION STATEMENT...
I'VE GOT NO REASON TO REFUSE. LET'S DO IT.
YOU MEAN IT?! THANK YOU SO MUCH!
YEP! I WAS JUST THINKING HOW SIR WOULD PROBABLY LIKE YOU.
WHOA, REALLY?! AWESOME!
THERE'S ALREADY SOMEONE HERE WHO WOULD MAKE THE PERFECT SUCCESSOR.
MIRIO TOGATA...?
HIS GRADES ARE NOTHING TO WRITE HOME ABOUT, BUT...
...HE'S CERTAINLY GOT PRESENCE.
WHEREVER HE GOES, LAUGHTER IS SURE TO FOLLOW.

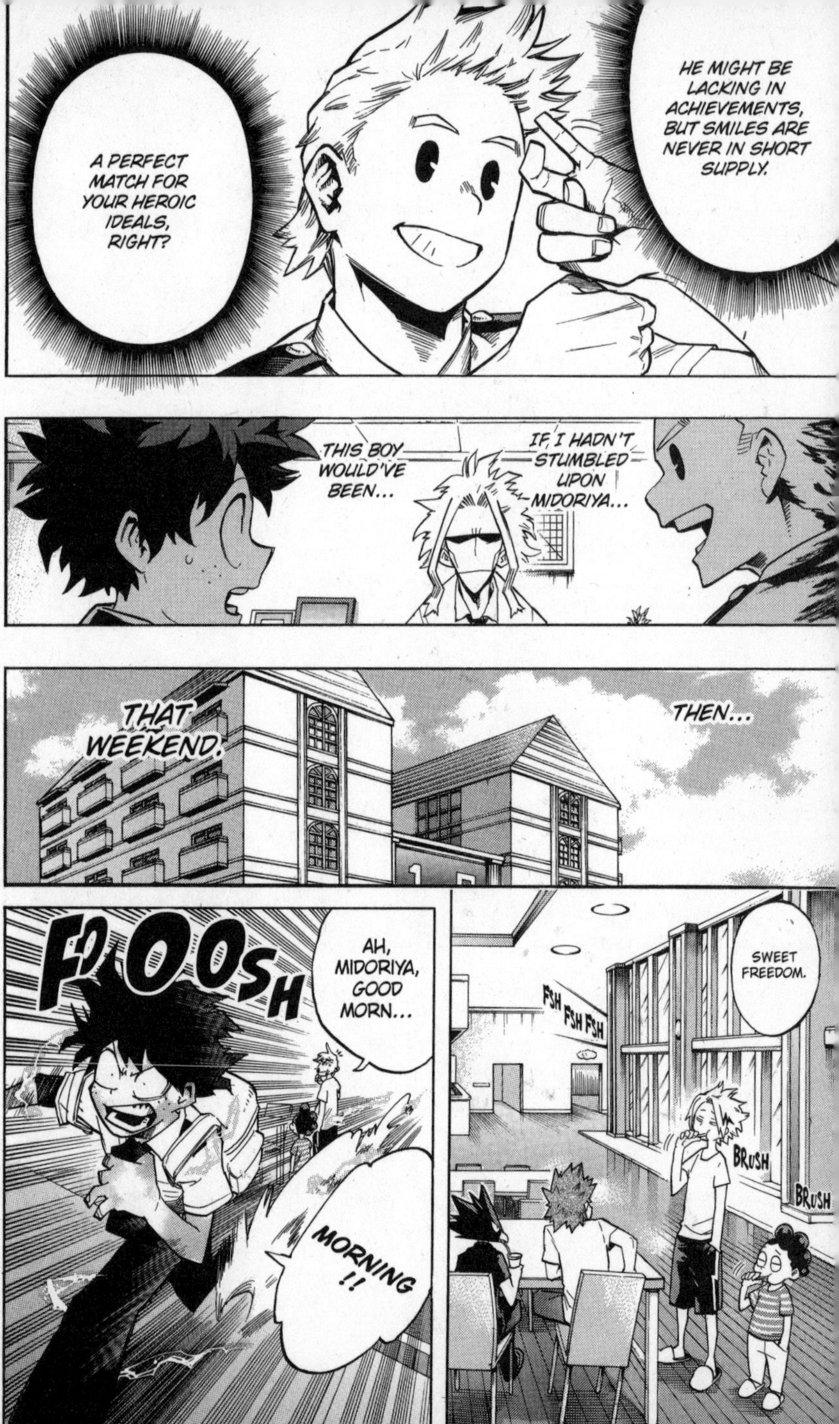
HE MIGHT BE LACKING IN ACHIEVEMENTS, BUT SMILES ARE NEVER IN SHORT SUPPLY.
A PERFECT MATCH FOR YOUR HEROIC IDEALS, RIGHT?
IF, I HADN'T STUMBLED UPON MIDORIYA...
THIS BOY WOULD'VE BEEN...
THAT WEEKEND.
THEN...
SWEET FREEDOM.
FSH FSH FSH
BRUSH
BRUSH
AH, MIDORIYA, GOOD MORN...
FOOSH
MORNING!!

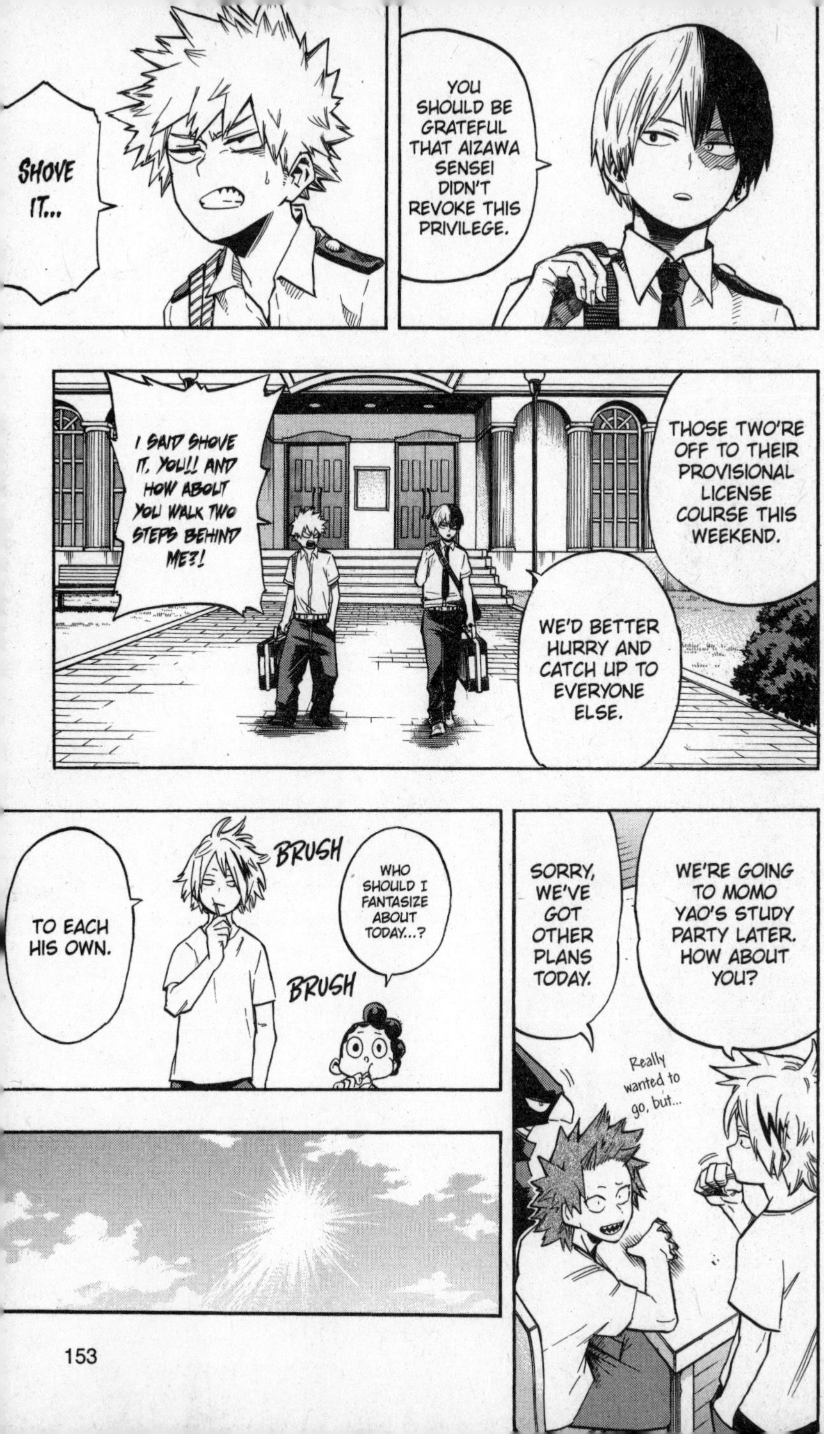

YOU SHOULD BE GRATEFUL THAT AIZAWA SENSEI DIDN'T REVOKE THIS PRIVILEGE.
SHOVE IT...
THOSE TWO'RE OFF TO THEIR PROVISIONAL LICENSE COURSE THIS WEEKEND.
WE'D BETTER HURRY AND CATCH UP TO EVERYONE ELSE.
I SAID SHOVE IT, YOU!! AND HOW ABOUT YOU WALK TWO STEPS BEHIND ME?!
WE'RE GOING TO MOMO YAO'S STUDY PARTY LATER. HOW ABOUT YOU?
SORRY, WE'VE GOT OTHER PLANS TODAY.
Really wanted to go, but...
WHO SHOULD I FANTASIZE ABOUT TODAY...?
BRUSH
BRUSH
TO EACH HIS OWN.

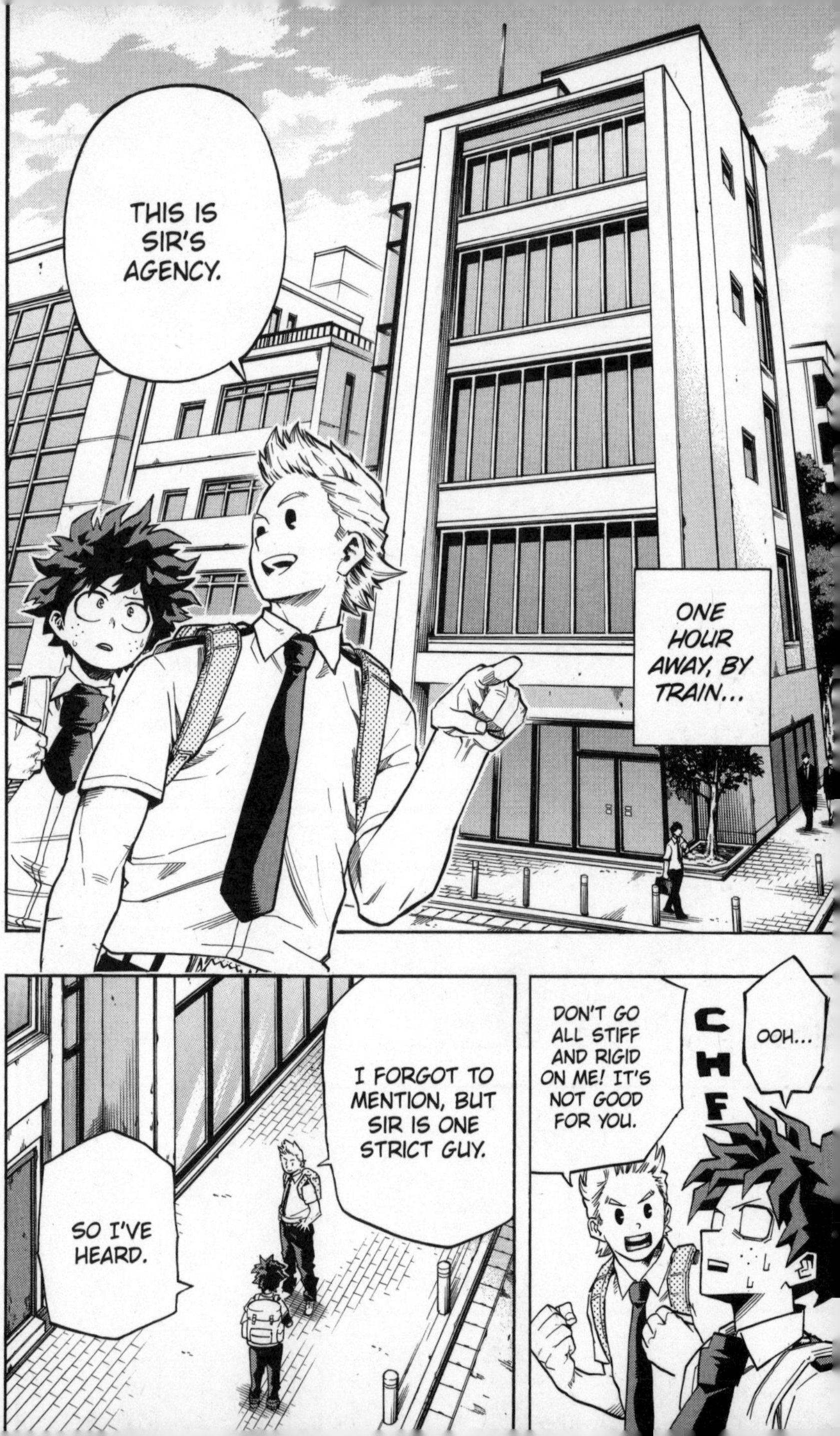
ONE HOUR AWAY, BY TRAIN...
THIS IS SIR'S AGENCY.
OOH...
CHF
DON'T GO ALL STIFF AND RIGID ON ME! IT'S NOT GOOD FOR YOU.
I FORGOT TO MENTION, BUT SIR IS ONE STRICT GUY.
SO I'VE HEARD.

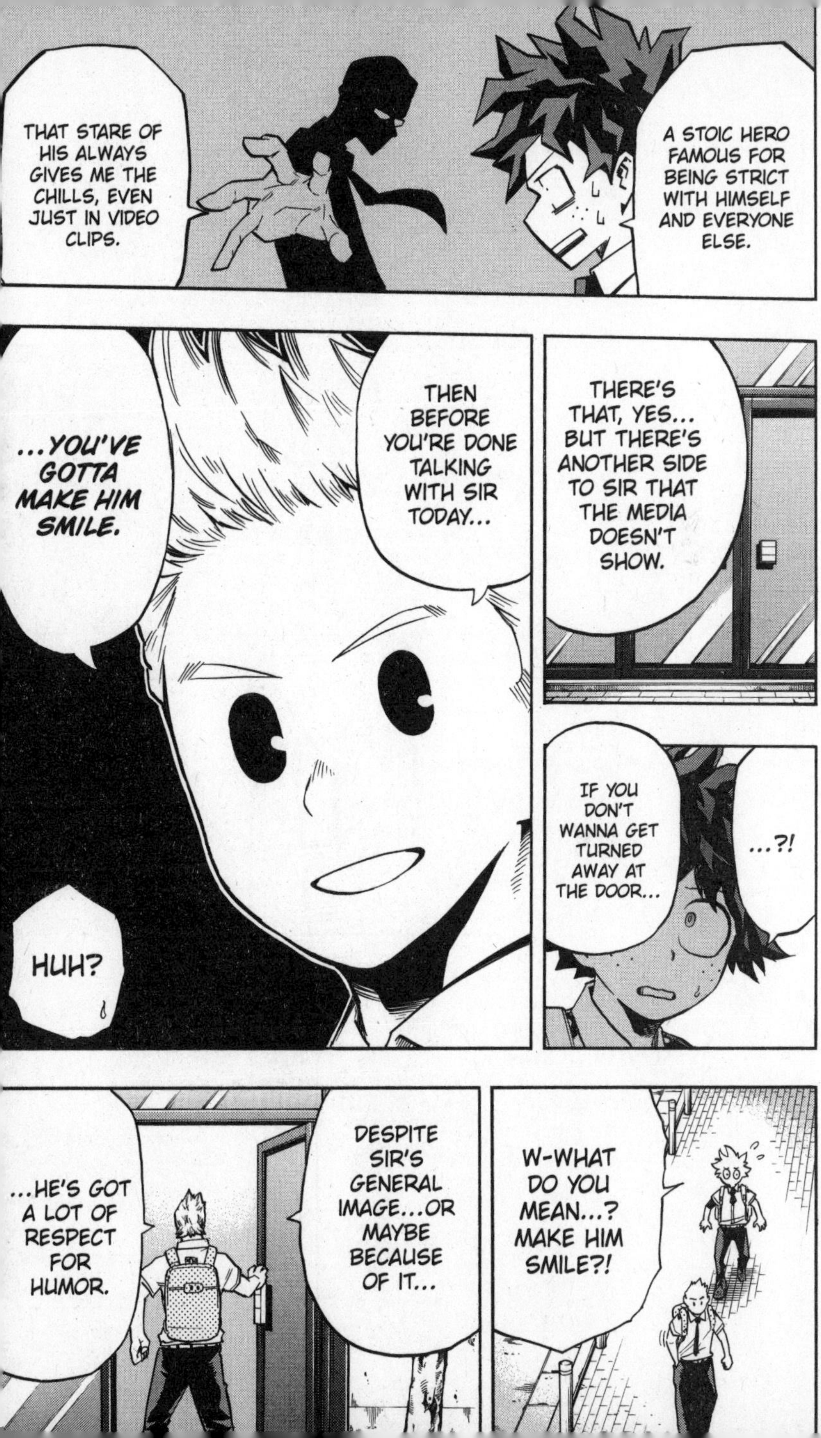
A STOIC HERO FAMOUS FOR BEING STRICT WITH HIMSELF AND EVERYONE ELSE.
THAT STARE OF HIS ALWAYS GIVES ME THE CHILLS, EVEN JUST IN VIDEO CLIPS.
THERE'S THAT, YES... BUT THERE'S ANOTHER SIDE TO SIR THAT THE MEDIA DOESN'T SHOW.
IF YOU DON'T WANNA GET TURNED AWAY AT THE DOOR...
...?!
THEN BEFORE YOU'RE DONE TALKING WITH SIR TODAY...
...YOU'VE GOTTA MAKE HIM SMILE.
HUH?
W-WHAT DO YOU MEAN...? MAKE HIM SMILE?!
DESPITE SIR'S GENERAL IMAGE...OR MAYBE BECAUSE OF IT...
...HE'S GOT A LOT OF RESPECT FOR HUMOR.

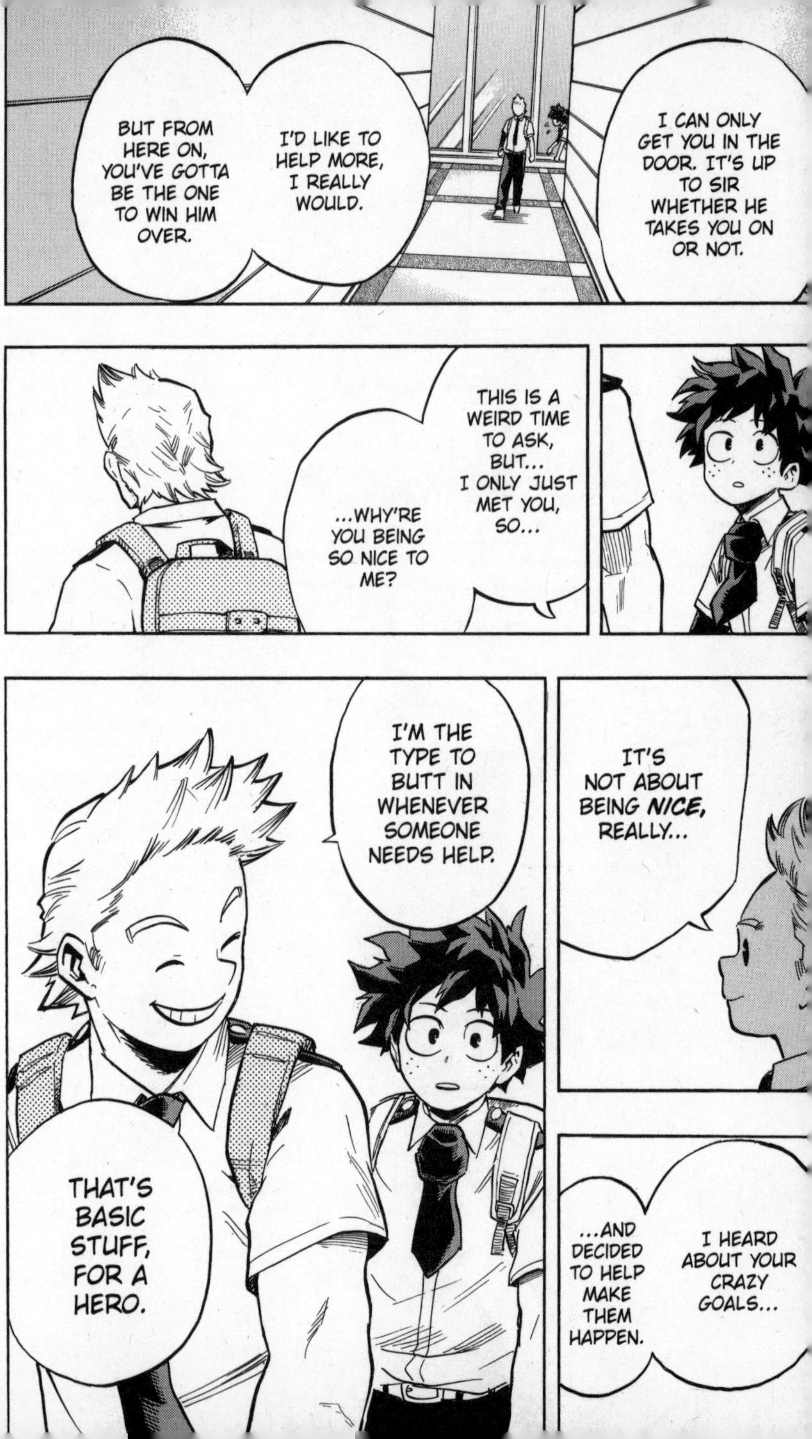
I CAN ONLY GET YOU IN THE DOOR. IT'S UP TO SIR WHETHER HE TAKES YOU ON OR NOT.
I'D LIKE TO HELP MORE, I REALLY WOULD.
BUT FROM HERE ON, YOU'VE GOTTA BE THE ONE TO WIN HIM OVER.
THIS IS A WEIRD TIME TO ASK, BUT... I ONLY JUST MET YOU, SO...
...WHY'RE YOU BEING SO NICE TO ME?
IT'S NOT ABOUT BEING *NICE*, REALLY...
I HEARD ABOUT YOUR CRAZY GOALS...
...AND DECIDED TO HELP MAKE THEM HAPPEN.
I'M THE TYPE TO BUTT IN WHENEVER SOMEONE NEEDS HELP.
THAT'S BASIC STUFF, FOR A HERO.

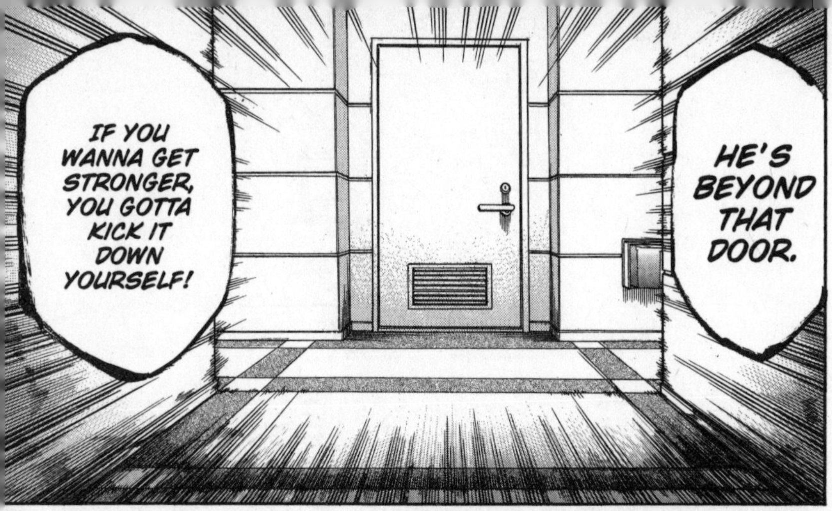
HE'S BEYOND THAT DOOR.
IF YOU WANNA GET STRONGER, YOU GOTTA KICK IT DOWN YOURSELF!

*BUBBLE GIRL WAS AGEN-SAN'S WINNING SUBMISSION IN THE FAN ART CONTEST!

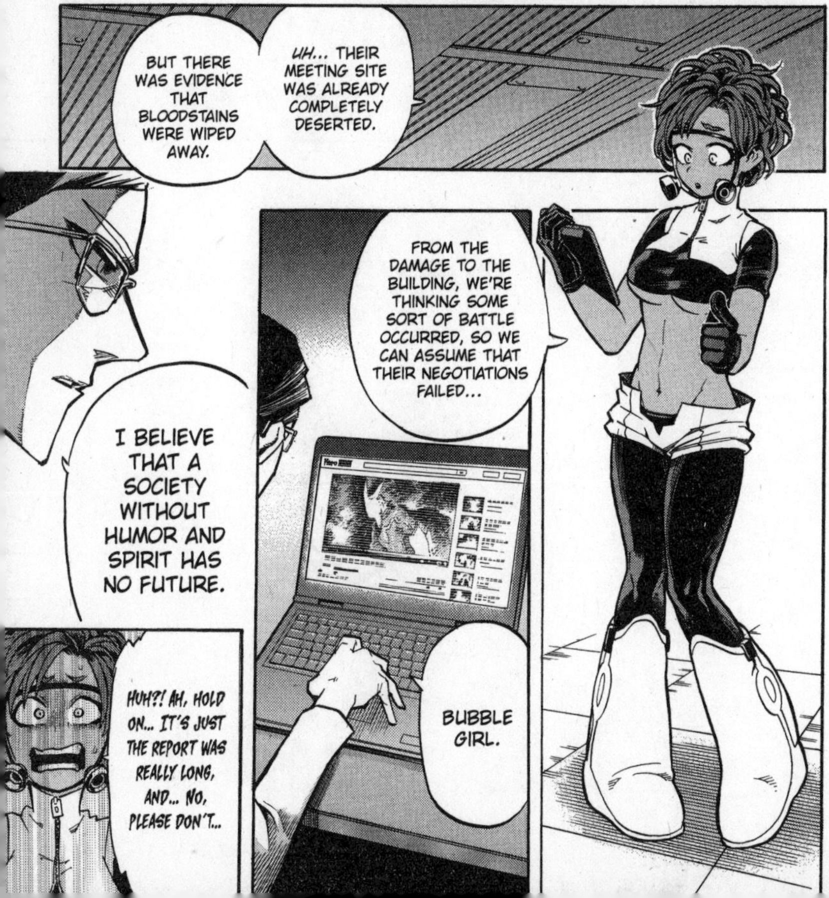
UH... THEIR MEETING SITE WAS ALREADY COMPLETELY DESERTED.
BUT THERE WAS EVIDENCE THAT BLOODSTAINS WERE WIPED AWAY.
FROM THE DAMAGE TO THE BUILDING, WE'RE THINKING SOME SORT OF BATTLE OCCURRED, SO WE CAN ASSUME THAT THEIR NEGOTIATIONS FAILED...
BUBBLE GIRL.
I BELIEVE THAT A SOCIETY WITHOUT HUMOR AND SPIRIT HAS NO FUTURE.
HUH?! AH, HOLD ON... IT'S JUST THE REPORT WAS REALLY LONG, AND... NO, PLEASE DON'T...

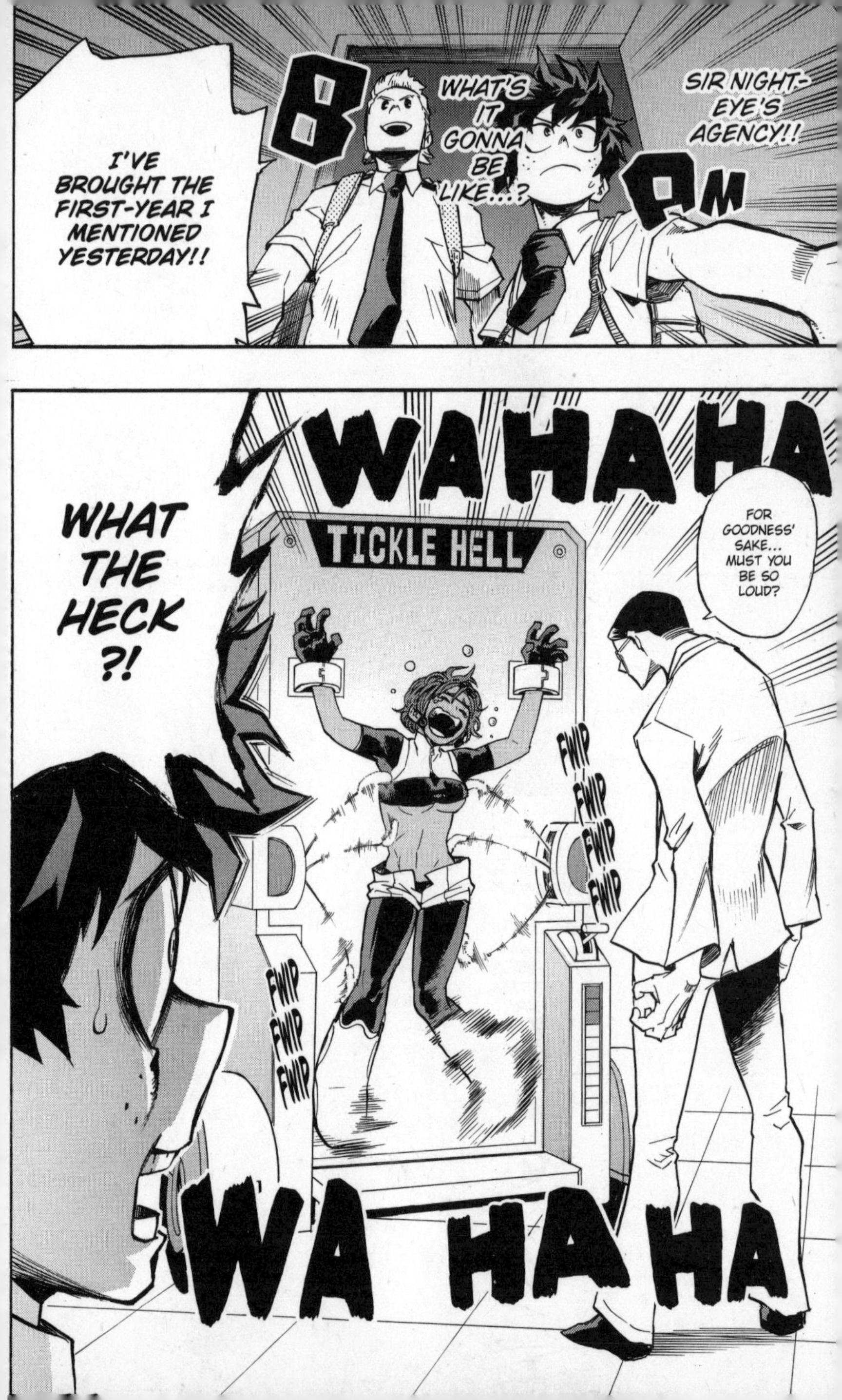

SIR NIGHT-EYE'S AGENCY!!
B
AM
WHAT'S IT GONNA BE LIKE...?
I'VE BROUGHT THE FIRST-YEAR I MENTIONED YESTERDAY!!
WAHAHA
FOR GOODNESS' SAKE... MUST YOU BE SO LOUD?
TICKLE HELL
WHAT THE HECK ?!
FWIP FWIP FWIP FWIP FWIP
FWIP FWIP FWIP
WA HA HA

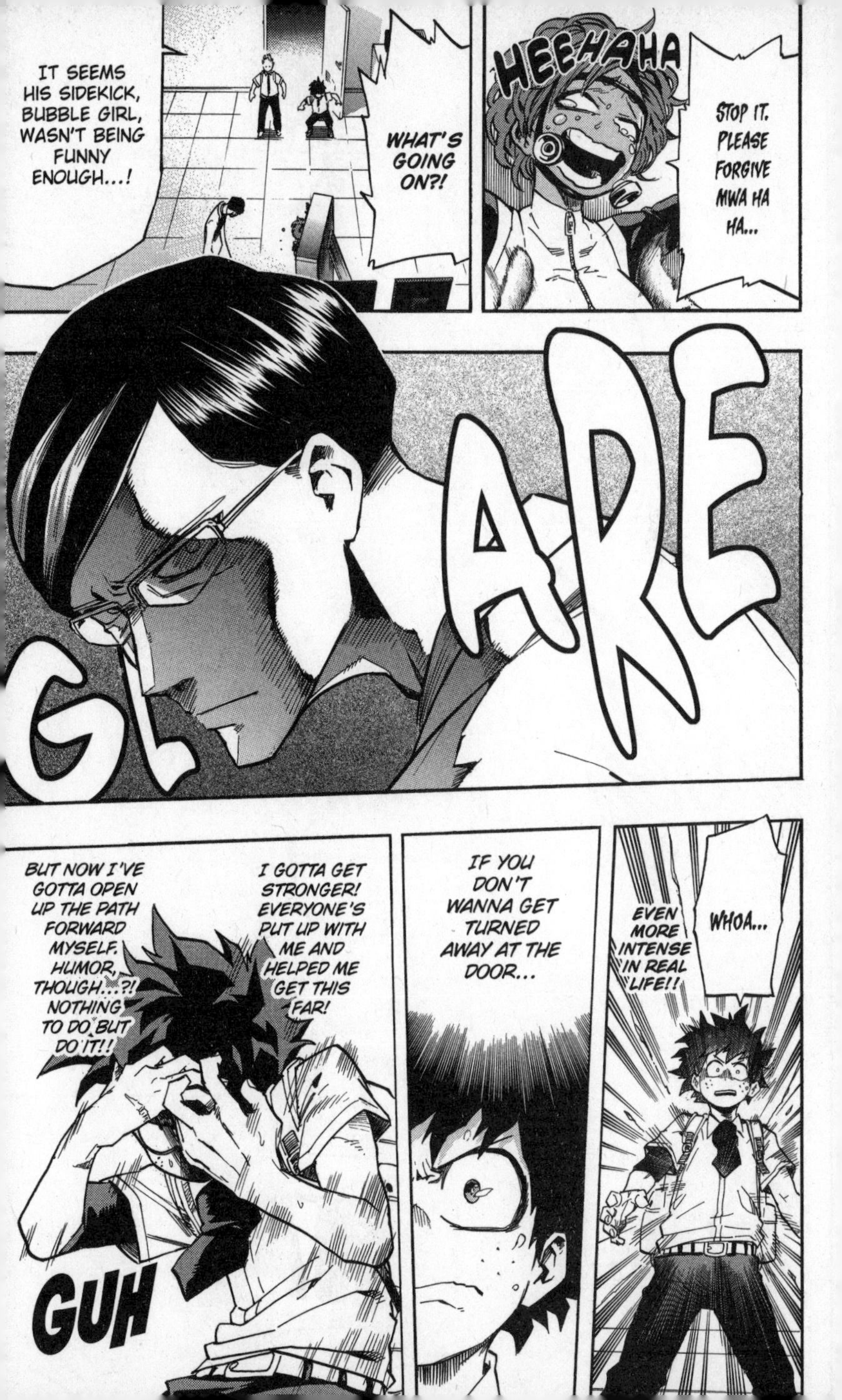
HEEHAHA
STOP IT. PLEASE FORGIVE MWA HA HA...
WHAT'S GOING ON?!
IT SEEMS HIS SIDEKICK, BUBBLE GIRL, WASN'T BEING FUNNY ENOUGH...!
GLARE
WHOA...
EVEN MORE INTENSE IN REAL LIFE!!
IF YOU DON'T WANNA GET TURNED AWAY AT THE DOOR...
I GOTTA GET STRONGER! EVERYONE'S PUT UP WITH ME AND HELPED ME GET THIS FAR!
BUT NOW I'VE GOTTA OPEN UP THE PATH FORWARD MYSELF. HUMOR, THOUGH...?! NOTHING TO DO BUT DO IT!!
GUH

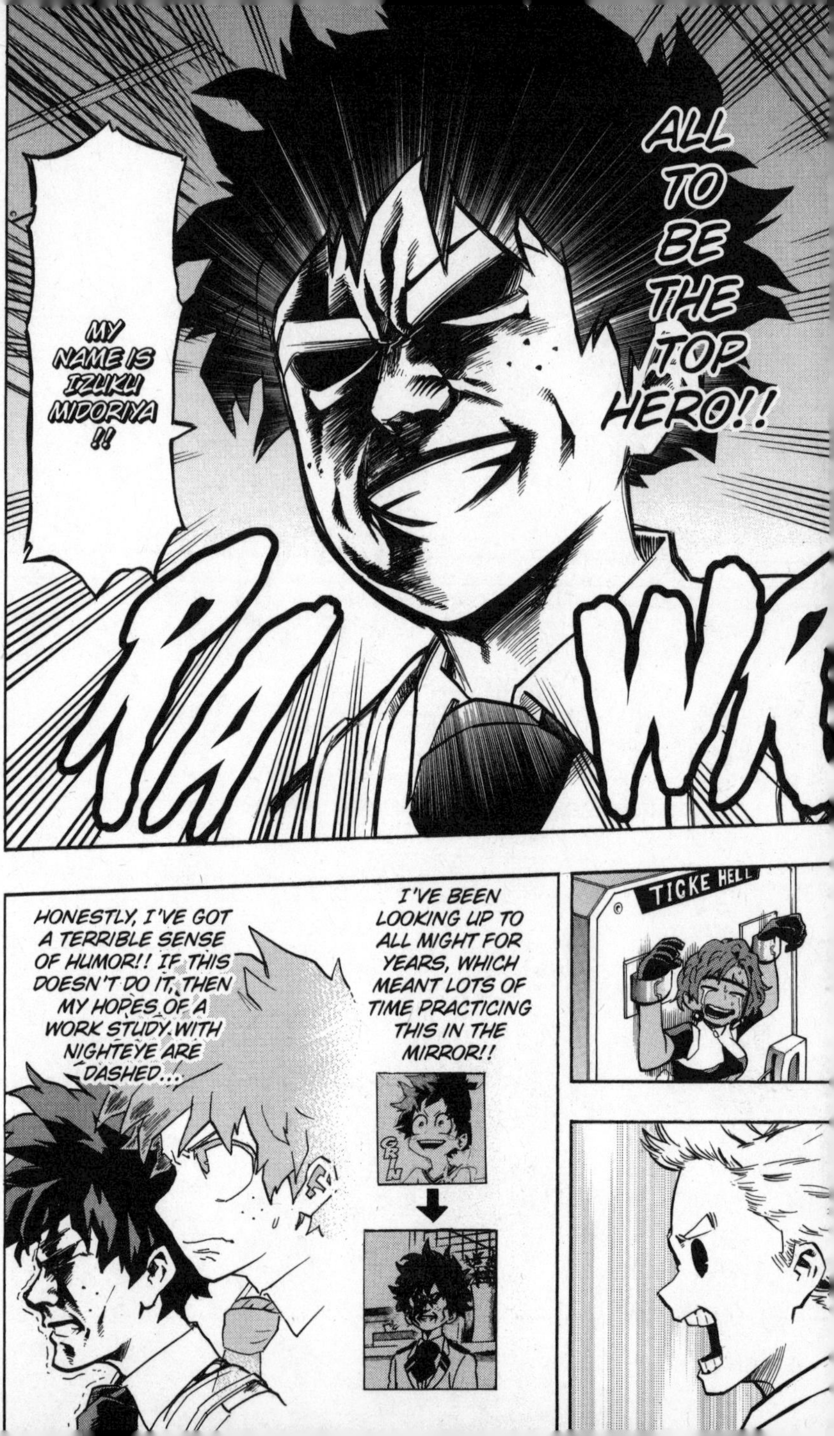

ALL TO BE THE TOP HERO!!
MY NAME IS IZUKU MIDORIYA!!
TICKE HELL
I'VE BEEN LOOKING UP TO ALL MIGHT FOR YEARS, WHICH MEANT LOTS OF TIME PRACTICING THIS IN THE MIRROR!!
HONESTLY, I'VE GOT A TERRIBLE SENSE OF HUMOR!! IF THIS DOESN'T DO IT, THEN MY HOPES OF A WORK STUDY WITH NIGHTEYE ARE DASHED...

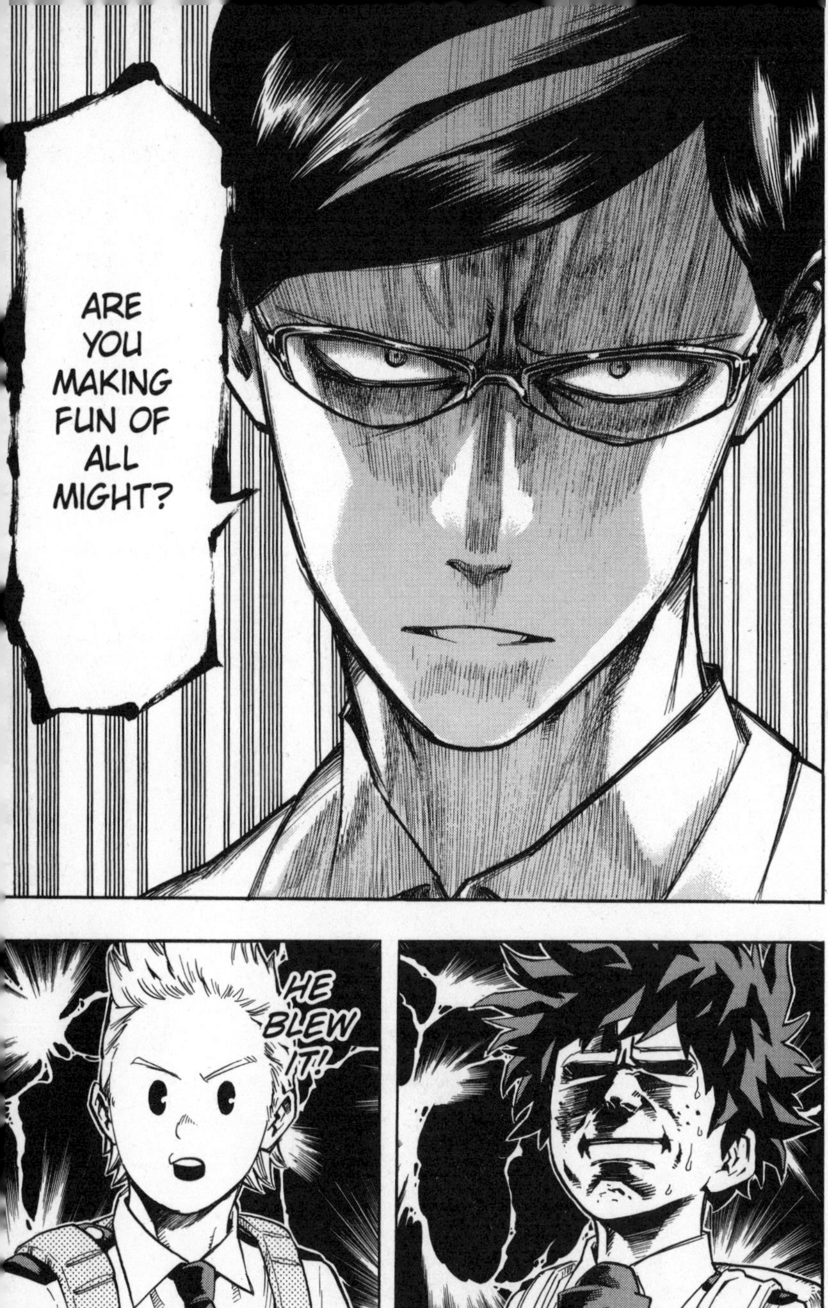
ARE YOU MAKING FUN OF ALL MIGHT?
HE BLEW IT!

HERO

NEJIRE HADO (17)

STREET CLOTHES

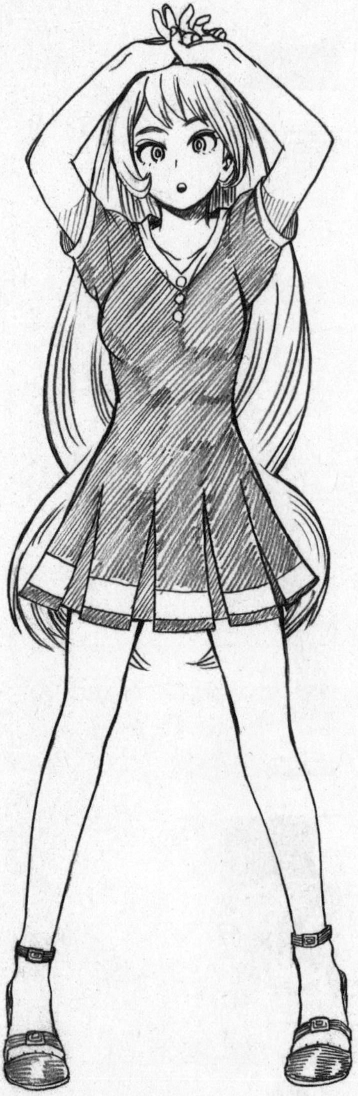

Birthday: 10/6
Height: 164 cm
Favorite Things: Lilies, jasmine tea

THE SUPPLEMENT

Brimming with curiosity, she wears her feelings on her sleeve. A very free spirit. Long hair is tough for me...

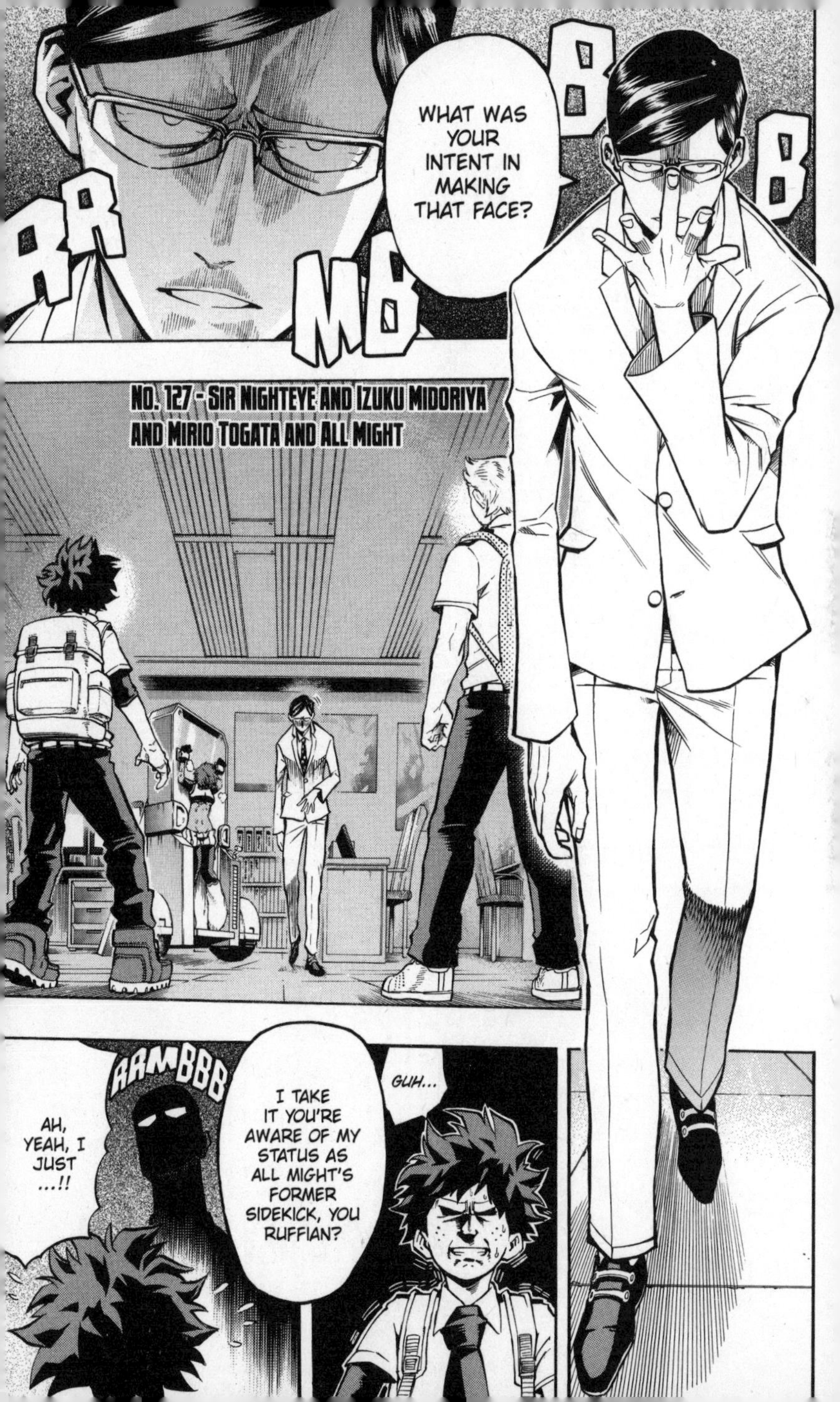
B
B
WHAT WAS YOUR INTENT IN MAKING THAT FACE?
MB
RR
No. 127 - Sir Nighteye and Izuku Midoriya and Mirio Togata and All Might
GUH...
I TAKE IT YOU'RE AWARE OF MY STATUS AS ALL MIGHT'S FORMER SIDEKICK, YOU RUFFIAN?
RRMBBB
AH, YEAH, I JUST ...!!

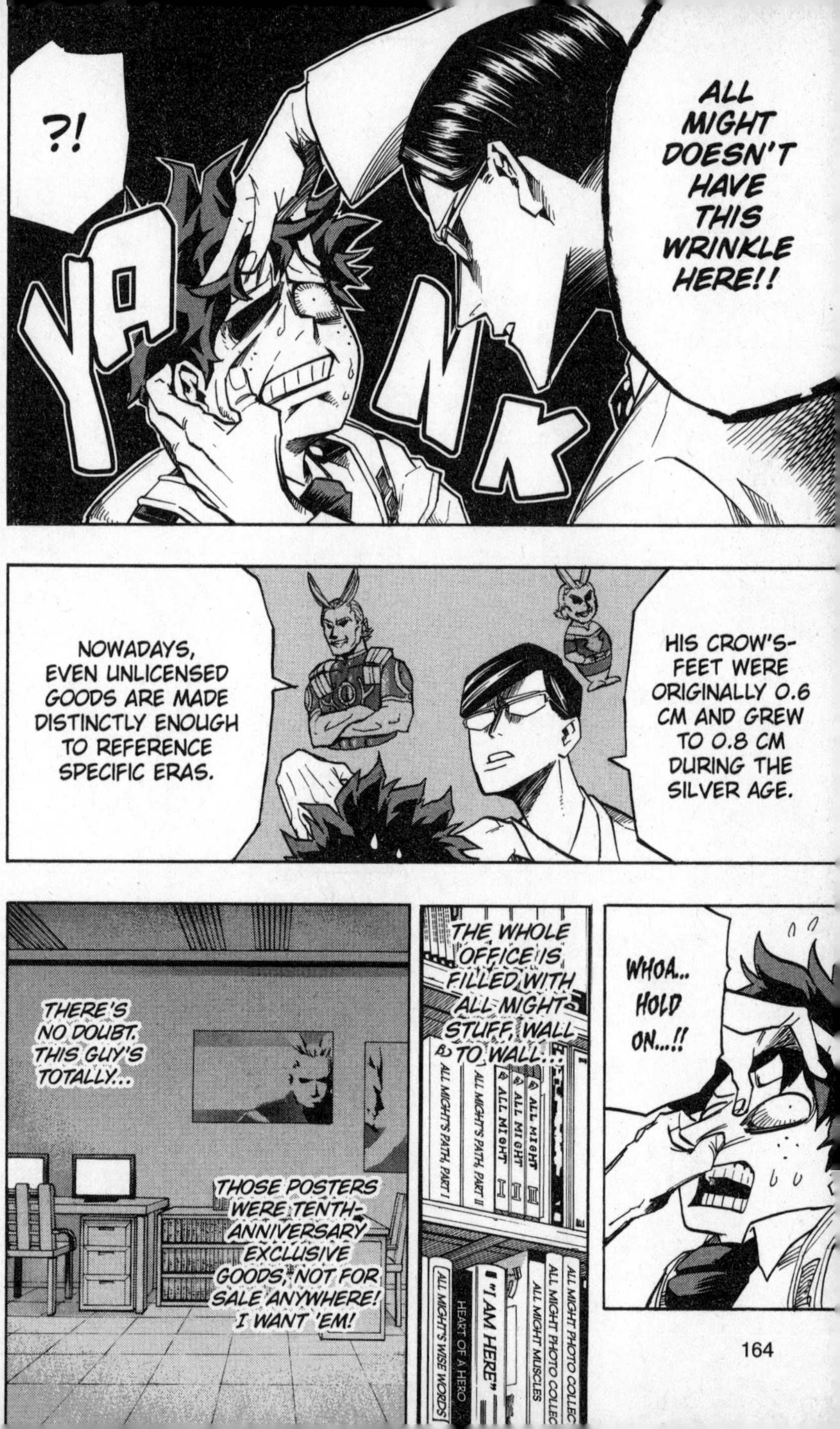
ALL MIGHT DOESN'T HAVE THIS WRINKLE HERE!!
?!
YANK
HIS CROW'S-FEET WERE ORIGINALLY 0.6 CM AND GREW TO 0.8 CM DURING THE SILVER AGE.
NOWADAYS, EVEN UNLICENSED GOODS ARE MADE DISTINCTLY ENOUGH TO REFERENCE SPECIFIC ERAS.
WHOA... HOLD ON...!!
THE WHOLE OFFICE IS FILLED WITH ALL MIGHT STUFF, WALL TO WALL...
ALL MIGHT III
ALL MIGHT II
ALL MIGHT
ALL MIGHT'S PATH, PART II
ALL MIGHT'S PATH, PART I
ALL MIGHT PHOTO COLLEC
ALL MIGHT MUSCLES
"I AM HERE"
HEART OF A HERO
ALL MIGHT'S WISE WORDS
THERE'S NO DOUBT. THIS GUY'S TOTALLY...
THOSE POSTERS WERE TENTH-ANNIVERSARY EXCLUSIVE GOODS, NOT FOR SALE ANYWHERE! I WANT 'EM!

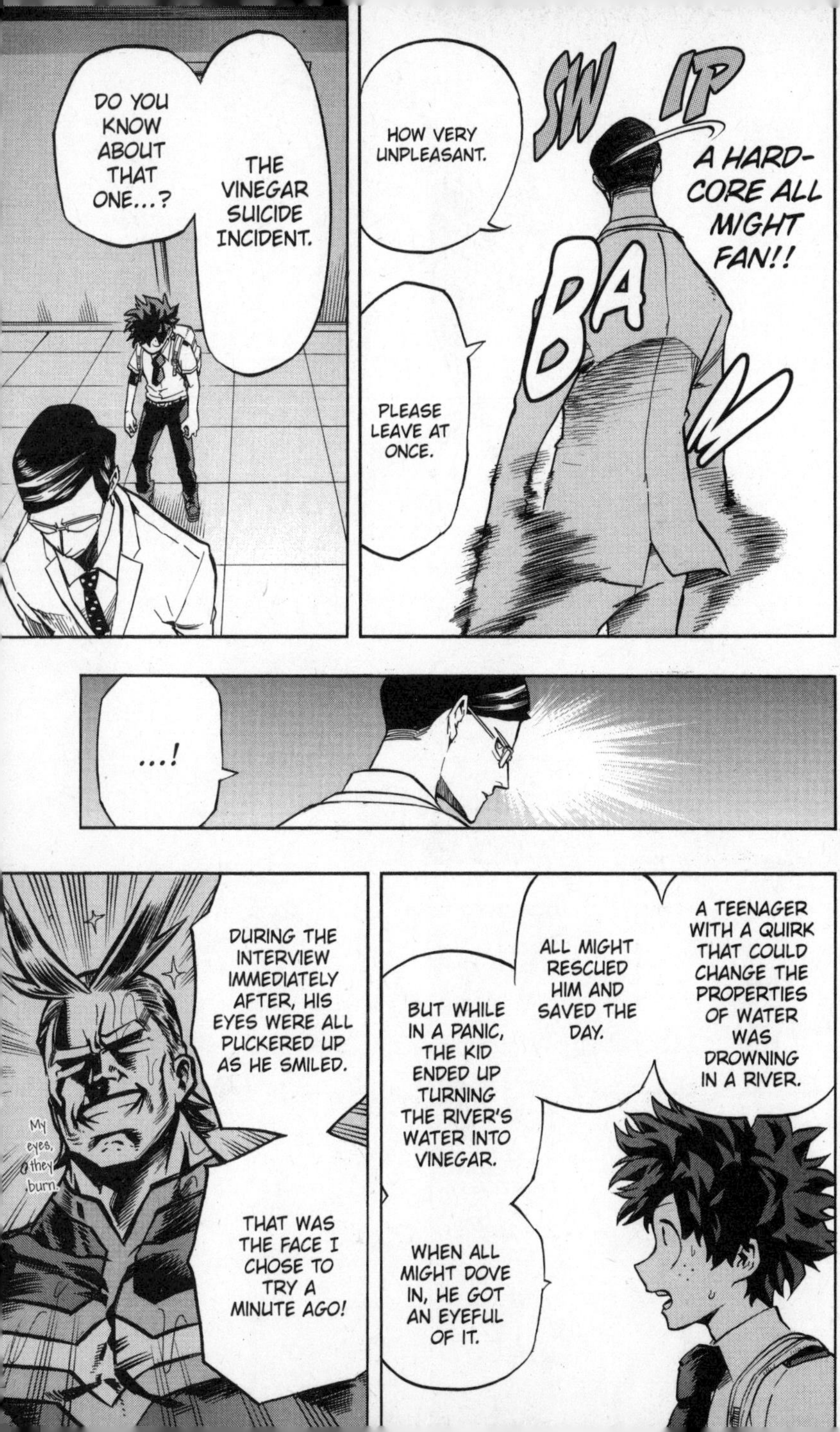
SWIP
A HARD-CORE ALL MIGHT FAN!!
HOW VERY UNPLEASANT.
BAM
PLEASE LEAVE AT ONCE.
THE VINEGAR SUICIDE INCIDENT.
DO YOU KNOW ABOUT THAT ONE...?
...!
A TEENAGER WITH A QUIRK THAT COULD CHANGE THE PROPERTIES OF WATER WAS DROWNING IN A RIVER.
ALL MIGHT RESCUED HIM AND SAVED THE DAY.
BUT WHILE IN A PANIC, THE KID ENDED UP TURNING THE RIVER'S WATER INTO VINEGAR.
WHEN ALL MIGHT DOVE IN, HE GOT AN EYEFUL OF IT.
DURING THE INTERVIEW IMMEDIATELY AFTER, HIS EYES WERE ALL PUCKERED UP AS HE SMILED.
THAT WAS THE FACE I CHOSE TO TRY A MINUTE AGO!
My eyes, they burn.

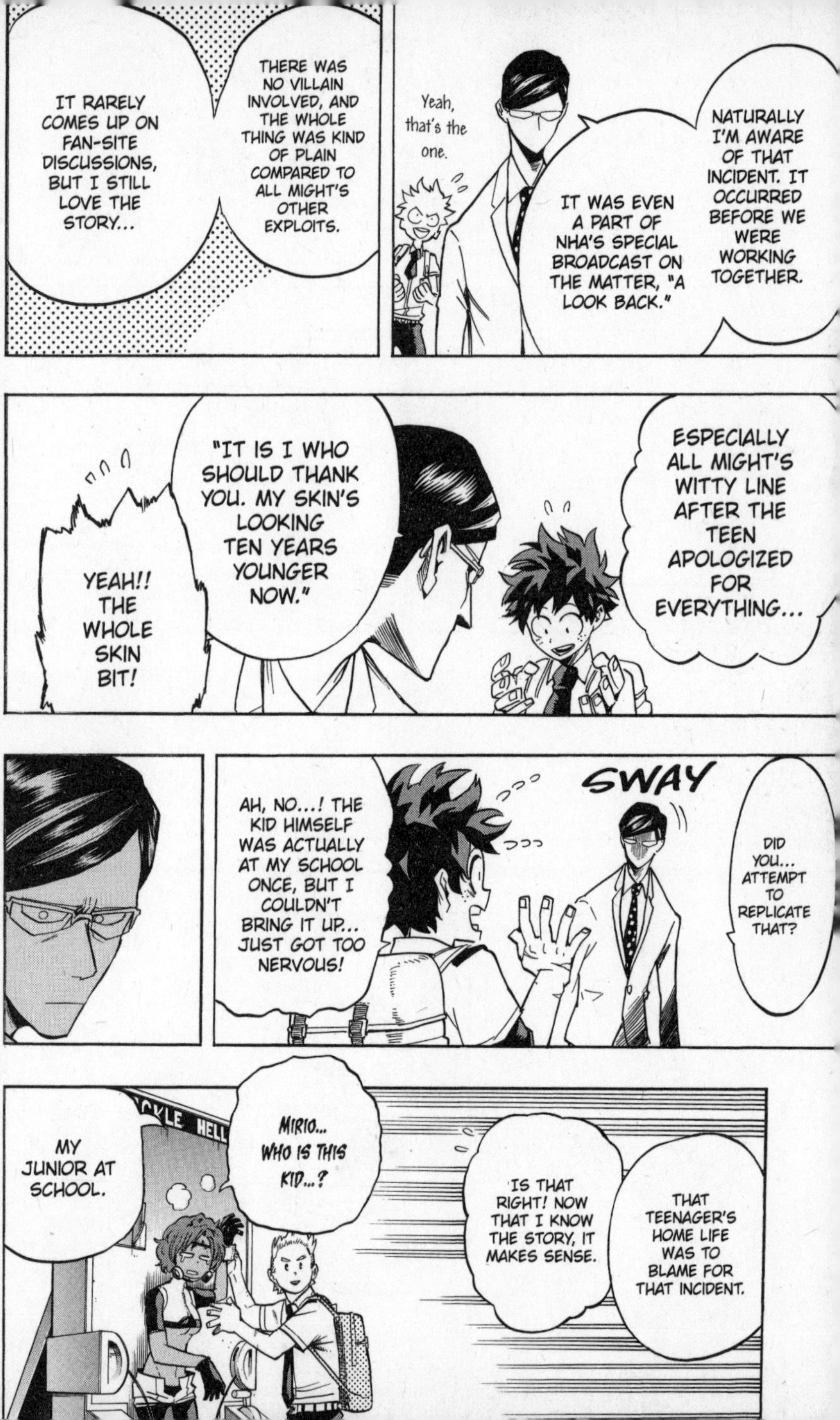
NATURALLY I'M AWARE OF THAT INCIDENT. IT OCCURRED BEFORE WE WERE WORKING TOGETHER.
IT WAS EVEN A PART OF NHA'S SPECIAL BROADCAST ON THE MATTER, "A LOOK BACK."
Yeah, that's the one.
THERE WAS NO VILLAIN INVOLVED, AND THE WHOLE THING WAS KIND OF PLAIN COMPARED TO ALL MIGHT'S OTHER EXPLOITS.
IT RARELY COMES UP ON FAN-SITE DISCUSSIONS, BUT I STILL LOVE THE STORY...
ESPECIALLY ALL MIGHT'S WITTY LINE AFTER THE TEEN APOLOGIZED FOR EVERYTHING...
"IT IS I WHO SHOULD THANK YOU. MY SKIN'S LOOKING TEN YEARS YOUNGER NOW."
YEAH!! THE WHOLE SKIN BIT!
SWAY
DID YOU... ATTEMPT TO REPLICATE THAT?
AH, NO...! THE KID HIMSELF WAS ACTUALLY AT MY SCHOOL ONCE, BUT I COULDN'T BRING IT UP... JUST GOT TOO NERVOUS!
THAT TEENAGER'S HOME LIFE WAS TO BLAME FOR THAT INCIDENT.
IS THAT RIGHT! NOW THAT I KNOW THE STORY, IT MAKES SENSE.
MIRIO... WHO IS THIS KID...?
MY JUNIOR AT SCHOOL.

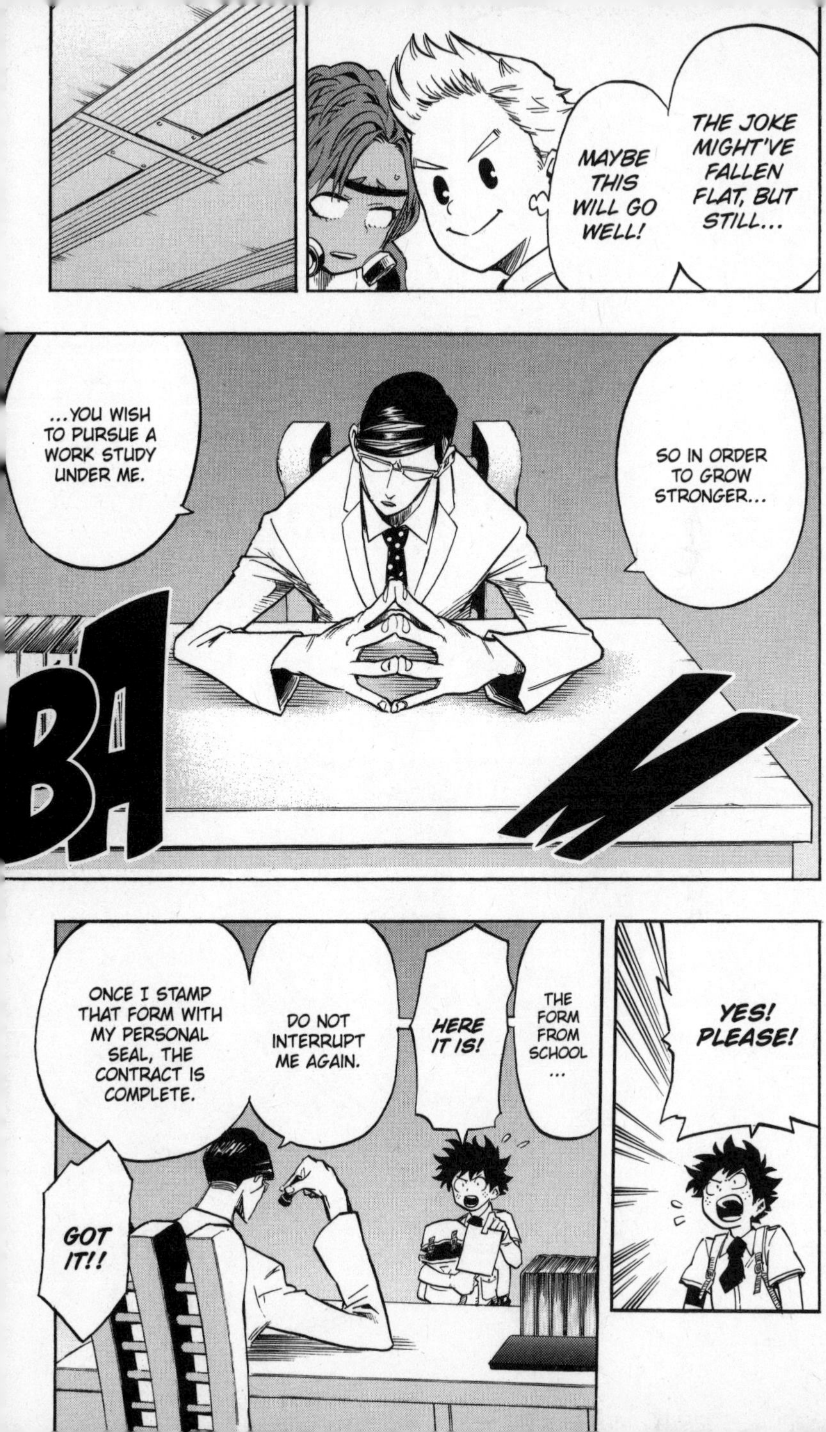
THE JOKE MIGHT'VE FALLEN FLAT, BUT STILL...
MAYBE THIS WILL GO WELL!
SO IN ORDER TO GROW STRONGER...
...YOU WISH TO PURSUE A WORK STUDY UNDER ME.
BAM
YES! PLEASE!
THE FORM FROM SCHOOL ...
HERE IT IS!
DO NOT INTERRUPT ME AGAIN.
ONCE I STAMP THAT FORM WITH MY PERSONAL SEAL, THE CONTRACT IS COMPLETE.
GOT IT!!

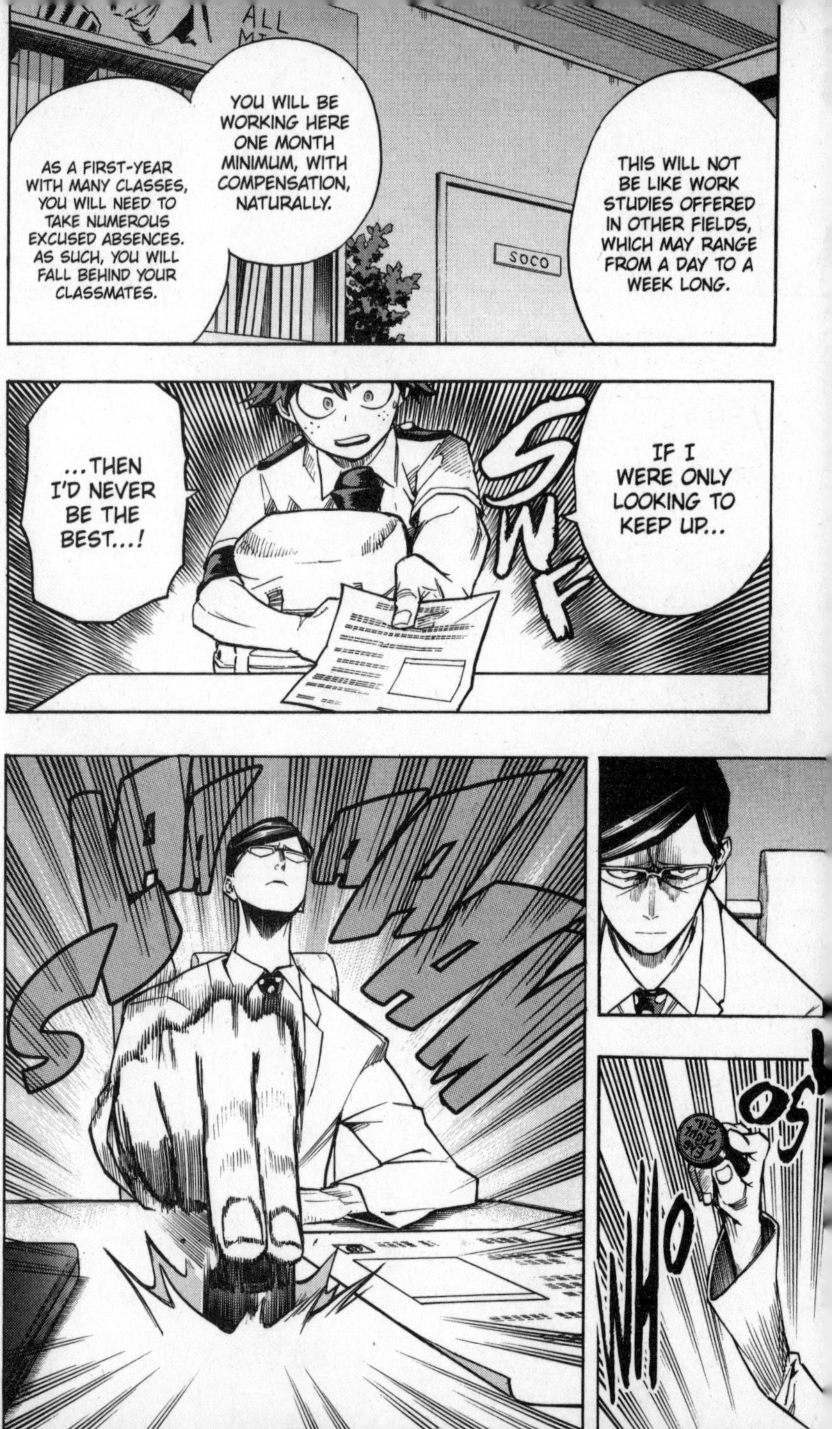
THIS WILL NOT BE LIKE WORK STUDIES OFFERED IN OTHER FIELDS, WHICH MAY RANGE FROM A DAY TO A WEEK LONG.
YOU WILL BE WORKING HERE ONE MONTH MINIMUM, WITH COMPENSATION, NATURALLY.
AS A FIRST-YEAR WITH MANY CLASSES, YOU WILL NEED TO TAKE NUMEROUS EXCUSED ABSENCES. AS SUCH, YOU WILL FALL BEHIND YOUR CLASSMATES.
SOCO
IF I WERE ONLY LOOKING TO KEEP UP...
SWF
...THEN I'D NEVER BE THE BEST...!

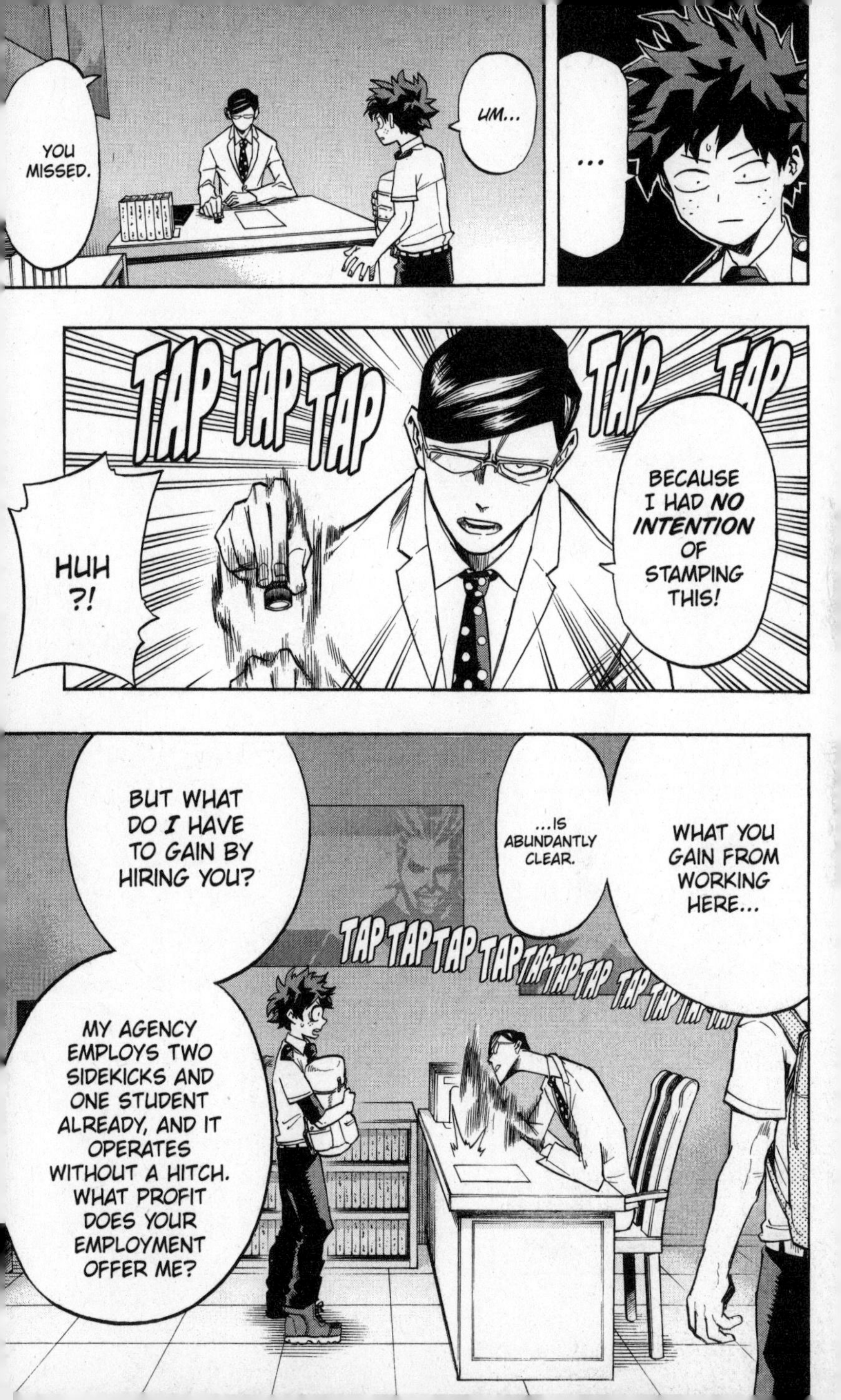
...
UM...
YOU MISSED.
TAP TAP
BECAUSE I HAD NO INTENTION OF STAMPING THIS!
TAP TAP TAP
HUH ?!
WHAT YOU GAIN FROM WORKING HERE...
...IS ABUNDANTLY CLEAR.
BUT WHAT DO I HAVE TO GAIN BY HIRING YOU?
TAP TAP TAP TAP TAP TAP TAP TAP TAP TAP TAP
MY AGENCY EMPLOYS TWO SIDEKICKS AND ONE STUDENT ALREADY, AND IT OPERATES WITHOUT A HITCH. WHAT PROFIT DOES YOUR EMPLOYMENT OFFER ME?

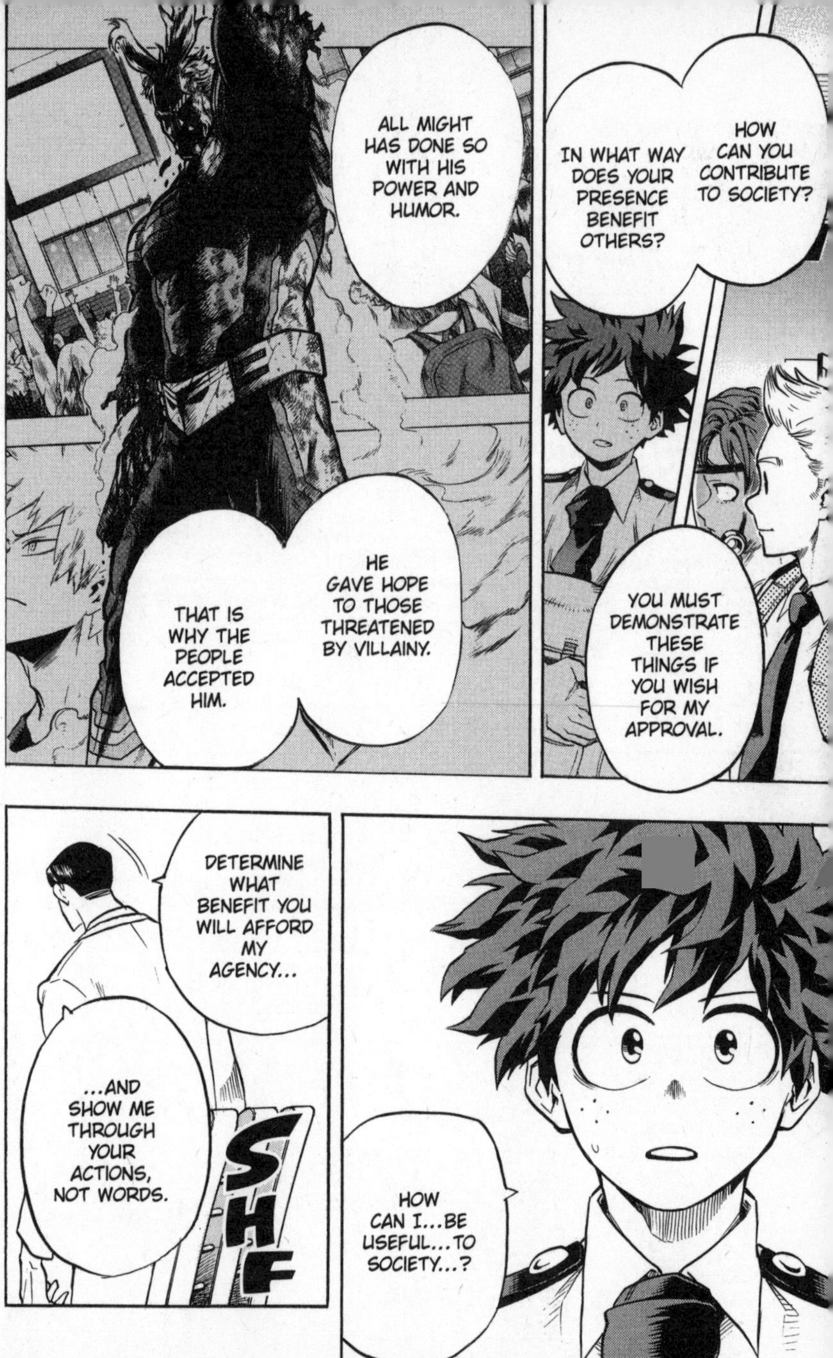
HOW CAN YOU CONTRIBUTE TO SOCIETY?
IN WHAT WAY DOES YOUR PRESENCE BENEFIT OTHERS?
YOU MUST DEMONSTRATE THESE THINGS IF YOU WISH FOR MY APPROVAL.
ALL MIGHT HAS DONE SO WITH HIS POWER AND HUMOR.
HE GAVE HOPE TO THOSE THREATENED BY VILLAINY.
THAT IS WHY THE PEOPLE ACCEPTED HIM.
HOW CAN I...BE USEFUL...TO SOCIETY...?
DETERMINE WHAT BENEFIT YOU WILL AFFORD MY AGENCY...
...AND SHOW ME THROUGH YOUR ACTIONS, NOT WORDS.
SHF

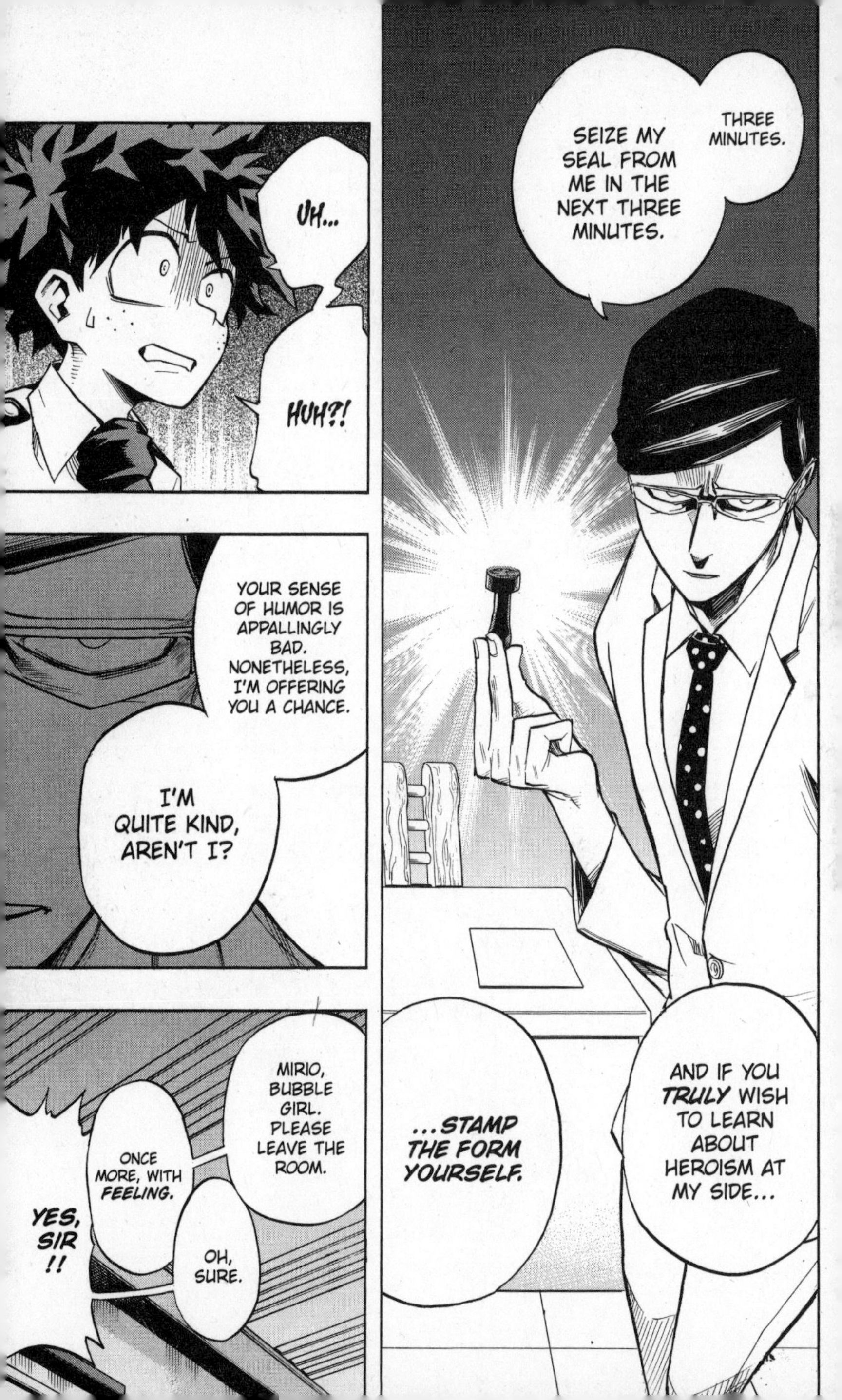
SEIZE MY SEAL FROM ME IN THE NEXT THREE MINUTES.
THREE MINUTES.
AND IF YOU *TRULY* WISH TO LEARN ABOUT HEROISM AT MY SIDE...
...STAMP THE FORM YOURSELF.
UH...
HUH?!
YOUR SENSE OF HUMOR IS APPALLINGLY BAD. NONETHELESS, I'M OFFERING YOU A CHANCE.
I'M QUITE KIND, AREN'T I?
MIRIO, BUBBLE GIRL. PLEASE LEAVE THE ROOM.
OH, SURE.
ONCE MORE, WITH *FEELING.*
YES, SIR!!

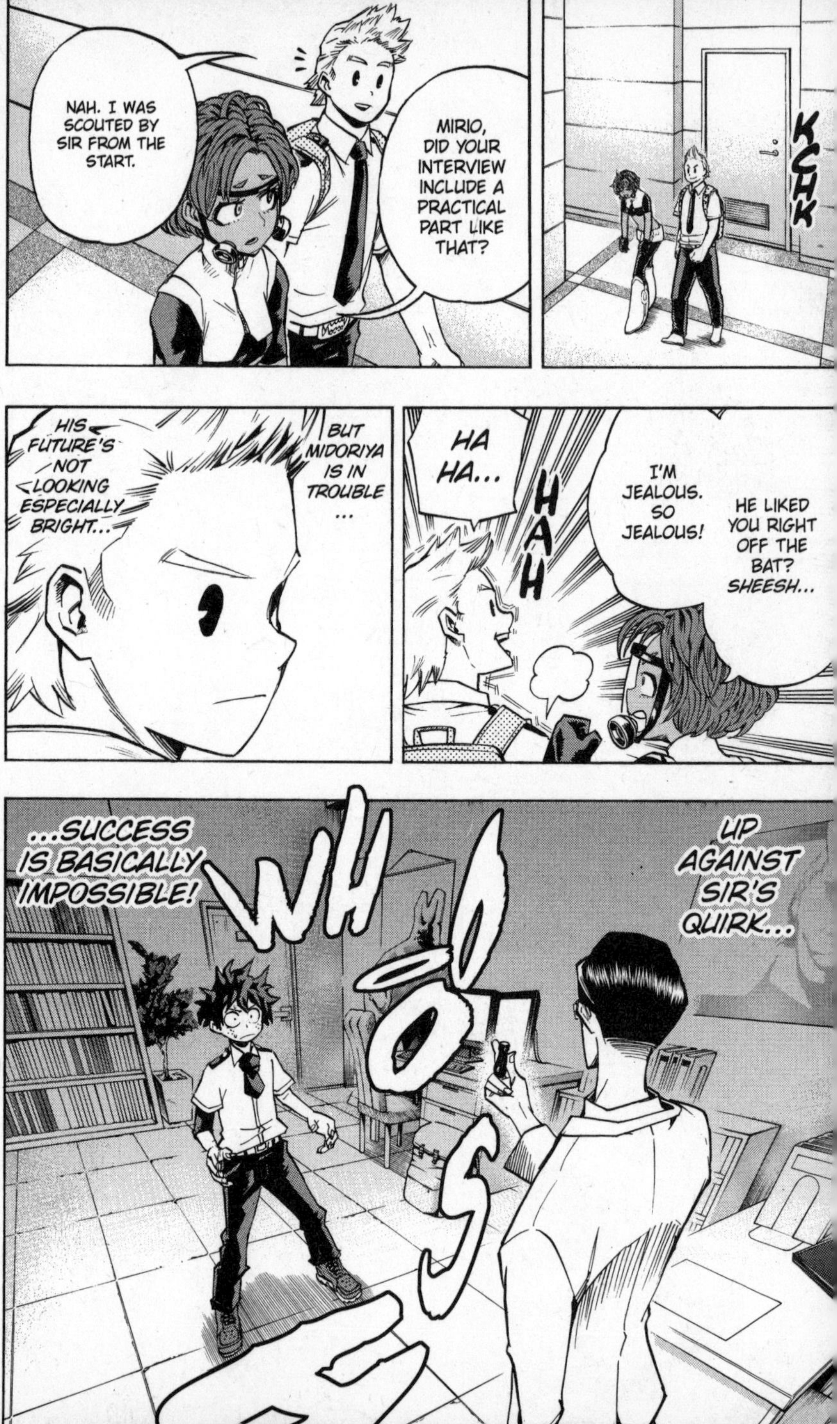
KCHK
MIRIO, DID YOUR INTERVIEW INCLUDE A PRACTICAL PART LIKE THAT?
NAH. I WAS SCOUTED BY SIR FROM THE START.
HE LIKED YOU RIGHT OFF THE BAT? SHEESH...
I'M JEALOUS. SO JEALOUS!
HAH
HA HA...
BUT MIDORIYA IS IN TROUBLE...
HIS FUTURE'S NOT LOOKING ESPECIALLY BRIGHT...
UP AGAINST SIR'S QUIRK...
WHOOOS
...SUCCESS IS BASICALLY IMPOSSIBLE!

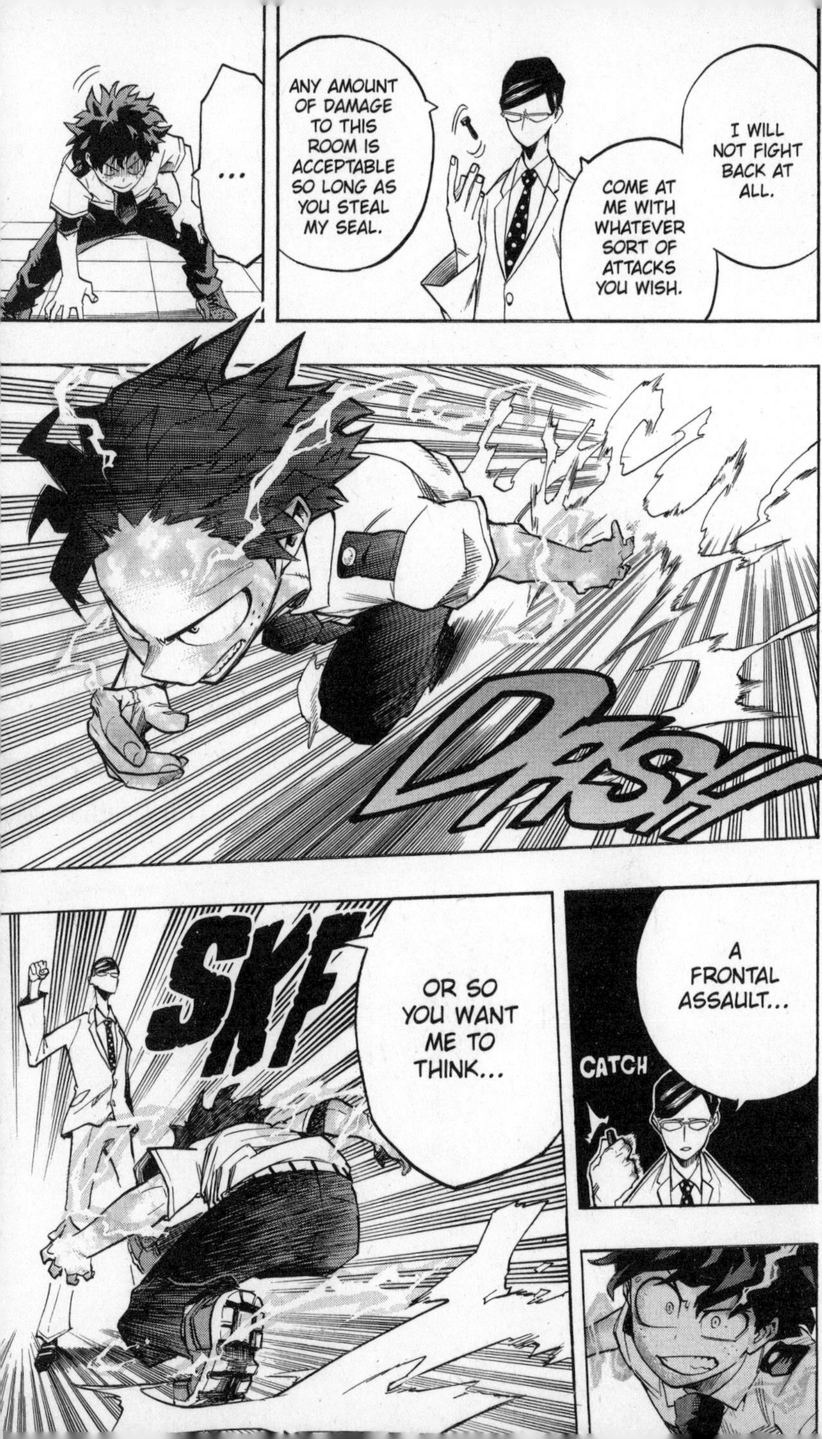
I WILL NOT FIGHT BACK AT ALL.
COME AT ME WITH WHATEVER SORT OF ATTACKS YOU WISH.
ANY AMOUNT OF DAMAGE TO THIS ROOM IS ACCEPTABLE SO LONG AS YOU STEAL MY SEAL.
...
DASH
A FRONTAL ASSAULT...
CATCH
OR SO YOU WANT ME TO THINK...
SKF

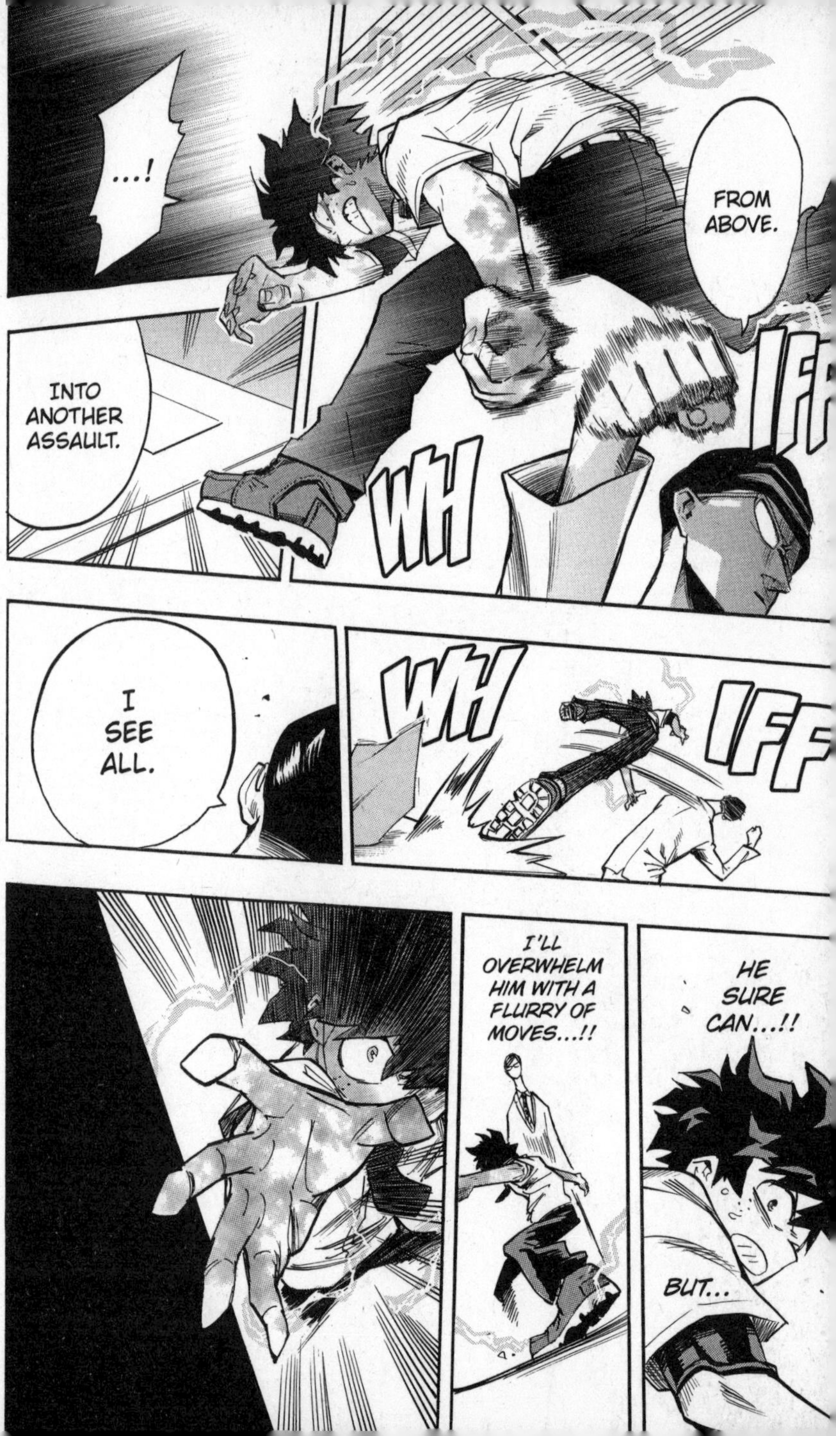
FROM ABOVE.
...!
INTO ANOTHER ASSAULT.
WHIFF
WHIFF
I SEE ALL.
HE SURE CAN...!!
BUT...
I'LL OVERWHELM HIM WITH A FLURRY OF MOVES...!!

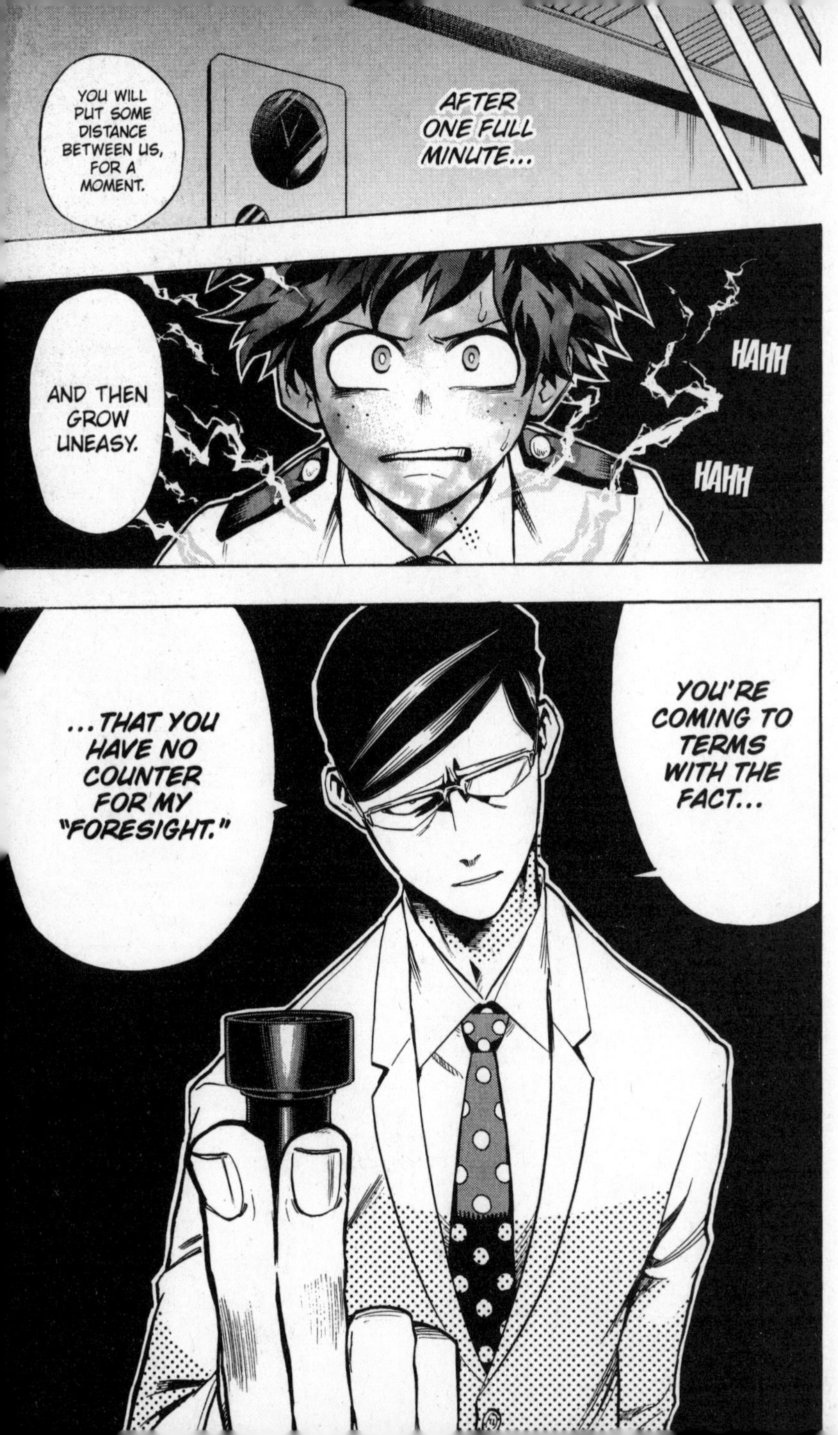
AFTER ONE FULL MINUTE...
YOU WILL PUT SOME DISTANCE BETWEEN US, FOR A MOMENT.
HAHH
HAHH
AND THEN GROW UNEASY.
YOU'RE COMING TO TERMS WITH THE FACT...
...THAT YOU HAVE NO COUNTER FOR MY "FORESIGHT."

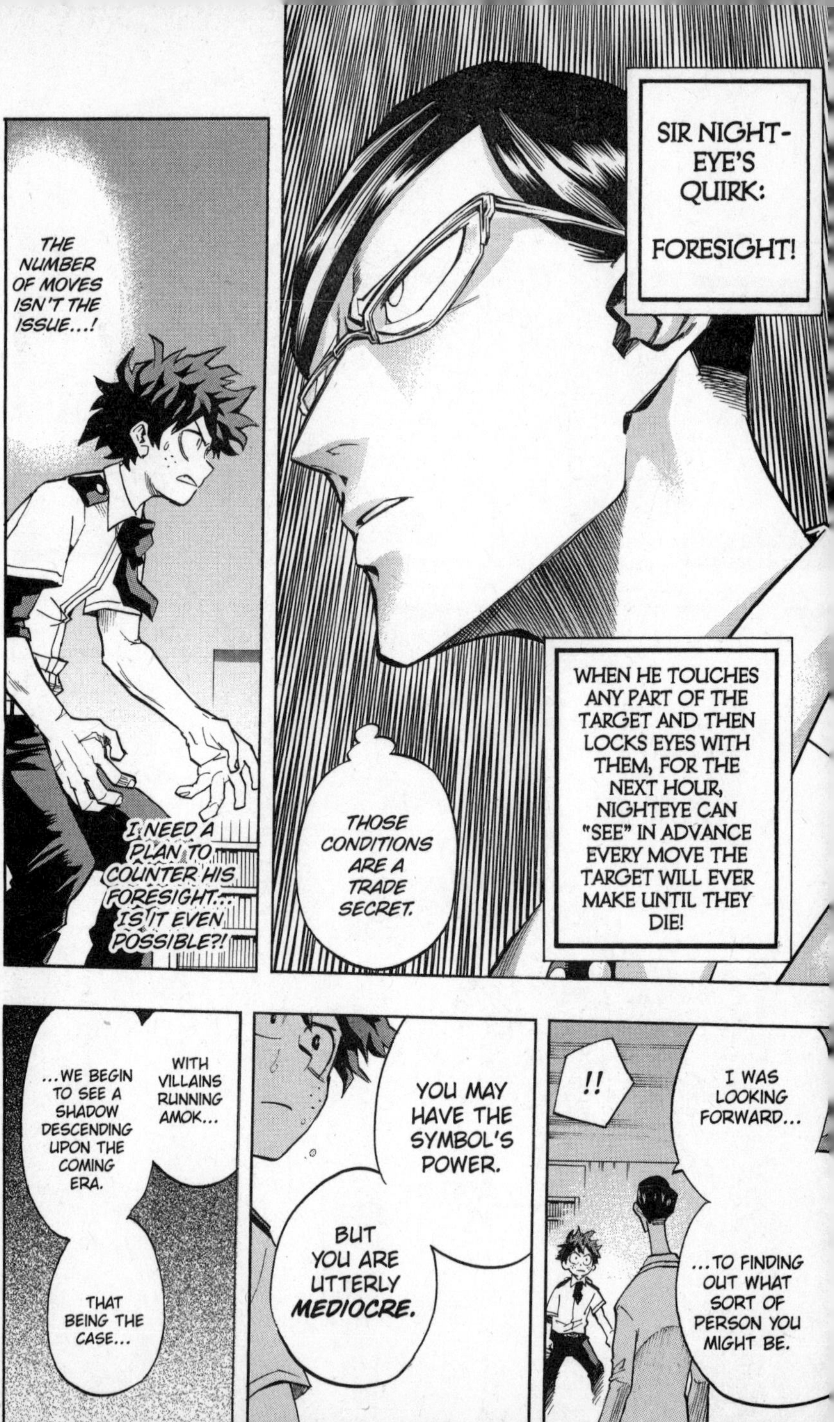
SIR NIGHT-EYE'S QUIRK: FORESIGHT!
WHEN HE TOUCHES ANY PART OF THE TARGET AND THEN LOCKS EYES WITH THEM, FOR THE NEXT HOUR, NIGHTEYE CAN "SEE" IN ADVANCE EVERY MOVE THE TARGET WILL EVER MAKE UNTIL THEY DIE!
THOSE CONDITIONS ARE A TRADE SECRET.
THE NUMBER OF MOVES ISN'T THE ISSUE...!
I NEED A PLAN TO COUNTER HIS FORESIGHT... IS IT EVEN POSSIBLE?!
I WAS LOOKING FORWARD...
!!
...TO FINDING OUT WHAT SORT OF PERSON YOU MIGHT BE.
YOU MAY HAVE THE SYMBOL'S POWER.
BUT YOU ARE UTTERLY *MEDIOCRE.*
WITH VILLAINS RUNNING AMOK...
...WE BEGIN TO SEE A SHADOW DESCENDING UPON THE COMING ERA.
THAT BEING THE CASE...

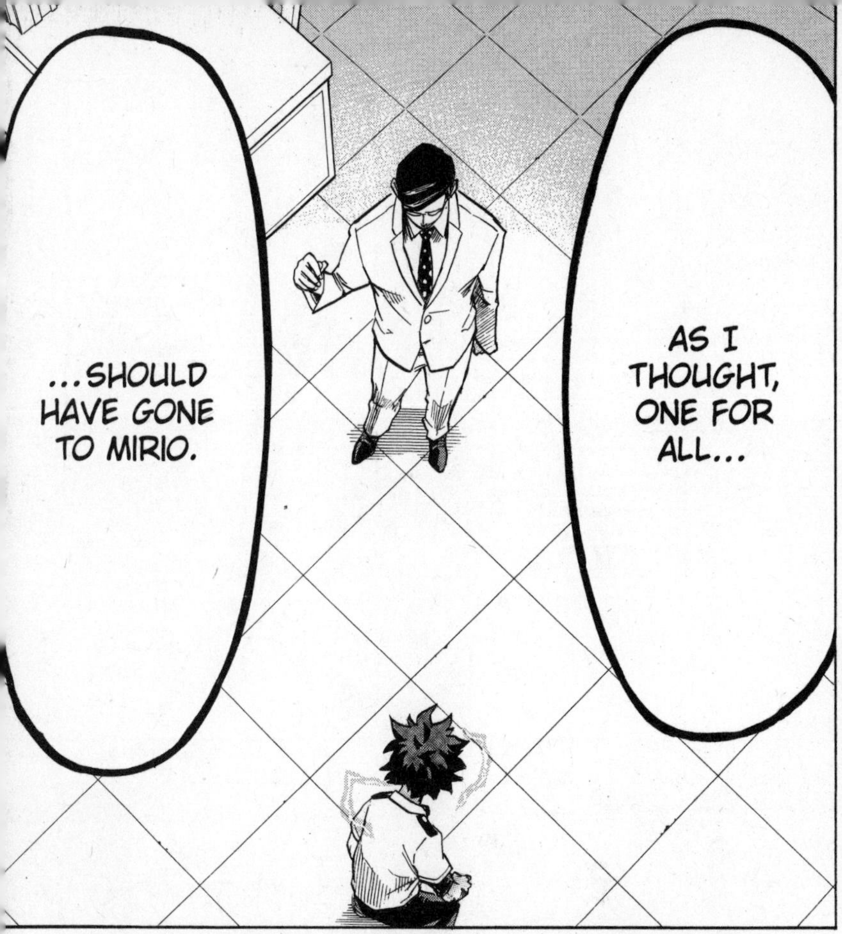
AS I THOUGHT, ONE FOR ALL...
...SHOULD HAVE GONE TO MIRIO.
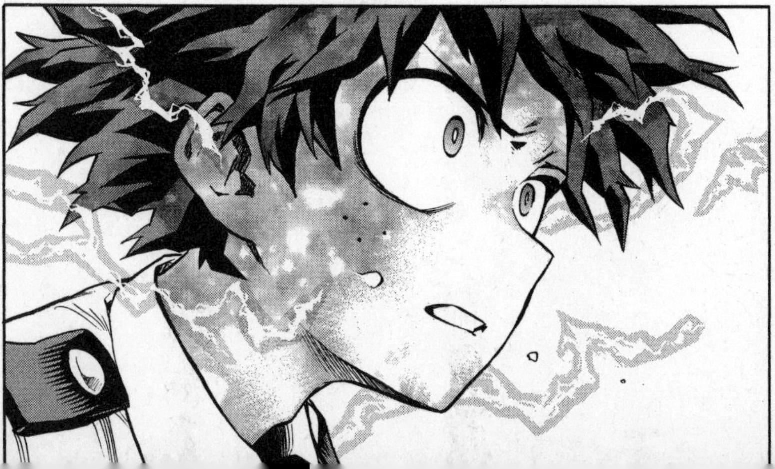

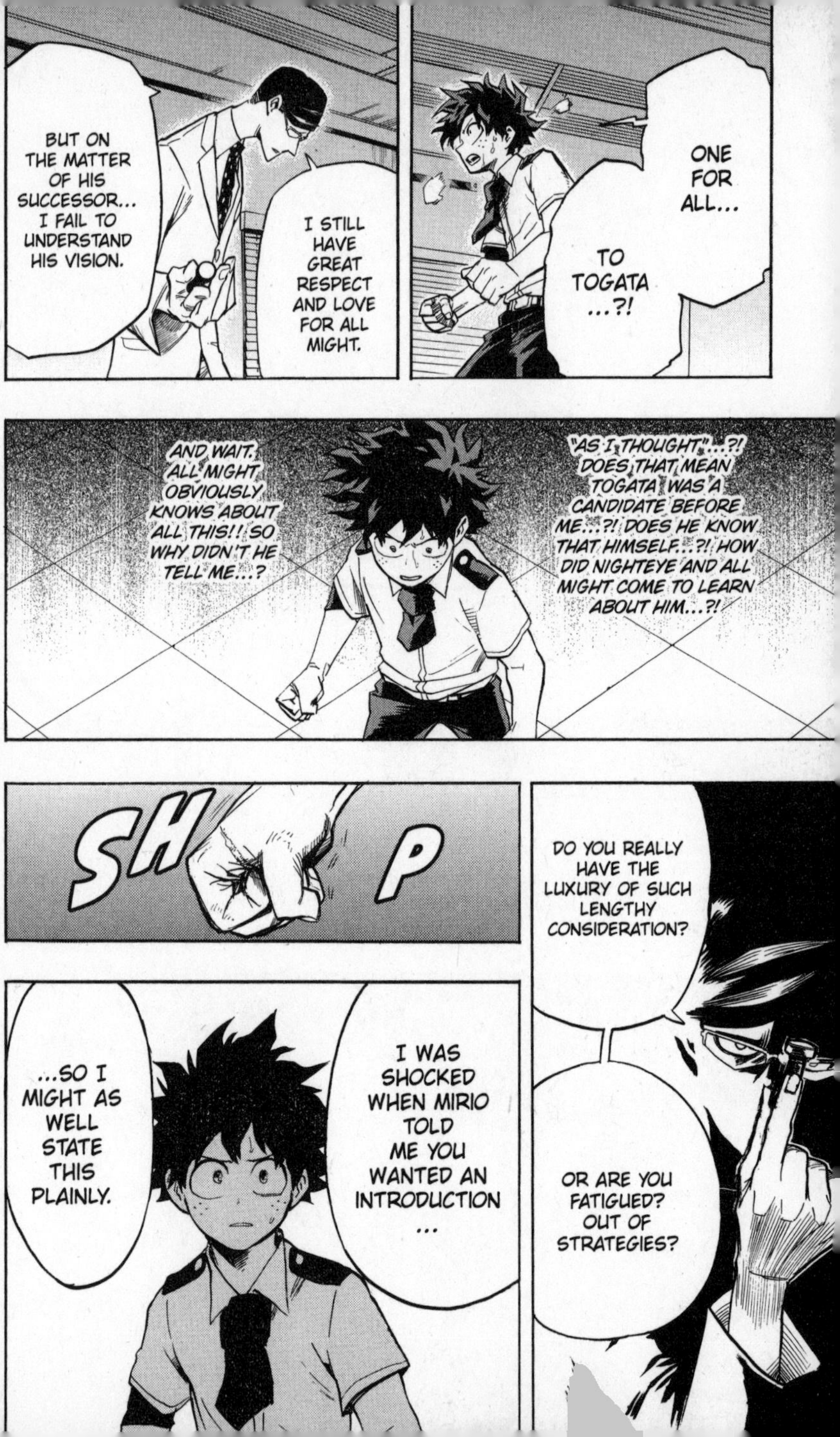
ONE FOR ALL...
TO TOGATA ...?!
I STILL HAVE GREAT RESPECT AND LOVE FOR ALL MIGHT.
BUT ON THE MATTER OF HIS SUCCESSOR... I FAIL TO UNDERSTAND HIS VISION.
"AS I THOUGHT"...?! DOES THAT MEAN TOGATA WAS A CANDIDATE BEFORE ME...?! DOES HE KNOW THAT HIMSELF...?! HOW DID NIGHTEYE AND ALL MIGHT COME TO LEARN ABOUT HIM...?!
AND WAIT. ALL MIGHT OBVIOUSLY KNOWS ABOUT ALL THIS!! SO WHY DIDN'T HE TELL ME...?
DO YOU REALLY HAVE THE LUXURY OF SUCH LENGTHY CONSIDERATION?
OR ARE YOU FATIGUED? OUT OF STRATEGIES?
SH P
I WAS SHOCKED WHEN MIRIO TOLD ME YOU WANTED AN INTRODUCTION ...
...SO I MIGHT AS WELL STATE THIS PLAINLY.

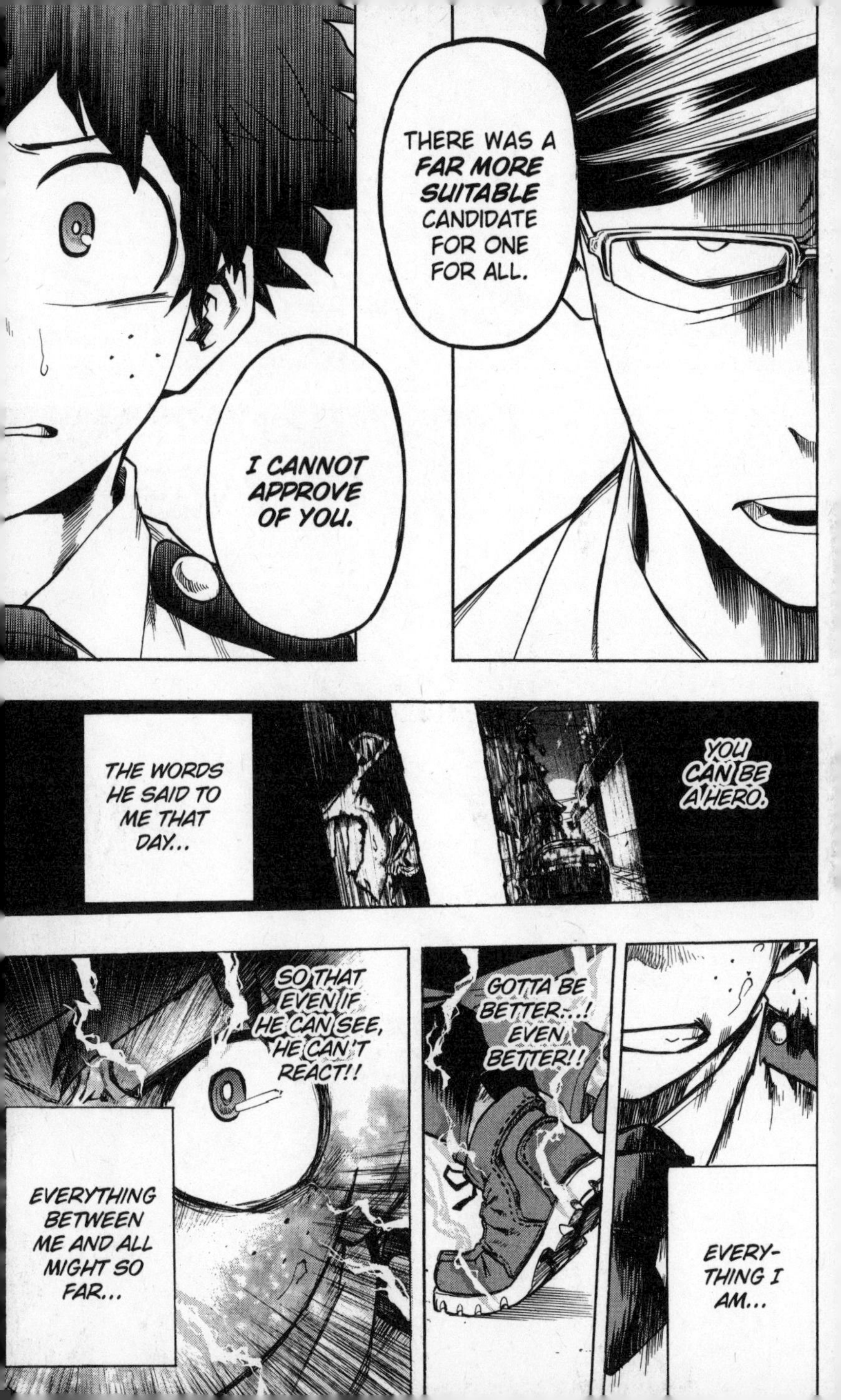
THERE WAS A FAR MORE SUITABLE CANDIDATE FOR ONE FOR ALL.
I CANNOT APPROVE OF YOU.
YOU CAN BE A HERO.
THE WORDS HE SAID TO ME THAT DAY...
EVERY-THING I AM...
GOTTA BE BETTER...! EVEN BETTER!!
SO THAT EVEN IF HE CAN SEE, HE CAN'T REACT!!
EVERYTHING BETWEEN ME AND ALL MIGHT SO FAR...

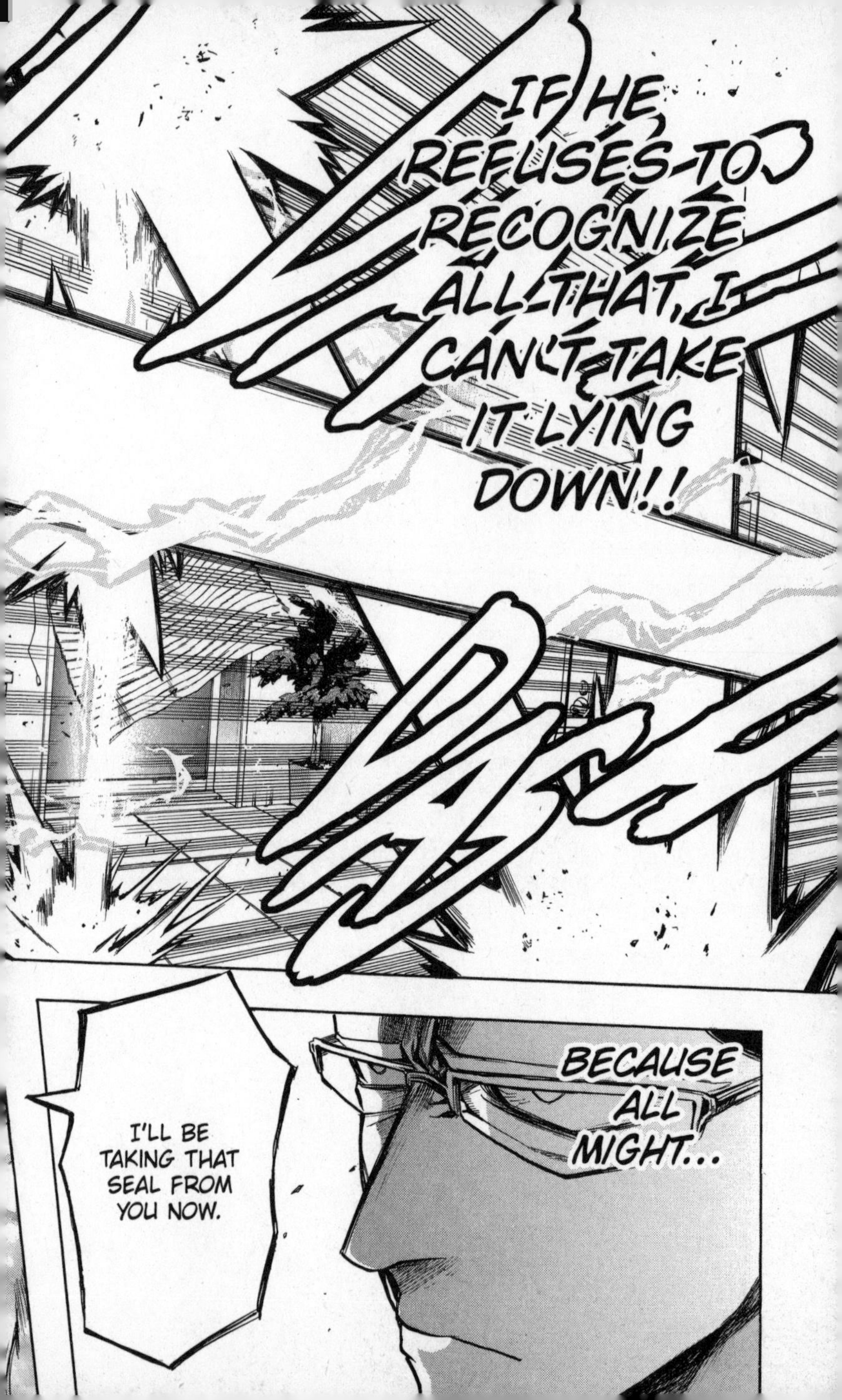
IF HE REFUSES TO RECOGNIZE ALL THAT, I CAN'T TAKE IT LYING DOWN!!
BECAUSE ALL MIGHT...
I'LL BE TAKING THAT SEAL FROM YOU NOW.

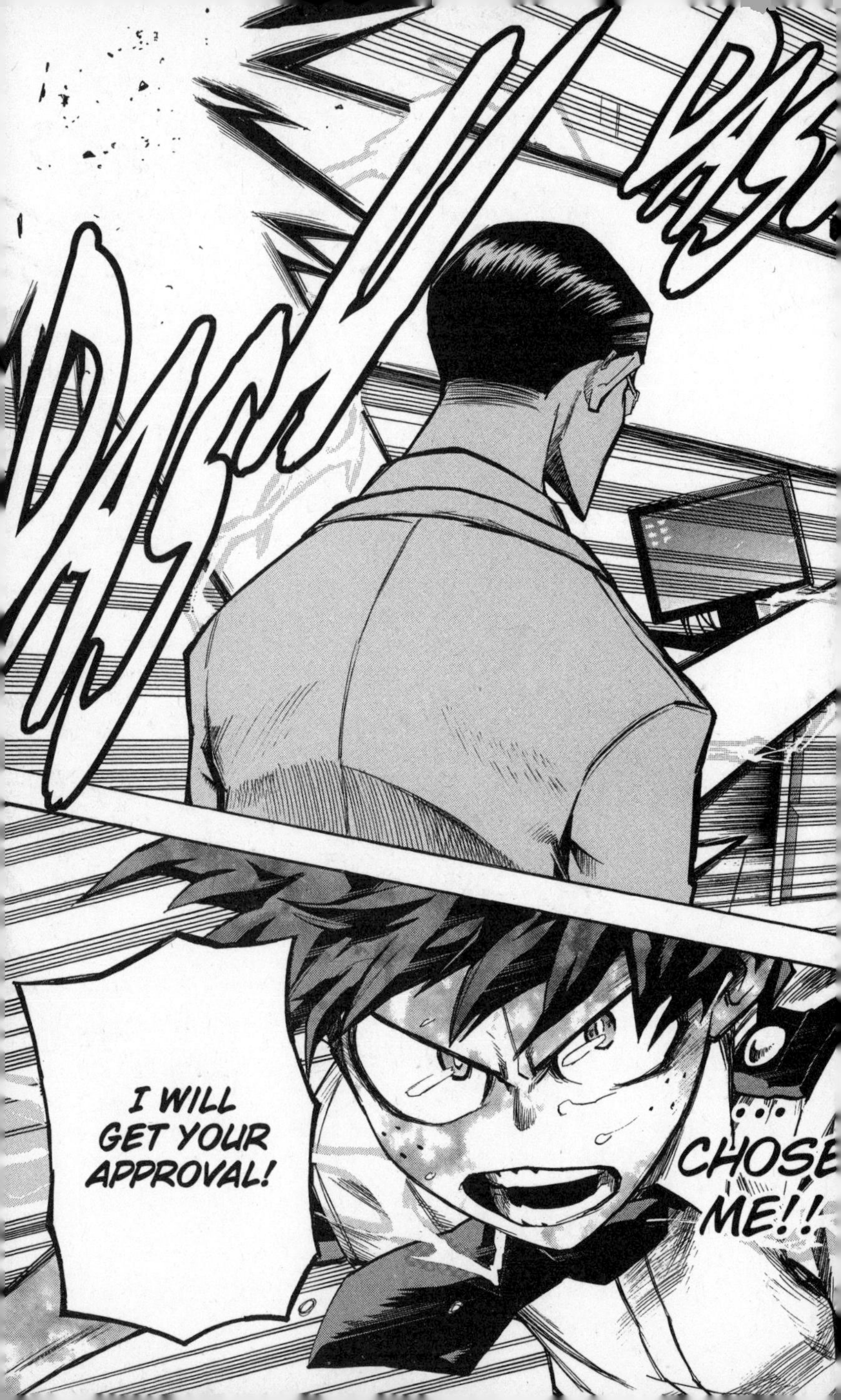
...CHOSE ME!!
I WILL GET YOUR APPROVAL!

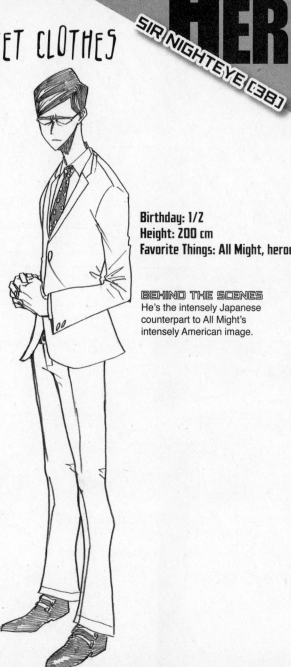

HERO

SIR NIGHTEYE (38)

STREET CLOTHES

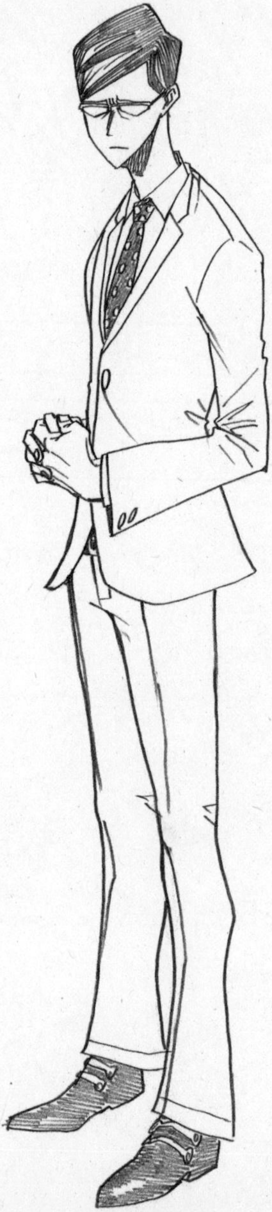

Birthday: 1/2
Height: 200 cm
Favorite Things: All Might, heroes

BEHIND THE SCENES

He's the intensely Japanese counterpart to All Might's intensely American image.

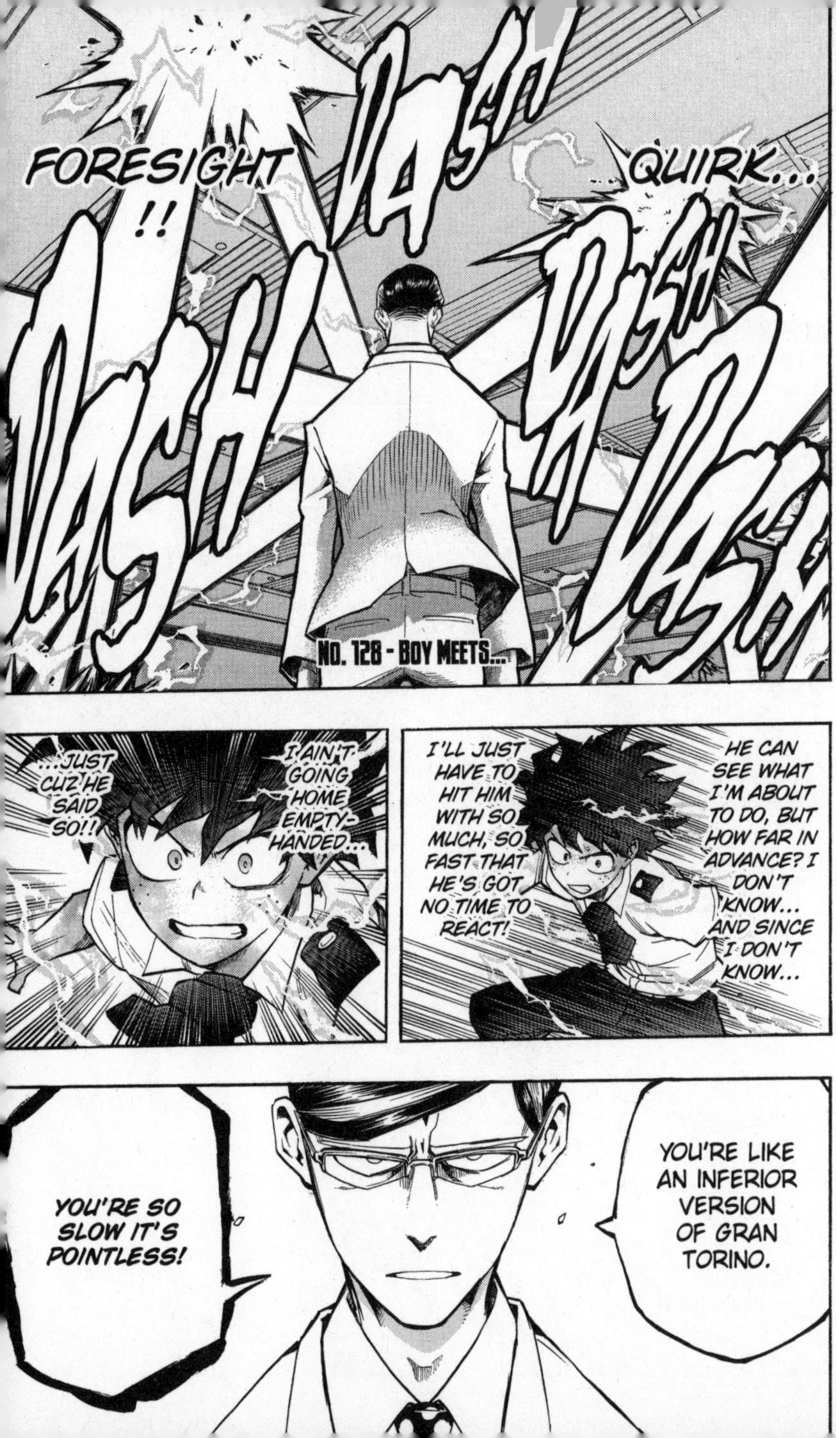

QUIRK...
FORESIGHT !!
DASH
DASH
DASH
DASH
NO. 128 - BOY MEETS...
HE CAN SEE WHAT I'M ABOUT TO DO, BUT HOW FAR IN ADVANCE? I DON'T KNOW... AND SINCE I DON'T KNOW...
I'LL JUST HAVE TO HIT HIM WITH SO MUCH, SO FAST THAT HE'S GOT NO TIME TO REACT!
I AIN'T GOING HOME EMPTY-HANDED...
...JUST CUZ HE SAID SO!!
YOU'RE LIKE AN INFERIOR VERSION OF GRAN TORINO.
YOU'RE SO SLOW IT'S POINTLESS!

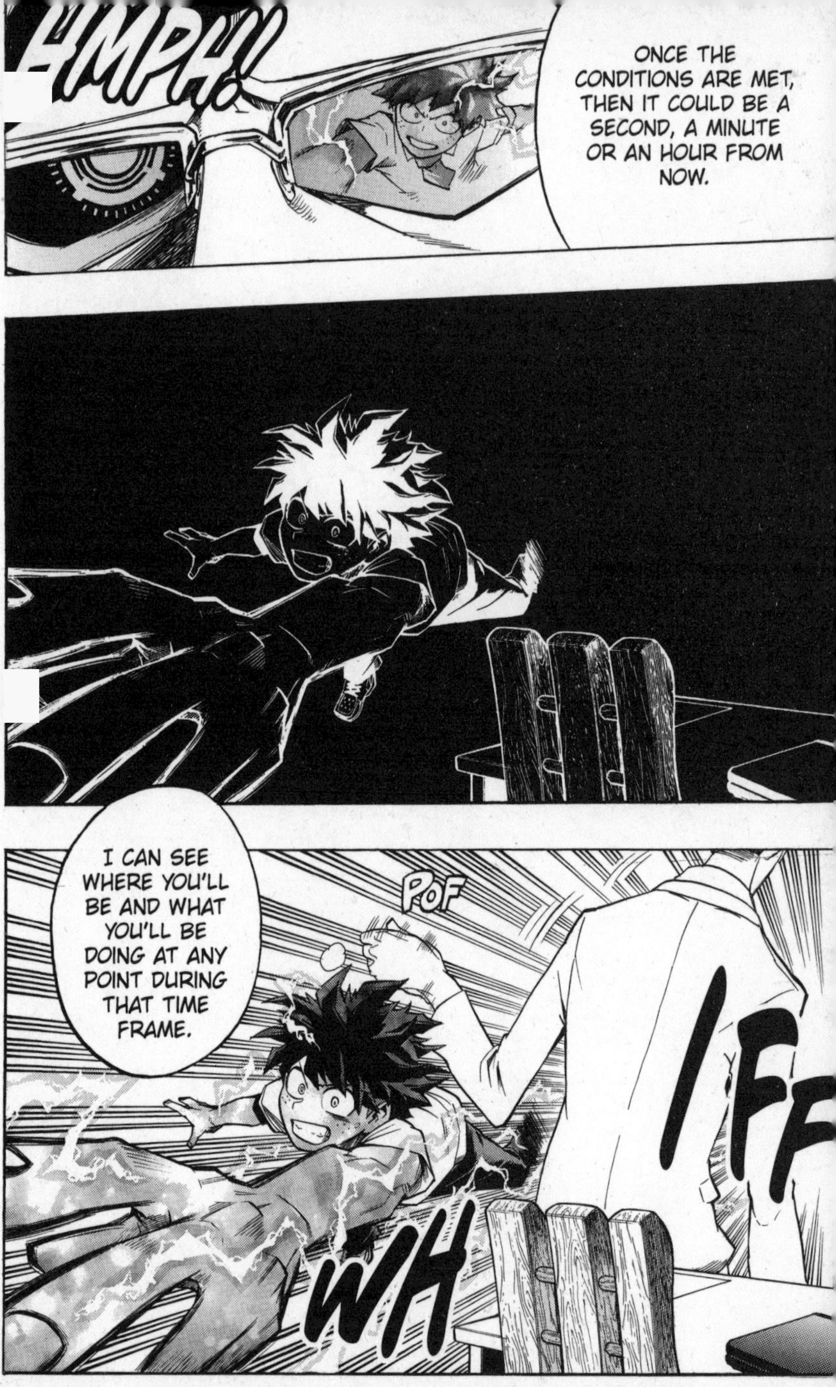
ONCE THE CONDITIONS ARE MET, THEN IT COULD BE A SECOND, A MINUTE OR AN HOUR FROM NOW.
HMPH!
I CAN SEE WHERE YOU'LL BE AND WHAT YOU'LL BE DOING AT ANY POINT DURING THAT TIME FRAME.
POF
IFF
WH

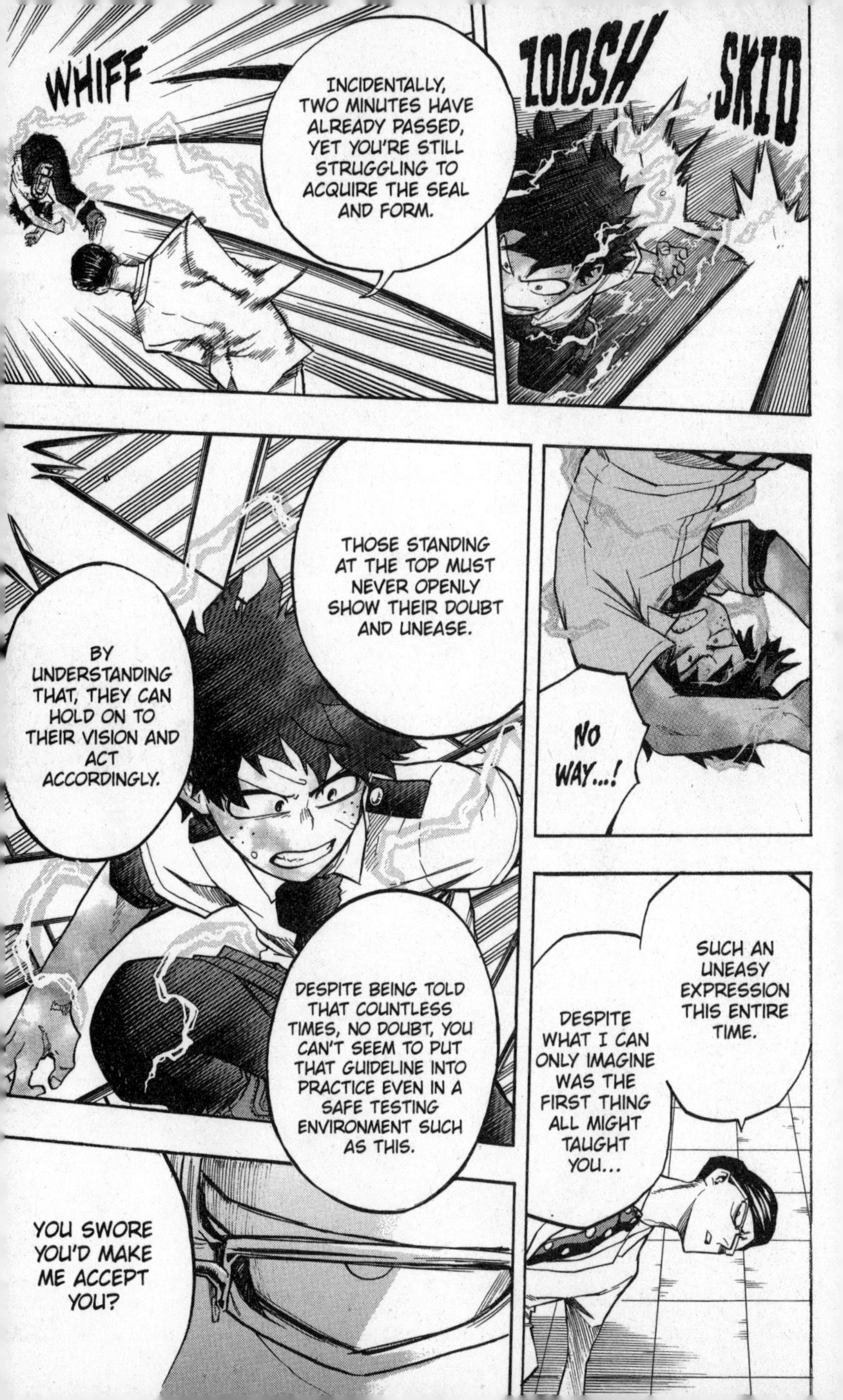
SKID
ZOOSH
INCIDENTALLY, TWO MINUTES HAVE ALREADY PASSED, YET YOU'RE STILL STRUGGLING TO ACQUIRE THE SEAL AND FORM.
WHIFF
NO WAY...!
SUCH AN UNEASY EXPRESSION THIS ENTIRE TIME.
DESPITE WHAT I CAN ONLY IMAGINE WAS THE FIRST THING ALL MIGHT TAUGHT YOU...
THOSE STANDING AT THE TOP MUST NEVER OPENLY SHOW THEIR DOUBT AND UNEASE.
BY UNDERSTANDING THAT, THEY CAN HOLD ON TO THEIR VISION AND ACT ACCORDINGLY.
DESPITE BEING TOLD THAT COUNTLESS TIMES, NO DOUBT, YOU CAN'T SEEM TO PUT THAT GUIDELINE INTO PRACTICE EVEN IN A SAFE TESTING ENVIRONMENT SUCH AS THIS.
YOU SWORE YOU'D MAKE ME ACCEPT YOU?

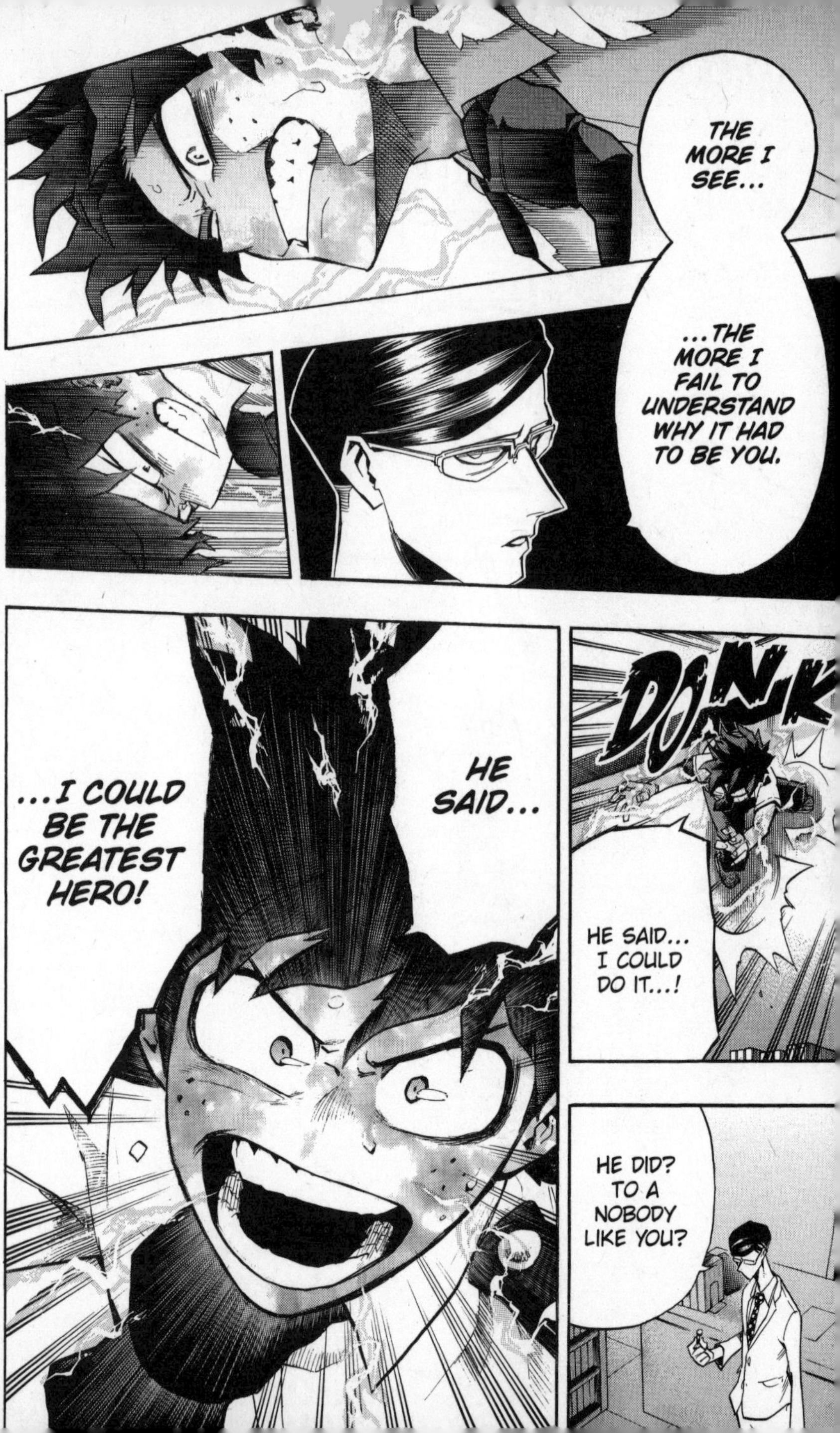
THE MORE I SEE...
...THE MORE I FAIL TO UNDERSTAND WHY IT HAD TO BE YOU.
DONK
HE SAID... I COULD DO IT...!
HE DID? TO A NOBODY LIKE YOU?
HE SAID...
...I COULD BE THE GREATEST HERO!

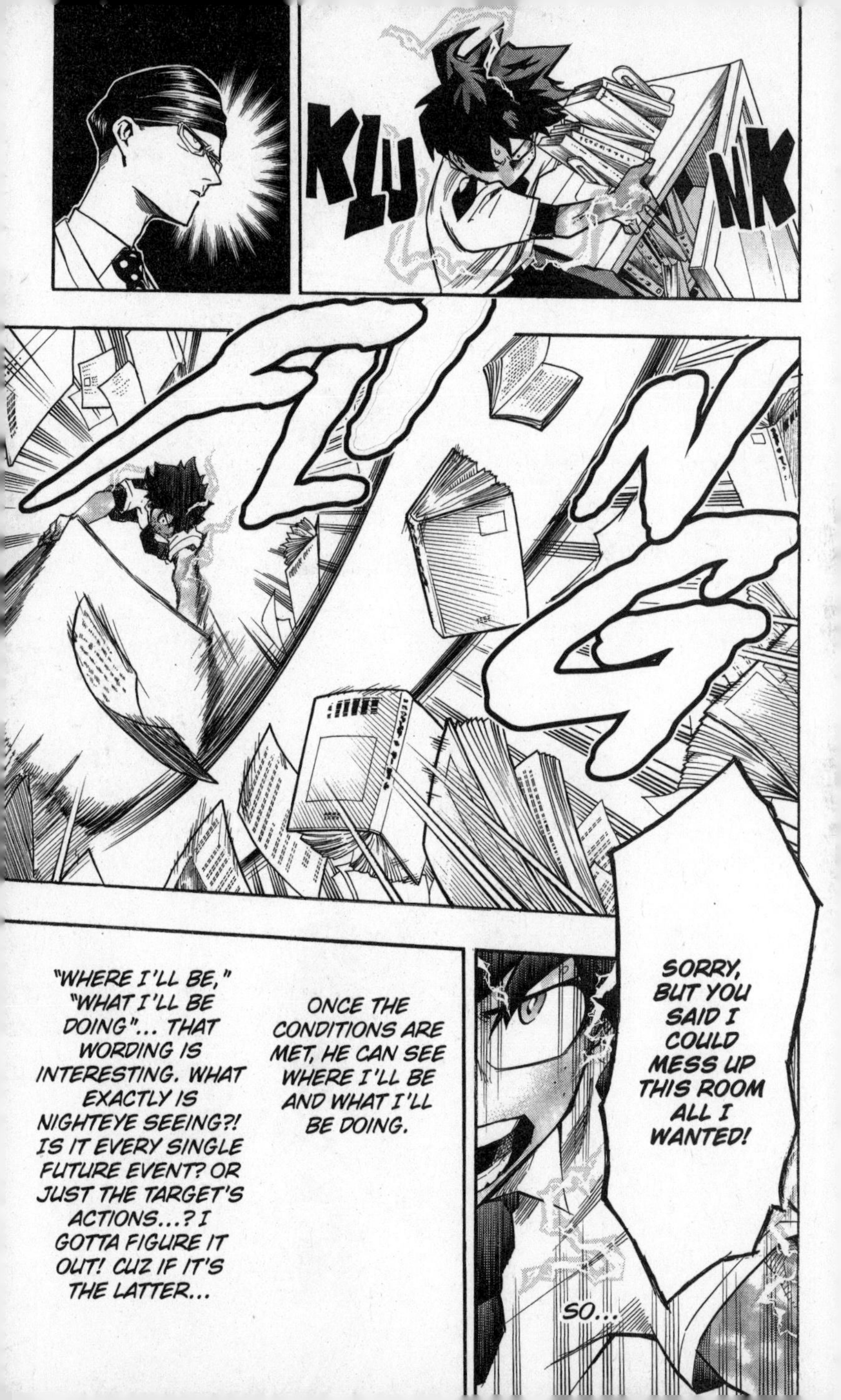
KLUNK
ZING
SORRY, BUT YOU SAID I COULD MESS UP THIS ROOM ALL I WANTED!
SO...
ONCE THE CONDITIONS ARE MET, HE CAN SEE WHERE I'LL BE AND WHAT I'LL BE DOING.
"WHERE I'LL BE," "WHAT I'LL BE DOING"... THAT WORDING IS INTERESTING. WHAT EXACTLY IS NIGHTEYE SEEING?! IS IT EVERY SINGLE FUTURE EVENT? OR JUST THE TARGET'S ACTIONS...? I GOTTA FIGURE IT OUT! CUZ IF IT'S THE LATTER...

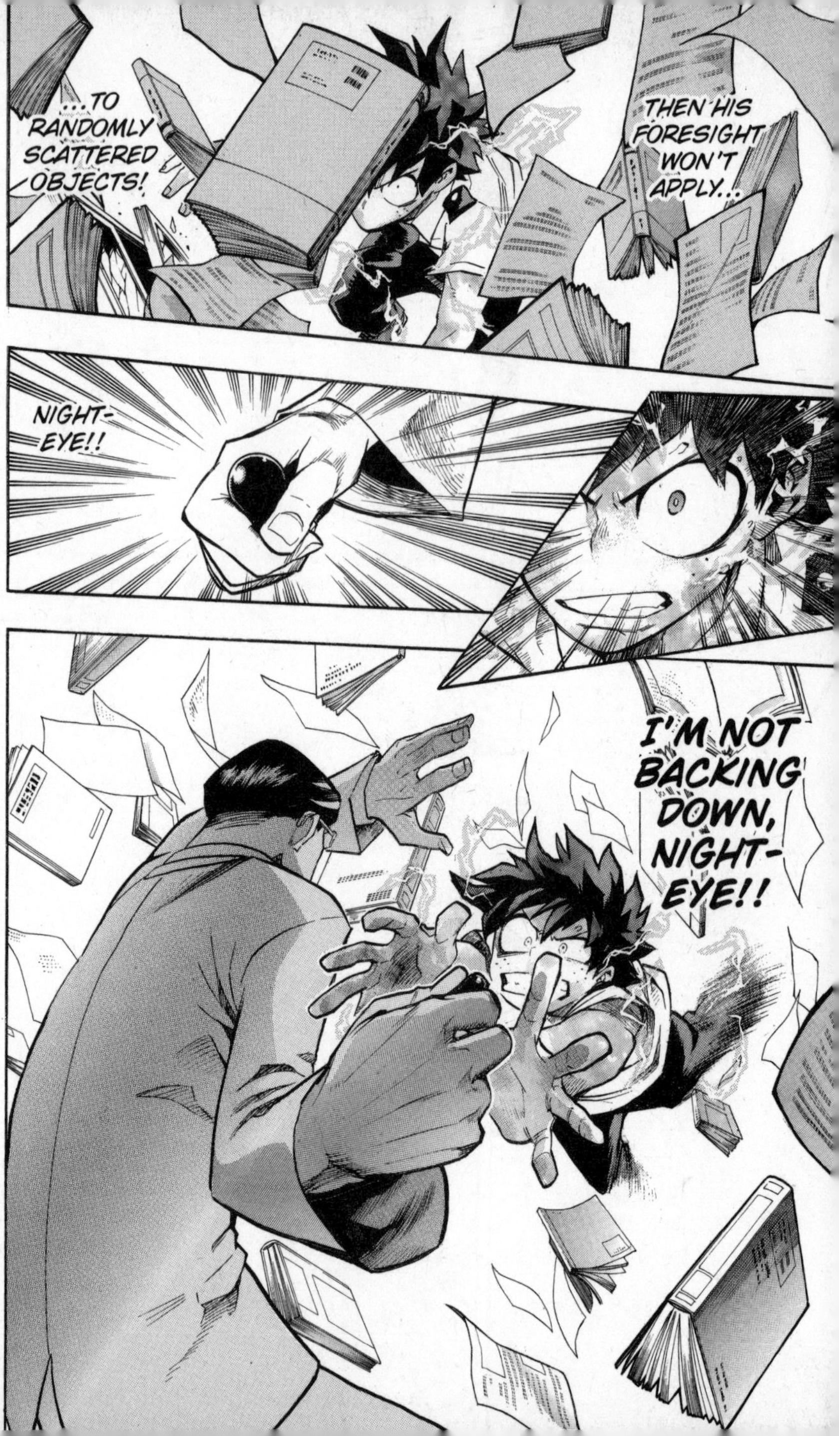
THEN HIS FORESIGHT WON'T APPLY...
...TO RANDOMLY SCATTERED OBJECTS!
NIGHT-EYE!!
I'M NOT BACKING DOWN, NIGHT-EYE!!

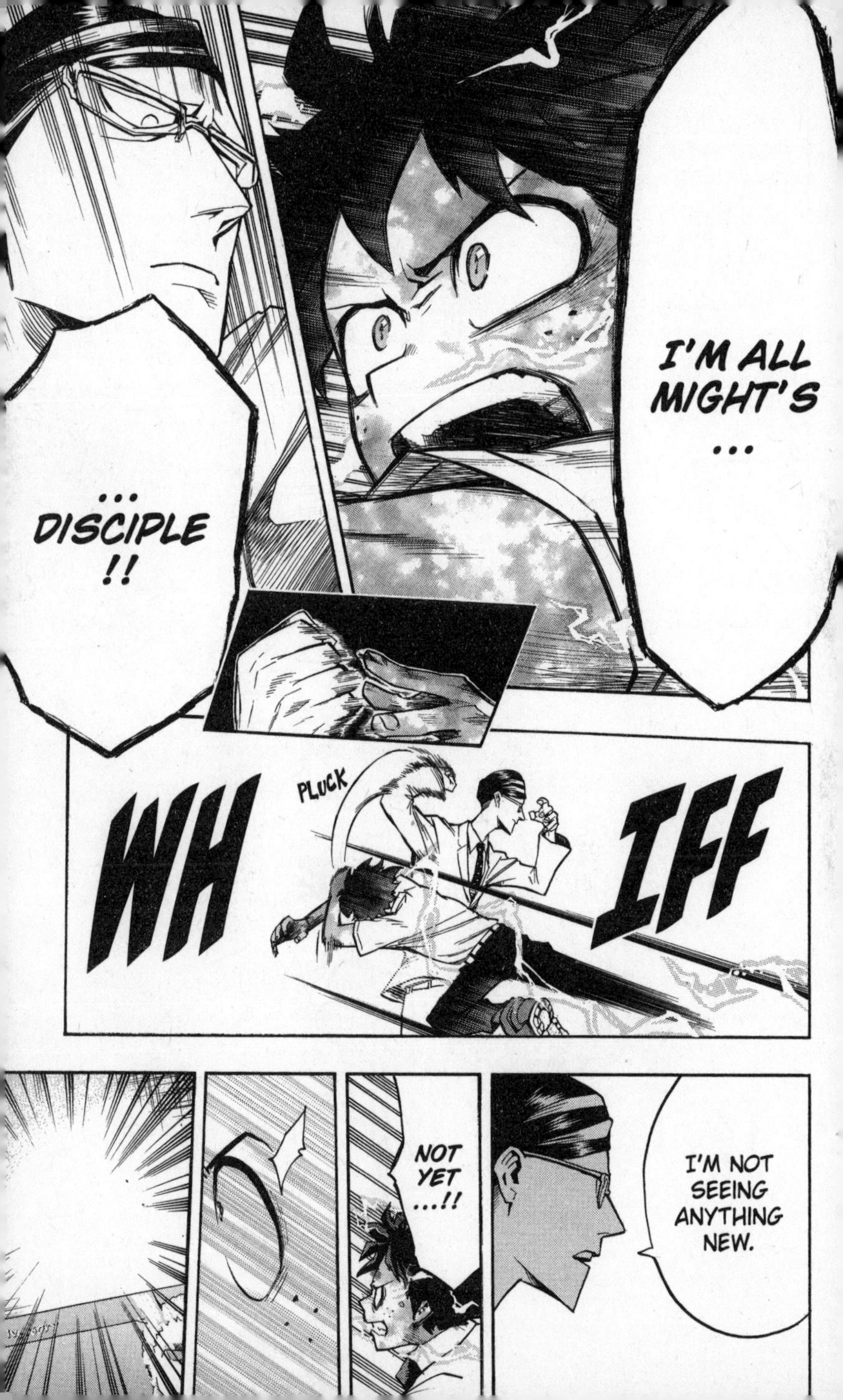
I'M ALL MIGHT'S ...
... DISCIPLE !!
WHIFF
PLUCK
I'M NOT SEEING ANYTHING NEW.
NOT YET ...!!

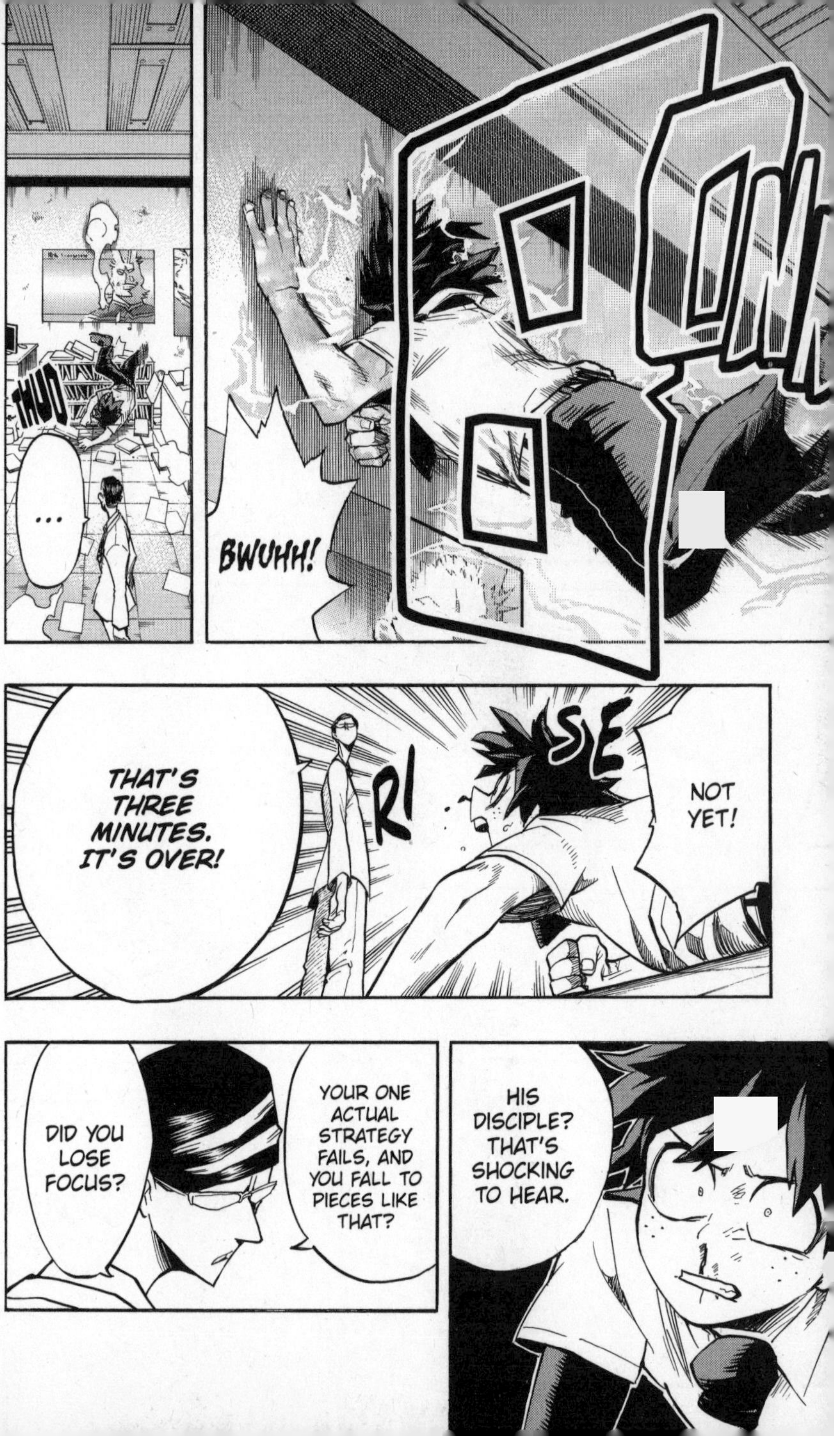
BWUHH!
THUD
...
NOT YET!
RISE
THAT'S THREE MINUTES. IT'S OVER!
HIS DISCIPLE? THAT'S SHOCKING TO HEAR.
YOUR ONE ACTUAL STRATEGY FAILS, AND YOU FALL TO PIECES LIKE THAT?
DID YOU LOSE FOCUS?

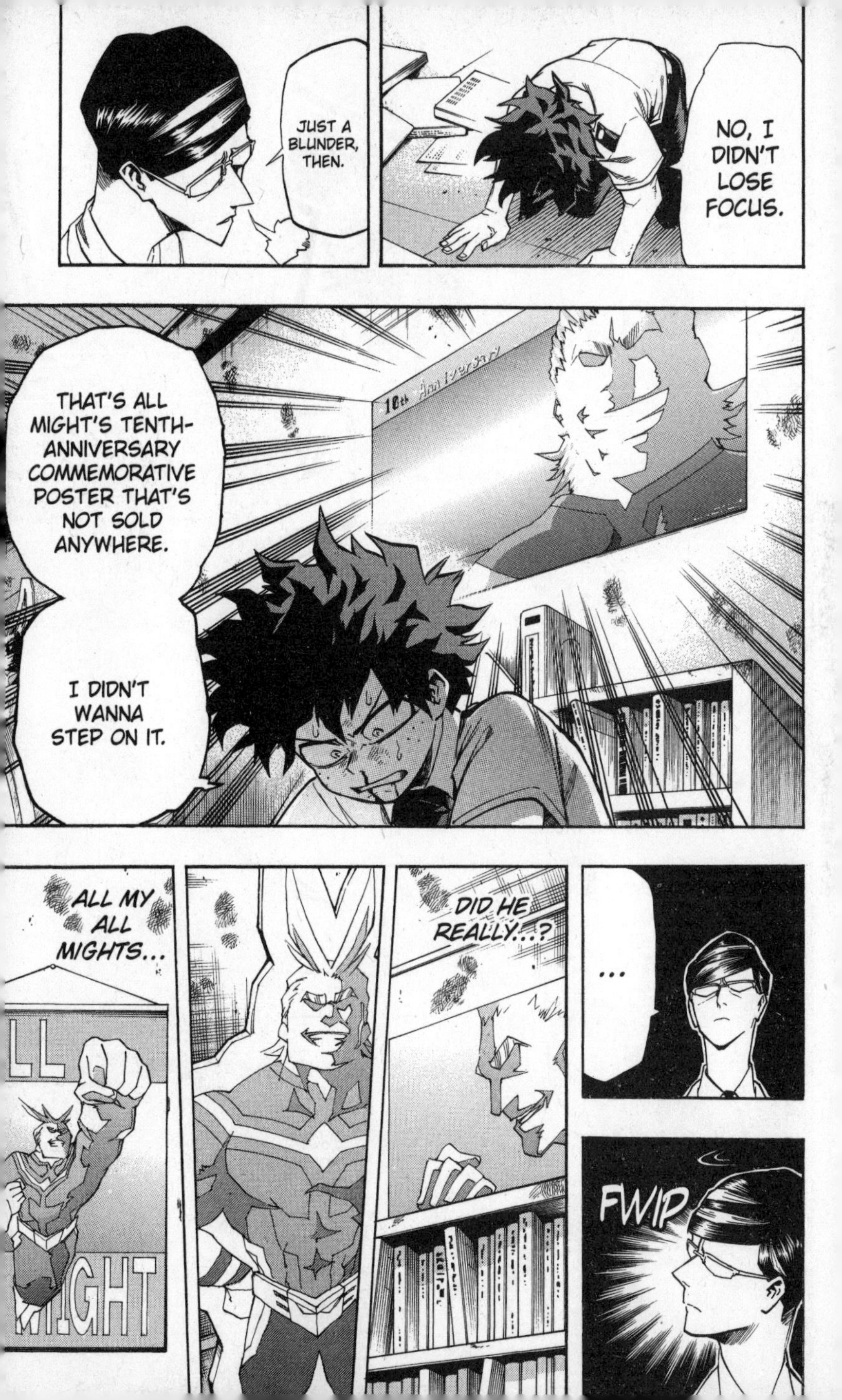
NO, I DIDN'T LOSE FOCUS.
JUST A BLUNDER, THEN.
THAT'S ALL MIGHT'S TENTH-ANNIVERSARY COMMEMORATIVE POSTER THAT'S NOT SOLD ANYWHERE.
I DIDN'T WANNA STEP ON IT.
...
FWIP
DID HE REALLY...?
ALL MY ALL MIGHTS...

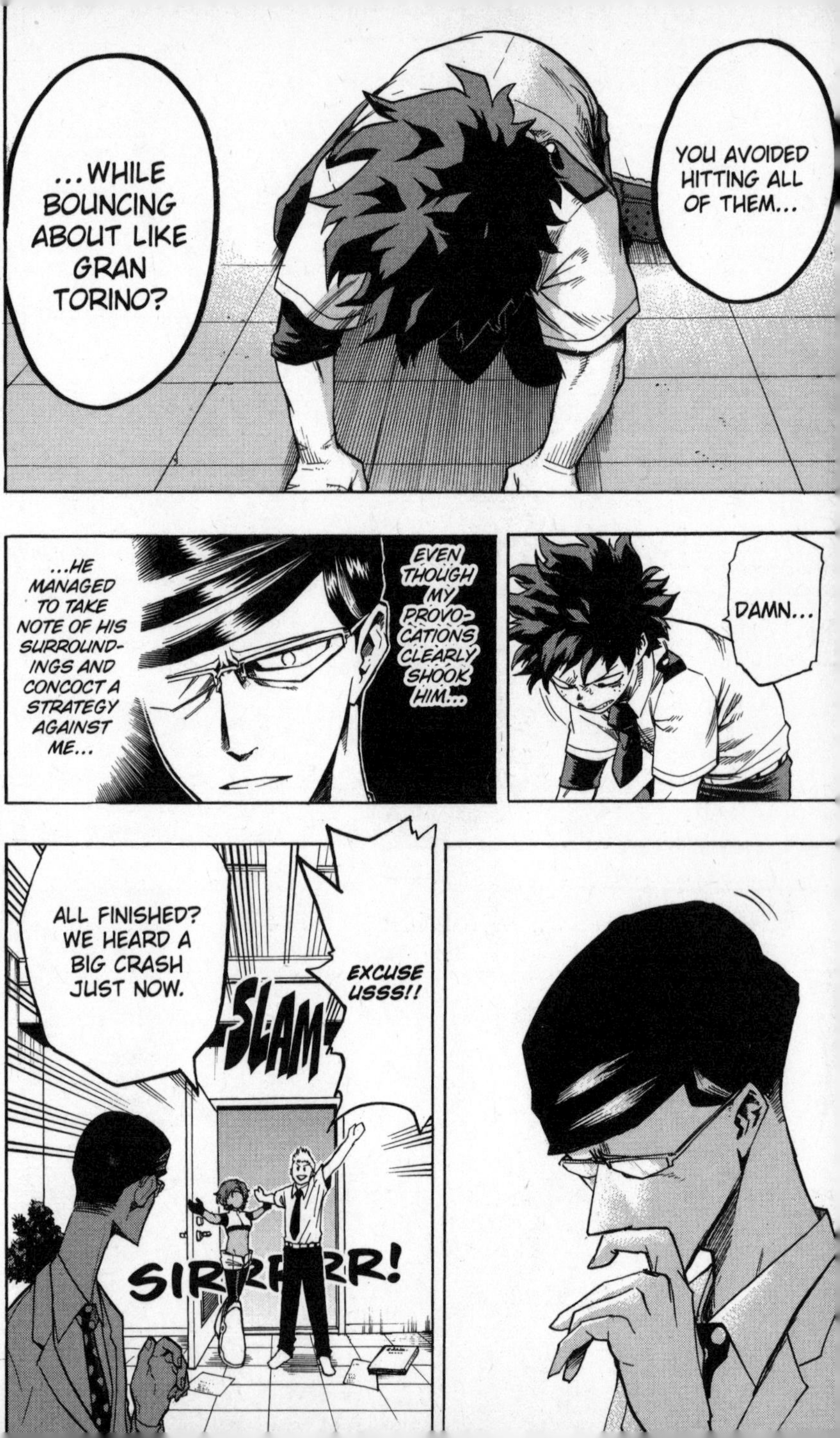
YOU AVOIDED HITTING ALL OF THEM...
...WHILE BOUNCING ABOUT LIKE GRAN TORINO?
DAMN...
EVEN THOUGH MY PROVOCATIONS CLEARLY SHOOK HIM...
...HE MANAGED TO TAKE NOTE OF HIS SURROUNDINGS AND CONCOCT A STRATEGY AGAINST ME...
EXCUSE USSS!!
SLAM
ALL FINISHED? WE HEARD A BIG CRASH JUST NOW.
SIRRRRR!

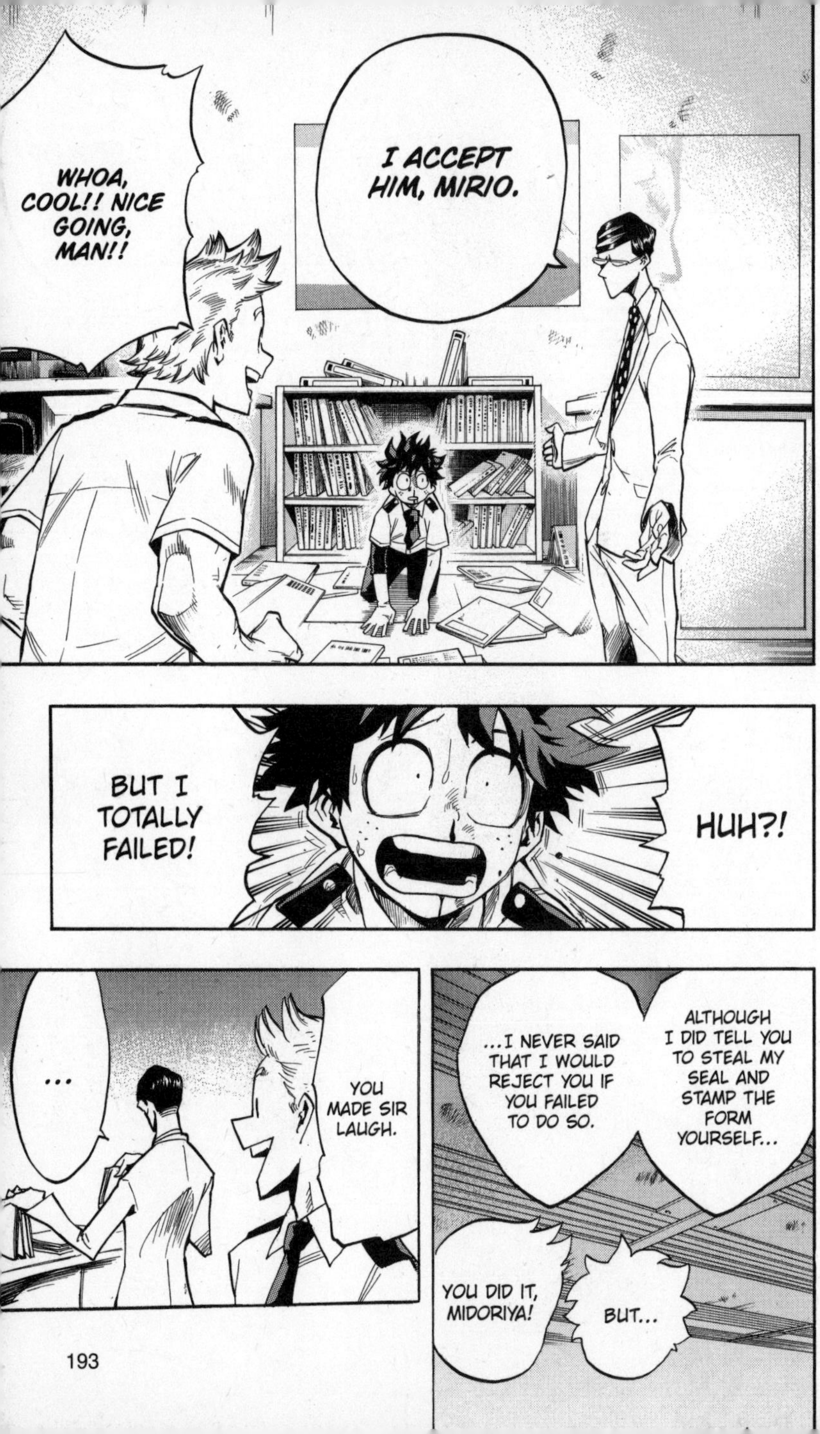
I ACCEPT HIM, MIRIO.
WHOA, COOL!! NICE GOING, MAN!!
HUH?!
BUT I TOTALLY FAILED!
ALTHOUGH I DID TELL YOU TO STEAL MY SEAL AND STAMP THE FORM YOURSELF...
...I NEVER SAID THAT I WOULD REJECT YOU IF YOU FAILED TO DO SO.
BUT...
YOU DID IT, MIDORIYA!
YOU MADE SIR LAUGH.
...

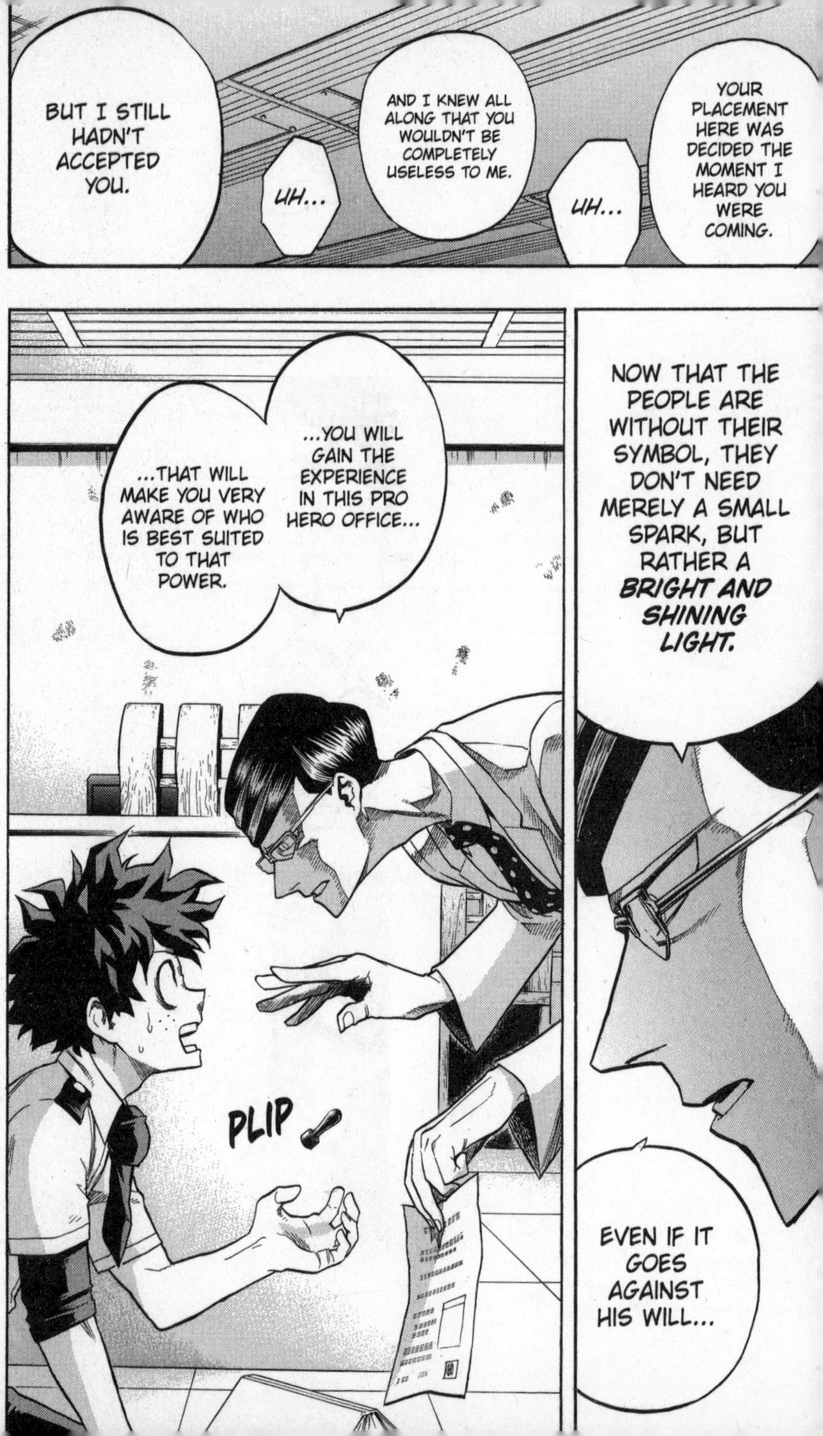
YOUR PLACEMENT HERE WAS DECIDED THE MOMENT I HEARD YOU WERE COMING.
UH...
AND I KNEW ALL ALONG THAT YOU WOULDN'T BE COMPLETELY USELESS TO ME.
UH...
BUT I STILL HADN'T ACCEPTED YOU.
NOW THAT THE PEOPLE ARE WITHOUT THEIR SYMBOL, THEY DON'T NEED MERELY A SMALL SPARK, BUT RATHER A ***BRIGHT AND SHINING LIGHT.***
EVEN IF IT GOES AGAINST HIS WILL...
...YOU WILL GAIN THE EXPERIENCE IN THIS PRO HERO OFFICE...
...THAT WILL MAKE YOU VERY AWARE OF WHO IS BEST SUITED TO THAT POWER.
PLIP

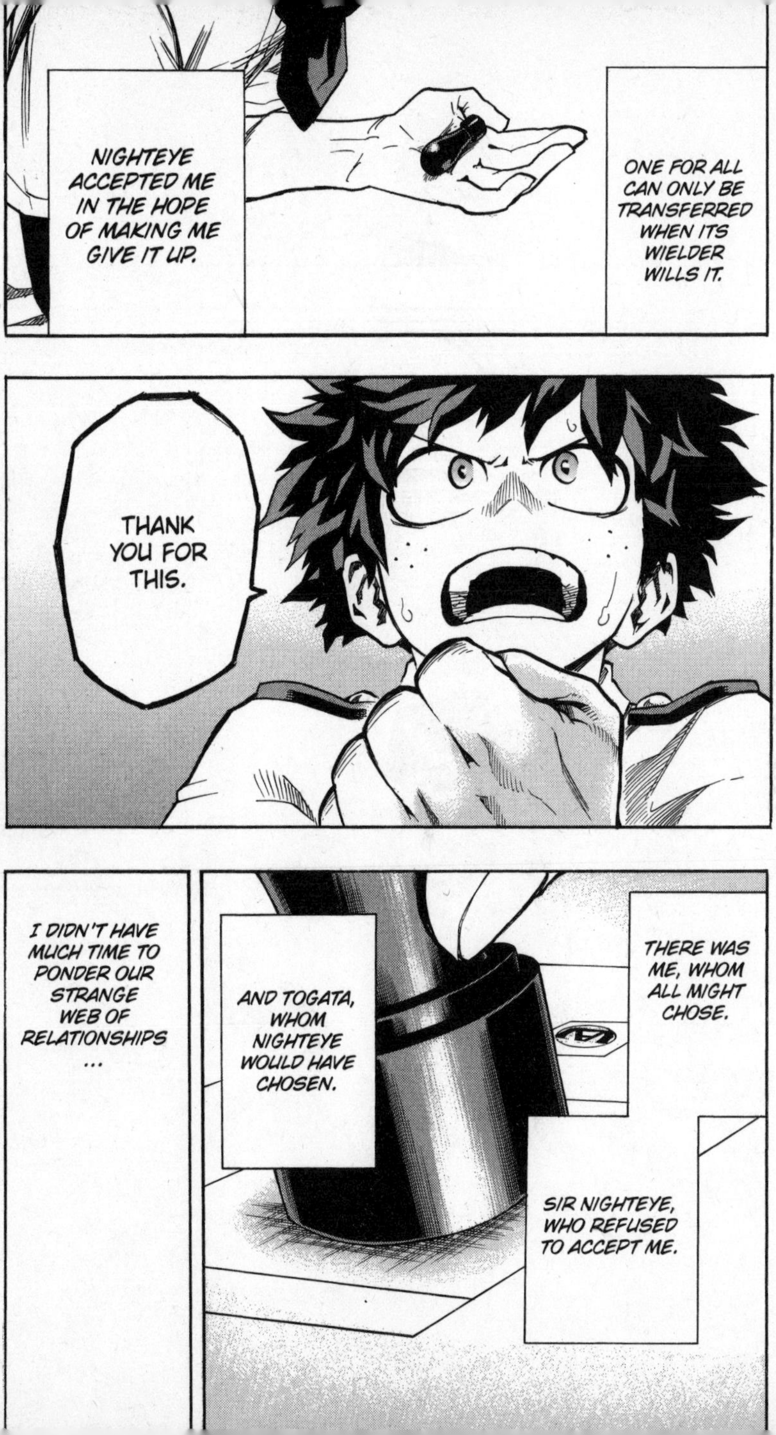
ONE FOR ALL CAN ONLY BE TRANSFERRED WHEN ITS WIELDER WILLS IT.
NIGHTEYE ACCEPTED ME IN THE HOPE OF MAKING ME GIVE IT UP.
THANK YOU FOR THIS.
THERE WAS ME, WHOM ALL MIGHT CHOSE.
AND TOGATA, WHOM NIGHTEYE WOULD HAVE CHOSEN.
SIR NIGHTEYE, WHO REFUSED TO ACCEPT ME.
I DIDN'T HAVE MUCH TIME TO PONDER OUR STRANGE WEB OF RELATIONSHIPS...

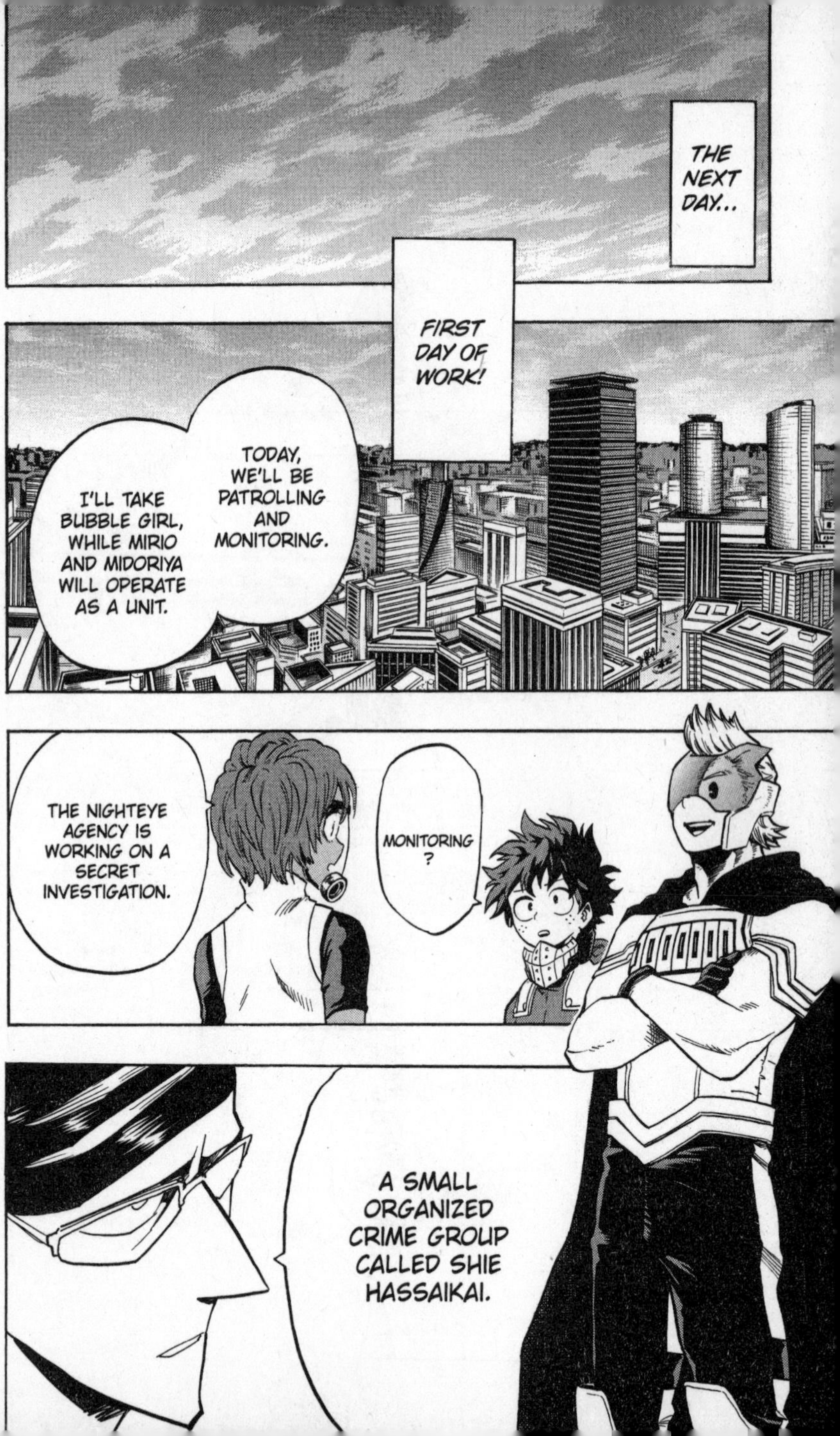
THE NEXT DAY...
FIRST DAY OF WORK!
TODAY, WE'LL BE PATROLLING AND MONITORING.
I'LL TAKE BUBBLE GIRL, WHILE MIRIO AND MIDORIYA WILL OPERATE AS A UNIT.
MONITORING?
THE NIGHTEYE AGENCY IS WORKING ON A SECRET INVESTIGATION.
A SMALL ORGANIZED CRIME GROUP CALLED SHIE HASSAIKAI.

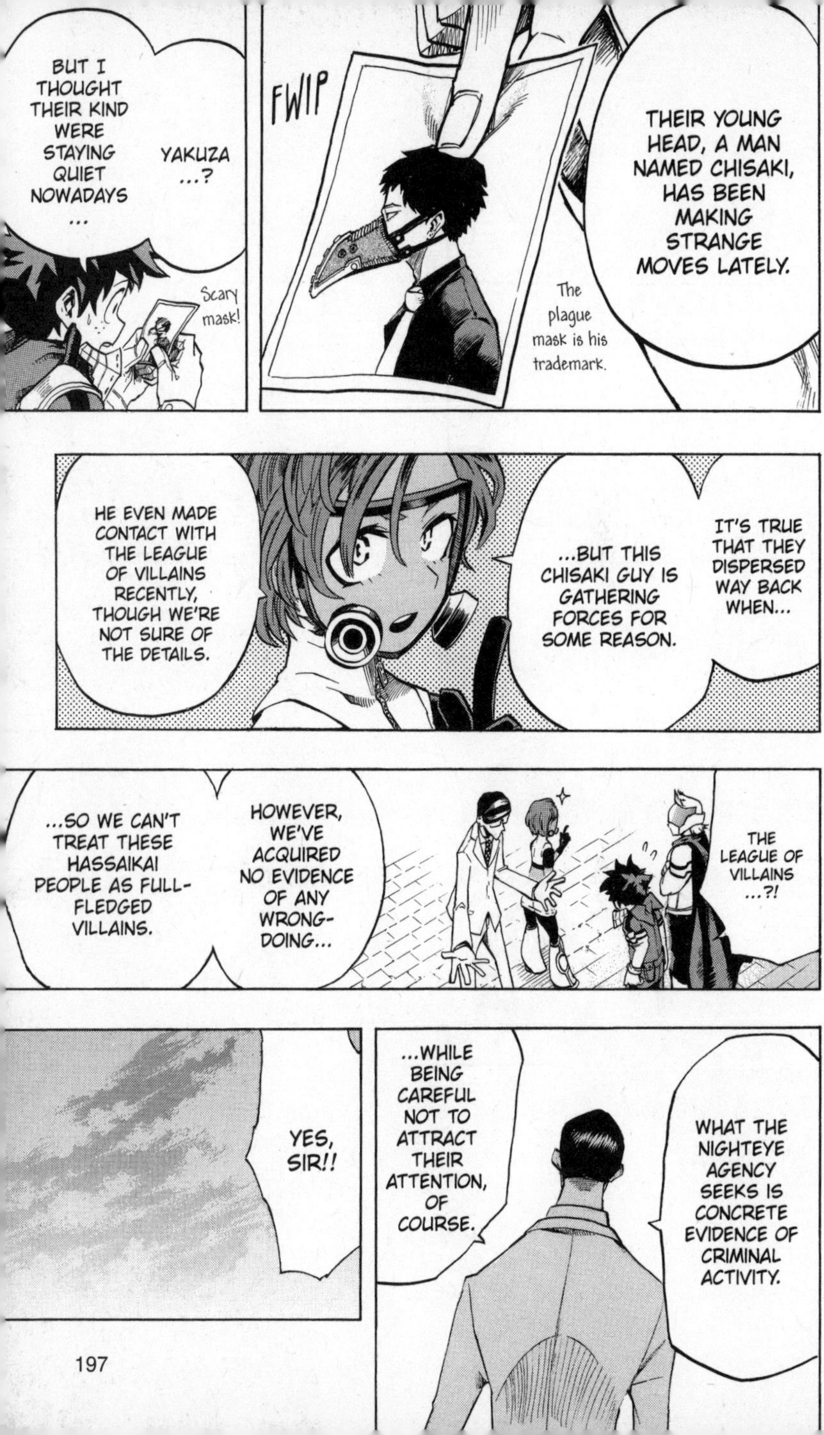

THEIR YOUNG HEAD, A MAN NAMED CHISAKI, HAS BEEN MAKING STRANGE MOVES LATELY.
FWIP
The plague mask is his trademark.
YAKUZA ...?
BUT I THOUGHT THEIR KIND WERE STAYING QUIET NOWADAYS ...
Scary mask!
IT'S TRUE THAT THEY DISPERSED WAY BACK WHEN...
...BUT THIS CHISAKI GUY IS GATHERING FORCES FOR SOME REASON.
HE EVEN MADE CONTACT WITH THE LEAGUE OF VILLAINS RECENTLY, THOUGH WE'RE NOT SURE OF THE DETAILS.
THE LEAGUE OF VILLAINS ...?!
HOWEVER, WE'VE ACQUIRED NO EVIDENCE OF ANY WRONG-DOING...
...SO WE CAN'T TREAT THESE HASSAIKAI PEOPLE AS FULL-FLEDGED VILLAINS.
WHAT THE NIGHTEYE AGENCY SEEKS IS CONCRETE EVIDENCE OF CRIMINAL ACTIVITY.
...WHILE BEING CAREFUL NOT TO ATTRACT THEIR ATTENTION, OF COURSE.
YES, SIR!!

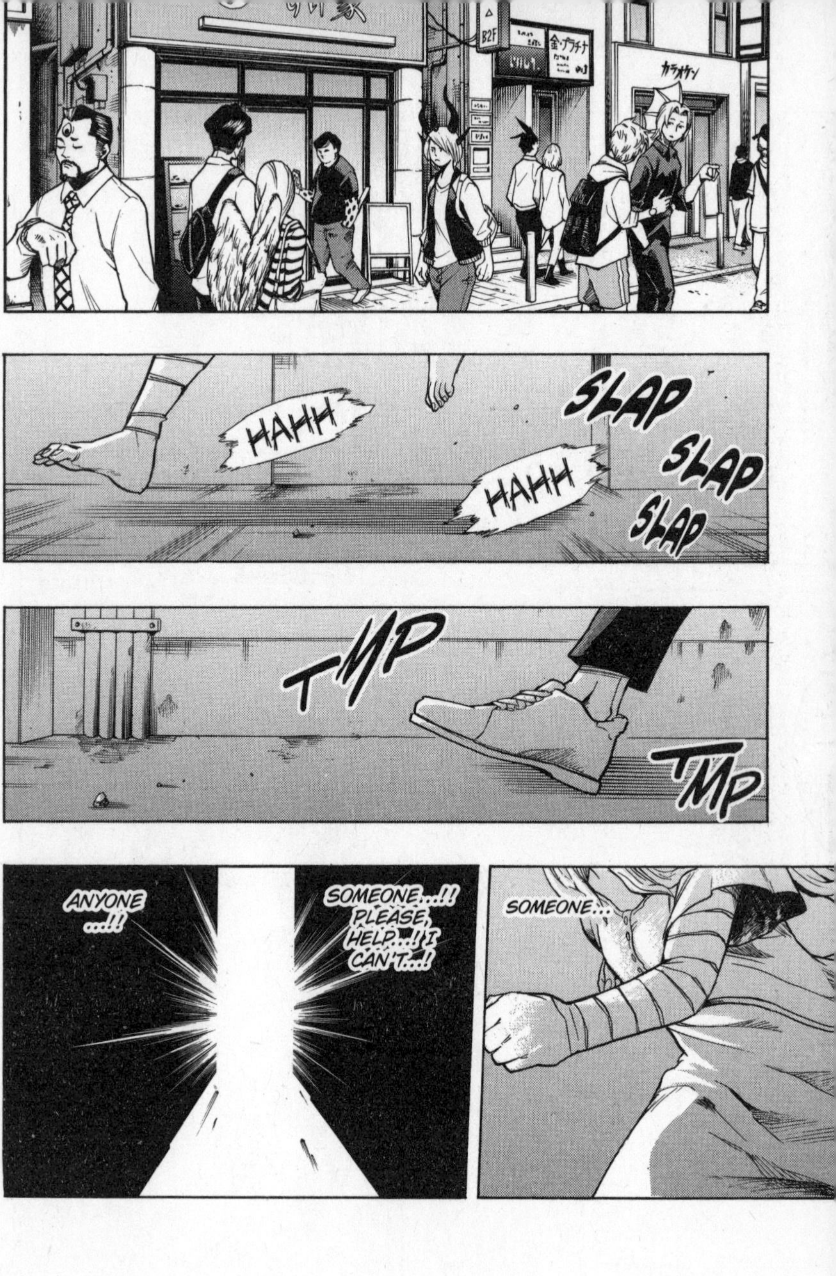

B2F
金・プラチナ
SLAP
SLAP
SLAP
HAHH
HAHH
TMP
TMP
SOMEONE...
SOMEONE...!! PLEASE, HELP...! I CAN'T...!
ANYONE ...!!

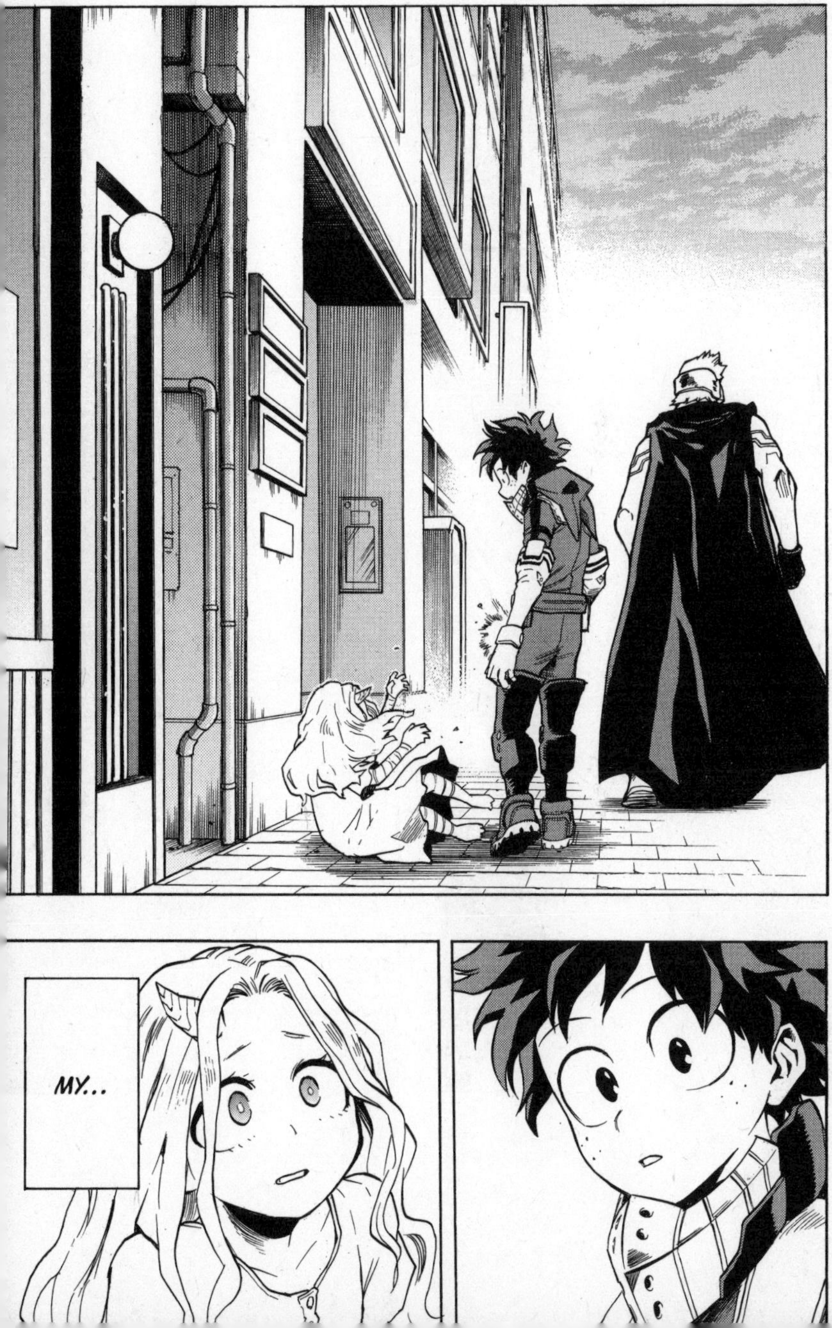
MY...

...LONG WORK STUDY HAD ONLY...

I'M SORRY. DID I HURT YOU?

AH...

TWITCH

SHAME ON YOU, CAUSING TROUBLE FOR THIS NICE HERO.

Can you stand up?

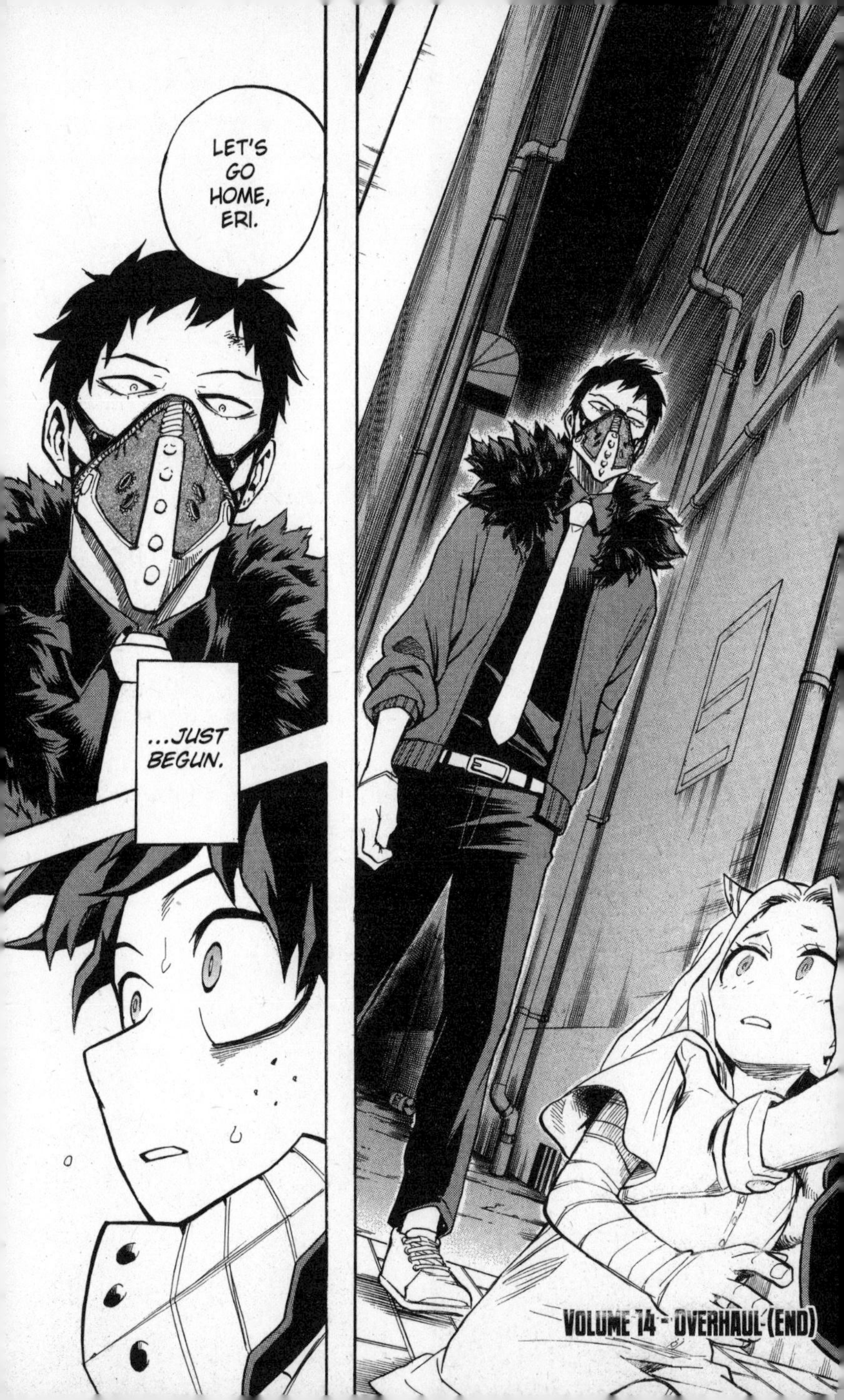
VOLUME 14 - OVERHAUL (END)
LET'S GO HOME, ERI.
...JUST BEGUN.

HERO

BUBBLE GIRL [21] [KAORUKO AWATA]

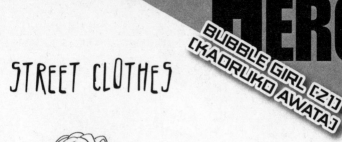

STREET CLOTHES

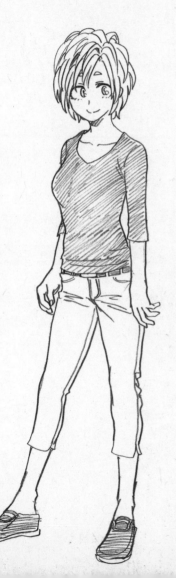

Birthday: 4/23
Height: 167 cm
Favorite Thing: Baths

THE PROCESS

A while back, I held a fan art contest where readers were asked to submit original designs for heroes. The plan was to introduce the winning design in the story.

This was that character.

Given all the work involved in bringing her into being, she won't be some forgettable, one-off character. I'm planning to use her a lot.

Q: WHO'S YOUR FAVORITE CHARACTER??

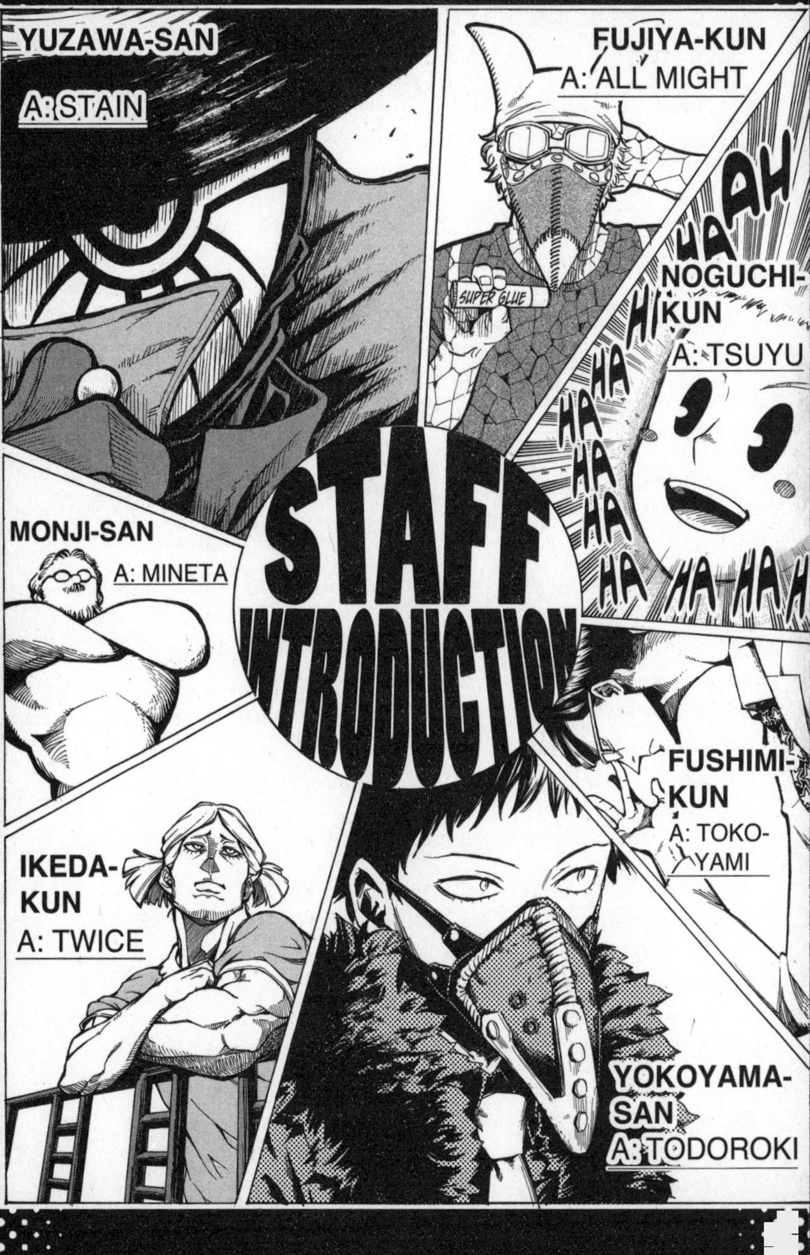

FUJIYA-KUN
A: ALL MIGHT
SUPER GLUE
YUZAWA-SAN
A: STAIN
HAHAH
NOGUCHI-KUN
A: TSUYU
HI
HA HA HA HA HA HA
HA HA HAH
STAFF INTRODUCTION
MONJI-SAN
A: MINETA
FUSHIMI-KUN
A: TOKO-YAMI
IKEDA-KUN
A: TWICE
YOKOYAMA-SAN
A: TODOROKI

SECOND ANNUAL CHARACTER POPULARITY POLL RESULTS

1ST KATSUKI BAKUGO — 3,020 VOTES

2ND IZUKU MIDORIYA — 2,217

3RD SHOTO TODOROKI — 1,795 VOTES

PLACE	NAME	VOTES
4TH	SHOTA AIZAWA	943
5TH	EIJIRO KIRISHIMA	722
6TH	ALL MIGHT	521
7TH	KYOKA JIRO	446
8TH	TENYA IDA	331
9TH	TSUYU ASUI	309
10TH	OCHACO URARAKA	292
11TH	DENKI KAMINARI	243
12TH	MASHIRAO OJIRO	211
13TH	MOMO YAOYOROZU	178
14TH	HITOSHI SHINSO	154
15TH	FUMIKAGE TOKOYAMI	127
16TH	TOMURA SHIGARAKI	125
17TH	PRESENT MIC	109
18TH	HANTA SERO	94
19TH	HIMIKO TOGA	75
20TH	YO SHINDO	58
21ST	MINA ASHIDO	36
	ORU HAGAKURE	
23RD	TETSUTETSU TETSUTETSU	30
	MEI HATSUME	
25TH	NEITO MONOMA	29
26TH	KOHEI HORIKOSHI (AUTHOR)	28
27TH	CEMENTOSS	27
	DABI	

PLACE	NAME	VOTES
29TH	STAIN	25
30TH	MANUAL	24
31ST	MINORU MINETA	23
	MEZO SHOJI	
33RD	BEST JEANIST	22
	ITSUKA KENDO	
35TH	MIDNIGHT	21
36TH	YUGA AOYAMA	17
37TH	NEZU (PRINCIPAL)	16
38TH	INASA YOARASHI	14
	MT. LADY	
40TH	ENDEAVOR	13
	SEIJI SHISHIKURA	
42ND	ECTOPLASM	12
43RD	NAOMASA TSUKAUCHI	11
44TH	INKO MIDORIYA	10
45TH	THIRTEEN	9
	GRAN TORINO	
	EDGESHOT	
	MIKUMO AKATANI (IZUKU'S EARLY DESIGN, FROM THE DATA BOOK)	
49TH	ALL FOR ONE	8
	MITSUKI BAKUGO	
	KOTA IZUMI	
	CAMIE	

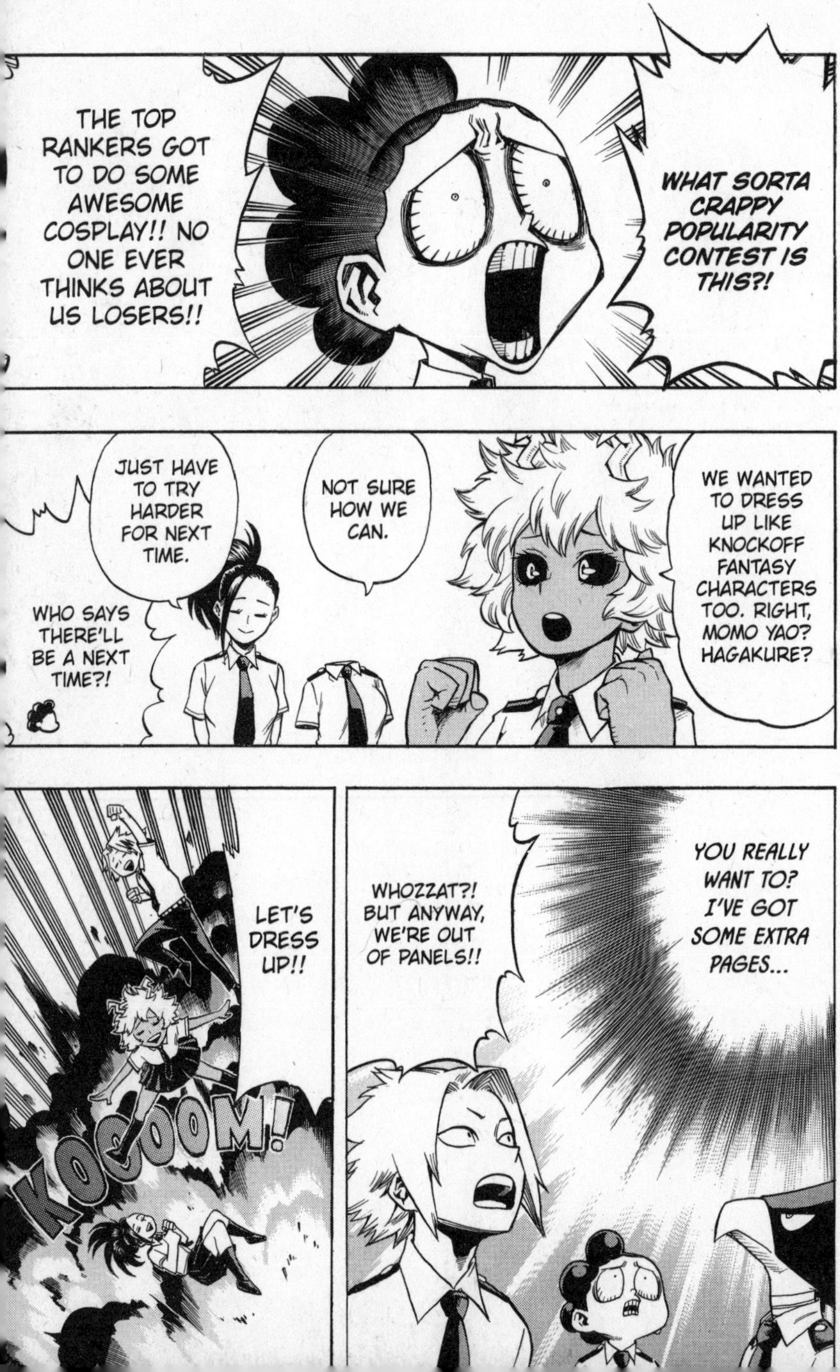
WHAT SORTA CRAPPY POPULARITY CONTEST IS THIS?!
THE TOP RANKERS GOT TO DO SOME AWESOME COSPLAY!! NO ONE EVER THINKS ABOUT US LOSERS!!
WE WANTED TO DRESS UP LIKE KNOCKOFF FANTASY CHARACTERS TOO. RIGHT, MOMO YAO? HAGAKURE?
NOT SURE HOW WE CAN.
JUST HAVE TO TRY HARDER FOR NEXT TIME.
WHO SAYS THERE'LL BE A NEXT TIME?!
YOU REALLY WANT TO? I'VE GOT SOME EXTRA PAGES...
WHOZZAT?! BUT ANYWAY, WE'RE OUT OF PANELS!!
LET'S DRESS UP!!
KOOOOM!

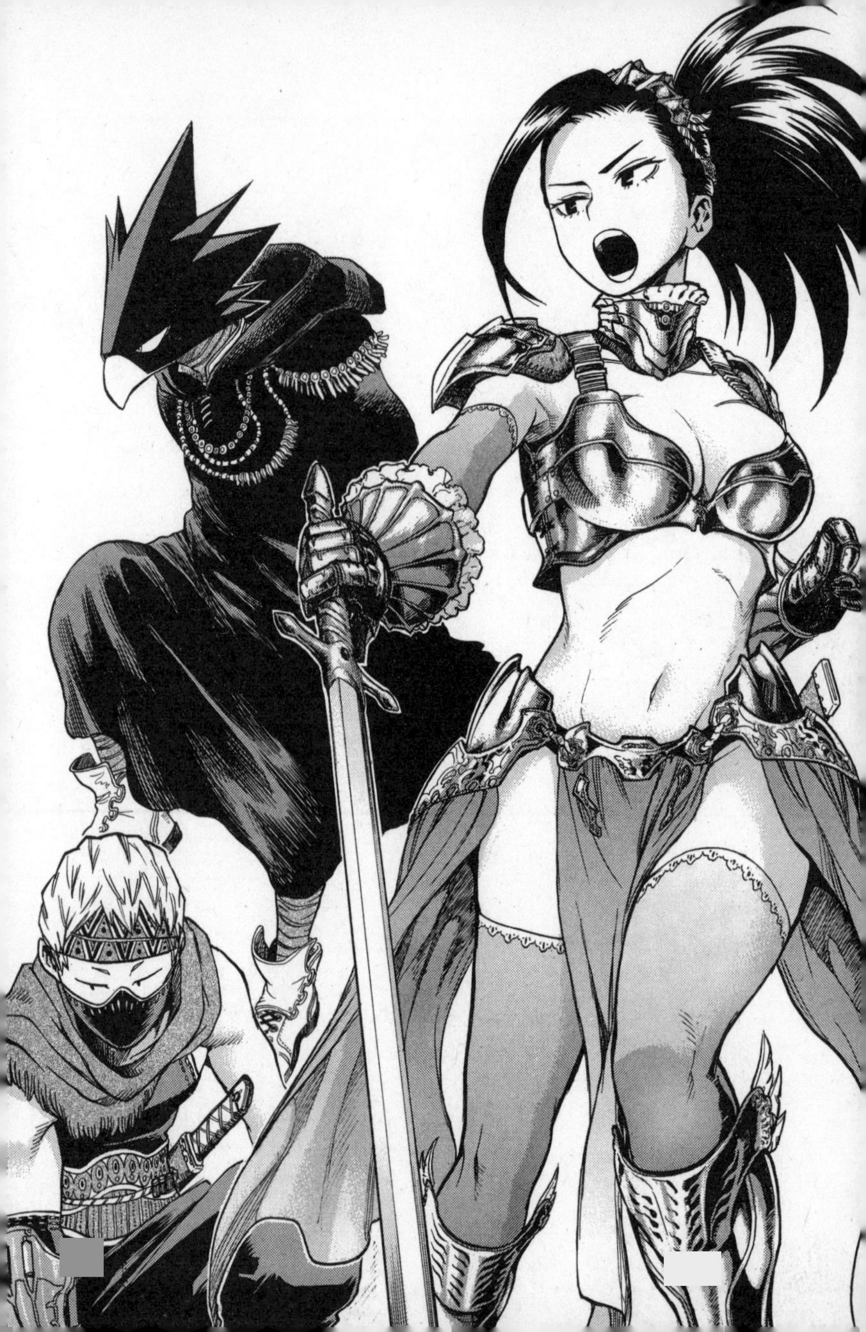

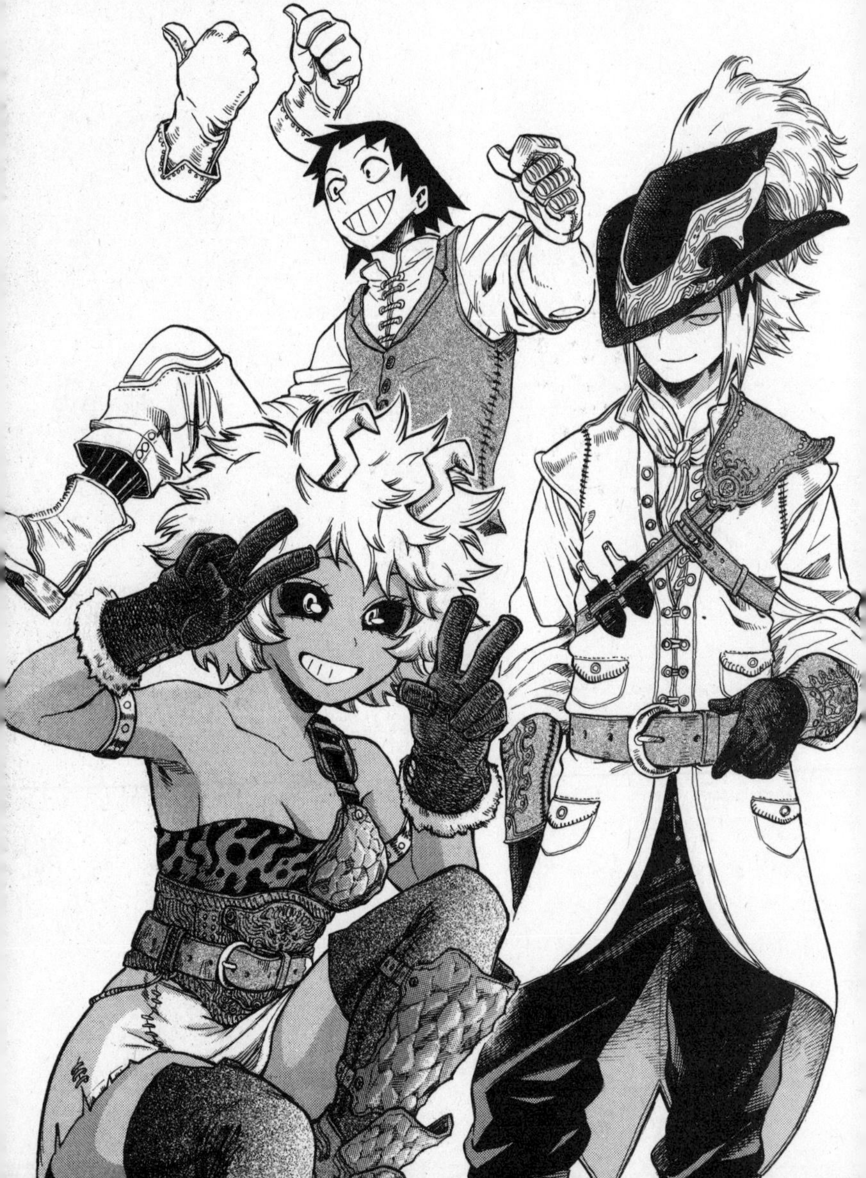

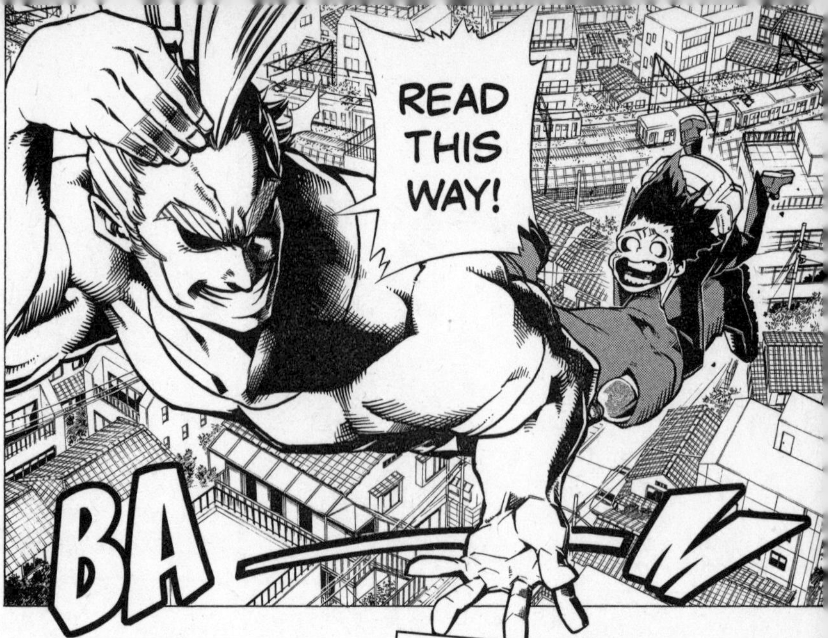
READ THIS WAY!
BA—M

MY HERO ACADEMIA

reads from right to left, starting in the upper-right corner. Japanese is read from right to left, meaning that action, sound effects and word-balloon order are completely reversed from English order.

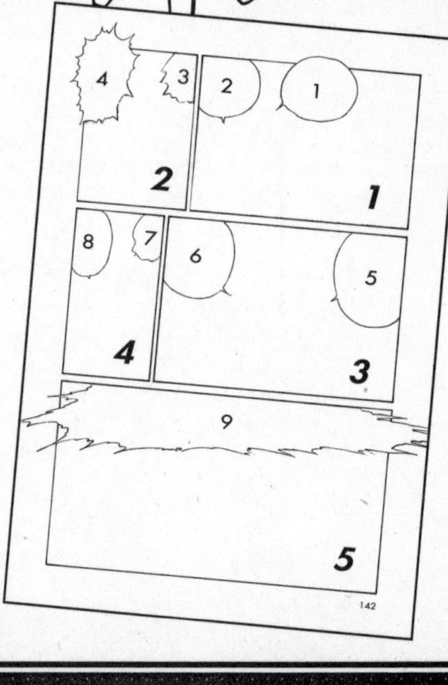